Sports Law

The West Legal Studies Series

Your options keep growing with West Legal Studies

Each year our list continues to offer you more options for every area of the law to meet your course or on-the-job reference requirements. We now have over 140 titles from which to choose in the following areas:

Accounting and Financials for the Law Office
Administrative Law
Alternative Dispute Resolution
Bankruptcy
Business Organizations/Corporations
Civil Litigation and Procedure
CLA Exam Preparation
Computer in the Law Office
Contract Law
Criminal Law and Procedure
Document Preparation
Elder Law
Employment Law
Environmental Law
Ethics
Evidence Law
Family Law

Intellectual Property
Interviewing and Investigation
Introduction to Law
Introduction to Paralegalism
Law Office Management
Law Office Procedures
Legal Nurse Consulting
Legal Research, Writing, and Analysis
Legal Terminology
Paralegal Employment
Product Liability
Real Estate Law
Reference Materials
Social Security
Sports Law
Torts and Personal Injury Law
Wills, Trusts, and Estate Administration

You will find unparalleled, practical support

Each book is augmented by instructor and student supplements to ensure the best learning experience possible. We also offer custom publishing and other benefits such as West's Student Achievement Award. In addition, our sales representatives are ready to provide you with dependable service.

We want to hear from you

Our best contributions for improving the quality of our books and instructional materials is feedback from the people who use them. If you have a question, concern, or observation about any of our materials, or you have a product proposal or manuscript, we want to hear from you. Please contact your local representative or write us at the following address:

West Legal Studies, 5 Maxwell Drive, Clifton Park, NY 12065-2919

For additional information point your browser at
www.WestLegalStudies.com

THOMSON
DELMAR LEARNING

Sports Law

Adam Epstein, Esq.

THOMSON

DELMAR LEARNING

Australia Canada Mexico Singapore Spain United Kingdom United States

THOMSON

DELMAR LEARNING

WEST LEGAL STUDIES

Sports Law
by Adam Epstein

Business Unit Executive Director:
Susan L. Simpfenderfer

Acquisitions Editor:
Pamela Fuller

Editorial Assistant:
Sarah Duncan

Executive Production Manager:
Wendy A. Troeger

Production Manager:
Carolyn Miller

Production Editor:
Matthew J. Williams

Executive Marketing Manager:
Donna J. Lewis

Channel Manager:
Wendy Mapstone

Cover Design:
TDB Publishing Services

Printed in Canada
1 2 3 4 5 XXX 06 05 04 03 02

For more information contact:
Delmar Learning
5 Maxwell Drive
Clifton Park, NY 12065-2919.

Or find us on the World Wide Web at
www.DelmarLearning.com or
www.WestLegalStudies.com

For permission to use material from this text or product, contact us by
Tel (800) 730-2214
Fax (800) 730-2215
www.thomsonrights.com

Library of Congress Cataloging-in-Publication Data

Epstein, Adam.
  Sports law / Adam Epstein.
    p. cm. -- (The West Legal Studies series)
  Includes index.
    ISBN 0-7668-2324-5
  1. Sports--Law and legislation--United States.
    I. Title. II. Series.
  KF3989 .E67 2002
  344.73'099--dc21

                            2002041017

ISBN: 0-7668-2324-5

NOTICE TO THE READER

Dedication

To the guidance and tutelage of Dr. Harry Rutledge, Emeritus Professor, Department of Classics, University of Tennessee.

Contents

CHAPTER 2

Sports Contracts 33

CHAPTER 3

Sports Torts   63

CHAPTER 6

Disabilities and Sports   127

CHAPTER 7

Drugs and Sports   163

CHAPTER 8

International Sports Issues   191

CHAPTER 9

Antitrust and Labor Issues in Sports   219

CHAPTER 10

Intellectual Property Issues in Sports   241

CHAPTER 11

Alternative Dispute Resolution in Sports   257

CHAPTER 12

Religion and Sports   277

Table of Cases

Preface

The goal of this book is to provide easy access to the legal issues involved in sport and the sport industry. The book's target audience is the nonlawyer and non-law student, though certainly this book should be enlightening for those trained in law as well. Sport management, legal studies, and paralegal students should find that this text is easy to read and covers the basics of the legal issues surrounding sports.

Sports Law includes 12 chapters. Some chapters, such as Sports Contracts, introduce the reader to skills sets, while other chapters, such as Sports Torts, present a more general view of that area of the law. The instructor is encouraged to provide course supplementation on the different chapters, though this text was written with the goal that no other supplementation would be necessary.

While one might debate the order of chapters or the order of importance of the issues, the author has given special attention to the needs of students who might study law only this once during their academic career. Clearly, though the focus of the book is on American jurisprudence, relative weight is given to international issues as well, particularly with regard to the Olympic Movement.

Actual cases have been included in the text so instructors and students need not copy cases from other books and can feel comfortable using this book as the sole course text. Questions have been included at the end of each chapter to allow students and instructors to ponder questions with clear-cut answers and others not so clear. Chapter summaries are also written with the expectation that readers could realize an overall appreciation of the context of the chapter.

Numerous Internet sites, additional cases, and statutes are provided throughout the book to enable students to further explore relevant issues and decisions. It is important to recognize that laws may change each year, and therefore students should beware to consult the latest cases and decisions since the writing of this text. In fact, it is highly recommended that the instructor note the latest versions of that particular state's laws to enhance (and verify) this text. Additionally, cases may be overruled or reversed; therefore, cases are meant to coalesce the concepts in the chapter rather than be used as the prime or "best" case that addresses a subject.

About the Author

Adam Epstein earned his B.A. (Classics), M.B.A. (Management) and J.D. from the University of Tennessee. He currently serves as the Chair of the Legal Studies Department at South College in Knoxville. He has served as an adjunct assistant professor at the University of Tennessee and Pellissippi State Technical Community College in Knoxville as well. Mr. Epstein is a Rule 31 General Civil Mediator in Tennessee.

Mr. Epstein has represented numerous professional athletes over the years, including several national champions and olympians primarily in the sports of swimming and triathlon. He co-authored *Sports Law and Legislation: An Annotated Bibliography* (1991), and has authored numerous articles that have been featured in the *Journal of Legal Aspects of Sport, Tennessee Bar Journal, The Paralegal Educator,* and Marquette University's *For the Record.* He has also served as a reviewer for numerous textbooks.

Acknowledgments

The author and Delmar Learning would like to thank the following reviewers:

Jeffrey A. Helewitz, Esq.

William J. Mulkeen
Essex County College

Robert Diotalevi
Florida Gulf Coast University

Les Sturdivant Ennis
Samford University

Kenneth Frank
Brenau University

Prof. Paul Anderson
Marquette University Law School

Introduction to Sports Law

Students who are interested in studying sports law are usually excited about the prospect. I am well aware of students across the country who have requested that such a subject be taught in their curriculum.

The target audience of this text is undergraduate legal studies, paralegal studies, and sport management students. This text may also complement studies in general business law and other special legal topics courses. This text is not written for the graduate law student, thought it certainly provides valuable information and fundamentals for such study.

Attempts to teach sports law are often met with mild resistance from faculty for several reasons. First, most educators have no experience in this area of the law. Second, many educators feel that students will not ultimately work in such an environment and therefore such study adds little or no value to preparation for participation in the legal profession. Finally, even though there are numerous sports law textbooks, most are designed for the graduate study of law or in law school. Few law schools consistently offer such a course.

Real-world cases, real-world documents, and special features are designed to show that working in an environment that influences or is affected by sports or athletes is likely to occur at some point during the course of one's career and is no longer considered just a "lucky" prospect.

Sports law is not considered a classic legal subject for law schools, and some traditionalists vehemently refuse to recognize it as a legitimate field of study in the legal profession. However, I have never met a lawyer or professor who was not interested in becoming involved in this field in some way whether on a full-time basis or merely to complement an already established civil or criminal practice or interest.

"Sports law" may be referred to as "sports and the law" in some circles. In other words, recognition that sports law is its own field might evoke strong debate, usually in the negative. However, realize that one will succeed in understanding sports law much better if it is clear that sports is a multibillion dollar industry with rules that are often not found in everyday life. Some students and educators might refuse to accept the fact that in the sports business the normality of the legal environment is difficult to comprehend, even twisted. Such resistance to accepting that rules are different in the sports industry will surely affect the study of this subject negatively. The importance and role of television cannot be underestimated in terms of its revenue streams, through advertising and sponsorship, for organizations, leagues, teams, colleges, and universities.

Rarely will a single employee of an organization outside of sports refuse to work or "hold out" from appearing for work due to the fact that other similarly situated employees are paid more for the same services. In the professional sports world, this is commonplace. In other fields, employees rarely have an agent. Employers might fire an insubordinate employee, and no one in the community would care. There would be no discussion in the newspaper, on the radio, or over the Internet. In the sports business, professional athletes and administrators may end up handsomely rewarded for outrageous behaviors. Sports law is about money. Sports law is about people. Sports law is about power. Sports law is about ego. These concepts sound remarkably similar to the descriptions often associated with the legal profession.

Professional and amateur sports leagues and organizations are recognized as profitable ventures involving large capital resources. They also regulate players and agents. Women have had a great influence in certain areas of sports and the law. Teenagers are becoming multimillionaires due to subsidies from athletic sponsors and organizations. Cities are taxing citizens to build stadiums and steal franchises from other cities. Fans are suing players and suing each other for injuries received during a sports contest, while local and state governments are seeking criminal sanctions against both fans' and athletes' misdeeds. Amateur associations and teams are increasingly becoming involved in debate over recruiting athletes and rules involving their sports, and fans are suing players for breaches of contract. The list goes on.

All in all, the study of sports law is still fun. It focuses on what many of us wish we could really do in any profession: get paid to play and have fun. Sports law evolves almost daily. Therefore, it is important that the reader use this book as a starting point for further research and to learn the fundamentals of an exciting area of the law.

CHAPTER ONE

Sports Agents

▮ Introduction

This chapter introduces the world of sports agency. One need not be a lawyer to be a sports agent, but many agents are lawyers. The word *agent* is a mysterious word, and *sports agent* is an even more intriguing term. What does that phrase actually mean? Usually the term connotes a power broker for a professional athlete. As a general rule, student-athletes with remaining eligibility may not have an agent to represent their interests in that particular sport.

Agents are notorious for becoming intense, occasionally overzealous, and persistent in furthering the athlete's interests to secure a contract with a team, event, league, or sponsor. Many lawyers are well known, even infamous, for such aggressive behavior and advocacy in the nonsports setting. The word *agent* has often been associated with the term *unscrupulous* in the context of the sports business. In fact, some lawyers prefer to be called *sports lawyers* or *sports managers* rather than "agents."

The law of sports agency continues to evolve. Players' unions in certain professional sports now regulate sports agents. At the time of this writing, 34 states have enacted laws regulating agents, and this number is quickly changing. Though no current federal law governs sports agency, it may have its day in the near future. The **Uniform Athlete Agents Act (UAAA)** has been drafted and approved and is available for adoption by states.

▮ Who Is a Sports Agent?

A **sports agent** advocates and represents the legal and business affairs of a professional athlete, usually for a fee. Generally speaking, the term *sports agent*

Uniform Athlete Agents Act (UAAA)   model act governing sports agents authored by the National Conference of Commissioners on Uniform State Laws

sports agent   individual who represents the interest of a professional athlete refers to someone who solicits the services of a **student-athlete** with remaining collegiate eligibility to represent that student-athlete when the time comes to negotiate a professional sports contract. The sports agent then charges the former student-athlete a fee or commission for the negotiation of such contract. Agents have a **fiduciary** relationship with their principals (clients), and maintaining a relation of trust and confidence is of utmost importance. Agents must be careful, skillful, and diligent.[1] Agents are sometimes referred to as "promoters," "managers," "contract advisors," or "player representatives." All of these terms are essentially synonymous.

Lawyers may be sports agents, though some lawyers who represent professional athletes prefer the label *sports lawyer*. However, successful sports agents who are also attorneys have often forgone renewal of their law license and law practice due to tougher laws governing lawyers compared to those applying to nonlawyer agents, particularly with regard to solicitation of clients.

States define the term *sports agent* differently. This myriad of definitions has led to confusion and misunderstanding in the legal profession. It is vital that the student research the definition of "sports agent" adopted in the state in question.

Qualifications to Become a Sports Agent

Generally speaking, there are no specific qualifications to become a sports agent.[2] In recent years, however, numerous states have attempted to define and ultimately regulate sports agents and their activities. Sports agents may need to attain certain minimum educational requirements if they wish to represent professional athletes in those sports governed by a collective bargaining agreement. The National Football League Players Association (**NFLPA**) now requires a four-year college degree from an accredited institution in order to represent professional football players in the National Football League (**NFL**).

Professional Leagues

In the major professional sports leagues of the NFL, Major League Baseball (**MLB**), National Basketball Association (**NBA**), and National Hockey League (**NHL**), players associations serve as unions and actually regulate fees that the agent may

---

student-athlete   student who participates as an individual or member of a college or university team

fiduciary   one who owes another a higher duty of good faith and care

NFLPA   National Football League Players Association

NFL   National Football League

MLB   Major League Baseball

NBA   National Basketball Association

NHL   National Hockey League

charge the player. These players associations are powerful and are capable of dismissing the agent from the ability to represent players within that sport for a violation of its policies and procedures.[3] Agents are now required to pay expensive fees to the players associations (unions) that regulate their own agents. Such costs can discourage a novice agent from entering the profession.[4]

Formal Education to Become an Agent

There is no typical, formal education program for sports agents. Many sports agents have law degrees. Others have no formal college education. Those who attend college earn degrees in a variety of fields, including legal studies, political science, sociology, and sports management.

Practically speaking, however, obtaining a law degree has become an unwritten prerequisite to break into the profession in terms of maintaining a competitive advantage. The dream of becoming an agent can still be realized without a law degree, but the upstart had better be financed well to compete with big firms that often induce clients with all sorts of cash and gifts.[5]

Agents without formal legal training will likely continue to recruit clients as long as those athletes find their services effective. Ultimately, the most important issue for sports agents is to keep their clients happy. On the other hand, this arena has grown in complexity and competitiveness to the point that the days of the "friend next door" or the parent of a professional athlete serving as a sports agent are in the past, with rare exceptions.[6]

■ General Agency Law Principles

Agency law has existed for hundreds of years. The basis of this law is to allow another to act on behalf of a **principal**. For example, an employee who acts within the "scope of his/her employment" furthers the business interest of the employer by creating a legally enforceable relationship that would hold the employer responsible for the actions of the employee. The phrase **scope of employment** is often referred to as *respondeat superior*, a Latin phrase meaning "let the master answer."

While the relationship of "master-servant" has been replaced with the less harsh phrase "principal-agent" or "employer-employee," the duties of the parties remain the same. An **agent** expressly enters into an agency agreement with a principal to further the interests of that principal. Sports agents serve in this capacity, though

---

principal   one who grants another, an agent, the right to act on his or her behalf

scope of employment   responsibilities an employee carries out on behalf of an employer

agent   individual authorized to act on behalf of a principal

one would not view the relationship between a sports agent and his or her client as "employer-employee."

Fiduciary Duties

Sports agents are subject to the same general legal duties such as duty of loyalty, duty of care, duty of accounting, and the general duty to act as a fiduciary for the client-principal. The agent as fiduciary must act in the best interests of the principal (athlete) and act in good faith to the principal, but breakdowns can occur in the relationship.[7]

Some agents are granted the power of attorney from the athlete-principal, but that is not usually recommended. The sports agent business is so competitive that it is common for agents to require the athlete to sign an **exclusive contract** or agency agreement as a condition of representation. However, **nonexclusive contracts** are acceptable when outsourcing media and marketing efforts to other firms for a flat fee.

■ History of Sports Agency

Historically speaking, most sports agents recognize the inception of the profession stemming from the work of several individuals during the 1960s.[8] However, sports agency can actually be traced back to 1925 when Red Grange hired an agent to negotiate his professional football contract.

In the 1960s, attorney Mark McCormack's work with young golfer Arnold Palmer forever changed the manner in which sponsors deal with professional athletes. Since the 1960s, many other remarkable sports agents have made an impression on the profession that is now dominated by high-profile individuals working for large sport management agencies.[9] Massive mergers offering economies of scale, in addition to the increased regulation of agents, have squeezed out many upstart agent hopefuls. However, an equally large number of smaller solo practitioners and small firms (sometimes simply law firms) handle particular aspects of the athlete's life, primarily legal affairs.

Once athletes have established themselves in their careers and established their market value, it is not uncommon for athletes to turn away from large sports agencies and instead use the services of smaller operations. Ultimately, since most professional sports careers last only a few years, choosing an effective representative can be one of the most important decisions athletes make and could greatly affect their income during the course of their career.

---

exclusive contract agreement for sole rights to sponsor, promote, and advertise between an agent and athlete

nonexclusive contract agreement allowing either party to pursue other similar contractual relationships

■ Agent Hierarchy

Becoming a sports agent (and staying in the industry) is a highly competitive venture. There are different levels of sports agents. Most agents we read about in the media represent professional athletes at the major league level in football, baseball, basketball and hockey, all of which have forms of minor leagues and/or alternative professional leagues of their own. Agents in the NFL, MLB, NBA, and NHL are subject to strict rules imposed by their respective players associations in addition to the myriad state regulations governing their activities.

However, an entirely different world of profitable sports agency relationships has developed among other sports, such as boxing, motor sports, soccer, tennis, golf, and numerous other traditionally Olympic sports. Agents serve both male and female athletes. Agents are predominantly male, though numerous successful female agents have made their mark in this industry. This is due to the gradual increase of the concept of the female as a professional athlete in this country, the effects of Title IX, the advent of the **WNBA**, and professinal women's teams.

Additionally, varied winter sports, bodybuilding and fitness competitors, and others enlist the help of representation from sports agents to assist them in managing their daily affairs and to obtain sponsorships, appearances, and other endorsements in exchange for cash and products in-kind. This also includes talented athletes whose primary purpose is to display their athletic prowess and charisma to arenas and television audiences in a "sports entertainment" format such as professional wrestling.[10]

In the 1996 film *Jerry Maguire*, actor Tom Cruise portrays a persistent yet struggling sports agent who must compete with his former employer, a sports super-agency.[11] His ultimate success rides on a professional football player who eventually secures a big contract. As a result, the agent secures a profitable fee or commission. Much of the movie portrays the real-world intense life of a sports agent. The movie correctly portrays the adage that a sports agent is only as effective as the client's athletic talents when it comes to marketing the athlete.

■ Agent Roles

Managing daily affairs of the athlete is the general role most sports agents play. This includes dealing with the media, negotiating contracts, and marketing the athlete's image to prospective future employers in the same league after the expiration of that player's contract. Moreover, the sports agent may assist in the selection of which events to compete in, what types of insurance the athlete should secure, and which sponsor or team best serves the athlete. Of course, lawyers who act as agents may conduct similar activities as nonlawyer agents, but if there is civil or criminal

---

WNBA   Women's National Basketball Association

litigation involving the athlete, sports agents who are lawyers usually enlist the services of outside counsel.

Unlike litigation lawyers whose function is to represent clients in an adversarial process within federal and state civil litigation rules, sports agents are often called upon to manage athletes and give advice outside the scope of the law and legal profession. Of course, licensed attorneys can give legal advice to athletes if and when requested, though nonattorney agents may not give legal advice.[12]

Due to the large sums of money that are involved in representing professional athletes, sports agents serve as a formidable go-between for the athlete and a team or a sponsor. Recently, contracts between professional teams and a single athlete have rivaled and even exceeded budgets and revenues of high-profile corporations.[13] This increase in cash and publicity appears to be without a ceiling as long as television continues to influence the exposure of these athletes and advertisers are willing to pay their advertising fees accordingly.

■ Other Sports Clients

Understanding the nature and business of sports is essential to becoming a successful sports agent. Coaches now have sports agents to manage and market them at the collegiate and professional level. Sports reporters on radio and television hire agents to manage their affairs and reach the largest available market of listeners. Agents may even act as the go-between for community sports corporations to attract revenue-generating events such as regional and national championships. Agents may also work with particular national governing bodies (NGBs) such as United States Swimming or the National Collegiate Athletic Association (**NCAA**) in order to market and promote the sport to obtain "official sponsor" status within that sport.[14]

■ Agent Regulation

Many lawyers and students of law would like to become sports agents. It is glamorous and profitable, and it certainly could assist lawyers in developing their practice in numerous other areas, including general civil litigation, criminal law, estate planning, workers compensation, and family law. Since there is no current federal regulation of sports agents, a myriad of state laws have created "chaos" in terms of regulation of agent activities. Refusal to follow particular state statutes has led to disbarment of lawyers in some circumstances and brought criminal charges and fines against an agent for failing to comply with state laws. Additionally, sports leagues that have players associations may regulate agent activity in addition to state laws.[15]

NCAA   National Collegiate Athletic Association

One focus of efforts to regulate agents and their activities is recruiting student-athletes from colleges and universities by agents' recruiters, sometimes called "runners."[16] Professional sports leagues "draft" these collegians (and sometimes even high school students with exceptional talent) with promises and sometimes guarantees of large salaries over a number of years. Thus, competition for recruiting student-athletes continues to become more fierce.

In sports such as gymnastics and tennis, agents scour the countryside looking to sign up potential clients even before they have reached high school to begin negotiation of deals well into the hundreds of thousands of dollars. The advent of the Internet has made the representation and recruitment of athletes as clients much easier but has added to the problem of regulating agent activity.

State Regulation of Sports Agents

The 34 states that currently regulate agents also provide for civil and criminal penalties (see Table 1–1). Agents are often required to register with the secretary of state of the state in which they recruit a student-athlete with remaining collegiate eligibility.

Though there is no current federal legislation governing sports agents, *The Sports Agent Responsibility and Trust Act* was introduced as a bill in 2002 in the United States House of Representatives which would allow the Federal Trade Commission (FTC) to regulate any deceptive or certain unfair conduct by sports agents relating to the signing of contracts with student-athletes. Only time will tell if such Act becomes federal law.

Push Toward Uniform Laws

The National Conference of Commissioners on Uniform State Laws (**NCCUSL**) adopted the final version of the UAAA in August 2000. The NCCUSL and the NCAA worked together to draft an act that could be adopted by all 50 states to avoid differences from state to state. The UAAA is included at the end of this chapter (see Exhibit 1–1) and has been approved for adoption purposes by many states. Utah was the first state to adopt the UAAA; other states and territories that have followed suit include Alabama, Arizona, Arkansas, Delaware, Idaho, Indiana, Mississippi, Nevada, Tennessee, U.S. Virgin Islands, and West Virginia.

Testing Sports Agents

Until recently, sports agents had to pass or follow no state tests or state codes of ethics unless the agent was also a licensed lawyer. Thus, virtually anyone could call himself or herself an agent without any formal training, and some still do. However, agents are required to pay state fees to recruit student-athletes in states with laws governing sports agents. One of the problems in enforcement, however, is that many sports agents refuse to pay the fees. Additionally, some players associations

---

NCCUSL   National Conference of Commissioners on Uniform State Laws

■ TABLE 1-1   States Regulating Sports Agents

As of June 2002, the UAAA had been passed in 14 states and two territories:	Eighteen states had existing, non-UAAA legislation designed to regulate athlete agents:
Alabama	
Arizona	California (UAAA introduced)
Arkansas	Colorado
Delaware	Connecticut
District of Columbia	Georgia (UAAA introduced)
Florida	Iowa (UAAA introduced)
Idaho	Kansas
Indiana	Kentucky
Minnesota	Louisiana
Mississippi	Maryland (UAAA introduced)
Nevada	Michigan (UAAA introduced)
Tennessee	Missouri (UAAA introduced)
Utah	North Carolina
U.S. Virgin Islands	North Dakota
Washington	Ohio
West Virginia	Oklahoma
	Oregon
Fifteen additional states had introduced the UAAA into their state legislatures:	Pennsylvania (UAAA introduced)
	Texas
California	
Georgia	
Hawaii	**Nine states and one territory had neither introduced the UAAA nor passed previous legislation regulating athlete agents:**
Illinois	
Iowa	
Maryland	Alaska
Michigan	Maine
Missouri	Massachusetts
Nebraska	Montana
New Jersey	Puerto Rico
New Mexico	Rhode Island
New York	South Dakota
Pennsylvania	Vermont
South Carolina	Virginia
Wisconsin	Wyoming

■ **EXHIBIT 1–1** *Uniform Athlete Agents Act*

UNIFORM ATHLETE AGENTS ACT (2000)
Drafted by the
NATIONAL CONFERENCE OF COMMISSIONERS
ON UNIFORM STATE LAWS

and by it
APPROVED AND RECOMMENDED FOR
ENACTMENT IN ALL THE STATES
at its
ANNUAL CONFERENCE
MEETING IN ITS ONE-HUNDRED-AND-NINTH
YEAR ST. AUGUSTINE, FLORIDA
JULY 28-AUGUST 4, 2000 *WITHOUT PREFATORY
NOTE AND COMMENTS*
Copyright © 2000
By
NATIONAL CONFERENCE OF COMMISSIONERS
ON UNIFORM STATE LAWS
August 9, 2000
UNIFORM ATHLETE AGENTS ACT

SECTION 1. SHORT TITLE. This [Act] may be cited
as the Uniform Athlete Agents Act.

SECTION 2. DEFINITIONS. In this [Act]:

(1) "Agency contract" means an agreement in which
a student-athlete authorizes a person to negotiate or solicit on behalf of the student-athlete a
professional-sports-services contract or an
endorsement contract.

(2) "Athlete agent" means an individual who enters
into an agency contract with a student-athlete or,
directly or indirectly, recruits or solicits a student-
athlete to enter into an agency contract. The
term does not include a spouse, parent, sibling,
[or] grandparent [or guardian] of the student-
athlete or an individual acting solely on behalf of
a professional sports team or professional sports
organization. The term includes an individual
who represents to the public that the individual is
an athlete agent.

(3) "Athletic director" means an individual responsible for administering the overall athletic program
of an educational institution or, if an educational
institution has separately administered athletic
programs for male students and female students,

the athletic program for males or the athletic
program for females, as appropriate.

(4) "Contact" means a communication, direct or
indirect, between an athlete agent and a student-
athlete, to recruit or solicit the student-
athlete to enter into an agency contract.

(5) "Endorsement contract" means an agreement
under which a student-athlete is employed or
receives consideration to use on behalf of the
other party any value that the student-athlete may
have because of publicity, reputation, following,
or fame obtained because of athletic ability or
performance.

(6) "Intercollegiate sport" means a sport played at the
collegiate level for which eligibility requirements
for participation by a student-athlete are established by a national association for the promotion
or regulation of collegiate athletics.

(7) "Person" means an individual, corporation,
business trust, estate, trust, partnership, limited
liability company, association, joint venture,
government; governmental subdivision, agency,
or instrumentality; public corporation, or any
other legal or commercial entity.

(8) "Professional-sports-services contract" means an
agreement under which an individual is
employed or agrees to render services as a
player on a professional sports team, with a professional sports organization, or as a professional
athlete.

(9) "Record" means information that is inscribed on a
tangible medium or that is stored in an electronic
or other medium and is retrievable in perceivable
form.

(10) "Registration" means registration as an athlete
agent pursuant to this [Act].

(11) "State" means a State of the United States, the
District of Columbia, Puerto Rico, the United
States Virgin Islands, or any territory or insular
possession subject to the jurisdiction of the
United States.

(12) "Student-athlete" means an individual who engages
in, is eligible to engage in, or may be eligible in
the future to engage in, any intercollegiate sport.

continued

If an individual is permanently ineligible to participate in a particular intercollegiate sport, the individual is not a student-athlete for purposes of that sport.

SECTION 3. ADMINISTRATION; SERVICE OF PROCESS; SUBPOENAS.

(a) The [Secretary of State] shall administer this [Act].

(b) By engaging in the business of an athlete agent in this State, a nonresident individual appoints the [Secretary of State] as the individual's agent to accept service of process in any civil action related to the individual's business as an athlete agent in this State.

(c) [The [Secretary of State] may issue subpoenas for any relevant material under this [Act].]

SECTION 4. ATHLETE AGENTS: REGISTRATION REQUIRED.

(a) Except as otherwise provided in subsection (b), an individual may not act as an athlete agent in this State before being issued a certificate of registration under Section 6 or 8.

(b) An individual may act as an athlete agent before being issued a certificate of registration for all purposes except signing an agency contract if:

(1) a student-athlete or another acting on behalf of the student-athlete initiates communication with the individual; and

(2) within seven days after an initial act as an athlete agent, the individual submits an application to register as an athlete agent in this State.

(c) An agency contract resulting from conduct in violation of this section is void. The athlete agent shall return any consideration received under the contract.

SECTION 5. REGISTRATION AS ATHLETE AGENT; FORM; REQUIREMENTS.

(a) An applicant for registration shall submit an application for registration to the [Secretary of State] in a form prescribed by the [Secretary of State]. [An application filed under this section is a public record.] Except as otherwise provided in subsection (b), the application must be in the name of an individual and signed by the applicant under penalty of perjury and must state or contain:

(1) the name of the applicant and the address of the applicant's principal place of business;

(2) the name of the applicant's business or employer, if applicable;

(3) any business or occupation engaged in by the applicant for the five years next preceding the date of submission of the application;

(4) a description of the applicant's:

   (A) formal training as an athlete agent;
   (B) practical experience as an athlete agent; and
   (C) educational background relating to the applicant's activities as an athlete agent;

(5) the names and addresses of three individuals not related to the applicant who are willing to serve as references;

(6) the name, sport, and last known team for each individual for whom the applicant provided services as an athlete agent during the five years next preceding the date of submission of the application;

(7) the names and addresses of all persons who are:

   (A) with respect to the athlete agent's business if it is not a corporation, the partners, officers, associates, or profit-sharers; and

   (B) with respect to a corporation employing the athlete agent, the officers, directors, and any shareholder of the corporation with a 5% or greater interest;

(8) whether the applicant or any other person named pursuant to paragraph (7) has been convicted of a crime that, if committed in this State, would be a felony or other crime involving moral turpitude, and identify the crime;

(9) whether there has been any administrative or judicial determination that the applicant or any other person named pursuant to paragraph (7) has made a false, misleading, deceptive, or fraudulent representation;

(10) any instance in which the conduct of the applicant or any other person named pursuant to paragraph (7) resulted in the imposition of a sanction, suspension, or declaration of ineligibility to participate in an interscholastic or intercollegiate athletic

event on a student-athlete or educational institution;

(11) any sanction, suspension, or disciplinary action taken against the applicant or any other person named pursuant to paragraph (7) arising out of occupational or professional conduct; and

(12) whether there has been any denial of an application for, suspension or revocation of, or refusal to renew, the registration or licensure of the applicant or any other person named pursuant to paragraph (7) as an athlete agent in any State.

(b) An individual who has submitted an application for, and received a certificate of, registration or licensure as an athlete agent in another State, may submit a copy of the application and a valid certificate of registration or licensure from the other State in lieu of submitting an application in the form prescribed pursuant to subsection (a). The [Secretary of State] shall accept the application and the certificate from the other State as an application for registration in this State if the application to the other State:

(1) was submitted in the other State within the six months next preceding the submission of the application in this State and the applicant certifies the information contained in the application is current;

(2) contains information substantially similar to or more comprehensive than that required in an application submitted in this State; and

(3) was signed by the applicant under penalty of perjury.

SECTION 6. CERTIFICATE OF REGISTRATION; ISSUANCE OR DENIAL; RENEWAL.

(a) Except as otherwise provided in subsection (c), the [Secretary of State] shall issue a certificate of registration to an individual who complies with Section 5(a).

(b) Except as otherwise provided in subsection (c), the [Secretary of State] shall issue a certificate of registration to an individual whose application has been accepted under Section 5(b).

(c) The [Secretary of State] may refuse to issue a certificate of registration if the [Secretary of State]

determines that the applicant has engaged in conduct that has a significant adverse effect on the applicant's fitness to serve as an athlete agent. In making the determination, the [Secretary of State] may consider whether the applicant has:

(1) been convicted of a crime that, if committed in this State, would be a felony or other crime involving moral turpitude;

(2) made a materially false, misleading, deceptive, or fraudulent representation as an athlete agent or in the application;

(3) engaged in conduct that would disqualify the applicant from serving in a fiduciary capacity;

(4) engaged in conduct prohibited by Section 14;

(5) had a registration or licensure as an athlete agent suspended, revoked, or denied or been refused renewal of registration or licensure in any State;

(6) engaged in conduct or failed to engage in conduct the consequence of which was that a sanction, suspension, or declaration of ineligibility to participate in an interscholastic or intercollegiate athletic event was imposed on a student-athlete or educational institution; or

(7) engaged in conduct that significantly adversely reflects on the applicant's credibility, honesty, or integrity. (d) In making a determination under subsection (c), the [Secretary of State] shall consider:

(A) how recently the conduct occurred;

(B) the nature of the conduct and the context in which it occurred; and

(C) any other relevant conduct of the applicant.

(e) An athlete agent may apply to renew a registration by submitting an application for renewal in a form prescribed by the [Secretary of State]. [An application filed under this section is a public record.] The application for renewal must be signed by the applicant under penalty of perjury and must contain current information on all matters required in an original registration.

(f) An individual who has submitted an application for renewal of registration or licensure in another State, in lieu of submitting an application for renewal in the form prescribed pursuant to subsection (e), may file a copy of the application for

continued

renewal and a valid certificate of registration from the other State. The [Secretary of State] shall accept the application for renewal from the other State as an application for renewal in this State if the application to the other State:

(1) was submitted in the other State within the last six months and the application certifies the information contained in the application for renewal is current;

(2) contains information substantially similar to or more comprehensive than that required in an application for renewal submitted in this State; and

(3) was signed by the applicant under penalty of perjury.

(g) A certificate of registration or a renewal of a registration is valid for [two] years.

SECTION 7. SUSPENSION, REVOCATION, OR REFUSAL TO RENEW REGISTRATION.

[(a)] The [Secretary of State] may suspend, revoke, or refuse to renew a registration for conduct that would have justified denial of registration under Section 6(c).

[(b) The [Secretary of State] may deny, suspend, revoke, or refuse to renew a registration only after proper notice and an opportunity for a hearing. The [Administrative Procedures Act] applies to this [Act].]

SECTION 8. TEMPORARY REGISTRATION. The
[Secretary of State] may issue a temporary certificate of registration while an application for registration or renewal is pending.

SECTION 9. REGISTRATION AND RENEWAL FEE.
An application for registration or renewal of registration must be accompanied by a fee in the following amount:

(1) [$] for an initial application for registration;

(2) [$] for an application for registration based upon a certificate of registration or licensure issued by another State;

(3) [$] for an application for renewal of registration; or

(4) [$] for an application for renewal of registration based upon an application for renewal of registration or licensure submitted in another State.

SECTION 10. FORM OF CONTRACT.

(a) An agency contract must be in a record, signed by the parties.

(b) An agency contract must state or contain:

(1) the amount and method of calculating the consideration to be paid by the student-athlete for services to be provided by the athlete agent under the contract and any other consideration the athlete agent has received or will receive from any other source for entering into the contract or for providing the services;

(2) the name of any person not listed in the application for registration or renewal who will be compensated because the student-athlete signed the agency contract;

(3) a description of any expenses that the student-athlete agrees to reimburse;

(4) a description of the services to be provided to the student-athlete;

(5) the duration of the contract; and

(6) the date of execution.

(c) An agency contract must contain, in close proximity to the signature of the student-athlete, a conspicuous notice in boldface type in capital letters stating:

WARNING TO STUDENT-ATHLETE

IF YOU SIGN THIS CONTRACT:

(1) YOU MAY LOSE YOUR ELIGIBILITY TO COMPETE AS A STUDENT-ATHLETE IN YOUR SPORT;

(2) BOTH YOU AND YOUR ATHLETE AGENT ARE REQUIRED TO TELL YOUR ATHLETIC DIRECTOR, IF YOU HAVE AN ATHLETIC DIRECTOR, WITHIN 72 HOURS AFTER ENTERING INTO AN AGENCY CONTRACT; AND

(3) YOU MAY CANCEL THIS CONTRACT WITHIN 14 DAYS AFTER SIGNING IT. CANCELLATION OF THE CONTRACT MAY NOT REINSTATE YOUR ELIGIBILITY.

(d) An agency contract that does not conform to this section is voidable by the student-athlete.

(e) The athlete agent shall give a copy of the signed agency contract to the student-athlete at the time of signing.

SECTION 11. NOTICE TO EDUCATIONAL INSTITUTION.

(a) Within 72 hours after entering into an agency contract or before the next scheduled athletic event in which the student-athlete may participate, whichever occurs first, the athlete agent shall give notice in a record of the existence of the contract to the athletic director of the educational institution at which the student-athlete is enrolled or the athlete agent has reasonable grounds to believe the student-athlete intends to enroll.

(b) Within 72 hours after entering into an agency contract or before the next athletic event in which the student-athlete may participate, whichever occurs first, the student-athlete shall inform the athletic director of the educational institution at which the student-athlete is enrolled that he or she has entered into an agency contract.

SECTION 12. STUDENT-ATHLETE'S RIGHT TO CANCEL.

(a) A student-athlete may cancel an agency contract by giving notice in a record to the athlete agent of the cancellation within 14 days after the contract is signed.

(b) A student-athlete may not waive the right to cancel an agency contract.

(c) If a student-athlete cancels an agency contract, the student-athlete is not required to pay any consideration under the contract or to return any consideration received from the agent to induce the student-athlete to enter into the contract.

SECTION 13. REQUIRED RECORDS.

(a) An athlete agent shall retain the following records for a period of five years:

(1) the name and address of each individual represented by the athlete agent;

(2) any agency contract entered into by the athlete agent; and

(3) any direct costs incurred by the athlete agent in the recruitment or solicitation of a student-athlete.

(b) Records required by subsection (a) to be retained are open to inspection by the [Secretary of State] during normal business hours.

SECTION 14. PROHIBITED ACTS.

(a) An athlete agent may not do any of the following with the intent to induce a student-athlete to enter into an agency contract:

(1) give any materially false or misleading information or make a materially false promise or representation;

(2) furnish anything of value to a student-athlete before the student-athlete enters into the agency contract, or

(3) furnish anything of value to any individual other than the student-athlete or another registered athlete agent.

(b) An athlete agent may not intentionally:

(1) initiate contact with a student-athlete unless registered under this [Act];

(2) refuse or willfully fail to retain or permit inspection of the records required by Section 13;

(3) violate Section 4 by failing to register;

(4) provide materially false or misleading information in an application for registration or renewal of registration;

(5) predate or postdate an agency contract; or

(6) fail to notify a student-athlete prior to the student-athlete's signing an agency contract for a particular sport that the signing by the student-athlete may make the student-athlete ineligible to participate as a student-athlete in that sport.

SECTION 15. CRIMINAL PENALTIES.

The commission of any act prohibited by Section 14 by an athlete agent is a [misdemeanor] [felony] punishable by [].

SECTION 16. CIVIL REMEDIES.

(a) An educational institution has a right of action against an athlete agent or a former student-athlete for damages caused by a violation of this [Act]. In an action under this section, the court may award to the prevailing party costs and reasonable attorney's fees.

(b) Damages of an educational institution under subsection (a) include losses and expenses incurred because, as a result of the activities of an athlete agent or former student-athlete, the educational institution was injured by a violation of this [Act] or was penalized, disqualified, or suspended from participation in athletics by a national association

continued

for the promotion and regulation of athletics, by an athletic conference, or by reasonable self-imposed disciplinary action taken to mitigate sanctions.

(c) A right of action under this section does not accrue until the educational institution discovers or by the exercise of reasonable diligence would have discovered the violation by the athlete agent or former student-athlete.

(d) Any liability of the athlete agent or the former student-athlete under this section is several and not joint.

(e) This [Act] does not restrict rights, remedies, or defenses of any person under law or equity.

SECTION 17. ADMINISTRATIVE PENALTY. The [Secretary of State] may assess a civil penalty against an athlete agent not to exceed [$25,000] for a violation of this [Act].

SECTION 18. APPLICATION AND CONSTRUCTION. In applying and construing this Uniform Act, consideration must be given to the need to promote uniformity of the law with respect to its subject matter of this [Act] among States that enact it.

SECTION 19. SEVERABILITY. If any provision of this [Act] or its application to any person or circumstance is held invalid, the invalidity does not affect other provisions or applications of this [Act] which can be given effect without the invalid provision or application, and to this end the provisions of this [Act] are severable.

SECTION 20. REPEALS. The following acts and parts of acts are hereby repealed:

SECTION 21. EFFECTIVE DATE. This [Act] takes effect _____.

are now testing agents in order to ensure that the agents are well versed in the nuances of that sports collective bargaining agreement.

Importance of Focus of Agent Laws

What if professional athletes ask a lawyer or sports agent, during the course of their professional career, to advise them, but the athletes are not student-athletes and were not recruited by the lawyer or agent? State agent laws appear not to regulate such relationships other than the standards imposed by collective bargaining agreements by the sports involved. It appears that the UAAA does not apply to an individual who does *not* solicit or recruit college athletes who have remaining eligibility. Thus, individuals can be sports agents in the states that have adopted the UAAA if they do not recruit student-athletes with remaining collegiate eligibility. It also appears that the UAAA does not apply to athletes or agents who have already exhausted their intercollegiate amateur eligibility in a specific sport.

Violators of State Agent Laws

It is regularly assumed that sports agents violate state rules and regulations when soliciting student-athletes in order to recruit a new crop of clients. In fact, many sports agents create a recruiting budget to solicit prospective clients. Any losses may even be characterized as part of the cost of doing business. Unfortunately, enforcement of state laws is extremely difficult, expensive, and often not pursued except in the most obvious or extreme cases. However, some agents eventually get caught and have had to pay the price.[17]

The state of Florida seems to be the toughest state in terms of regulation of sports agents; agents in this state have been charged with crimes and punished more often than in any other state.[18] However, other states such as Georgia, Texas, Alabama, South Carolina, and Tennessee have powerful laws that provide for imprisonment for a violation of their laws pursued by state attorneys general.

In a well-known sports agency case, recruiters of student-athletes at Florida State University faced criminal sanctions for failing to file with the state as sports agents. Characterized as scandalous, several agents paid $6,000 to finance a shopping spree at a local Footlocker store. A man from Las Vegas named Raul Bey allegedly financed the FSU scandal by using the services of a man named Nate Cebrun[19] who enlisted the help of numerous individuals, including a Tallahassee high school football coach. None of the individuals filed with the state of Florida to register as an "athlete agent," none paid the mandatory state fees, and all were charged with the crime of failing to register as an athlete agent ($250 at that time), which was a felony in Florida.[20]

Statutory Framework

Most states now have a statute that provides for penalties for violations of the state's sports agent act, which includes enabling the college or university affected by the illegal recruitment of student-athletes to sue both the former student-athletes and their sports agents for damages. Adoption of the UAAA provides a model framework as well.

Sports Agent as Lawyer

All states have codes that govern lawyer conduct. If a lawyer violates the state code of ethics, the lawyer may be disbarred, suspended, reprimanded, or publicly censured.[21] However, this code applies only to a licensed attorney. Many individuals obtain a law degree but do not sit for the bar exam (or do not pass); therefore the question arises as to whether such nonlicensed lawyers may face a penalty for ethical improprieties. Clearly, licensed lawyers face stiff penalties if their sports agent activity falls under the "practice of law" category as defined by the state.

Professional Codes of Ethics

Licensed lawyers who represent professional athletes may actually be at a disadvantage to nonlawyer agents when it comes to recruiting clients. Whether one is licensed in a state that subscribes to the **Model Code of Professional Responsibility**

Model Code of Professional Responsibility   model act for ethical conduct by attorneys adopted by the American Bar Association in 1969

(1969) or the **Model Rules of Professional Conduct** (1983), licensed lawyers are subject to numerous provisions that nonlawyer sports agents are not with regard to advertising, solicitation, and splitting fees.

For example, in Florida, attorneys who are agents must follow the Rules Regulating the Florida Bar.[22] Sports agents who are not lawyers are not subject to this ethical code. Since it is arguably unclear to the client as to when a lawyer-agent is acting as a lawyer or acting as an agent, the rules are enforceable to the lawyer and can present serious dilemmas.[23] According to the Florida Bar,

> A lawyer shall not solicit professional employment from a prospective client with whom the lawyer has no family or prior professional relationship, in person or otherwise, when a significant motive for the lawyer's doing so is the lawyer's pecuniary gain. A lawyer shall not permit employees or agents of the lawyer to solicit in the lawyer's behalf. . . . The terms "solicit" includes contact in person, by telephone, telegraph, or facsimile . . . " R. Regulating Florida Bar 4–7.4

Clearly such a statute puts a licensed attorney-agent at a disadvantage when it comes to recruiting athletes as opposed to nonlicensed or nonlawyer agents. Additionally, it is clear in the legal profession that lawyers may not split or share fees with nonlawyers. However, sports agents who are not lawyers apparently may do so without fear of harm at this point in time in numerous jurisdictions.[24]

It would be prudent for sports agents who are lawyers to join the Sports Lawyer's Association in order to stay abreast of changes in the law in the area of agent regulation nationally. It would also be prudent (and mandatory) to join players associations if the lawyer or nonlawyer agent wishes to represent athletes in the NFL, MLB, NBA, and NHL.

■ Sports Agent Fees

The fees that agents may charge their clients are both regulated and nonregulated. When an agent is required to register with the NFLPA, **MLBPA**, **NBPA**, or **NHLPA**, the players unions often require the agents to complete lengthy applications and pay a fee. This affords the opportunity to regulate the agents' activities with players in the union especially if the behavior becomes illegal or represents clear conflicts of interests. Caps regulate fees in these sports that agents may charge for negotiation of salaries and sometimes endorsements.[25] Many states have not attempted to regulate agent fees.

Model Rules of Professional Conduct   approved by the American Bar Association in 1983, these rules have been adopted by many states to replace the Model Code of Professional Responsibility

MLBPA   Major League Baseball Players Association

NBPA   National Basketball Players Association

NHLPA   National Hockey League Players Association

States Regulating Fees

In addition to regulation of agents by players associations and rules imposed on colleges and universities by the NCAA,[26] 34 states currently regulate sports agents, and that number is continually on the rise. For example, Alabama regulates fees for any "professional sports services contracts,"[27] but the statute is unclear as to whether this applies to endorsement contracts.

Outside the NFL, MLB, NBA, and NHL, no cap restricts the fee an agent may charge an athlete for representation, though market forces generally have indicated that fees between 10 percent and 20 percent of an endorsement contract are reasonable. To many people this may seem high, but the money generated in endorsements is not guaranteed and agents may spend considerable amounts of time and financial resources to promote an athlete in this area. Accordingly, most athletes do not object to higher fees.

■ Regulation by Players Associations/Unions

Regulating sports agents allows for the free exchange of important salary information and for punishing unethical or unprofessional conduct by or on behalf of the agent. In addition, regulation proscribes a standard representation agreement between the athlete and agent.

The NFLPA regulates contract advisors in the NFL.[28] The MLBPA regulates player agents in Major League Baseball, as do the NHLPA and NBPA in their respective sports. These associations are the exclusive bargaining agents for the players and are subject to the rules and procedures set for in the National Labor Relations Act.[29] Recently, sports agent William "Tank" Black was stripped of his certification with the NFLPA for violating solicitation codes of ethics and state laws in numerous states, as he faced criminal charges in South Carolina and under federal laws.[30]

NFLPA

Before an agent may represent an NFL player, the agent must register with the NFLPA. To represent players in this league, the agent or "contract advisor" must receive a degree from a four-year accredited college or university.[31] Additionally, the NFLPA has recently required a written take-home test to remain in good standing; an agent who does not pass the test or who does not pay the fee can be suspended by the NFLPA. Similar to state statutes governing lawyers, NFLPA contract advisors may not offer a monetary inducement to any player or prospective player to encourage that person to use his or her services.[32]

MLBPA

As in the NFL, agents who wish to conduct business in baseball as a player agent must be certified by the MLBPA. However, a college degree is not required and there is no limit as to the fee an agent may charge in this league as long as, after the agent's fee is deducted, the player still is entitled to the minimum salary for that particular player's position in the league.[33] Player agents in this league may not induce clients with money.[34]

NHLPA

The NHL players union regulates agent activity as well. Similar to MLB, the NHL does not cap agent fees as long as the player earns the minimum salary after the agent is paid.

NBPA

The NBA's players association certifies agents. Players must use certified agents to represent them during contract negotiation or players may negotiate contracts themselves. Teams not negotiating with certified agents may be fined.

■ Breach of Fiduciary Duty

Sometimes a conflict regarding the role of the agent may lead to litigation. Most disagreements focus on financial disputes. Such cases are often settled without the necessity of legal action, but in some instances there appears to be no acceptable alternative other than litigation.

California prohibits agents from maintaining an ownership or financial interest in any entity that is directly involved in the same sport as a person with whom the athlete agent has entered into an agent contract.[35] Alabama and California have comprehensive statutes that an agent may not split fees with a team or league due to the appearance of impropriety.[36]

Other legal disputes have resulted when agents of a former sports management group have left the agency to form their own business. These agents have been served with injunctions and lawsuits alleging that such conduct was unethical, fraudulent, and a breach of contract with the former employer.

■ NCAA Student-Athletes Turning Professional

In addition to state laws, the NCAA has expressed serious concerns over the abuse by agents with regard to nonprofessional student-athletes who have remaining eligibility in their particular sport.[37] Agents who are adept at recruiting student-athlete clients can use a variety of resources to get to know a student-athlete with the expectation of retaining the student-athlete as a professional client. It is not against NCAA regulations (see Exhibit 1–2) for an agent to contact a student-athlete, but some state laws prohibit such conduct.

However, the NCAA has been adamant in its resolve to maintain its integrity as an amateur organization. According to the NCAA Division I manual, the basic purpose of the NCAA is to "maintain intercollegiate athletics as an integral part of the educational program and the athlete as an integral part of the student body and, by so doing, retain a clear line of demarcation between intercollegiate athletics and professional sports" (Rule 1.3.1).

If a student-athlete merely agrees to be represented by an agent orally or in writing, that student-athlete may have to forfeit his or her remaining collegiate eligibility. This punishes the student-athlete and may also force the college or university to forfeit games, prevent an appearance in a post-season bowl, lose scholarships over time, and even prevent the college or university from sharing in revenues with other members of the NCAA.[38] It is the latter concern that is often the most important in terms of state regulation of agents.

Case 1 represents one of the most egregious instances of impropriety in sports agency history. **Norby Walters** and **Lloyd Bloom** were indicted in federal district court in Chicago for violation of NCAA rules by inducing student-athletes to sign professional contracts before their collegiate eligibility had expired. The athletes were showered with cash and products, as were their families.

Professional Sports Counseling Panels

In 1984, the NCAA adopted legislation that permits its member institutions to establish **professional sports counseling panels**. This legislation was intended to encourage member institutions to provide guidance to their student-athletes regarding future professional athletic careers. The panels were designed to assist student-athletes in making a decision regarding whether to remain in school or turn professional and to provide guidance to student-athletes regarding contacts and agreements with player agents.

student-athletes need objective advice from individuals at institutions who have no vested interest in their careers. Their coaches or other athletic department members may be biased in favor of student-athletes remaining in their programs to further the athletic interests of the college or university. The NCAA notes that such panels should attempt to provide information to student-athletes regarding professional athletics that they may not be able to obtain or understand sufficiently on their own.

Norby Walters and **Lloyd Bloom**   sports agents charged with racketeering, conspiracy, and fraud in recruiting student-athletes

professional sports counseling panels   groups formed by colleges and universities to advise student-athletes on potential careers in professional sports

■ **EXHIBIT 1–2**   *Excerpt of NCAA Rules Governing Agents*

II. AGENTS.

A. General Rule. An individual shall be ineligible for participation in an intercollegiate sport if he or she ever has agreed (orally or in writing) to be represented by an agent for the purpose of marketing his or her athletics ability or reputation in that sport. Further, an agency contract not specifically limited in writing to a sport or particular sports shall be deemed applicable to all sports, and the individual shall be ineligible to participate in any sport. [12.3.1]

1. Student-Athlete Signing Agreement with Attorney. A student-athlete is not permitted to sign an agreement with an attorney to represent the student-athlete in screening inquiries and analyzing offers from agents, inasmuch as it would be contrary to 12.3.1 (representation by an agent). [01/27/89 legislative services staff (cited in this document as "Staff"), item 1-c]

2. Relationship between Student-Athlete and Lawyer who Contacted Professional Football Teams on Student-Athlete's Behalf. The staff agreed that an agency relationship existed between a student-athlete and a lawyer, contrary to the provisions of 12.3.1, in a situation in which the student-athlete received a "tryout" with one professional team as a result of the lawyer's efforts, and the student-athlete and the lawyer communicated with each other over a five-month period regarding the reaction of the professional teams. [08/14/87 Staff, item 1-c]

3. Student-Athlete Signing Agreement with Agent and Participating in an All-Star Contest. A student-athlete who has signed with an agent subsequent to the completion of the student-athlete's eligibility in that sport (including post-season team competition) still would be permitted to participate in an individual all-star contest. [01/09/81, NCAA Council (cited in this document as "Council") and 12/09/91 Legislative Assistance Column No. 44 (cited in this document as "LAC"), Item No. 4.]

4. Student-Athletes Having Agreements with Financial Advisors. A financial advisor can be treated as an agent for purpose of the application of NCAA legislation if he or she acts as an agent. Accordingly, NCAA rules do not prohibit student-athletes from agreeing to be represented by a financial advisor, whose responsibilities are limited solely to the functions of a money manager. [04/26/95 Council, Item No. 4-k-(1)]

5. Student-Athlete Retaining Agent to Pursue Radio/Television/Theatre Appearances. A student-athlete who is seeking a degree in the performing arts (e.g., theatre, drama) may retain an entertainment agent for the purposes of pursuing appearances on radio, television, and theatre, provided the student-athlete's athletics reputation or ability is not used in any manner to secure such appearances and any compensation received by the student-athlete is at a rate commensurate with the individual's skills and experience as a performer and not based in any way on the individual's athletics ability or reputation. Any compensation received by the student-athlete must be consistent with applicable NCAA limitations on a student-athlete's maximum amount of financial aid. [03/11/96 NCAA Interpretations Committee (cited in this document as "IC"), Item No. 1]

B. Coaches Involvement.

1. Marketing Student-Athletes to Professional Teams/Organizations. Staff members of the athletics department of a member institution shall not represent, directly or indirectly, any individual in the marketing of athletics ability or reputation to an agent, a professional sports team or a professional sports organization, except as specified in 11.1.5.1, and shall not receive compensation or gratuities of any kind, directly or indirectly, for such services. [11.1.5]

2. Exception—Professional Sports Counseling Panel and Head Coach. An institution's professional sports counseling panel or a head coach in a sport may contact agents, professional sports teams or professional sports organizations on behalf of a student-athlete, provided no compensation is received for such services. The head coach shall consult with and report his or her activities on behalf of the student-athlete to the institution's professional sports counseling panel. If the institution has no such panel, the head coach shall consult with and report his or her activities to the chief executive officer, [or an individual or group (e.g., athletics advisory board) designated by the chief executive officer]. The professional sports counseling panel and the head coach may: [11.1.5.1]

   a. Communicate directly (e.g., in-person, by mail or telephone) with representatives of a professional athletics team to assist in securing a tryout with that team for a student-athlete;

b. Assist the student-athlete in the selection of an agent by participating with the student-athlete in interviews of agents, by reviewing written information player agents send to the student-athlete and by having direct communication with those individuals who can comment about the abilities of an agent (e.g., other agents, a professional league's players association); and

c. Visit with player agents or representatives of professional athletics teams to assist the student-athlete in determining his or her market value (e.g., potential salary, draft status).

3. Coach/Parent — Negotiations. A parent, who is an institution's coaching staff member, may participate in the activities listed in 12.2.4.3 (e.g., negotiations with professional team) on behalf of his or her child without jeopardizing the individual's amateur status. The coach, however, is not permitted to engage in any activities related to the marketing of his or her son's or daughter's athletics ability or reputation except as permitted in 11.1.5.1. [03/08/95 Staff, item 1-e]

C. Representation for Future Negotiations. An individual shall be ineligible per 12.3.1 if he or she enters into a verbal or written agreement with an agent for representation in future professional sports negotiations that are to take place after the individual has completed his or her eligibility in that sport. [12.3.1.1]

D. Benefits from Prospective Agents. An individual shall be ineligible per 12.3.1 if he or she (or his or her relatives or friends) accepts transportation or other benefits from any person who represents the individual in the marketing of his or her athletics ability, or any agent, even if the agent has indicated that he or she has no interest in representing the student-athlete in the marketing of his or her athletics ability or reputation and does not represent individuals in the student-athlete's sport. The receipt of such expenses constitutes compensation based on athletics skill and is an extra benefit not available to the student body in general. [12.3.1.2]

1. For example, a student-athlete would jeopardize his or her intercollegiate eligibility in a particular sport if he or she accepted from a prospective agent automobile transportation from the member institution's campus to the prospective agent's office to discuss services the agent could provide to the student-athlete.

2. Student-Athlete Who is a Multisport Participant Receives Money from an Agent. A student-athlete may sign an agency contract for a particular sport, but by doing so, the student-athlete would render himself or herself ineligible in that sport. A student-athlete who receives money (or other benefits) from an agent who is representing the student-athlete only in a particular sport would remain eligible to participate in a second sport at the member institution. Under such circumstances, the student-athlete's financial aid would be required to be gradated in an amount equal to the loan or the value of the benefits. [04/26/91 IC, Item No. 1]

3. Agent Charging Fee to Student-Athlete on Deferred Payment Schedule. A student-athlete jeopardizes his or her eligibility if an agent provides advice to the student-athlete about a professional contract with the understanding that the student-athlete will pay the agent for such services once the student-athlete has been drafted by a professional sports organization, regardless of the fact that the agent provides the service only to student-athletes and has the same fee arrangement for all clients. [12/16/92 Staff, item 1-a]

4. Agent Employing Student-Athlete. It would be necessary to sponsor legislation in order to preclude the employment of a prospect or a student-athlete by an agent under any circumstances. [04/20/95 IC, Item No. 1]

5. Receipt of Improper Benefits. A student-athlete is determined to have received an improper benefit at the time the student-athlete accepts a benefit associated with an item that is not otherwise permissible under NCAA legislation. In situations in which a student-athlete accepts but does not actually use the impermissible item, such information may be considered as a mitigating factor in any appeal for restoration of the student-athlete's eligibility. [10/23/95 IC, Item No. 2]

E. Legal Counsel. Securing advice from a lawyer concerning a proposed professional sports contract shall not be considered contracting for representation by an agent under this rule, unless the lawyer also represents the student-athlete in negotiations for such a contract. [12.3.2]

■ CASE 1 *United States v. Walters (Excerpt)*

UNITED STATES COURT OF APPEALS,
SEVENTH CIRCUIT.

UNITED STATES of America, Plaintiff-Appellee,

v.

Norby WALTERS, Defendant-Appellant.

No. 92-3420.

Argued June 11, 1993.

Decided June 30, 1993.

Defendant was charged with mail fraud and other offenses. Following reversal of initial conviction, 913 F.2d 388, and denial of motion to dismiss, United States District Court for the Northern District of Illinois, Harry D. Leinenweber, J., 775 F.Supp. 1173, defendant pleaded guilty to mail fraud, conceding that record of first trial supplied factual basis for conviction, while reserving right to contest sufficiency of that evidence. Defendant appealed. The Court of Appeals, Easterbrook, Circuit Judge, held that: (1) forms mailed by colleges to the National Collegiate Athletic Association (NCAA) verifying college football players' eligibility were not sufficiently integral to defendant's scheme, to sign players secretly to agency contracts prior to expiration of their college eligibility, to support a mail fraud conviction; (2) even if mailings were sufficient, defendant did not cause universities to use the mails; and (3) in any event, conviction could not be sustained on basis that defendant deprived universities of scholarship funds paid to athletes who were no longer eligible, where defendant did not obtain any property from the victim universities by fraud.

Reversed.

Robert S. Rivkin, Asst. U.S. Atty. (argued), Barry R. Elden, Asst. U.S. Atty., Chicago, IL, for U.S.

Andrew L. Frey (argued), Kerry Lynn Edwards, Mayer, Brown & Platt, Washington, DC, Tyrone C. Fahner, Mayer, Brown & Platt, Chicago, IL, for defendant-appellant.

Before EASTERBROOK and MANION, Circuit Judges, and ALDISERT, Senior Circuit Judge.*

EASTERBROOK, Circuit Judge.

Norby Walters, who represents entertainers, tried to move into the sports business. He signed 58 college football players to contracts while they were still playing. Walters offered cars and money to those who would agree to use him as their representative in dealing with professional teams. Sports agents receive a percentage of the players' income, so Walters would profit only to the extent he could negotiate contracts for his clients. The athletes' pro prospects depended on successful completion of their collegiate careers. To the NCAA, however, a student who signs a contract with an agent is a professional, ineligible to play on collegiate teams. To avoid jeopardizing his clients' careers, Walters dated the contracts after the end of their eligibility and locked them in a safe. He promised to lie to the universities in response to any inquiries. Walters inquired of sports lawyers at Shea & Gould whether this plan of operation would be lawful. The firm rendered an opinion that it would violate the NCAA's rules but not any statute.

Having recruited players willing to fool their universities and the NCAA, Walters discovered that they were equally willing to play false with him. Only 2 of the 58 players fulfilled their end of the bargain; the other 56 kept the cars and money, then signed with other agents. They relied on the fact that the contracts were locked away and dated in the future, and that Walters' business depended on continued secrecy, so he could not very well sue to enforce their promises. When the 56 would neither accept him as their representative nor return the payments, Walters resorted to threats. One player, Maurice Douglass, was told that his legs would be broken before the pro draft unless he repaid Walters' firm. A 75-page indictment charged Walters and his partner Lloyd Bloom with conspiracy, RICO violations (the predicate felony was extortion), and mail fraud. The fraud: causing the universities to pay scholarship funds to athletes who had become ineligible as a result of the agency contracts. The mail: each university required its athletes to verify their eligibility to play, then sent copies by mail to conferences such as the Big Ten.

After a month-long trial and a week of deliberations, the jury convicted Walters and Bloom. We reversed, holding that the district judge had erred in declining to instruct the jury that reliance on Shea & Gould's advice could prevent the formation of intent to defraud the universities. 913 F.2d 388, 391–92 (1990). Any dispute about the adequacy of Walters' disclosure to his lawyers and the bona fides of his reliance was for the jury, we concluded. Because Bloom declined to waive his own attorney-client privilege, we held that the defendants must be retried separately. *Id.* at 392–93. On remand, Walters asked the district court to dismiss the indictment, arguing that the evidence presented at trial is insufficient to support the convictions. After the judge denied this motion, 775 F.Supp. 1173 (N.D.Ill.1991), Walters agreed to enter a conditional *Alford* plea: he would plead guilty to mail fraud, conceding that the record of the first trial supplies a factual basis for a conviction while reserving his right to contest the sufficiency of that evidence. In return, the prosecutor agreed to dismiss the RICO and conspiracy charges and to return to Walters all property that had been forfeited as a result of his RICO conviction. Thus a case that began with a focus on extortion has become a straight mail fraud prosecution and may undergo yet another transformation. The prosecutor believes that Walters hampered the investigation preceding his indictment. *See In re Feldberg*, 862 F.2d 622 (7th Cir.1988) (describing some of the investigation). The plea agreement reserves the prosecutor's right to charge Walters with perjury and obstruction of justice if we should reverse the conviction for mail fraud.

[1] [2] "Whoever, having devised . . . any scheme or artifice to defraud, or for obtaining money or property by means of false or fraudulent pretenses, representations, or promises . . . places in any post office or authorized depository for mail matter, any matter or thing whatever to be sent or delivered by the Postal Service . . . or knowingly causes [such matter or thing] to be delivered by mail" commits the crime of mail fraud. 18 U.S.C. § 1341. Norby Walters did not mail anything or cause anyone else to do so (the universities were going to collect and mail the forms no matter what Walters did), but the Supreme Court has expanded the statute beyond its literal terms, holding that a mailing by a third party suffices if it is "incident to an essential part of the scheme," *Pereira v. United States*, 347 U.S. 1, 8, 74 S.Ct. 358, 363, 98 L.Ed. 435 (1954). While stating that such mailings can turn ordinary fraud into mail fraud, the Court has cautioned that the statute "does not purport to reach all frauds, but only those limited instances in which the use of the mails is a part of the execution of the fraud". *Kann v. United States*, 323 U.S. 88, 95, 65 S.Ct. 148, 151, 89 L.Ed. 88 (1944). Everything thus turns on matters of degree. Did the schemers foresee that the mails would be used? Did the mailing advance the success of the scheme? Which parts of a scheme are "essential"? Such questions lack obviously right answers, so it is no surprise that each side to this case can cite several of our decisions in support. Compare *United States v. McClain*, 934 F.2d 822, 835 (7th Cir.1991), and *United States v. Kwiat*, 817 F.2d 440, 443–44 (7th Cir.1987), among cases reversing convictions because use of the mails was too remote or unforeseeable, with *Messinger v. United States*, 872 F.2d 217 (7th Cir.1989), among many cases holding that particular uses of the mails were vital to the scheme and foreseeable.

"The relevant question . . . is whether the mailing is part of the execution of the scheme as conceived by the perpetrator at the time". *Schmuck v. United States*, 489 U.S. 705, 715, 109 S.Ct. 1443, 1450, 103 L.Ed.2d 734 (1989). Did the evidence establish that Walters conceived a scheme in which mailings played a role? We think not—indeed, that no reasonable juror could give an affirmative answer to this question. Walters hatched a scheme to make money by taking a percentage of athletes' pro contracts. To get clients he signed students while college eligibility remained, thus avoiding competition from ethical agents. To obtain big pro contracts for these clients he needed to keep the deals secret, so the athletes could finish their collegiate careers. Thus deceit was an ingredient of the plan. We may assume that Walters knew that the universities would ask athletes to verify that they were eligible to compete as amateurs. But what role do the mails play? The plan succeeds so long as the athletes conceal their contracts from their schools (and remain loyal to Walters). Forms verifying eligibility do not help the plan *succeed*; instead they create a risk that it will be discovered if a student should tell the truth. Cf. *United States v. Maze*, 414 U.S. 395, 94 S.Ct. 645, 38 L.Ed.2d 603 (1974). And it is the forms, not their mailing to the Big Ten, that pose the risk. For all Walters cared, the forms

continued

could sit forever in cartons. Movement to someplace else was irrelevant. In *Schmuck*, where the fraud was selling cars with rolled-back odometers, the mailing was essential to obtain a new and apparently "clean" certificate of title; no certificates of title, no marketable cars, no hope for success. Even so, the Court divided five to four on the question whether the mailing was sufficiently integral to the scheme. A college's mailing to its conference has less to do with the plot's success than the mailings that transferred title in *Schmuck*.

[3] [4] [5] [6] To this the United States responds that the mailings were essential because, if a college had neglected to send the athletes' forms to the conference, the NCAA would have barred that college's team from competing. Lack of competition would spoil the athletes' pro prospects. Thus the use of the mails was integral to the profits Walters hoped to reap, even though Walters would have been delighted had the colleges neither asked any questions of the athletes nor put the answers in the mail. Let us take this as sufficient under *Schmuck* (although we have our doubts). The question remains whether Walters caused the universities to use the mails.[1] A person "knowingly causes" the use of the mails when he "acts with the knowledge that the use of the mails will follow in the ordinary course of business, or where such use can reasonably be foreseen." *United States v. Kuzniar*, 881 F.2d 466, 472 (7th Cir.1989), quoting *Pereira*, 347 U.S. at 8–9, 74 S.Ct. at 363. The paradigm is insurance fraud. Perkins tells his auto insurer that his car has been stolen, when in fact it has been sold. The local employee mails the claim to the home office, which mails a check to Perkins. Such mailings in the ordinary course of business are foreseeable. E.g., *United States v. Richman*, 944 F.2d 323 (7th Cir.1991). Similarly, a judge who takes a bribe derived from the litigant's bail money causes the use of the mails when the ordinary course is to refund the bond by mail. E.g., *United States v. Murphy*, 768 F.2d 1518, 1529–30 (7th Cir.1985). The prosecutor contends that the same approach covers Walters.

No evidence demonstrates that Walters *actually* knew that the colleges would mail the athletes' forms. The record is barely sufficient to establish that Walters knew of the forms' existence; it is silent about Walters' knowledge of the forms' disposition. The only evidence implying that Walters knew that the colleges had students fill out forms is an ambiguous reference to "these

forms" in the testimony of Robert Perryman. Nothing in the record suggests that Perryman, a student-athlete, knew what his university did with the forms, let alone that Perryman passed this information to Walters. So the prosecutor is reduced to the argument that mailings could "reasonably be foreseen." Yet why should this be so? Universities frequently collect information that is stashed in file drawers. Perhaps the NCAA just wants answers available for inspection in the event a question arises, or the university wants the information for its own purposes (to show that it did not know about any improprieties that later come to light). What was it about these forms that should have led a reasonable person to foresee their mailing? Recall that Walters was trying to break into the sports business. Counsel specializing in sports law told him that his plan would not violate any statute. These lawyers were unaware of the forms (or, if they knew about the forms, were unaware that they would be mailed). The prosecutor contends that Walters neglected to tell his lawyers about the eligibility forms, spoiling their opinion; yet why would Walters have to brief an expert in sports law if mailings were foreseeable even to a novice?

[7] In the end, the prosecutor insists that the large size and interstate nature of the NCAA demonstrate that something would be dropped into the mails. To put this only slightly differently, the prosecutor submits that all frauds involving big organizations necessarily are mail frauds, because big organizations habitually mail things. No evidence put before the jury supports such a claim, and it is hardly appropriate for judicial notice in a criminal case. Moreover, adopting this perspective would contradict the assurance of *Kann*, 323 U.S. at 95, 65 S.Ct. at 151, and many later cases that most frauds are covered by state law rather than § 1341. That statute has been expanded considerably by judicial interpretation, but it does not make a federal crime of every deceit. The prosecutor must *prove* that the use of the mails was foreseeable, rather than calling on judicial intuition to repair a rickety case.

[8] [9] There is a deeper problem with the theory of this prosecution. The United States tells us that the universities lost their scholarship money. Money is property; this aspect of the prosecution does not encounter a problem under *McNally v. United States*, 483 U.S. 350, 107 S.Ct. 2875, 97 L.Ed.2d 292 (1987). Walters emphasizes that the universities put his 58 athletes on

scholarship long before he met them and did not pay a penny more than they planned to do. But a jury could conclude that had Walters' clients told the truth, the colleges would have stopped their scholarships, thus saving money. So we must assume that the universities lost property by reason of Walters' deeds. Still, they were not out of pocket *to Walters*; he planned to profit by taking a percentage of the players' professional incomes, not of their scholarships. Section 1341 condemns "any scheme or artifice to defraud, or *for obtaining* money or property" (emphasis added). If the universities were the victims, how did he "obtain" their property?, Walters asks.

According to the United States, neither an actual nor a potential transfer of property from the victim to the defendant is essential. It is enough that the victim lose; what (if anything) the schemer hopes to gain plays no role in the definition of the offense. We asked the prosecutor at oral argument whether on this rationale practical jokes violate § 1341. *A* mails *B* an invitation to a surprise party for their mutual friend *C*. *B* drives his car to the place named in the invitation. But there is no party; the address is a vacant lot; *B* is the butt of a joke. The invitation came by post; the cost of gasoline means that *B* is out of pocket. The prosecutor said that this indeed violates § 1341, but that his office pledges to use prosecutorial discretion wisely. Many people will find this position unnerving (what if the prosecutor's policy changes, or *A* is politically unpopular and the prosecutor is looking for a way to nail him?). Others, who obey the law out of a sense of civic obligation rather than the fear of sanctions, will alter their conduct no matter what policy the prosecutor follows. Either way, the idea that practical jokes are federal felonies would make a joke of the Supreme Court's assurance that § 1341 does not cover the waterfront of deceit.

Practical jokes rarely come to the attention of federal prosecutors, but large organizations are more successful in gaining the attention of public officials. In this case the mail fraud statute has been invoked to shore up the rules of an influential private association. Consider a parallel: an association of manufacturers of plumbing fixtures adopts a rule providing that its members will not sell "seconds" (that is, blemished articles) to the public. The association proclaims that this rule protects consumers from shoddy goods. To remain in good standing, a member must report its sales monthly. These

reports flow in by mail. One member begins to sell "seconds" but reports that it is not doing so. These sales take business away from other members of the association, who lose profits as a result. So we have mail, misrepresentation, and the loss of property, but the liar does not get any of the property the other firms lose. Has anyone committed a federal crime? The answer is yes—but the statute is the Sherman Act, 15 U.S.C. § 1, and the perpetrators are the firms that adopted the "no seconds" rule. *United States v. Trenton Potteries Co.*, 273 U.S. 392, 47 S.Ct. 377, 71 L.Ed. 700 (1927). The trade association we have described is a cartel, which the firm selling "seconds" was undermining. Cheaters depress the price, causing the monopolist to lose money. Typically they go to great lengths to disguise their activities, the better to increase their own sales and avoid retaliation. The prosecutor's position in our case would make criminals of the cheaters, would use § 1341 to shore up cartels.

Fanciful? Not at all. Many scholars understand the NCAA as a cartel, having power in the market for athletes. E.g., Arthur A. Fleisher III, Brian L. Goff & Robert D. Tollison, *The National Collegiate Athletic Association: A Study in Cartel Behavior* (1992); Joseph P. Bauer, *Antitrust and Sports: Must Competition on the Field Displace Competition in the Marketplace?*, 60 Tenn.L.Rev. 263 (1993); Roger D. Blair & Jeffrey L. Harrison, *Cooperative Buying, Monopsony Power, and Antitrust Policy*, 86 Nw.U.L.Rev. 331 (1992); Lee Goldman, *Sports and Antitrust: Should College Students be Paid to Play?*, 65 Notre Dame L.Rev. 206 (1990); Richard B. McKenzie & E. Thomas Sullivan, *Does the NCAA Exploit College Athletes? An Economic and Legal Reinterpretation*, 32 Antitrust Bull. 373 (1987); Stephen F. Ross, *Monopoly Sports Leagues*, 73 Minn.L.Rev. 643 (1989). See also *NCAA v. University of Oklahoma*, 468 U.S. 85, 104 S.Ct. 2948, 82 L.Ed.2d 70 (1984) (holding that the NCAA's arrangements for the telecasting of college football violated the Sherman Act); *Banks v. NCAA*, 977 F.2d 1081 (7th Cir.1992) (showing disagreement among members of this court whether the NCAA's restrictions on athletes violate the Sherman Act). The NCAA depresses athletes' income—restricting payments to the value of tuition, room, and board, while receiving services of substantially greater worth. The NCAA treats this as desirable preservation of amateur sports; a more jaundiced eye would see it as the use of monopsony power to obtain athletes' services for less than the

continued

competitive market price. Walters then is cast in the role of a cheater, increasing the payments to the student-athletes. Like other cheaters, Walters found it convenient to hide his activities. If, as the prosecutor believes, his repertory included extortion, he has used methods that the law denies to persons fighting cartels, but for the moment we are concerned only with the deceit that caused the universities to pay stipends to "professional" athletes. For current purposes it matters not whether the NCAA *actually* monopsonizes the market for players; the point of this discussion is that the prosecutor's theory makes criminals of those who consciously cheat on the rules of a private organization, even if that organization is a cartel. We pursue this point because any theory that makes criminals of cheaters raises a red flag.

Cheaters are not self-conscious champions of the public weal. They are in it for profit, as rapacious and mendacious as those who hope to collect monopoly rents. Maybe more; often members of cartels believe that monopoly serves the public interest, and they take their stand on the platform of business ethics, e.g., *National Society of Professional Engineers v. United States*, 435 U.S. 679, 98 S.Ct. 1355, 55 L.Ed.2d 637 (1978), while cheaters' glasses have been washed with cynical acid. Only Adam Smith's invisible hand turns their self-seeking activities to public benefit. It is cause for regret if prosecutors, assuming that persons with low regard for honesty must be villains, use the criminal laws to suppress the competitive process that undermines cartels. Of course federal laws have been used to enforce cartels before; the Federal Maritime Commission is a cartel-enforcement device. Inconsistent federal laws also occur; the United States both subsidizes tobacco growers and discourages people from smoking. So if the United States simultaneously forbids cartels and forbids undermining cartels by cheating, we shall shrug our shoulders and enforce both laws, condemning practical jokes along the way. But what is it about § 1341 that labels as a crime all deceit that inflicts any loss on anyone? Firms often try to fool their competitors, surprising them with new products that enrich their treasuries at their rivals' expense. Is this mail fraud because large organizations inevitably use the mail? "[A]ny scheme or artifice to defraud, or for obtaining money or property by means of false or fraudulent pretenses, representations, or promises" reads like a description of schemes to *get* money or property by fraud rather than methods of doing business that incidentally cause losses.

None of the Supreme Court's mail fraud cases deals with a scheme in which the defendant neither obtained nor tried to obtain the victim's property. It has, however, addressed the question whether 18 U.S.C. § 371, which prohibits conspiracies to defraud the United States, criminalizes plans that cause incidental loss to the Treasury. *Tanner v. United States*, 483 U.S. 107, 130, 107 S.Ct. 2739, 2752, 97 L.Ed.2d 90 (1987), holds that § 371 applies only when the United States is a "target" of the fraud; schemes that cause indirect losses do not violate that statute. *McNally* tells us that § 371 covers a broader range of frauds than does § 1341, see 483 U.S. at 358–59 n. 8, 107 S.Ct. at 2881, n. 8, and it follows that business plans causing incidental losses are not mail fraud. We have been unable to find any appellate cases squarely resolving the question whether the victim's loss must be an objective of the scheme rather than a byproduct of it, perhaps because prosecutions of the kind this case represents are so rare.[2] According to the prosecutor, however, there have been such cases, and in this circuit. The United States contends that we have already held that a scheme producing an incidental loss violates § 1341. A representative sample of the cases the prosecutor cites shows that we have held no such thing.

For example, *United States v. Ashman*, 979 F.2d 469, 477–83 (7th Cir.1992), affirms convictions for fraud in a matched-order scheme on the floor of the Chicago Board of Trade. Customers sent orders for execution "at the market." Traders paired some of these orders off the market at times chosen to divert profits to themselves. This deprived the customers of the benefits provided by an open-outcry auction; more important, it moved money directly from customers' accounts to the traders' accounts. The transfers were the objective of the scheme. Nothing comparable took place here; no money moved from the universities to Walters. There is, however, some parallel in *Ashman*: we held that trades executed after the market was limit-up or limit-down could not support mail fraud convictions. *Id.* at 479. Once the market had moved the limit for the day, customers received the same price no matter when or with whom they traded. A customer willing to trade at a known price is like a university willing to give a scholarship to a known athlete. A customer who loses the honesty of the traders, but no money, has not been defrauded of property; a university that loses the benefits of amateurism likewise has been deprived only of an intangible right, which per *McNally* does not support a conviction.[3]

United States v. Richman sustained mail fraud convictions arising out of a lawyer's attempt to bribe the claims adjuster for an insurance company. Retained to represent the victim of an accident, the lawyer offered the adjuster 5% of any settlement. Here was a fraud aimed at obtaining money from the insurer—a settlement was the objective rather than a byproduct of the scheme. The lawyer defended by contending that, because his client really *had* been injured, the insurer would have paid anyway. 944 F.2d at 330. This was highly implausible; why was the lawyer willing to bribe the adjuster? The scheme was designed to increase the settlement, or to induce the insurer to pay even if its insured was not negligent. At all events, we observed, the statute prohibits schemes that are designed to bilk other persons out of money or other property; the lawyer's scheme had this objective even though the deceit might have been unnecessary. 944 F.2d at 330–31. Walters lacked any similar design to separate the universities from their money. Then there is *United States v. Jones*, 938 F.2d 737 (7th Cir.1991). The Joneses impersonated loan brokers. In exchange for $4,000 paid up front, they promised to procure large loans for their clients. Although they accepted almost $10 million in fees, they never found funding for a single client. Next they dispersed the money in an effort to prevent the assessment and collection of taxes on the booty. Our holding that the scam violated both § 371 and § 1343 (wire fraud) by preventing the United States from taking its cut of the proceeds does not support a conclusion that any deceit that incidentally causes a loss to someone also violates federal law.

Many of our cases ask whether a particular scheme deprived a victim of property. E.g., *Lombardo v. United States*, 865 F.2d 155, 159–60 (7th Cir.1989). They do so not with an emphasis on "deprive" but with an emphasis on "property"—which, until the enactment of 18 U.S.C. § 1346 after Walters' conduct, was essential to avoid the "intangible rights" doctrine that *McNally* jettisoned. No one doubted that the schemes were designed to enrich the perpetrators at the victims'

expense; the only difficulty was the proper characterization of the deprivation.[4] Not until today have we dealt with a scheme in which the defendants' profits were to come from legitimate transactions in the market, rather than at the expense of the victims. Both the "scheme or artifice to defraud" clause and the "obtaining money or property" clause of § 1343 contemplate a transfer of some kind. Accordingly, following both the language of § 1341 and the implication of *Tanner*, we hold that only a scheme to obtain money or other property from the victim by fraud violates § 1341. A deprivation is a necessary but not a sufficient condition of mail fraud. Losses that occur as byproducts of a deceitful scheme do not satisfy the statutory requirement.

[10] Anticipating that we might come to this conclusion, the prosecutor contends that Walters is nonetheless guilty as an aider and abettor. If Walters did not defraud the universities, the argument goes, then the athletes did. Walters put them up to it and so is guilty under 18 U.S.C. § 2, the argument concludes. But the indictment charged a scheme *by Walters* to defraud; it did not depict Walters as an *aide de camp* in the students' scheme. The jury received a boilerplate § 2 instruction; this theory was not argued to the jury, or for that matter to the district court either before or after the remand. Independent problems dog this recasting of the scheme—not least the difficulty of believing that the students hatched a plot to employ fraud to receive scholarships that the universities had awarded them long before Walters arrived on the scene, and the lack of evidence that the students knew about or could foresee any mailings. Walters is by all accounts a nasty and untrustworthy fellow, but the prosecutor did not prove that his efforts to circumvent the NCAA's rules amounted to mail fraud.

REVERSED.

FOOTNOTES

*Hon. Ruggero J. Aldisert, of the Third Circuit, sitting by designation.

1. The United States contends that Walters has waived the causation argument by failing to raise it with sufficient specificity after remand. Yet the judge addressed this subject and rejected Walters' argument on the merits. 775 F.Supp. at 1181. An argument presented clearly enough to draw a response from the district judge has been

continued

preserved for decision on appeal. Moreover, causation is an element of the offense, and Walters expressly contended that the evidence was deficient. Both the plea agreement and the letter of understanding negotiated by the parties preserve this contention.

2. Cases such as *United States v. Goodrich*, 871 F.2d 1011, 1013 (11th Cir.1989); *United States v. Evans*, 844 F.2d 36, 39–40 (2d Cir.1988), and *United States v. Baldinger*, 838 F.2d 176, 180 (6th Cir.1988), contain language implying support for Walters' position, but none of these cases directly confronted the question. Other cases contain language seeming to undermine that position, e.g., *United States v. Gimbel*, 830 F.2d 621, 627 (7th Cir.1987), but again the court did not confront the issue. (*Gimbel* reversed the conviction on *McNally* grounds; the panel's passing observation that the scheme "resulted in the [victim] being deprived of money or property" hardly settles the question in our case.) One district court has held that the victim's loss must be an objective of the scheme. *United States v. Regan*, 713 F.Supp. 629, 636–38 (S.D.N.Y.1989). The district court's opinion in Walters' case appears to be the only expressly contrary authority.

3. The United States recasts this argument by contending that the universities lost (and Walters gained) the "right to control" who received the scholarships. This is an intangible rights theory once removed—weaker even than the position rejected in *Toulabi v. United States*, 875 F.2d 122 (7th Cir.1989), and *United States v. Holzer*, 840 F.2d 1343 (7th Cir.1988), because Walters was not the universities' fiduciary. *Borre v. United States*, 940 F.2d 215 (7th Cir.1991), did not purport to overrule *Toulabi* and *Holzer*, and is at all events a case in which the fraud (a) transferred property from victim to perpetrator, and (b) was committed by a group of schemers that includes the victim's fiduciary.

4. In *Lombardo* the plan was to bribe a Senator by selling him, for $1.4 million, a piece of property worth $1.6 million. Had the scheme succeeded, the Senator would have been $200,000 richer and the Teamsters pension fund $200,000 poorer, although it might have received some "legislative appreciation." The defendants would have been among the beneficiaries of that "appreciation" and thus stood to receive, indirectly, a portion of the fund's loss.

■ Summary

Sports agents serve a valuable role for the professional athlete. Most agents require exclusive agency contracts. General agency law principles prevail in sports agency as well. No federal laws regulate sports agents, but 34 states have adopted sports agent regulations. The Uniform Athlete Agents Act (UAAA) has been drafted and approved by the National Conference of Commissioners on Uniform State Laws as a model to ensure uniformity throughout the nation. Many states have adopted it already.

Sports agents need not be lawyers and lawyers may actually be at a disadvantage when it comes to ethical and solicitation issues compared to nonlawyer sports agents. The sports agent plays a fiduciary role for the athlete. There are numerous examples of egregious conduct by sports agents in violation of state laws, including the infamous case of Norby Walters and Lloyd Bloom. The NCAA does not allow student-athletes to have agents represent their interest in the particular sport in which the student-athlete participates at the amateur level. Major league players associations have added a regulatory framework for agents who wish to represent athletes in their respective sports through the collective bargaining process.

■ Key Terms

agent
exclusive contract
fiduciary
Lloyd Bloom
MLB
MLBPA
Model Code of Professional
  Responsibility
Model Rules of Professional Conduct
NBA
NBPA
NCAA
NCCUSL

NFL
NFLPA
NHL
NHLPA
nonexclusive contract
Norby Walters
principal
professional sports counseling panels
scope of employment
sports agent
student-athlete
Uniform Athlete Agents Act (UAAA)
WNBA

■ Additional Cases

Detroit Lions, Inc. v. Argovitz, 580 F. Supp. 542 (E.D. Mich. 1984) *aff'd in part and remanded,*
  767 F.2d 919 (6th Cir. (1985)
Gregory v. Rosenhaus, 1996 U.S. Dist. LEXIS 21321 (N.D. Miss. (1996)
In the Matter of Frederick J. Henley, Jr., case no. S96Y1735 (Sup. Ct. Ga. Dec. 5, 1996)
Lustig Pro Sports Enterprises, Inc., v. Kelley, 1992 WL 369289 (Ohio Ct. App. 1992)
Norby Walters and Lloyd Bloom v. Brent Fullwood, 675 F. Supp. 155 (S.D.N.Y. 1987)
Speakers of Sport, Inc., v. ProServ, Inc., 1998 WL 473469 (N.D. Ill. 1998)
Zinn v. Parrish, 644 F.2d 360 (7th Cir. 1981)

■ Review Questions

1. Should there be a uniform federal law that governs sports agents or is this field better regulated by individual states?
2. Should college athletes be allowed to have sports agents for the sport in which they participate?
3. Why did the concept of professional athletes having agents gather steam in the 1960s?
4. Should all sports agents be lawyers?
5. Should players unions be allowed to regulate the fees that agents charge for their services?
6. Why is the agent profession considered a glamour profession?

■ Endnotes

1 *See* Also *Black's Law Dictionary* (8th Ed. 2001).

2 To represent football players in the NFL, "contract advisors" must have a four-year degree from an accredited college or university and must pass a written take-home test.

3 NFLPA, MLBPA, and NHLPA.

4 More discussion of players associations found later in the chapter.

5 Inducement by money or goods to sign up clients is a violation of the Model Rules of Professional Conduct (1983), the Model Code of Professional Responsibility (1969), the NFLPA and MLBPA rules, and many state laws.

6 Hockey star Eric Lindros and golf star Tiger Woods have extreme parental agent advice and influence.

7 *See Detroit Lions, Inc. v. Argovitz*, 580 F.Supp. 542 (E.D. Mich. 1984) aff'd in part and remanded, 767 F.2d 919 (6th Cir.1985) discussed later in the chapter. See also *Zinn v. Parrish*, 644 F.2d 360 (7th Cir. 1981).

8 Attorneys Mark McCormack and Bob Woolf are established icons who provided legal, financial, and marketing advice to professional athletes.

9 David Falk, Scott Boras, Leigh Steinberg, Tom Condon just to name a few, while IMG, SFX, Octagon, and others represent influential athletes at the corporate conglomerate level as mergers in the industry continue to prevail.

10 World Wrestling Entertainment, Inc. (WWE) for example.

11 Successful film with $275 million in worldwide receipts.

12 This would be considered the unauthorized practice of law and would violate state statutes.

13 Baseball player Derek Jeter signed a contract in 2001 with the New York Yankees for 10 years and $189 million dollars. However, Alex Rodriguez signed a contract for $252 million for 10 years, which is the largest in sports history.

14 The United States Olympic Committee (USOC) is the sole National Olympic Committee (NOC) for the Olympic Games, and national governing bodies oversee several Olympic sports (e.g., United States Swimming, USA Triathlon, USA Track and Field, just to name a few).

15 *See* NFLPA Regulations Governing Contract Advisors (1998) and MLBPA Regulations Governing Player Agents.

16 Some runners are paid up to $5,000 per month and obtain a percentage of the fee that an unscrupulous agent may charge the client.

17 For example, Paul Williams was sentenced to 30 days in jail for the Footlocker shopping spree incident involving Nate Cebrun and Florida State University student-athletes.

18 University of Florida athletic director Jeremy Foley has been quoted as saying that the University of Florida will vigorously pursue sports agents in a state that is "inhospitable" for violators of state law. See David Jones, *Florida Today*, March 31, 2000.

19 Cebrun is also noted for having been arrested for a violation of an Alabama law for the recruitment of a star Auburn University student-athlete.

20 Fines and a prison sentence were handed out and several student-athletes were suspended.

21 States abide by either the Model Code of Professional Responsibility or Model Rules of Professional Conduct.

22 *See* Rules Regulating the Fla. Bar chs. 3–5 (Mar. 2000); See Also the Model Rules of Professional Conduct and Model Code of Professional Responsibility.

23 *See* R. Regulating Fla. Bar 4-7.2 (Advertising) and 7.4 (Direct Contact with Prospective Clients).

24 However, agents who are members of the NFLPA and MLBPA are subject to additional recruiting rules.

25 3% according to NFLPA Regulations 6, sec. 4.B.

26 The National Collegiate Athletic Association based in Indianapolis, Indiana, is a voluntary, non-profit organization composed of over 1,200 colleges and universities around the country and has three levels of competition with Division I being the most influential in terms of television exposure and revenue.

27 Ala. Code sec. 8-26-24 (Supp. 1999) sets a maximum total fee of 10% compensation per calendar year under any negotiated sports services contract. Additionally, Connecticut's statute mandates that the issue of fee regulation must be addressed. Conn. Gen. Stat. Ann. sec. 20-556 (West 1999).

28 The NFLPA began regulating agents in 1983 while the MLBPA started in 1998.

29 This act gives the NFLPA, for example, the exclusive right to bargain collectively for NFL players. See 29 U.S.C.A. sec. 141-197.

30 Money laundering.

31 *See* NFLPA Regulations 6, sec. 2. G.

32 *Id.*, 6, sec. 4.B.(4).

33 MLBPA Regulations note 6, sec. 4.F.

34 *Id.*, sec's. 3.B.(5)-(8).

35 Cal. Bus. & Prof. Code sec. 18897.27 (Michie 2000).

36 Ala. Code sec. 8-26-34 (Supp. 1999), and Cal. Bus. & Prof. Code sec. 18897.47 (Michie 2000).

37 The NCAA's purpose is further discussed in the Chapter, 2.

38 NCAA rules governing agents are provided at the end of this chapter in Exhibit 1–2.

CHAPTER TWO

Sports Contracts

■ Introduction

Contracts in sports are no different than contracts in everyday life: Athletes are compensated for their services as employees or independent contractors via a paycheck just as you and I are rewarded for our own efforts in our jobs. The primary differences might be that professional athletes' services are usually seasonal in nature, the athletes participate in a "game," there are no playoffs in our jobs, and you and I pay large sums of money to watch the athletes work (i.e., play). Additionally, our employers usually have not signed a television contract with a major network.

This chapter examines the nature of personal services contracts of professional athletes. However, even the amateur athlete deals with important contract-related issues. Amateur athletes often have to make tough choices about changing their status from "amateur" to "professional" given the dramatic increase in money that may be available to be earned in their sports.

Some professional athletes are paid a lot more money in one year than most people ever earn in their lifetimes. Participation in a sport for financial remuneration is the fundamental difference between professional and amateur athletes. Depending upon the sport, an athlete may have a greater market or potential to secure contracts due to the international (or purely national) nature of the game. Understanding the formation of contracts and general contract terms certainly would benefit all parties involved in a contractual relationship.

■ Sports Agents and Contracts

Sports agents serve a valuable role in terms of securing and negotiating contracts for the professional athlete. Lawyers who represent athletes have been trained in the fundamentals of contract drafting and formation and should be familiar with the current market value of their client relative to other athletes within the same sport. However, it should be noted that hiring a lawyer is not required (nor is an agent for that matter) to secure deals for the athlete. Some athletes do not wish to hire an agent for a variety of reasons, including having to pay commissions or other fees associated with the representation.

However, it is generally accepted that when athletes wish to represent themselves, there may be too close of a relationship between the players and team or sponsor to maintain an objective approach to negotiation. A similar situation arises when a close family member represents the athlete's interests. This may result in increased tensions during contract formation due to family or personal (as opposed to professional) pressures. Additionally, one must be concerned with possible unauthorized practice of law issues if one is acting as an advocate for another but does not have a law license to do so.

■ Personal Services Nature of Sports Contracts

Since the athlete has unique talents, abilities, and skills, such contracts for athletes services are categorized as **personal services contracts** and may not be assigned or delegated to another person. For example, a professional tennis player sponsored by a shoe, clothing, or racquet company could not assign or delegate her rights or duties to another player since her talents are so unique. However, many contracts in the sports industry do not involve personal services contracts of the professional athlete. Such contracts may simply involve the delivery of goods or provision of services and are treated no differently than contracts in any other industry.

Public Nature of Sports Contracts

Though general contract principles may apply in sports contracts, often such contracts are so important to the particular league, industry, or community that pressure to negotiate or renegotiate often becomes a matter of public debate. Additionally, the "going rate" for the athlete's services often becomes a matter of public discussion, depending on the sport. Let's face it: Communities have a vested financial and emotional interest in seeing their team perform well. In sports that do not receive the same sort of public centerpiece such as swimming, triathlon, and other sports industries that do not receive substantial television revenue, the athletes often share salary and/or endorsement information among themselves to establish a going rate for their services.[1]

The Occupation of "Athlete"

The occupation of "professional athlete" has become recognized as one of the most financially rewarding professions in the country, though it is becoming increasingly

---

personal services contract   special, nonassignable contract providing unique talents, abilities, and skills

unclear as to who is a professional and who is an amateur. Since sports sponsors often tie thousands of dollars into subsidizing an athlete to promote its own products or services, the sports contract often has an impact on many, many individual lives. One athlete contract may affect the well-being of an entire organization in the sports industry in both team and individual sports.

However, even today's amateurs must face crucial issues such as whether to continue to compete as an amateur or be lured away by money to accept cash rewards for performance by turning professional during their sophomore or junior year of college. Though not all amateur athletes are in college and therefore voluntarily subject to NCAA rules and regulations, college sports such as football, basketball, baseball, and hockey are often regarded as proving grounds for the major professional leagues.

As competition and demand for athletes continue to increase the value of sports contracts, more individuals and firms—including law firms—have attempted to add value to the formation and transformation of sports contracts and bid competitively for the use of their services (see Chapter 1). Many student-athletes are urged to abandon amateur status to be compensated for their services as a professional. However, this may not always be the best course of action, especially if the athlete is not thereafter drafted into a professional league that would have guaranteed some income in the form of a salary or signing bonus.

■ General Contract Law Principles

Definition

A **contract** is a legally binding agreement. A contract represents the **meeting of the minds** of the parties. Contracts in sports are subject to the same principles of contract formation as any other form of employment agreement. Paralegals are likely to play many different roles in assisting the sports lawyer in the traditional sports agent practice, though negotiation will not likely be one of them. However, a general understanding of contract law and standard player contracts would certainly serve any assistant well in terms of understanding the nature and effect of contract terms.

Offer and Acceptance

Students of law recognize that all contracts are subject to the principles of offer, acceptance, and consideration and that the contract must be for a legal purpose with the legal capacity by both parties in order to enter into the agreement. If any of these elements are missing in the contractual relationship, then no contract exists. An

---

contract   legally binding agreement

meeting of the minds   phrase used to describe agreement between offeror and offeree

offer is made by the **offeror** to an **offeree**. The offeror is the "master of the offer." This means that the offeror can create the parameters of the who, when, where, and how of the proposed contractual relationship. Once an offer is made, an offeree can respond in four ways:

1. Accept (a legally binding contract is created).
2. Reject (the offer is automatically terminated).
3. Counteroffer (in which case the original offeror is now the offeree).
4. Nothing (the law will terminate the contract offer after a reasonable time).

Any ambiguities created when making an offer will be construed against the offeror if an **acceptance** is made. The offeror can create the time, the manner, and the place of the contract. With the advent of improved technology such as facsimile and electronic communication (e-mail), contracts can even be made over the Internet effectively.

Consideration

The **consideration** element is most interesting in sports contracts since the "price of the promise" may be extremely high financially. Though sports contracts must be for a legal purpose, just as is any contract in order to be enforceable, an issue can arise with regard to the legal "capacity" aspect of a minor signing a contract. Sports such as gymnastics, swimming, and tennis often involve contractual issues regarding minors. Proof of legal capacity may require the signature of a parent or guardian. Even though minors may enter into contractual arrangements, minors hold the ability to make such contracts voidable at their option. However, the other party must be placed in the same position as prior to entering into the agreement, or at least at no worse position.

Most sports contracts are express contracts; that is, there are virtually no more implied contracts in the sports industry. This is likely the result of increased professional services by lawyers and agents and due to the large increase of dollars that have entered into the sports world. Athletes, too, are sophisticated enough to rely mostly on a written agreement that involves their professional career.

Statute of Frauds

As a general rule, contracts may be either oral or written. However, the law requires a written agreement in specific situations. For contracts that by their terms will last more than one year, the statute of frauds will apply and a writing is required. Also,

---

offer   element of contract that creates the power of acceptance in the offeree

offeror   one who makes an offer

offeree   one who receives an offer and has the power to accept

acceptance   agreement to the terms of an offer that creates a legally binding agreement

consideration   the price, usually in monetary terms, of a promise

all contracts for the sale of real estate, contracts involving the sale of goods costing more than $500, and promises to answer for the debt of another (i.e., cosigners) must be in writing.

Valid, Void, Voidable

All contracts are **valid**, **void**, or **voidable**. With regard to voidability, sports contracts are often wrapped with "voidability" clauses, particularly when the athlete reaches certain goals and objectives in terms of performance. Such goals are often referred to as incentives and can be an excellent way to reward the athlete for outstanding performance. Additionally, minors (persons under the age of 18) may void a contract while still a minor but must put the other party back in the position it was in prior to forming the contract.

Though most employees in the United States do not receive a formal, express contract in writing from their employer, sports contracts almost always are in writing and often represent the complete "meeting of the minds" between the employer or endorser and the athlete. When the athlete and the employer or sponsor merely sign a deal prior to performance, such a deal is characterized as being *fully executed* and is valid though in other industries this term implies that each party has fully performed its obligations.

Good Faith

The Uniform Commercial Code (UCC) requires good faith in the buying and selling of goods. However, the UCC does not apply to services. Therefore, the UCC does not apply to personal services contracts *per se*.

Still, in any contract there must be an underlying theme of good faith, reasonableness, and trust. When a party violates the sanctity of the contractual relationship or breaches the duties required under the contract, such a breakdown of the contract can lead to litigation. Additionally, ambiguities created when a contract is formed or issues that were not foreseen by a contract drafter can lead to serious problems. It is important to remember that the offeror is the "master of the offer" and has the duty to avoid creating ambiguities in an offer. Otherwise, such ambiguities will likely be construed against the offeror by a judge.

Even if parties are acting in good faith, the advent of league salary caps and free agency issues have caused athletes to seek employment with another team even if it is not in either party's best interest. Changing market conditions, especially for publicly traded companies, may force cutbacks in terms of offering endorsement contracts to athletes.

---

valid   term used to describe a legally binding contract

void   contract that is not enforceable

voidable   contract that may be voided by one of the parties

■ Categories of Contracts

Sports contracts can be divided into three general categories: (1) professional services contracts (sometimes called *standard player contracts* or *personal services*), (2) endorsement contracts, and (3) appearance contracts. If an individual athlete is a member of a team, the athlete's contract may be affected by other members of that team due to a league salary cap or other structure. There is no dollar limit as to the amount that an individual athlete may request for his or her own services when it comes to endorsement and appearance contracts.

Team Contracts versus Individual Contracts

If a professional athlete is part of a team, usually the athlete receives a standard player contract. The only difference between his contract and other members of the team are usually salary, bonuses, and the option to renegotiate. Exceptional team athletes or "stars" are also able to secure private deals with individual companies for endorsement and appearance contracts.

The Professional Services (Standard Player) Contract

The **standard player contract (SPK)** is usually in a "**boilerplate**" form, regardless of whether the athlete is involved in a league with a players association or not. Such a contract is usually offered to the athlete and other athletes with all the same terms other than the salary and bonus. While all contracts may be negotiated, many agreements use standardized contract forms with different dollar amounts only depending upon the "value" of the individual athlete. This contract is usually the written by-product of a history of negotiation between the league and the players in that league and is contained within that league's **collective bargaining agreement (CBA)**. Many sports, such as track and field, ice skating, swimming, and gymnastics, are not subject to "league" status, and therefore professional services contracts are usually replaced with an endorsement contract by a sponsor of a special team or individual. These contracts may, too, be boilerplate in nature if both offeror and offeree agree to such regular and consistently similar terms.

Problems have arisen when professional athletes unite, refuse to work and "strike" due to alleged poor working conditions, unfair labor practices, or the natural expiration of the collective bargaining agreement. Additional problems have arisen when certain teams in larger markets can spend more money than teams in smaller markets with smaller television contracts. As such, owners and players have agreed to a salary cap in the NFL, for example, in order to

---

standard player contract (SPK)   boilerplate contract between a league and a professional athlete

boilerplate   fixed or standard contract terms that generally are not negotiable

collective bargaining agreement (CBA)   contract between a league and players association

maintain a competitive balance in that league and control escalating player salaries.

Newly formed leagues often model their own contracts after one of the Big Four (NFL, MLB, NBA, and NHL) in order to recognize contemporary issues relevant to team owners and athletes. Some start-up leagues, however, have taken a newer approach to professional services contracts by establishing minimal salaries for the athletes in that sport and rewarding the team and athlete on a per game basis for incentive play. The now defunct Xtreme Football League (XFL), for example, offered modest salaries to its players. Such wages were comparable to most Americans' wages. This is primarily due to the fact that the league owned all of the teams rather than each team serving as a franchise for the league. None of the Big Four sports leagues are run by a single entity, and therefore each team is a franchise and competes for players. That is a primary contributor to the escalation of player salaries.

Endorsement Contracts

Unlike the professional services contract, the **endorsement contract** is usually not conducted as an employer-employee relationship. Rather, it is one of contractor-independent contractor. As such, tax withholding, insurance, and workers compensation are usually not afforded in this arrangement. An endorsement contract is essentially a contract that grants the sponsor or endorser the right to use (i.e., license) the athlete's name, image, or likeness in connection with advertising the endorser's products or services. In most professional sports, the leagues prohibit individual players from endorsing alcoholic beverages or tobacco products other than for public service announcements such as "Don't drink and drive." Additionally, the NFL recently established a policy that players may not endorse certain nutritional supplements.

The endorsement contract's terms and conditions are virtually left up to the financial resources of the endorser or sponsor and the creativity of the parties. There are no set rules or parameters for such an agreement other than that they be legal. It is a generally held principle that the more an endorser (or sponsor) feels that the sponsored athlete can assist in the sales of the particular product, the greater the likelihood of a higher stipend and bonus structure. The underlying assumption is that the sponsor wishes to increase sales or market share of its own products by pushing a visible athlete to the forefront of an advertising campaign.

Appearance Contracts

The final form of professional sports contract is the **appearance contract**. Such arrangement compensates the athlete for appearing at a group function, assembly,

---

endorsement contract   contract in which a sponsor agrees to pay a fee or provide product to an athlete in exchange for using the athlete's name or image in its promotions

appearance contract   agreement that the athlete will appear in person on behalf of a sponsor's promotion or instructional session. Sometimes appearences are included in the endorsement contract. Athletes often command nice fees for such an appearance, and the sponsor of the event usually compensates the athlete in terms of airfare or other transportation, food, and modest expenses. Only the finest athletes in a particular sport are in demand for such an appearance in exchange for a fee. However, it should be noted that many athletes appear without a fee on behalf of themselves or their team.

■ Drafting the Sports Contract

All professional services contracts address key common clauses. According to the NFLPA, MLBPA, NBPA, and NHLPA, all contract provisions have been established, except for salary and bonuses. Additionally, the players associations have group licensing arrangements in which players are compensated by licensing their names and likenesses in group package deals to trading card companies and video games, for example. Good contract drafters are aware of fundamental contract drafting techniques and realize that it is an acceptable art to borrow clauses from one contract that may suit the needs of their own agreement.

It is important to remember that when drafting a contract, it is often a solid policy to be a pessimist: Think of what can go wrong. Though most contracts begin as a beneficial relationship between the parties, it is well known that over time attitudes and behaviors can change. Therefore, the contract drafter should use exceptional care to ensure that policies and procedures are provided to address situations and legal issues that might arise when something goes wrong. Good contract drafters protect their client in the event such a situation might occur.

Sports Contract Drafting Suggestions

The following clauses might be a model for the contract drafter to follow.

1. *Title*: It is always important to name the agreement. Keep the description to a minimum, but the title identifies the type of contractual agreement. Phrases such as "Sponsorship Agreement," "Sports Contract," "Agreement for Athletic Services," or "Representation Agreement" are simple suggestions. Giving subheadings their own title proves useful for all relevant parties as well.
2. *Describe the Parties*: Establish the name and address of the parties to the contract. Sports contracts often paraphrase the athlete's name. For example, an athlete named "Sabrina Jameson" may be abbreviated as "the athlete" or "Sabrina" throughout the contract rather than continuing to repeat the full name. Important information, such as mailing address, phone numbers, dates of birth, and social security numbers, might be included here as well.
3. *Term*: It is always important to establish the duration of the agreement from the beginning date to the end date. Since many contracts last more than one year, the writing requirement of the statute of frauds is satisfied.

4. *Purpose*: Traditional contract drafters became enamored with providing numerous "Whereas" clauses to establish the purpose of an agreement. Modern-day drafters still use this technique to demonstrate the intent of the parties, but it is no longer necessary to use *Whereas.* Contemporary drafters do not use such terminology and instead simply give each paragraph a name or heading to assist the parties and other readers in the interpretation of the agreement and the purpose of each paragraph. Usually this paragraph delineates why or how the athlete will endorse the company's products or services.

5. *Duties and Obligations*: Once the parties, term of the agreement, and purpose have been established, it is important to outline the rights, duties, and responsibilities of each party. This can include compensation, but usually compensation has its own paragraph for clarification purposes.

6. *Compensation*: This is often referred to as legal *consideration.* An exhibit or an addendum attached to the contract is often helpful, specifically delineating salary, bonuses, and other incentives. Outlining in-kind compensation is important, as is including provision of a reasonable amount of product or "capping" the amount of product that the athlete may use and require.

7. *Exclusivity*: Due to the personal and unique nature of the sports contract, most employers and sponsors (including agents) require an exclusive arrangement with the athlete in order to most effectively promote their product or talent during the term of the agreement. Additionally, it is common for a sponsor in this paragraph to require the athlete to use the products or services exclusively at all times, especially in public, or the endorser may have the right to terminate the agreement as a breach of good faith or failure to use "best efforts."

8. *Confidentiality*: Though a confidentiality clause is often considered valuable to both the team and the athlete, players unions have somewhat undermined such a clause with respect to athletes under contract while represented by a players union by making salaries public. In nonunion contracts, confidentiality is an important consideration for the sponsor and the athlete to prevent similarly situated athletes from comparing their agreements. This will undoubtedly create concern for a party to the contract if the terms are revealed.

9. *Termination*: Though discussion of termination seems awkward to address at the beginning of the contractual relationship, it is important to include such a clause. If one party does not live up to its end of the bargain, anger may turn into rage and one party may be released from the agreement. Interesting topics covered in many termination clauses include one party's refusal to keep the terms of the agreement confidential, the athlete's voluntary discontinuation of participation in the sport, or cases in which the athlete is found guilty of a crime or is found to have been a part of unethical or immoral conduct (sometimes called a "morals clause"). Additionally, termination may occur if the athlete is unable to compete. For example, if a swimmer signs a contract to promote a swim product and then injures himself while waterskiing (and is unable to compete in swimming again), the sponsor may wish to terminate the agreement because the sponsor can no longer promote that swimmer's unique talents.

10. *Nonassignment*: It is important to establish that such an agreement is a personal services contract and therefore is nonassignable or nondelegable.

11. *Alternative Dispute Resolution* (ADR): Though alternative dispute resolution may be effective to resolve disputes via mediation or arbitration, the traditional method of resolving a breach of contract issue is through litigation. Collective bargaining agreements address issues related to arbitration and/or mediation and giving consideration to ADR is always important.

12. *Modification*: It is also productive to provide flexibility in any contract. One useful method is to allow both parties to amend their agreement in the form of an addendum during the course of the term of the contract in the event circumstances change. Though it is usually not obligatory for either party to agree to a modification, most parties who enter into good faith agreements will agree to this in the spirit of cooperation.

13. *Governing Law*: Since many sports contracts affect parties from different states, agreeing upon controlling law ahead of time can save jurisdictional issues from becoming problematic.

14. *Merger*: *Merger* is a legal term that essentially means that any other prior oral or written agreements or statements are null and void, and that this contract constitutes the final and complete agreement between the parties. This is vital to include, especially given that the parol evidence rule excludes prior oral or written statements that contradict the terms of the agreement. The rule will allow, however, evidence that may help the court understand the meaning of peculiar terms.

15. *Signature Line*: The signature is of great importance, of course. Since many parties require possession of an original copy of the contract, signing in blue ink can avoid issues as to which contract is the original. Modern photocopy quality is so good that it can virtually be impossible to determine the original if it is signed in black ink.

16. *Waivers*: A waiver may limit liability to the team or sponsor in the event of the occurrence of a condition. For example, an athletic sponsor does not normally maintain an insurance policy on the athlete during the participation of a sporting event. The waiver clause may release or limit liability if the athlete is injured while competing.

17. *Covenants Not to Compete*: Sometimes referred to as "no-compete clauses," such clauses prevent an employee from leaving one company and working for another for a specified time period or within a particular geographic location. Such clauses are used frequently in coaching contracts and other contracts where information may be vital to the success of the previous organization that trained the former employee. Most covenants not to compete will be upheld unless they are clearly unreasonable or too restrictive. A judge or jury often must decide the reasonability of such clauses.

18. *Exhibits and Other Addenda*: This section makes the contract most unique relative to other similar contracts. Bonuses, schedules, numbers of product, and other incentives may be listed here. From the endorser's point of view, this allows similar contracts to be produced in mass quantities with only the final clause or page to differentiate between major terms in the agreement.

Exhibit 2–1 offers a sample endorsement contract.

■ **EXHIBIT 2–1** *Example of Endorsement Agreement*

SPONSORSHIP AGREEMENT

This Sponsorship Agreement ("Agreement") is made and entered into as of the _____ day of _____ 2002, by and between *AMANDA JACOBS*, of 3900 Middlebrook Pike, Knoxville, Tennessee 37923 ("Jacobs"), and *HEART RATE MONITORS, INCORPORATED* ("HRM, Inc."), a Delaware corporation with a principal place of business at P.O. Box 8310, Mizpah, Montana 06762.

WITNESSETH:

WHEREAS, Jacobs is a professional athlete who competes regularly in competitive triathlon events;

WHEREAS, Jacobs desires to have HRM, Inc. sponsor Jacobs's participation in all of the triathlon events in which Jacobs competes during the term of this Agreement (referred to hereinafter individually as a "Triathlon" and collectively as the "Triathlons"); and

WHEREAS, HRM, Inc. desires to sponsor Jacobs's participation in all of the Triathlons in which Jacobs competes during the term of this Agreement; and

WHEREAS, Jacobs and HRM, Inc. desire to enter into an Agreement whereby HRM, Inc. will be a secondary sponsor of Jacobs and, as such secondary sponsor, HRM, Inc. will receive certain other promotional rights (referred to hereinafter collectively as the "Promotional Rights").

NOW, THEREFORE, for and in consideration of the covenants and promises contained herein, and for other good and valuable consideration, the receipt and sufficiency of which is hereby acknowledged, the parties mutually agree as follows:

1. *Sponsorship.* HRM, Inc. shall sponsor Jacobs's participation in every Triathlon in which Jacobs competes, in any capacity other than as a member of the 2004 United States Olympic Team, during the Term (as such term is hereinafter defined) of this Agreement upon the terms and conditions set forth herein.

2. *Term.* This Agreement will commence as of January 1, 2002, and will continue through and including December 31, 2004 (the "Term"), unless terminated sooner pursuant to the terms of this Agreement. For the purpose of this Agreement, each January 1 – December 31 shall be deemed to be a separate "Sponsorship Year".

3. *Promotional Obligations of Jacobs.* Jacobs agrees to cooperate with and provide assistance to HRM, Inc. in all matters relating to its promotional activities. Jacobs's obligations hereunder (referred to hereinafter as "Promotional Obligations"), shall include, but are not limited to, the following:

   (a) *Personal Apparel.* Jacobs shall prominently display the HRM, Inc. name and logo (which name and logo, together with the names and logos of any affiliates of HRM, Inc. are sometimes referred to hereinafter as the "HRM, Inc. Name and Logo" or as the "HRM, Inc. Name" or the "HRM, Inc. Logo"), in the locations shown or described on *Exhibit A*, attached hereto and made a part hereof (as the same may be amended and supplemented from time to time by the agreement of the parties) on the front chest and lower back of all race and training uniforms and uniform changes, including, without limitation, all swim wear, bicycle racing uniforms and running apparel and on all casual wear worn to and from race events and at all other appropriate times, including, but not limited to, all interviews and media and other publicity sessions (referred to hereinafter collectively as "Promotional Appearances" and individually as a "Promotional Appearance").

   (b) *Triathlons and Promotional Appearances.* Jacobs shall compete in no fewer than eight (8) Triathlons during each Sponsorship Year. HRM, Inc. and Jacobs shall agree upon a calendar of Triathlons in which Jacobs will participate during the applicable Sponsorship Year (which Triathlons are sometimes referred to hereinafter as the "Required Triathlons"), a copy of which shall be attached hereto as *Exhibit B* and made a part hereof (as the same may be amended and supplemented from time to time by the agreement of the parties), on or before March 10, 2002 (for Triathlons to be held during Sponsorship Year 2002) and on or before December 31, 2002 (for Triathlons to

continued

be held during Sponsorship Year 2003). In addition to competing in the Required Triathlons, Jacobs shall make not less than three (3) Promotional Appearances on behalf of HRM, Inc. during the Term of this Agreement, which Promotional Appearances shall take place at such times and in such places as the parties may agree. HRM, Inc. shall have no obligation to pay Jacobs for the Promotional Appearances referenced herein; however, it shall pay all of Jacobs's reasonable expenses, including but not limited to reasonable travel, food and housing expenses (up to a maximum of $3,500 per Promotional Appearance) that pertain to or are caused by HRM, Inc.'s requiring that Jacobs make a particular Personal Appearance other than in connection with a Triathlon.

4. *Compensation.* Jacobs shall be paid a fee of $10,000 as compensation for this endorsement agreement. In consideration of and in payment for the Promotional Rights and as compensation for the right to sponsor Jacobs's participation in the Required Triathlons and to serve as Jacobs's exclusive heart rate monitor, HRM, Inc. shall pay to Jacobs this fee (referred to hereinafter as the "Sponsorship Fee") by January 15, 2002 in a lump-sum check.

5. *Additional Rights of HRM, Inc.* HRM, Inc. has the right to use Jacobs's photograph, with no additional payment to Jacobs in advertising, promotional and other sales-related undertakings, including, without limitation on the HRM, Inc. Internet website;

6. *Other Sponsors.* Jacobs shall not enter into any agreement with any other manufacturer, supplier, wholesaler and/or distributor of heart rate monitors.

7. *Ownership and Protection of Intellectual Properties.* Jacobs and HRM, Inc. acknowledge that HRM, Inc. owns the HRM, Inc. Name and Logo whether or not registered on the federal principal register by HRM, Inc. and all goodwill associated with or symbolized by the HRM, Inc. Name and Logo and any and all trade names/trademarks associated therewith.

8. *Limitations on Rights Granted and Rights Reserved to HRM, Inc.* Jacobs has no right to grant any sublicense, concession, right or privilege relating to the HRM, Inc. Name and Logo. Any right to use the HRM, Inc. Name and Logo granted hereunder is not transferable or assignable by Jacobs, either directly, indirectly or by operation of law for any reason.

9. *Third Party Infringement.* Jacobs shall immediately give notice to HRM, Inc., by telephone and in writing, of any infringement or misuse of the HRM, Inc. Name and Logo by any other party of which Jacobs becomes aware. HRM, Inc. shall have the right, but not the obligation, to commence legal action regarding any infringement or misuse.

10. *Non-Disparagement.* During the term of this Agreement other parties, including members of the general public, may come to associate Jacobs with HRM, Inc. In recognition thereof Jacobs agrees that Jacobs shall conduct herself in a professional manner that is in keeping with HRM, Inc.'s reputation and shall act in the best interests of HRM, Inc. at all times during the term of this Agreement, including, without limitation, when dealing with members of the general public and representatives of the mass media.

11. *Confidential Information.* During the term of this Agreement, and for three (3) years thereafter, Jacobs agrees that she will not disclose to any third party any of the procedures, technical data, confidential or proprietary information or trade secrets of HRM, Inc. or of any of its affiliates without the prior written permission of the applicable party. The foregoing obligations of confidentiality shall not apply to information that:

(i) is, or subsequently may become, available to the public through no fault of Jacobs;

(ii) Jacobs can show was previously known to it at the time of disclosure;

(iii) is required to be disclosed by Jacobs pursuant to a requirement, order or directive of a court or government agency or by operation of law, provided that Jacobs notifies HRM, Inc. in advance of any such disclosure and takes steps to maintain the confidentiality of such information that are no less rigorous than those that Jacobs would take to protect her own confidential and proprietary information, including, without limitation and in consultation with HRM, Inc.'s legal counsel, obtaining a protective order with respect to such disclosure; or

(iv) is otherwise approved in writing by HRM, Inc.

12. *Termination.* HRM, Inc. shall have the right to terminate this Agreement if:

(a) Jacobs ceases to be ranked within the top ten (10) professional female triathletes as determined by the World Triathlon Corporation;

(b) Jacobs fails to perform any term or condition of this Agreement and such failure is not cured within thirty (30) days after Jacobs receives written notice from HRM, Inc. thereof; or

(c) Jacobs suffers an injury that prevents her from competing in any additional Required Triathlons during the Sponsorship Year in question or from fulfilling Jacobs's Promotional Obligations.

13. *No Liability.* Upon the expiration or termination of this Agreement, Jacobs shall not be entitled to termination payments, compensation, reimbursement or damages on account of any loss of prospective profits on anticipated sales or on account of expenditures for advertising or promotional activities or other commitments relating to the business or goodwill of Jacobs or Jacobs's reliance upon further continuance of this Agreement.

14. *Indemnification.* Jacobs shall indemnify and hold harmless HRM, Inc., its affiliates, their directors, officers, employees and agents, and their respective successors and assigns, against any losses, claims, damages, liabilities, costs or expenses, including, without limitation, attorneys' fees and court costs, that HRM, Inc. may incur as the result of any claim, suit or other proceeding made or brought by or against HRM, Inc. or Jacobs (excluding, however, costs and expenses that HRM, Inc. may incur in connection with any claim, suit or other proceeding brought by Jacobs against HRM, Inc. to enforce this Agreement, unless such costs or expenses are awarded to HRM, Inc. by the body having jurisdiction over such claim, suit or other proceeding), based upon, relating to or arising out of: (i) Jacobs's participation in a Triathlon; (ii) Jacobs's performance or non-performance of this Agreement; and/or (iii) HRM, Inc.'s having to bring a suit, action or other proceeding against Jacobs to enforce this Agreement.

15. *Warranties.* Each party warrants and represents that it has the full corporate right and authority or the legal capacity to enter into and perform this Agreement in accordance with all its provisions.

16. *Relationship of Parties.* The parties to this Agreement are independent contractors under this Agreement. Except as may be provided for in this Agreement, neither party will have any right or authority and will not attempt to enter into any contract, commitment or agreement, or incur any debt or obligation of any nature in the name of or on behalf of the other party.

17. *Assignment.* Neither this Agreement, nor any interest herein, nor any rights hereunder shall be assigned by Jacobs

18. *Notices.* All notices, requests, demands and other communications hereunder shall be in writing and shall be deemed to have been given (i) when hand-delivered, including delivery by messenger or carrier service (or if delivery is refused, at the time of refusal), addressed as set forth below; (ii) when received or refused as evidenced by the postal receipt if sent by United States mail as certified mail, return receipt requested, with proper postage prepaid, addressed as set forth below; or (iii) when received as evidenced by the transmission report of the facsimile machine of the transmitting party acknowledging a good transmission if sent by facsimile to the number set forth below:

If to Jacobs:
Amanda Jacobs
3900 Middlebrook Pike
Knoxville, TN 37923

If to HRM, Inc.:
HRM, Inc. Corporation
P.O. Box 8310
Mizpah, Montana 59301

19. *Governing Law and Consent to Jurisdiction.* This agreement is made in the State of Montana and shall be governed by and construed and interpreted in accordance with the laws of the State of Montana, excluding, however, its choice of law provisions. Any arbitration or other legal proceedings shall have venue in the State of Montana and, in connection therewith, each of the parties hereto hereby irrevocably submits to the jurisdiction of

continued

and agrees that any action, suit or other proceeding may be brought in the courts of the State of Montana or in the United States District Courts for the District of Montana for the purpose of the resolution of any claim, controversy or dispute arising between the parties regarding this Agreement or the transactions contemplated hereby. HRM, Inc. and Jacobs each further agree that any final judgment rendered in connection with any such suit, action or other proceeding shall be conclusive and may be enforced against such party in any other jurisdiction by suit on a judgment or in any other manner permitted by applicable law.

20. *Additional Terms.*

(a) *Binding Effect.* The terms and conditions herein contained will apply to and bind the successors and permitted assigns of the parties hereto.

(b) *Modification.* This agreement may not be amended or modified in any respect unless in writing signed by Jacobs and by a duly authorized officer or representative of HRM, Inc.

(c) *Waiver.* Failure or delay on the part of either party to exercise any right, remedy, power or privilege hereunder shall not operate or be construed to operate as a waiver hereof. A waiver, to be affective, must be in writing and be signed by the party making the waiver. No written waiver of any term or condition of this Agreement shall operate or be construed to operate as a waiver of any other term or condition, nor shall any written waiver of any breach or default operate or be construed to operate as a waiver of any other breach of default or of the same type of breach or default on a subsequent occasion.

(d) *Severability.* If any one or more of the provisions of this Agreement is held to be invalid or unenforceable under the laws of any jurisdiction, such invalidity or unenforceability shall not affect any other provision of this Agreement, and this Agreement shall be construed as if the invalid or unenforceable provisions had not been contained herein and the parties shall negotiate in good faith to replace the invalid or unenforceable provisions with such enforceable provisions which has the effect nearest to that of the provisions being replaced.

(e) *Entire Agreement.* This Agreement constitutes the final expression of the agreement of the parties; is intended as a complete and exclusive statement of the terms of their agreement, and supersedes all prior and concurrent proposals, promises, representations, negotiations, discussions and agreements that may have been made in connection with the subject matter hereof.

IN WITNESS WHEREOF, the parties hereto by their duly authorized officers have executed this Agreement as of the date first above written.

_____

Amanda Jacobs

HRM, INC. CORPORATION

BY: _____

Bob Shore

Courts generally do not favor private parties agreeing to give up certain rights when it comes to contractual relationships. However, a **waiver** (sometimes called a *release, disclaimer,* or *exculpatory clause*) can effectively allow the parties to avoid liability in the event of a certain condition occurring. Often waivers that give up the right of players to sue other players or a league for negligence are offered to its participants as a condition of participation. This is prevalent in Little League sports, recreational activities such as skydiving, and even through the professional ranks. This subject is more thoroughly discussed in Chapter 3.

_____

waiver   the voluntary relinquishment of certain legal rights

Implied Contracts

Students of the law are aware that sometimes a court may find an **implied contract** (as opposed to an express contract) to avoid unfairness in a contractual relationship under the concepts of substantial performance and *quantum meruit*. In sports, implied contracts have become almost nonexistent since most athletes have become sophisticated to the extent that one of the athlete's first considerations is to put virtually all relationships in writing. However, courts may still exercise *quantum meruit* in the event a contract is breached or is begun under uncertain terms.

■ Damages and Remedies for Breach

Generally speaking, when there is a breach of contract, contract law uses a variety of methods to repair the **damages**. Courts attempt to place the injured party in the position that he or she would have been in had the contract been fully performed. Case 2 provides an example of a lawsuit resulting from a breach of a coaching contract.

Types of Remedies

Several kinds of contract **remedies** are available to the victim of a breach of contract:

■ specific performance
■ compensatory damages
■ consequential damages
■ liquidated damages
■ punitive damages

Specific Performance

Specific performance is an order by a court requiring the party that breached the contract to perform its obligation. The breaching party must do what it agreed to do in the contract. Most professional sports contracts are not subject to specific performance as a remedy, however, since professional athletes are considered to

---

implied contract   contract created by the courts as an obligation in the absence of an agreement to prevent unjust enrichment by one of the parties

quantum meruit   term used to describe amount of compensation that must be paid under an implied contract to prevent unjust enrichment of one party by another.

damages   amount of money recoverable by a person for a loss or injury, usually due to negligence or a breach of contract

remedies   one of various methods to enforce a contract if a breach or default occurs

specific performance   remedy as ordered by a court to enforce a contract in its exact form where money damages would be an inadequate form of compensation for a breach

■ **CASE 2** *Vanderbilt University v. DiNardo*

UNITED STATES COURT OF APPEALS,
Sixth Circuit.

VANDERBILT UNIVERSITY, Plaintiff-Appellee,
v.
Gerry DiNARDO, Defendant-Appellant.
No. 97-5935.
Argued Oct. 27, 1998.
Decided April 14, 1999.

University brought state court action against its former head football coach, seeking liquidated damages for coach's alleged breach of employment contract. Former coach removed action to federal court. The United States District Court for the Middle District of Tennessee, Robert L. Echols, J., 974 F.Supp. 638, entered summary judgment in favor of university. Former coach appealed. The Court of Appeals, Gibson, Circuit Judge, sitting by designation, held that: (1) liquidated damages provision was not unenforceable penalty; (2) university did not waive its right to liquidated damages; and (3) addendum extending coach's five-year employment contract for two years extended contract's liquidated damages provision.

Affirmed in part, reversed in part, and remanded.

Nelson, Circuit Judge, concurred in part, dissented in part, and filed opinion.

Clay, Circuit Judge, concurred in part, dissented in part, and filed opinion.

Thomas J. Piskorski (argued and briefed), David E. Metz (briefed), Seyfarth, Shaw, Fairweather & Geraldson, Chicago, Illinois, for Defendant-Appellant.

William N. Ozier (argued and briefed), J. Davidson French (briefed), Bass, Berry & Sims, Nashville, Tennessee, for Plaintiff-Appellee.

Before: NELSON, CLAY, and GIBSON, Circuit Judges.*

GIBSON, J., delivered the opinion of the court. NELSON and CLAY, JJ., delivered separate opinions concurring in part and dissenting in part.

GIBSON, Circuit Judge.

Gerry DiNardo resigned as Vanderbilt's head football coach to become the head football coach for Louisiana State University. As a result, Vanderbilt University brought this breach of contract action. The district

court entered summary judgment for Vanderbilt, awarding $281,886.43 pursuant to a damage provision in DiNardo's employment contract with Vanderbilt. DiNardo appeals, arguing that the district court erred in concluding: (1) that the contract provision was an enforceable liquidated damage provision and not an unlawful penalty under Tennessee law; (2) that Vanderbilt did not waive its right to liquidated damages; (3) that the Addendum to the contract was enforceable; and (4) that the Addendum applied to the damage provision of the original contract. DiNardo also argues that there are disputed issues of material fact precluding summary judgment. We affirm the district court's ruling that the employment contract contained an enforceable liquidated damage provision and the award of liquidated damages under the original contract. We conclude, however, that there are genuine issues of material fact as to whether the Addendum was enforceable. We therefore reverse the judgment awarding liquidated damages under the Addendum and remand the case to the district court.[1]

On December 3, 1990, Vanderbilt and DiNardo executed an employment contract hiring DiNardo to be Vanderbilt's head football coach. Section one of the contract provided:

The University hereby agrees to hire Mr. DiNardo for a period of five (5) years from the date hereof with Mr. DiNardo's assurance that he will serve the entire term of this Contract, a long-term commitment by Mr. DiNardo being important to the University's desire for a stable intercollegiate football program. . . .

The contract also contained reciprocal liquidated damage provisions. Vanderbilt agreed to pay DiNardo his remaining salary should Vanderbilt replace him as football coach, and DiNardo agreed to reimburse Vanderbilt should he leave before his contract expired. Section eight of the contract stated:

Mr. DiNardo recognizes that his promise to work for the University for the entire term of this 5-year Contract is of the essence of this Contract to the University. Mr. DiNardo also recognizes that the University is making a highly valuable investment in his continued employment by entering into this Contract and its investment would be lost were he to resign or otherwise terminate his employment as Head Football Coach with the University prior to the expiration of this Contract. Accordingly, Mr. DiNardo agrees that in the event he resigns or otherwise terminates his employment as Head Football Coach (as opposed to his resignation or termination from another position at the University to which he may have been reassigned), prior to the expiration of this Contract, and is employed or performing services for a person or institution other than the University, he will pay to the University as liquidated damages an amount equal to his Base Salary, less amounts that would otherwise be deducted or withheld from his Base Salary for income and social security tax purposes, multiplied by the number of years (or portion(s) thereof) remaining on the Contract.

During contract negotiations, section eight was modified at DiNardo's request so that damages would be calculated based on net, rather than gross, salary.

Vanderbilt initially set DiNardo's salary at $100,000 per year. DiNardo received salary increases in 1992, 1993, and 1994.

On August 14, 1994, Paul Hoolahan, Vanderbilt's Athletic Director, went to Bell Buckle, Tennessee, where the football team was practicing, to talk to DiNardo about a contract extension. (DiNardo's original contract would expire on January 5, 1996). Hoolahan offered DiNardo a two-year contract extension. DiNardo told Hoolahan that he wanted to extend his contract, but that he also wanted to discuss the extension with Larry DiNardo, his brother and attorney.

Hoolahan telephoned John Callison, Deputy General Counsel for Vanderbilt, and asked him to prepare a contract extension. Callison drafted an addendum to the original employment contract which provided for a two-year extension of the original contract, specifying a termination date of January 5, 1998. Vanderbilt's Chancellor, Joe B. Wyatt, and Hoolahan signed the Addendum.

On August 17, Hoolahan returned to Bell Buckle with the Addendum. He took it to DiNardo at the practice field where they met in Hoolahan's car. DiNardo stated that Hoolahan did not present him with the complete two-page addendum, but only the second page, which was the signature page. DiNardo asked, "what am I signing?" Hoolahan explained to DiNardo, "[i]t means that your contract as it presently exists will be extended for two years with everything else remaining exactly the same as it existed in the present contract." Before DiNardo signed the Addendum, he told Hoolahan, "Larry needs to see a copy before this thing is finalized." Hoolahan agreed, and DiNardo signed the document. DiNardo explained that he agreed to sign the document because he thought the extension was the "best thing" for the football program and that he "knew ultimately, Larry would look at it, and before it would become finalized he would approve it." Hoolahan took the signed document without giving DiNardo a copy.

On August 16, Larry DiNardo had a telephone conversation with Callison. They briefly talked about the contract extension, discussing a salary increase. Larry DiNardo testified that as of that date he did not know that Gerry DiNardo had signed the Addendum, or even that one yet existed.

DiNardo stated publicly that he was "excited" about the extension of his contract, and there was an article in the August 20, 1994, newspaper, *The Tennessean*, reporting that DiNardo's contract had been extended by two years.

On August 25, 1994, Callison faxed to Larry DiNardo "a copy of the draft Addendum to Gerry's contract." Callison wrote on the fax transmittal sheet: "[l]et me know if you have any questions." The copy sent was unsigned. Callison and Larry DiNardo had several telephone conversations in late August and September, primarily discussing the television and radio contract. Callison testified that he did not recall discussing the Addendum, explaining: "[t]he hot issue . . . was the radio and television contract." On September 27, Callison sent a fax to Larry DiNardo concerning the television and radio contract, and also added: "I would like your comments on the contract extension." Larry DiNardo testified that he neither participated in the drafting nor suggested any changes to the Addendum.

In November 1994, Louisiana State University contacted Vanderbilt in hopes of speaking with DiNardo about becoming the head football coach for L.S.U. Hoolahan gave DiNardo permission to speak to L.S.U. about the position. On December 12, 1994, DiNardo announced that he was accepting the L.S.U. position.

Vanderbilt sent a demand letter to DiNardo seeking payment of liquidated damages under section eight of the contract. Vanderbilt believed that DiNardo was

continued

liable for three years of his net salary: one year under the original contract and two years under the Addendum. DiNardo did not respond to Vanderbilt's demand for payment.

Vanderbilt brought this action against DiNardo for breach of contract. DiNardo removed the action to federal court, and both parties filed motions for summary judgment. The district court held that section eight was an enforceable liquidated damages provision, not an unlawful penalty, and that the damages provided under section eight were reasonable. *Vanderbilt University v. DiNardo*, 974 F.Supp. 638, 643 (M.D.Tenn.1997). The court held that Vanderbilt did not waive its contractual rights under section eight when it granted DiNardo permission to talk to L.S.U. and that the Addendum was enforceable and extended the contract for two years. *Id.* at 643–45. The court entered judgment against DiNardo for $281,886.43. *Id.* at 645. DiNardo appeals.

I.

[1] DiNardo first claims that section eight of the contract is an unenforceable penalty under Tennessee law. DiNardo argues that the provision is not a liquidated damage provision but a "thinly disguised, overly broad non-compete provision," unenforceable under Tennessee law.

We review the district court's summary judgment de novo, using the same standard as used by the district court. *See Birgel v. Bd. of Comm'rs.*, 125 F.3d 948, 950 (6th Cir.1997), *cert. denied*, 522 U.S. 1109, 118 S.Ct. 1038, 140 L.Ed.2d 104 (1998). We view the evidence in the light most favorable to the non-moving party to determine whether there is a genuine issue as to any material fact. *See id.* Summary judgment is proper if the record shows that "there is no genuine issue as to any material fact and that the moving party is entitled to judgment as a matter of law." Fed.R.Civ.P. 56(c).

[2][3][4][5] Contracting parties may agree to the payment of liquidated damages in the event of a breach. *See Beasley v. Horrell*, 864 S.W.2d 45, 48 (Tenn.Ct.App.1993). The term "liquidated damages" refers to an amount determined by the parties to be just compensation for damages should a breach occur. *See id.* Courts will not enforce such a provision, however, if the stipulated amount constitutes a penalty. *See id.* A penalty is designed to coerce performance by

punishing default. *See id.* In Tennessee, a provision will be considered one for liquidated damages, rather than a penalty, if it is reasonable in relation to the anticipated damages for breach, measured prospectively at the time the contract was entered into, and not grossly disproportionate to the actual damages. *See Beasley*, 864 S.W.2d at 48; *Kimbrough & Co. v. Schmitt*, 939 S.W.2d 105, 108 (Tenn.Ct.App.1996). When these conditions are met, particularly the first, the parties probably intended the provision to be for liquidated damages. However, any doubt as to the character of the contract provision will be resolved in favor of finding it a penalty. *See Beasley*, 864 S.W.2d at 48.

The district court held that the use of a formula based on DiNardo's salary to calculate liquidated damages was reasonable "given the nature of the unquantifiable damages in the case." 974 F.Supp. at 642. The court held that parties to a contract may include consequential damages and even damages not usually awarded by law in a liquidated damage provision provided that they were contemplated by the parties. *Id.* at 643. The court explained:

The potential damage to [Vanderbilt] extends far beyond the cost of merely hiring a new head football coach. It is this uncertain potentiality that the parties sought to address by providing for a sum certain to apply towards anticipated expenses and losses. It is impossible to estimate how the loss of a head football coach will affect alumni relations, public support, football ticket sales, contributions, etc. . . . As such, to require a precise formula for calculating damages resulting from the breach of contract by a college head football coach would be tantamount to barring the parties from stipulating to liquidated damages evidence in advance.

Id. at 642.

DiNardo contends that there is no evidence that the parties contemplated that the potential damage from DiNardo's resignation would go beyond the cost of hiring a replacement coach. He argues that his salary has no relationship to Vanderbilt's damages and that the liquidated damage amount is unreasonable and shows that the parties did not intend the provision to be for liquidated damages.

DiNardo's theory of the parties' intent, however, does not square with the record. The contract language establishes that Vanderbilt wanted the five-year contract because "a long-term commitment" by DiNardo was "important to the University's desire for a stable intercollegiate football program," and that this commitment was of "essence" to the contract. Vanderbilt offered the two-year contract extension to DiNardo well over a year before his original contract expired. Both parties understood that the extension was to provide stability to the program, which helped in recruiting players and retaining assistant coaches. Thus, undisputed evidence, and reasonable inferences therefrom, establish that both parties understood and agreed that DiNardo's resignation would result in Vanderbilt suffering damage beyond the cost of hiring a replacement coach.

[6] This evidence also refutes DiNardo's argument that the district court erred in presuming that DiNardo's resignation would necessarily cause damage to the University. That the University may actually benefit from a coaching change (as DiNardo suggests) matters little, as we measure the reasonableness of the liquidated damage provision at the time the parties entered the contract, not when the breach occurred, *Kimbrough & Co.*, 939 S.W.2d at 108, and we hardly think the parties entered the contract anticipating that DiNardo's resignation would benefit Vanderbilt.

The stipulated damage amount is reasonable in relation to the amount of damages that could be expected to result from the breach. As we stated, the parties understood that Vanderbilt would suffer damage should DiNardo prematurely terminate his contract, and that these actual damages would be difficult to measure. *See Kimbrough & Co.*, 939 S.W.2d at 108.

Our conclusion is consistent with a decision by the Tennessee Court of Appeals in *Smith v. American General Corporation*, No 87–79-II, 1987 WL 15144 (Tenn.Ct.App. Aug.5, 1987). In that case, an individual sued his former employer for breach of an employment contract. *Id.* at *1. The employee had a three-year contract, and the contract provided for a single lump sum payment of all remaining compensation in the event of a breach by the employer. *Id.* at *1–2. When the employer reduced the employee's duties, he quit, and sued seeking to enforce the liquidated damage provision. The employer argued the provision was a penalty, and that the employee should only be able to recover his total salary under the contract reduced by the employee's earnings in his new job. The Tennessee court rejected these arguments, concluding that even

though the usual measure of damage is the difference between an employee's old and new salaries, here, the parties reasonably contemplated "special damage," including the intangible damage to the employee's prestige and career. *Id.* at *6. The court found that the parties expressly recognized the importance to the employee of the continuation of his employment, and it was "clearly within the contemplation of the parties that, if [the employee] should not be retained in his position . . . he would suffer unliquidated damages which would be difficult of proof." *Id.* at *7.

Our reasoning follows that of *Smith*. Vanderbilt hired DiNardo for a unique and specialized position, and the parties understood that the amount of damages could not be easily ascertained should a breach occur. Contrary to DiNardo's suggestion, Vanderbilt did not need to undertake an analysis to determine actual damages, and using the number of years left on the contract multiplied by the salary per year was a reasonable way to calculate damages considering the difficulty of ascertaining damages with certainty. *See Kimbrough & Co.*, 939 S.W.2d at 108. The fact that liquidated damages declined each year DiNardo remained under contract, is directly tied to the parties' express understanding of the importance of a long-term commitment from DiNardo. Furthermore, the liquidated damages provision was reciprocal and the result of negotiations between two parties, each of whom was represented by counsel.

We also reject DiNardo's argument that a question of fact remains as to whether the parties intended section eight to be a "reasonable estimate" of damages. The liquidated damages are in line with Vanderbilt's estimate of its actual damages. *See Kimbrough & Co.*, 939 S.W.2d at 108–09. Vanderbilt presented evidence that it incurred expenses associated with recruiting a new head coach of $27,000.00; moving expenses for the new coaching staff of $86,840; and a compensation difference between the coaching staffs of $184,311. The stipulated damages clause is reasonable under the circumstances, and we affirm the district court's conclusion that the liquidated damages clause is enforceable under Tennessee law.

II.

[7][8] DiNardo next argues that Vanderbilt waived its right to liquidated damages when it granted DiNardo permission to discuss the coaching position with L.S.U.

continued

Under Tennessee law, a party may not recover liquidated damages when it is responsible for or has contributed to the delay or nonperformance alleged as the breach. *See V.L. Nicholson Co. v. Transcon Inv. and Fin. Ltd., Inc.*, 595 S.W.2d 474, 484 (Tenn.1980).

Vanderbilt did not waive its rights under section eight of the contract by giving DiNardo permission to pursue the L.S.U. position. *See Chattem, Inc. v. Provident Life & Accident Ins. Co.*, 676 S.W.2d 953, 955 (Tenn.1984) (waiver is the intentional, voluntary relinquishment of a known right). First, Hoolahan's permission was quite circumscribed. Hoolahan gave DiNardo permission to talk to L.S.U. about their coaching position; he did not authorize DiNardo to terminate his contract with Vanderbilt. Second, the employment contract required DiNardo to ask Vanderbilt's athletic director for permission to speak with another school about a coaching position,[2] and Hoolahan testified that granting a coach permission to talk to another school about a position was a "professional courtesy." Thus, the parties certainly contemplated that DiNardo could explore other coaching positions, and indeed even leave Vanderbilt, subject to the terms of the liquidated damage provision. *See Park Place Ctr. Enterprises, Inc. v. Park Place Mall Assoc.*, 836 S.W.2d 113, 116 (Tenn.Ct.App.1992) ("All provisions of a contract should be construed as in harmony with each other, if such construction can be reasonably made . . ."). Allowing DiNardo to talk to another school did not relinquish Vanderbilt's right to liquidated damages.

III.

DiNardo claims that the Addendum did not become a binding contract, and therefore, he is only liable for the one year remaining on the original contract, not the three years held by the district court.

A.

[9] DiNardo argues that the Addendum did not extend section eight, or that there is at least a question of fact as to whether the Addendum extended section eight.

[10] [11] Under Tennessee law, the rights and obligations of contracting parties are governed by their written agreements. *Hillsboro Plaza Enterprises v. Moon*, 860 S.W.2d 45, 47 (Tenn.Ct.App.1993). When the agreement is unambiguous, the meaning is a question of law, and we should enforce the agreement according

to its plain terms. *Richland Country Club, Inc. v. CRC Equities, Inc.*, 832 S.W.2d 554, 557 (Tenn.Ct.App.1991).

DiNardo argues that the original employment contract explicitly provides that section eight is limited to "the entire term of this five-year contract," and the plain, unambiguous language of the Addendum did not extend section eight. He points out that the Addendum did not change the effective date in section eight, unlike other sections in the contract.

The plain and unambiguous language of the Addendum read in its entirety, however, provides for the wholesale extension of the entire contract. Certain sections were expressly amended to change the original contract expiration date of January 5, 1996, to January 5, 1998, because those sections of the original contract contained the precise expiration date of January 5, 1996. The district court did not err in concluding that the contract language extended all terms of the original contract.

B.

[12] [13] DiNardo also claims that the Addendum never became a binding contract because Larry DiNardo never expressly approved its terms.[3] DiNardo contends that, at the very least, a question of fact exists as to whether the two-year Addendum is an enforceable contract.

The district court concluded that the Addendum was enforceable as a matter of law because the parties acted as though the contract had been extended and because Larry DiNardo never objected to the Addendum. *See* 974 F.Supp. at 644.

[14] Under Tennessee law, parties may accept terms of a contract and make the contract conditional upon some other event or occurrence. *See Disney v. Henry*, 656 S.W.2d 859, 861 (Tenn.Ct.App.1983). DiNardo argues that the Addendum is not enforceable because it was contingent on Larry DiNardo's approval.

Vanderbilt responds that the undisputed facts establish that there was no condition precedent to the Addendum's enforceability. Vanderbilt first points out that DiNardo did not make this argument until late in the litigation, and more importantly did not make this argument when Vanderbilt initially requested payment from DiNardo in January 1995. Vanderbilt also contends that if Larry DiNardo found any of the language in the simple two-page Addendum objectionable, he should have objected immediately. Finally, Vanderbilt argues that if we decide that Larry DiNardo's approval was a condition precedent to enforceability, the condition was satisfied by Larry DiNardo's failure to object.

In *Disney*, the defendants sent a mailgram accepting a buyer's offer on their house "subject to review" of the actual sales contract. Although the court held that the contract could be conditioned on final approval of the sales contract, the court enforced the contract because the defendants' failure to object within a reasonable time validated the acceptance. *Id.* at 860.

Viewing the evidence in the light most favorable to DiNardo, as we must, we are convinced that there is a disputed question of material fact as to whether the Addendum is enforceable. There is a factual dispute as to whether Larry DiNardo's approval of the contract was a condition precedent to the Addendum's enforceability. Gerry DiNardo testified that he told Hoolahan that the contract extension was not "final" until Larry DiNardo looked at it.[4] Hoolahan's testimony on this point was consistent with DiNardo's: "He [Gerry DiNardo] said that he wanted to discuss the matter with you [Larry DiNardo], which I said certainly." Furthermore, although Callison's version of Larry DiNardo's role in the preparation of the contract extension differs from DiNardo's, it is undisputed that on August 25, nine days after Gerry DiNardo signed the Addendum, Callison sent Larry DiNardo an unsigned copy of the "draft Addendum." The cover sheet on a fax sent by Callison to DiNardo on September 27 closes with: "I would like your comments on the contract extension." From these facts, a jury could conclude that Larry DiNardo's approval was required before the Addendum became a binding contract.

Of course, there is evidence that the Addendum was not contingent on Larry DiNardo's approval. Gerry DiNardo told others that he was happy with his contract extension, and Larry DiNardo never objected to the Addendum. This evidence, however, does not carry the day, because we view the evidence on summary judgment in the light most favorable to DiNardo and resolve all factual disputes in his favor. *See Birgel*, 125 F.3d at 950.

Likewise, Larry DiNardo's failure to object to the Addendum may have constituted acceptance of the Addendum's terms, *see, e.g., Disney*, 656 S.W.2d at 861,

but on this record, we cannot resolve the issue on summary judgment. There is evidence from which a jury could find that Larry DiNardo's failure to object did not amount to acceptance of the Addendum. First, in contrast to *Disney*, 656 S.W.2d at 860–61, there is evidence explaining DiNardo's delay. The parties were primarily negotiating the radio and television contract during the fall of 1994. Callison testified that he could not recall whether he had any conversations with DiNardo in September about the contract extension. He explained: "The hot issue, if you will, was the radio and television contract. That was what was on my mind." It is not unreasonable to infer that the parties had not completely negotiated the details of the contract extension; the original contract did not expire for another year. On September 27, Callison asked Larry DiNardo for "his comments" on the contract extension. A jury could conclude from this solicitation that even Vanderbilt did not believe that the Addendum had been approved and was enforceable as of that time. We cannot say that Larry DiNardo's failure to object by December 12, 1994, constitutes an acceptance of the Addendum as a matter of law.

Accordingly, we affirm the district court's judgment that the contract contained an enforceable liquidated damage provision, and we affirm the portion of the judgment reflecting damages calculated under the original five-year contract. We reverse the district court's judgment concluding that the Addendum was enforceable as a matter of law. We remand for a resolution of the factual issues as to whether Larry DiNardo's approval was a condition precedent to the enforceability of the Addendum and, if so, whether the condition was satisfied by Larry DiNardo's failure to object.

We affirm in part, reverse in part, and remand the case to the district court for further proceedings consistent with this opinion.

DAVID A. NELSON, Circuit Judge, concurring in part and dissenting in part.

If section eight of the contract was designed primarily to quantify, in an objectively reasonable way, damages that the university could be expected to suffer in the event of a breach, such damages being difficult to measure in the absence of an agreed formula, the provision is enforceable as a legitimate liquidated damages clause. If section eight was designed primarily to punish

continued

Coach DiNardo for taking a job elsewhere, however, the provision is a penalty unenforceable under Tennessee law. My colleagues on the panel and I are in agreement, I believe, on both of these propositions. We disagree, however, as to section eight's primary function.

It seems to me that the provision was designed to function as a penalty, not as a liquidation of the university's damages. Insofar as the court holds otherwise, I am constrained to dissent. In all other respects, I concur in Judge Gibson's opinion and in the judgment entered pursuant to it.

My principal reasons for viewing section eight as a penalty are these: (1) although the damages flowing from a premature resignation would normally be the same whether or not Coach DiNardo took a job elsewhere, section eight does not purport to impose liability for liquidated damages unless the coach accepts another job; (2) the section eight formula incorporates other variables that bear little or no relation to any reasonable approximation of anticipated damages; and (3) there is no evidence that the parties were attempting, in section eight, to come up with a reasonable estimate of the university's probable loss if the coach left. I shall offer a few words of explanation on each of these points.

Section eight does not make Coach DiNardo liable for any liquidated damages at all, interestingly enough, unless, during the unexpired term of his contract, he "is employed or performing services for a person or institution other than the University. . . ." But how the coach spends his post-resignation time could not reasonably be expected to affect the university's damages; should the coach choose to quit in order to lie on a beach somewhere, the university would presumably suffer the same damages that it would suffer if he quit to coach for another school. The logical inference, therefore, would seem to be that section eight was intended to penalize the coach for taking another job, and was not intended to make the university whole by liquidating any damages suffered as a result of being left in the lurch.

This inference is strengthened, as I see it, by a couple of other anomalies in the stipulated damages formula. First, I am aware of no reason to believe that damages arising from the need to replace a prematurely departing coach could reasonably be expected to vary in direct proportion to the number of years left on the coach's

contract. Section eight, however, provides that for every additional year remaining on the contract, the stipulated damages will go up by the full amount of the annual take-home pay contemplated under the contract. Like the "other employment" proviso, this makes the formula look more like a penalty than anything else.

Second, the use of a "take-home pay" measuring stick suggests that the function of the stick was to rap the coach's knuckles and not to measure the university's loss. Such factors as the number of tax exemptions claimed by the coach, or the percentage of his pay that he might elect to shelter in a 401(k) plan, would obviously bear no relation at all to the university's anticipated damages.

Finally, the record before us contains no evidence that the contracting parties gave any serious thought to attempting to measure the actual effect that a premature departure could be expected to have on the university's bottom line. On the contrary, the record affirmatively shows that the university did not attempt to determine whether the section eight formula would yield a result reasonably approximating anticipated damages. The record shows that the university could not explain how its anticipated damages might be affected by the coach's obtaining employment elsewhere, this being a subject that the draftsman of the contract testified he had never thought about. And the record shows that the question of why the number of years remaining on the contract would have any bearing on the amount of the university's damages was never analyzed either.

In truth and in fact, in my opinion, any correspondence between the result produced by the section eight formula and a reasonable approximation of anticipated damages would be purely coincidental. What section eight prescribes is a penalty, pure and simple, and a penalty may not be enforced under Tennessee law. On remand, therefore, in addition to instructing the district court to try the factual questions identified in Judge Gibson's opinion, I would instruct the court to determine the extent of any actual damages suffered by the university as a result of Coach DiNardo's breach of his contract. Whether more than the section eight figure or less, I believe, the university's actual damages should be the measure of its recovery.

CLAY, Circuit Judge, concurring in part and dissenting in part.

continued

Because I would affirm the ruling below in all respects, I dissent from Part III.B of the court's opinion. Even if we conclude that the approval of the contract extension by Larry DiNardo, Gerry DiNardo's brother and attorney, was a condition precedent to the enforceability of the Addendum, a grant of summary judgment on behalf of Vanderbilt was appropriate because relevant circumstantial and direct evidence support the conclusion that the contract was agreed upon. This evidence, combined with Larry DiNardo's failure to object to the contract extension, causes me to conclude that summary judgment was properly granted.

The Court's opinion correctly notes that in *Disney v. Henry*, 656 S.W.2d 859 (Tenn.Ct.App.1983), the state court held that where enforcement of a sales contract was expressly conditioned on the sellers' final approval, the sellers' failure to object to the terms and conditions of the contract within a reasonable time validated the acceptance. *Disney*, 656 S.W.2d at 861. However, the Court's opinion fails to note that in determining that a reasonable time had lapsed, the state court relied exclusively on the fact that the sellers had allowed the buyers to take concrete steps in reliance on the contract. *Id.* at 860–61.

Particularly in this light, the facts on record establish that Larry DiNardo's failure to object validated his brother's acceptance of the contract. Following lopsided losses by Vanderbilt's football team to close out the 1993 season, there was rampant speculation that Gerry DiNardo would be fired. The magazine *Sports Illustrated* listed him as a coach on the "hot seat." By early 1994, Vanderbilt's athletic department became aware that the coach's status was becoming "more and more of an issue in recruiting." This evidence indicates that due to this concern about the coach's status, Vanderbilt initiated contract extension discussions specifically in order to quiet speculation of instability in the football program.

As a result, Vanderbilt announced the signing of the Addendum almost immediately—presumably to quell the rumors of Gerry DiNardo's impending dismissal. Local sports columnists applauded the move precisely because it put to rest rumors of the coach's firing and the possibility of ensuing instability. Even more significantly, the coach himself confirmed that the deal was done. In remarks published on August 20, 1994, Gerry DiNardo expressed his happiness with the contract extension and his relief that this issue had been settled. Among other things, the coach said: [The extension] sends a message publicly that I've known right along, that [the athletic director] and the chancellor are very supportive of us. . . . I want less distraction, less public controversy, and the best way to do that is to keep myself out of the picture with the public as much as possible. I don't want people talking about me, about external parts of football. I want our players to be the focus.

* * * *

I always felt they were committed, but actually having it makes me feel big time happy. I remember when we were at Colorado and they gave [the head coach an extension] after three years. It means a lot to our assistants. It's pretty important when someone does that for you. Then, it's easy to circle the wagons and identify the enemy. There is no second-guessing.

Vanderbilt and Gerry DiNardo thus both took steps immediately in reliance on the Addendum by moving forcefully to put to rest any uncertainty about the coach's job security and potential instability in the football program.

Indeed, Gerry DiNardo's pronouncement embracing the contract extension renders Larry DiNardo's failure to object to Vanderbilt's announcement of the extension particularly significant. Vanderbilt asked Larry DiNardo in late August and again in late September of 1994 for any comments he might have on the Addendum. (This occurred after Gerry DiNardo had already signed the Addendum extending his contract on August 17, 1994, but had informed Vanderbilt that notwithstanding the fact that he had signed the extension, he still would like to have his brother review it.) Larry DiNardo said nothing—even though the coach had already publicly expressed his happiness that the extension was complete and Vanderbilt had announced the extension to the world.

Taking all of these facts into account, and viewing this evidence in the light most favorable to the defendant, I would hold that Larry DiNardo's failure to object to the Addendum validated the coach's acceptance, even assuming that Gerry DiNardo's acceptance was initially conditional in nature, and so put the Addendum into effect. Accordingly, I concur in the Court's opinion

continued

with the exception of Part III.B, from which I dissent for the reasons set forth above.

174 F.3d 751, 134 Ed. Law Rep. 766, 14 IER Cases 1702, 1999 Fed.App. 0135P

FOOTNOTES

* The Honorable John R. Gibson, Circuit Judge of the United States Court of Appeals for the Eighth Circuit, sitting by designation.

1. Judge Clay's separate opinion concurs in Parts I and II and dissents from Part III of the court's opinion. Judge Nelson's separate opinion concurs in Parts II and III and dissents from Part I of the court's opinion.

2. Section nine provided: The parties agree that should another coaching opportunity be presented to Mr. DiNardo or should Mr. DiNardo be interested in another coaching position during the term of this Contract, he must notify the University's Director of Athletics of such opportu-nity or interest and written permission must be given to Mr. DiNardo by the Director of Athletics before any discussions can be held by Mr. DiNardo with the anticipated coaching- position principal.

3. Vanderbilt contends that DiNardo waived this defense because it was not suggested until DiNardo's deposition on October 28, 1996, and not brought before the court until DiNardo filed his amended answer in May, 1997. The district court considered DiNardo's theory of defense, however, and we review the district court's grant of leave to amend under an abuse of discretion standard. *See United States v. Midwest Suspension and Brake*, 49 F.3d 1197, 1201 (6th Cir.1995).

4. In general, parol evidence is admissible to show that a condition must be satisfied before a written contract will take effect. *See Ware v. Allen*, 128 U.S. 590, 594, 9 S.Ct. 174, 32 L.Ed. 563 (1888) (written contract subject to approval by attorney).

Reprinted with permission from West Group.

have unique talents, abilities, and skills. Therefore, to force an athlete to perform such personal services contract would constitute a modern-day form of enslave-ment. However, sales of goods and products would certainly fall within the scope of specific performance as a remedy.

Compensatory Damages

Compensatory damages can be defined as the amount of money necessary to make up for the economic loss caused by breach of contract. Such damages are often available in the sports industry.

Consequential Damages

Consequential damages are economic loss caused indirectly by a breach of contract. For example, if a party to a contract refused to perform and ticket sales decreased accordingly, such damages may be recoverable.

---

compensatory damages   remedy to compensate a plaintiff for actual loss or expense due to negligence or breach of contract

consequential damages   damages for an injury arising from special circumstances that were not ordinarily foreseeable but result from the consequences of an act by a defendant

Liquidated Damages

Liquidated damages are damages specified in the contract itself and are often referred to as "agreed-upon" damages. They may operate as a "penalty" for breach of contract; that is, the amount of the agreed-upon damages may or may not have any relation to the contract as a whole. For example, late delivery of jerseys to a club or organization might have a clause that each day late constitutes a fine of $100 per day.

Punitive Damages

Punitive damages, sometimes called *exemplary damages*, are damages that punish the wrongdoer in a breach of contract action. Such damages are often used to prevent a future breach by the same parties and/or to send a message to the community (or society) at large that such conduct is unacceptable. Unlike compensatory damages, punitive damages are not based only on actual economic loss. They are designed to make an example out of the party and punish them for their wrongful conduct. However, punitive damages are *not* recoverable in a contract action since the goal of contract law is to make "whole" rather than to punish, which is the goal of criminal law.

Mitigation of Damages

The duty to **mitigate damages** means that the victim of a breach of contract cannot simply let economic losses pile up and later sue the other party to pay all of those subsequent losses as well. The victim of a breach of contract must attempt to reduce the amount of economic loss. Failing to reduce one's damages leads to waste. Such conduct is not favored by courts.

■ NCAA Contracts and Amateurism

Though the Indianapolis-based National Collegiate Athletic Association (NCAA) is considered a nonprofit organization, its billion-dollar television contract and its rules and policies affect the sports industry in numerous ways and often present a conflict between the concepts of amateurism and professionalism.

The NCAA was originally established to address safety issues involved in the sport of football. The organization has grown to become the largest amateur organization in the United States related to the regulation of student-athletes. These student-athletes may compete for a maximum of four years while attending a college or university. Membership in the NCAA is divided into Divisions I, II,

---

liquidated damages   agreed-upon remedy for breach of contract found within the contract itself

punitive damages   damages designed to punish the misconduct of a civil defendant; not available for breach of contract

mitigation of damages   reducing or keeping one's damages to a minimum

and III. Division I is the largest and offers the most scholarships to student-athletes. Each sport has its own rules and limits the number of scholarships in a given sport. Sports such as football and basketball are characterized as "revenue" sports while soccer, gymnastics, track and field, and other sports are considered "nonrevenue sports."

Membership in the NCAA is entirely voluntary, and some colleges or universities have chosen not to become a member of this organization. However, more than 1,200 schools abide by the policies of the member-driven organization and therefore share in revenues generated by the NCAA, similar to a shareholder distribution plan. This "sharing of the wealth" is driven by television contracts with the organization for post-season football bowl championships and the "March Madness" contract with CBS television for the NCAA Division I Mens' Basketball Tournament.[2]

Recognizing the evolution of the professional sports industry and the minor leagues as competitors, the NCAA has recently modified its rules regarding amateurism to allow a professional athlete to participate in a college or university sports program if the athlete has remaining eligibility, and the participation is in a different sport. Thus, a 27-year-old football quarterback who played professionally as a minor league baseball player may still be able to compete as an amateur in football for a college or university. It will be interesting to see if the NCAA changes its position further on "amateurism" in the near future.

Evolution of Amateurism

Sports contracts revolve around the athletic participants. An amateur athlete used to be defined as someone who participated purely for the love of the sport and did not expect compensation for athletic performance. For numerous years, the **United States Olympic Committee (USOC)** prevented professional athletes from participating in the Olympic Games just as the NCAA disallows professional athletes to participate in college as amateurs within that particular sport. The USOC has modified its nonprofessional agenda, however, and actually endorses professionals to participate in its Olympic events. However, the NCAA continues to refuse to allow student-athletes to be paid in cash or in kind for their services as student-athletes.

Professional athletes often have careers spanning only a few years, so each year as an amateur may count as a year unearned as a professional. Due to the nature of intercollegiate athletics and its current emphasis on the definition of *amateur*, collegiate athletes may *not* currently represent a college or university if that individual is considered a professional in that particular sport.

USOC　United States Olympic Committee

Other NCAA Contract Issues

Still, numerous rules and regulations surround the student-athlete. student-athletes agree to rules that regulate transferring to another institution, being randomly tested for performance-enhancing drugs, and earning a minimum number of credit hours in their studies. These and other rules are important aspects of the contractual relationship between the NCAA and the student-athlete. The NCAA and USOC have recently agreed to examine ways to ensure that talented amateur athletes who have remaining collegiate eligibility may actually earn a stipend from an Olympic national governing body (**NGB**) such as United States Swimming and still retain amateur status. Many student-athletes decide to turn professional during or after a successful collegiate career or season. When student-athletes decide to turn professional, this may cause them to lose their amateur status.

Letter of Intent

student-athletes are the beneficiaries of athletic scholarships (more specifically referred to as "grants-in-aid"). These gifted individuals sign an agreement with the college or university in the form of a **letter of intent**, which is a binding agreement between the student-athlete and an institution. This agreement provides that in exchange for the student-athlete's services in their sport, the student shall have tuition, room and board, and books paid for by the institution. However, no financial compensation may be awarded to student-athletes in exchange for their athletic talents in that particular sport.

Legal questions remain, however, as to the validity of such agreements if a letter of intent were challenged in court. It appears that such an agreement need not be signed as a prerequisite to participation in NCAA-governed sports, though the NCAA manual does refer to the letter of intent program. The National Letter of Intent Program is actually not administered by the NCAA but rather through the College Commissioners Association (CCA). The CCA has administered this program for 30 years and has no reported lawsuits against it. However, hundreds of "appeals" are filed each year with respect to letters of intent, particularly when prospective student-athletes sign to play with a college or university and the coach who recruited them is no longer employed at the college when the student-athletes arrive and the student-athlete desires to transfer to another school.

There may be jurisdictional issues related to the validity of such an agreement as well. Many letters of intent are signed by high school seniors who may not have yet reached the age of 18; therefore, the legal capacity of the minor might be taken into consideration if he or she desires to void this agreement.

NGB   national governing body, such as United States Swimming

letter of intent   form prospective student athletes sign committing to attend a college or university

■ Health Club Contracts

Most states now regulate the terms of a **health club contract**. Many states have limits on the length of health club contracts. Numerous states cap the length of a health club contract to no more than three years. Many states also allow the member to void a health club contract within three business days of signing the contract. This three-day, cooling-off period is similar to the **Federal Trade Commission's (FTC)** three-day rule, which allows consumers a unilateral right to **rescind** without penalty purchase agreements for in-home, door-to-door sales of goods or services for personal, family, or household use with a purchase price of $25 or more. Due to the extremely competitive nature of health club contracts and the temptation for fraud, health club regulations often are found within a particular state's consumer protection laws and may include a mandatory warning on the contract in bold lettering such as:

"YOU, THE BUYER, MAY CANCEL THIS TRANSACTION AT ANY TIME PRIOR TO MIDNIGHT OF THE THIRD BUSINESS DAY AFTER THE DATE OF THIS TRANSACTION. SEE THE ATTACHED NOTICE OF CANCELLATION FORM FOR AN EXPLANATION OF THIS RIGHT."

Violation of a state health club act and/or the FTC rule constitutes an unfair and deceptive act or practice that can subject the health club to federal or state prosecution or civil liability including treble (triple) damages.

■ Major League Contracts

One nuance of some sports contracts is that when the athlete is a member of a player's union in the NFL, MLB, NBA, or NHL, the contract terms have virtually become uniformly settled. The only issue is the term of the agreement (i.e., number of years or seasons) and the salary and bonuses for the athlete. Such uniform player contracts are established through negotiation between the management of the league (usually the owners) and the laborers of the league (the players) in the form of a CBA. This agreement serves the same purpose as that of any other union in this country and is governed by the rules of the National Labor Relations Act (NLRA).

In baseball, for example, alternative dispute resolution in the form of arbitration is offered to athletes after a certain number of years as part of the negotiation

---

health club contract   agreements typically regulated by state consumer protection acts to protect health club members from potential abuses

Federal Trade Commission (FTC)   Federal agency that enforces laws against false, deceptive, and other unfair advertising and trade practices

rescind   to cancel or nullify a contract due to another's breach

process for their salary. Students of labor law recognize that wages, hours, and working conditions are mandatory subjects for collective bargaining agreements, while all other aspects of the contract are left up to the management and labor to hash out. If disagreements arise between players and management and a collective bargaining agreement is in place, the player must file a grievance with the league (see Chapter 9 for further discussion).

■ Summary

Sports and contracts are vitally interrelated. A contract is a legally binding agreement that represents the meeting of the minds of the parties involved. While many contracts in sports involve the individual coach or athlete and a team, league, or sponsor, numerous contracts involving television and sporting goods affect the sports world on a daily basis. The fundamental elements of any contract must include an offer, acceptance of the offer, and the legal concept of consideration. Contracts are only enforceable if they are formed for a legal purpose. All contracts are valid, void, or voidable. Minors may enter into contracts. Waivers are often necessary to prevent legal liability.

Many professional sports contracts are boilerplate standard player contracts and governed by that sport's collective bargaining agreement. However, endorsement and appearance contracts generally may take any shape. Contract drafters are wise to predict what might happen in the future, provide for it in the contract, and protect their client accordingly.

When a contract is breached, the nonbreaching party has numerous options, or remedies. Though a lawsuit may be used to enforce obligations, other remedies such as liquidated damages may serve as private methods to resolve breach of contract disputes in addition to alternative forms of dispute resolution such as mediation and arbitration.

Health clubs around the country use varied forms of contracts. While there is no uniformity, many health clubs are regulated by states under the state consumer protection act.

■ Key Terms

acceptance	endorsement contract
appearance contract	Federal Trade Commission (FTC)
boilerplate	health club contract
collective bargaining agreement (CBA)	implied contract
compensatory damages	letter of intent
consequential damages	liquidated damages
consideration	meeting of the minds
contract	mitigation of damages
damages	NGB

offer

offeree

offeror

personal services contract

punitive damages

quantum meruit

remedies

rescind

specific performance

standard player contract (SPK)

USOC

valid

void

voidable

waiver

■ Additional Cases

Athletes and Artists, Inc. v. Millen, 1999 LEXIS 11911

Banks v. NCAA, 977 F. 2d 1081 (7th Cir. 1992)

Boston Celtics v. Brian Shaw, 908 F.2d 1041 (1st Cir. 1990)

Brown v. Woolf, 554 F. Supp. 1206 (S.D. Ind. 1983)

Cooper v. Peterson, 626 N.Y.S.2d 432 (Sup. Ct. 1995)

Knap v. Northwestern Univ., 101 F.3d 473 (7th Cir. 1996)

Lewis v. Don King Productions, Inc., 94 F.Supp. 2d 430 (2000)

Living Well (North) Inc. v. Pennsylvania Human Relations Comm'n, No. 2676 C.D.
(Commonwealth Ct. of Penn. 1992)

McKenzie v. Wright Univ., 683 N.E. 2d 381 (Ohio Ct. App. 1996)

Ross v. Creighton Univ., 957 F. 2d 410 (7th Cir. 1992)

Total Economic Athletic Management of America, Inc. v. Pickens, 898 S.W. 2d 98 (Mo. Ct. App. 1995)

Wallace v. Texas Tech Univ., 80 F. 3d 1042 (5th Cir. 1996)

■ Review Questions

1. Why is having a written contract so important in the sports industry?
2. Why is a personal services contract so different than a contract for a product?
3. Why do most agents charge their clients a higher fee for an endorsement contract than a contract with a league or team?
4. What is the significance of a merger clause at the end of a contract?
5. Why are punitive damages not offered for breaches of contracts?
6. Why are health club contracts so heavily regulated by many states?

■ Endnotes

1 Major league players associations encourage such activity.
2 The NCAA budget for 2000–2001 was $325.6 million.

CHAPTER THREE

Sports Torts

■ Introduction

Tort law is the comprehensive study of the intentional or negligent injury to a person or his or her property. **Tort** law is the study of private lawsuits involving plaintiffs and defendants. Tort law is designed to *compensate* the plaintiff monetarily due to the tortfeasor's misdeeds whereas the fundamental purpose of criminal law is to *punish* the perpetrator-defendant. While the government must prove its case beyond a reasonable doubt in a criminal case, a private plaintiff in tort litigation must prove its case by a **preponderance of the evidence**. Tort law presents some of the most interesting cases for the law student to study.

Sports torts, of course, involve personal injuries that normally occur during a sports contest. Violent sports such as boxing, football, and hockey involve duels that outside of the sports contest would likely represent many different violent torts and even crimes. However, contestants in these sports often view such activity as an inherent part of the game.

Many courts view torts in sports as part of the game and refuse to award damages under the theory of *consent*. In other words, the participants themselves consent to what otherwise might be considered a harmful or offensive physical contact with another. Though most sports injuries are physical, one may sue for emotional and psychological damages and for damages to the athlete's reputation.

Is it obvious that sports fans who attend a contest expose themselves to injury? Are some sports more dangerous than others? Should athletes have the right to sue each other for their conduct, or do courts classify such behavior as an inherent risk in sports? Does it matter if the game is played in a professional sports contest or merely during a recreational afternoon? This chapter addresses such issues keeping in mind that as a general rule, courts are reluctant to interfere with sports contests and having to settle such disputes in a courtroom.

---

tort   civil injury or wrong that violates a legal duty owed to another

preponderance of the evidence   test in a civil case that plaintiff must prove the defendant is "more likely than not" responsible for the injuries sustained

Most sports involve some degree of contact between participants. Often, this results in serious, and sometimes permanent, injuries among participants and even spectators. Who should pay, then, for such injuries, if at all? Are professional athletes entitled to workers compensation for injuries that occur within the scope of their employment?

■ General Tort Theories

When an individual is injured and believes that the injury is the fault of another, the plaintiff may sue under several legal theories. These tort theories are not mutually exclusive. In other words, plaintiffs may sue under one or more of the legal theories with the hope that a judge or jury will award some sort of monetary damages to compensate them for the loss.

The concept of negligence is the hallmark of tort law. When a defendant is found to be negligent, the plaintiff may be compensated for some (if not all) damages. More closely related to criminal law are **intentional torts**. The intentional torts are usually the civil version of most criminal cases since assault, battery, defamation, and the like regard the voluntary action or **intent** as a factor in assessing whether damages should be awarded, as opposed to negligence's **reasonable person standard**.[1]

Products liability is certainly regarded as one of the areas of tort law most likely to result in a lawsuit given the fact that the sports industry and its participants use all different types of sports-related equipment. **Strict (absolute) liability** is not often considered in sports torts, but it is a viable option depending upon the facts of each case.

Negligence

Negligence is the hallmark of tort law and involves the most sports-related litigation among the major classes of torts. Important to the discussion of negligence is whether or not the defendant acted as a reasonable person would have acted in that same situation. Sometimes negligence is called *ordinary negligence* because the plaintiff attempts to demonstrate that the defendant failed to use the ordinary care of a reasonable person.

---

intentional tort　tort closely related with crimes in which the tortfeasor intended to commit an injury to another

intent　desire to bring about a particular result

reasonable person standard　test used to determine whether, in hindsight, a person acted reasonably

products liability　tort law focusing on a defect in design, manufacture, or warning

strict (absolute) liability　liability for an activity that involves an ultra-hazardous activity

negligence　failure to act as an ordinary, reasonably prudent person

If the defendant acted as a reasonable person in the mind of the judge or jury, then no liability is imposed on the defendant. If the defendant did not act as a reasonable person, then the defendant may be completely or partially liable for damages. Ultimately a judge or jury must decide this issue first and then, if negligence is found, determine the amount of damages.

During an analysis of negligence, the plaintiff must demonstrate

1. that the defendant owed a duty of care to the plaintiff;
2. that the defendant breached that duty to the plaintiff in the form of unreasonable conduct;
3. that the defendant was the proximate cause of the breach of duty; and
4. that there is evidence of damages.

If the plaintiff fails in proving any of these points, the plaintiff's claim will not succeed.

Contributory Negligence versus Comparative Negligence (Fault)

In a jurisdiction that recognizes **contributory negligence**,[2] if the plaintiff is found to have contributed to his or her own injuries in any way, the plaintiff's claim will fail. This is a harsh result, especially if the plaintiff's contribution is slight. One of the strongest defenses to injuries to sports participants is that the participants "assumed the risks" of being participants or spectators at that event. In a contributory negligence state, such assumption of risk would often limit the liability of the defendant to no liability at all.

However, most states now recognize **comparative negligence**, sometimes called **comparative fault**. Under the doctrine of comparative fault, plaintiffs may be partially to blame for their own injuries, but as long as they are not more at fault than the defendant, they can still recover damages minus their percentage of fault. Percentages of fault are allocated to the parties by a judge or jury. This is known as the *49 percent rule* though some jurisdictions use the *50 percent rule*. The trier of fact (either the judge or jury) actually allocates a numerical percentage of fault to the litigants in the case.

Most jurisdictions now recognize (though sometimes reluctantly) that sports may be prime areas for personal injuries, whether at the professional, amateur, or recreational level. The extent of physical contact that occurs during any sports contest varies from sport to sport. As such, many states only allow recovery for sports injuries when the level of conduct on the part of the defendant far exceeds that of the ordinary rules of the game. This encourages vigorous participation by weekend

---

contributory negligence   failure of plaintiffs to take reasonable precautions for their own safety

comparative negligence (fault)   standard in which damages are rewarded based on the degree of fault among plaintiff and defendant; typically, plaintiff's degree of fault must be 49 percent or less to recover damages

warriors in the most trivial basketball games, for example, while at the same time avoiding the flood of litigation that might ensue for each and every injury suffered during a sports contest.

Gross Negligence and Recklessness

What happens when sports participants act so outside the scope of the rules of the game that it appears the sole purpose of the play was to injure another player intentionally without concern for the play itself? In such instances, defendants may be so lacking in their care to the injured party that the plaintiff attempts to show that defendant acted recklessly, or was **grossly negligent**. In other words, the defendant allegedly used so little care when dealing with the plaintiff that the defendant essentially intended to injure the plaintiff. The standard of **recklessness** is difficult to prove. However, if the plaintiff is successful, the plaintiff may recover punitive damages for the outrageous conduct of the defendant in addition to the general damages (pain and suffering) and special damages (medical bills). Case 3 provides an example in which a golfer argued that the defendant golfer acted recklessly during the sports activity.

■ Spectator Injuries

While most sports torts involve personal injuries brought by participants against each other, often a spectator to a sporting event might be injured by the events originating on the field. Foul balls, deflected hockey pucks, and flying debris from a race car might hit spectators. In such an event, who is responsible for the spectator's injuries? Does the owner of a stadium have a duty to warn or protect spectators from foul balls or other foreseeable injuries? American courts refuse to allow recovery for injuries to spectators caused by the open and obvious rules of the game, particularly when it comes to foul balls. This has been referred to as the **universal rule**.

On the other hand, what about other sports, such as golf, hockey, and football when an activity on the field might impact the fans in the stands? Does an owner of a stadium owe a duty to spectators to prevent all foreseeable injuries, or does common sense impose some duties on the spectators themselves? Do cities and counties have to warn recreational swimmers that diving into shallow water could expose them to a risk of danger? It is wise to post signs that warn of potential dangers but to warn of all possible dangers is clearly not possible in the sports context. If a sign is at issue, however, the adequacy of the posting of the sign is usually the focus of the analysis.

---

gross negligence   failure to use a small amount of care to avoid harm to a plaintiff

recklessness   such a high degree of carelessness that most courts view the harm to the plaintiff as intentional, making punitive damage awards likely

universal rule   concept whereby courts expect that all spectators who watch baseball or softball games have a reasonable expectation that foul balls are part of the risk of watching a game.

■ **CASE 3** *Schick v. Ferolito*

Superior Court of New Jersey,
Appellate Division.

Jeffrey SCHICK, Plaintiff-Appellant,
v.
John **FEROLITO**, Defendant-Respondent.

Argued Jan. 11, 2000.
Decided Jan. 26, 2000.

Plaintiff golfer sued defendant golfer who hit him in the face with a golf ball. The Superior Court, Law Division, Essex County, granted summary judgment against plaintiff golfer, and he appealed. The Superior Court, Appellate Division, Arnold, J.S.C. (temporarily assigned), held that genuine issue of material fact existed as to whether defendant golfer was negligent in hitting an unannounced second tee shot, precluding summary judgment.

Reversed.

Richard M. Chisholm, for plaintiff-appellant.

James M. DeMarzo, Morristown, for defendant-respondent (O'Donnell, McCord, Helfrich & DeMarzo, attorneys; Mr. DeMarzo, on the brief).

Before Judges PRESSLER, CIANCIA and ARNOLD.

The opinion of the court was delivered by

ARNOLD, J.S.C. (temporarily assigned).

[1] Plaintiff Jeffrey Schick was hit in the face by a golf ball. He appeals from an order of summary judgment entered September 16, 1998, in favor of defendant John Ferolito, who hit the ball. The motion judge granted the motion for summary judgment because he found that "the undisputed facts in this record does [sic] not support a finding of willful, wanton or intentional acts" pursuant to the reckless standard of care applied to sports in *Crawn v. Campo*, 136 *N.J.* 494, 643 A.2d 600 (1994). We disagree that the reckless standard of care for sports applies to the factual circumstances in this case involving an alleged unannounced second shot (a Mulligan) hit from the tee after plaintiff, two other members of the foursome and defendant had already teed off.

Because the motion judge granted defendant's motion for summary judgment, we must consider plaintiff's version of the facts. *R.* 4:46–2(c); *Brill v. Guardian Life Ins. Co.*, 142 *N.J.* 520, 540, 666 A.2d 146 (1995). Briefly, those facts are as follows. On July 27, 1994, plaintiff and his father were playing golf at the East Orange Golf course. They joined up with defendant and his playing partner, Tom Gonella, at the tenth tee. At the sixteenth tee, plaintiff teed off first, followed by his father, then Gonella and finally, defendant. The three stood behind defendant when he teed off. Defendant sliced his drive into the woods on the right but it was not out of bounds. After defendant hit this drive, plaintiff and his father moved to their golf cart in front of the tee, perhaps ten to sixteen feet away from the tee area and at a forty-five degree angle to the left. Because defendant's ball was not out of bounds, plaintiff assumed that defendant would play his second shot from the woods. Instead, unbeknownst to plaintiff and his father, defendant unexpectedly hit a second shot from the tee (a Mulligan). The heel of the golf club hit the ball so that the ball hooked to the left and struck plaintiff in the face causing serious personal injury.[1] The motion judge concluded that the applicable standard of care was that set forth in *Crawn, supra*, 136 *N.J.* at 508, 643 A.2d 600, where the court held that the "duty of care in establishing liability arising from informal sports activities should be based on a standard that requires, under the circumstances, conduct that is reckless or intentional."[2] The motion judge held that plaintiff's version of the facts did not meet that standard.

In *Crawn*, the plaintiff, while playing catcher in a softball game with a no-sliding rule, was injured when defendant "approached the plate . . . lowered his body and barreled into plaintiff's left side." Plaintiff sued defendant for his personal injuries alleging that defendant was liable because his conduct had been either negligent, reckless or intentional.[3] The principal issue before the New Jersey Supreme Court centered on the applicable standard of care: negligence or the heightened recklessness standard. Justice Handler, writing for a unanimous court, initially noted that physical contact was "an inherent or integral part of the game in many sports." *Id.* at 504, 643 A.2d 600. Relying upon case law throughout the country analyzing the standard of care applicable to contact sports such as football, hockey, basketball and softball, the court

continued

held that the heightened standard of recklessness or intentional conduct was applicable to sports. *Id.* at 497, 508, 643 A.2d 600. There is no reference in the opinion to either golf or other non-contact sports.

Plaintiff argues that the reckless standard of *Crawn*, is meant only to apply to physical contact or rough and tumble sports and should not be applied to golf. Specifically, plaintiff relies on *Zurla v. Hydel*, 289 *Ill.App.*3d 215, 224 *Ill.Dec.* 166, 681 *N.E.*2d 148 (1997) where the Illinois court held that since golf is not a contact sport, "a golfer injured by a golf ball need only allege and prove traditional negligence in order to recover damages, rather than willful and wanton conduct." *Id.* 224 *Ill.Dec.* 166, 681 *N.E.*2d at 152. Connecticut also does not apply a reckless standard to golf. *See Jaworski v. Kiernan*, 241 *Conn.* 399, 696 *A.2d* 332, 339 (1997) (discussing the decision in *Walsh v. Machlin*, 128 *Conn.* 412, 23 *A.2d* 156 (1941)). However, California, Texas and Ohio have extended the reckless standard to injuries caused by "shanked" or errant shots. *Dilger v. Moyles*, 54 *Cal.App.*4th 1452, 63 *Cal.Rptr.*2d 591 (1997); *Hathaway v. Tascosa Country Club, Inc.*, 846 *S.W.*2d 614 (Tex.Ct.App.1993); *Thompson v. McNeill*, 53 *Ohio St.*3d 102, 559 *N.E.* 2d 705 (1990). Texas has even applied the reckless standard to an unannounced Mulligan tee shot in circumstances similar to those found in this case. *Allen v. Donath*, 875 *S.W.*2d 438 (Tex.Ct.App.1994).

New Jersey has long held golfers to the ordinary negligence standard, that is, a golfer hitting a ball has a duty to use reasonable care before executing a swing, to first observe whether there is anybody else in the line of fire, and if so, to provide an adequate warning. *Toohey v. Webster*, 97 *N.J.L.* 545, 547, 117 *A.* 838 (E. & A. 1922); *Carrigan v. Roussell*, 177 *N.J.Super.* 272, 275–76, 426 *A.2d* 517 (App.Div.1981). This has been the general rule elsewhere. *See* David M. Holliday, Annotation, *Liability to One Struck By Golf Ball*, 53 *A.L.R.*4th 282, 293 (1987) (noting "the generally accepted view that a golfer is only required to exercise

ordinary care and give an adequate and timely warning of his intention to play to those persons reasonably within the range of danger of being struck by the ball").

As we read *Crawn v. Campo, supra*, the standard among sports participants has generally been raised from that of "negligence" to "recklessness or intent to do harm" but only as to anticipated risks which are "an inherent or integral part of the game." *Id.* at 504, 643 *A.2d* 600. This standard would apply to the risk of an errant golf ball straying from its intended course, the unintentional hitting of a "slice" or "hook", or the "shanking" of a golf ball. However, we conclude that hitting an unannounced and unexpected Mulligan from the tee after all members of the foursome have teed off creates such an unanticipated risk to the other members of the foursome, from which they cannot protect themselves, that it cannot be considered an "inherent or integral part of the game." It should, therefore, be measured by an ordinary negligence standard.

[2] Under plaintiff's version of the facts, defendant's conduct cannot be considered "wantonly reckless" so punitive damages are not awardable. *Allendorf v. Kaiserman Enter.*, 266 *N.J.Super.* 662, 675, 630 *A.2d* 402 (App.Div.1993).

Reversed.

744 A.2d 219, 327 N.J.Super. 530

FOOTNOTES

1. In his deposition, defendant insisted that he had warned plaintiff and his father that he was about to hit a second shot and suggested that they move their golf cart, which he regarded as being parked in a hazardous location.

2. Plaintiff does not allege that defendant's conduct was intentional.

3. Prior to trial, plaintiff voluntarily dismissed the count alleging intentional conduct.

Reprinted with permission from West Group.

Recently, a 13-year-old girl died after she was hit in the head by a puck that shot over the glass during an NHL game. She died two days after she was hit in the stands during the Columbus Blue Jackets NHL hockey game in March 2002. Though ticket stubs have warnings and arenas warn of dangers due to flying pucks, it is unlikely that such warnings provide an absolute defense to death from flying pucks. It will be interesting to see the outcome of litigation in this case (if at all) because this death appears to be the first of its kind in an NHL game.[3] Case 4 involves a negligence analysis of a spectator injury at a baseball game.

■ No Fly Zones

When large crowds gather for sporting events, there is a greater likelihood of injuries to spectators. Balancing fun, safety and security have been an issue for organizers of events for many years. In November 2000, the Federal Aviation Administration (FAA) proposed a rule that would add a provision to the existing regulations to allow more flexibility in designating temporary flight restriction (TFR) zones in the vicinity of aerial demonstrations or major sporting events. The temporary **no fly zone** may be used to protect spectators at sporting events from potential tragic accidents (and future lawsuits) and to avoid aerial nuisances in general. The proposed rule lists several events that would qualify as a major sporting event, such as the Rose Bowl, the Olympics, and the World Series.

Recently, the NCAA asked that the FAA allow colleges and universities to petition for a TFR during regular season games if a substantial number of individuals might be impacted by an aerial accident. The FAA granted numerous requests. The University of Michigan and other institutions with large sports stadiums reported as many as 15 small aircraft carrying banner advertising while flying above its football stadium. Concerns over stadium security in general have been heightened particularly since the New York City World Trade Center tragedy on September 11, 2001 an incident involving more of the criminal law.

■ Wrongful Death

When someone dies as the result of personal injury, the individual's estate may have a claim for **wrongful death**. This is the civil equivalent of the criminal charge of one of the varied forms of homicide, including murder. Should a sports participant be held liable for the death of another athlete or a spectator? Virtually all sports involve an activity and an aspect of risk that could lead to the death of a participant. It is important for architects and administrators to provide protective screening and appropriate warnings for participants and spectators related to such concerns.

■ Malpractice in Sports

One of the more curious areas of sports torts involves team physicians and trainers. What if a trainer or physician employed by a team recommends that the injured

---

no fly zone   areas established by the FAA in which airplanes and helicopters may not travel without prior consent

wrongful death   death caused by a tort

■ **CASE 4**　*Benejam v. Detroit Tigers, Inc.*

Court of Appeals of Michigan.

Alyssia Maribel **BENEJAM**, a minor; Ysabel
Benejam and Robert **Benejam**,
Individually, Jointly and as Next Friends of Alyssia
Maribel **Benejam**,
Plaintiffs-Appellees,
v.
DETROIT TIGERS, INC., a Michigan Corporation,
Defendant-Appellant.

Docket No. 217727.

Submitted April 11, 2001, at Detroit.
Decided July 10, 2001, at 9:00 a.m.
Released for Publication Oct. 9, 2001.

Minor and her parents brought negligence action against baseball stadium proprietor, after minor suffered injuries when she was hit by a fragment of a baseball bat during a game. The Circuit Court, Wayne County, Paul S. Teranes, J., entered judgment on jury verdict for minor. Stadium proprietor appealed. The Court of Appeals, Bandstra, C.J., held that: (1) as a matter of first impression, proprietor was not liable, under "limited duty" rule, for minor spectator's injuries, and (2) proprietor had no duty to provide a warning regarding the risk of injury from objects leaving the baseball field.

Reversed and remanded.

James O. Elliott, Bloomfield Hills (Sommers, Schwartz, Silver & Schwartz, P.C. by Patrick Burkett, Southfield, of Counsel), for the plaintiffs.

Dickinson Wright PLLC (by Barbara H. Erard and Paul R. Bernard), Detroit, for the defendant.

Thomas, DeGrood, Witenoff & Hoffman, P.C. (by Gary N. Felty, Jr., and John J. Hoffman), Southfield, amicus curiae for Office of the Commissioner of Major League Baseball.

Before BANDSTRA, C.J., and ZAHRA and METER, JJ.

BANDSTRA, C.J.

In this case, we are asked to determine whether we should adopt, as a matter of Michigan law, the "limited duty" rule that other jurisdictions have applied with respect to spectator injuries at baseball games. Under that rule, a baseball stadium owner is not liable for injuries to spectators that result from projectiles leaving the field during play if safety screening has been provided behind home plate and there are a sufficient number of protected seats to meet ordinary demand. We conclude that the limited duty doctrine should be adopted as a matter of Michigan law and that there was no evidence presented at trial that defendants failed to meet that duty. Further, we conclude that there is no duty to warn spectators at a baseball game of the well-known possibility that a bat or ball might leave the field. We therefore conclude that there is no evidence to support the verdict rendered on behalf of plaintiffs against defendant and we reverse and remand.

FACTS

Plaintiff Alyssia M. Benejam, a young girl, attended a Tigers game with a friend and members of the friend's family and was seated quite close to the playing field along the third base line. The stadium was equipped with a net behind home plate, and the net extended part of the way down the first and third base lines. Although Alyssia was behind the net, she was injured when a player's bat broke and a fragment of it curved around the net.[1] There was no evidence, and plaintiffs do not contend, that the fragment of the bat went through the net, that there was a hole in the net, or that the net was otherwise defective.

Plaintiffs sued the Tigers, claiming primarily[2] that the net was insufficiently long and that warnings about the possibility of projectiles leaving the field were inadequate.[3] The Tigers responded with motions before, during, and after trial arguing that, as a matter of law, plaintiffs could not or did not present any viable legal claim. Those motions were all denied by the trial court. Alyssia suffered crushed fingers as a result of the accident and the jury awarded plaintiffs noneconomic damages (past and future) totaling $917,000, lost earning capacity of $56,700 and $35,000 for past and future medical expenses. Damages are not at issue on appeal.

STANDARD OF REVIEW

[1] Defendant's arguments concern the duty of care and duty to warn applicable in this case. Questions regarding the nature and extent of a tortfeasor's duty are issues of

law subject to review de novo. *Groncki v. Detroit Edison Co.*, 453 Mich. 644, 649, 557 N.W.2d 289 (1996).

STANDARD OF CARE/PROTECTIVE SCREENING

Defendant argues that although there is no Michigan law directly on point, other jurisdictions have balanced the safety benefits of providing a protective screen against the fact that such screening detracts from the allure of attending a live baseball game by placing an obstacle or insulation between fans and the playing field. The rule that emerges in these cases is that a stadium proprietor cannot be liable for spectator injuries if it has satisfied a "limited duty"—to erect a screen that will protect the most dangerous area of the spectator stands, behind home plate, and to provide a number of seats in this area sufficient to meet the ordinary demand for protected seats. In this case, there is no dispute that the Tigers constructed a protective screen behind home plate, and there was no evidence that the screen was insufficient to meet the ordinary demand for protected seating. Defendant argues the circuit court erred in failing to recognize the limited duty doctrine and in denying motions based on that doctrine for summary disposition, a directed verdict, and judgment notwithstanding the verdict.

Plaintiffs argue against application of the limited duty doctrine and contend that, under usual principles of premises liability, the circuit court correctly concluded that a jury question was presented. Defendant (an invitor) had a duty to exercise ordinary care and prudence and maintain premises reasonably safe for invitees like Alyssia. Plaintiffs argue that the jury verdict was supported by sufficient evidence that the defendant failed to fulfill this duty because it did not provide a screen extending long enough along the third (and first) base lines.

There is no Michigan case law directly on point.[4] Our review of precedents from other jurisdictions finds overwhelming, if not universal,[5] support for the limited duty rule that defendant advocates. See, e.g., *Lawson v. Salt Lake Trappers, Inc.*, 901 P.2d 1013, 1015 (Utah, 1995); *Bellezzo v. Arizona*, 174 Ariz. 548, 553–554, 851 P.2d 847 (Ariz.App., 1992); *Arnold v. City of Cedar Rapids*, 443 N.W.2d 332, 333 (Iowa, 1989); *Friedman v. Houston Sports Ass'n*, 731 S.W.2d 572, 574–575 (Tex.App., 1987); *Swagger v. City of Crystal*, 379 N.W.2d 183, 185 (Minn.App., 1985); *Rudnick v. Golden West Broadcasters*, 156 Cal.App.3d 793, 796, 202 Cal.Rptr. 900 (1984).[6]

The logic of these precedents is that there is an inherent risk of objects leaving the playing field that people know about when they attend baseball games. See, e.g., *Swagger, supra* at 185 ("[n]o one of ordinary intelligence could see many innings of the ordinary league [baseball] game without coming to a full realization that batters cannot and do not control the direction of the ball"), quoting *Brisson v. Minneapolis Baseball & Athletic Ass'n*, 185 Minn. 507, 509–510, 240 N.W. 903 (1932).[7] Also, there is inherent value in having most seats unprotected by a screen because baseball patrons generally want to be involved with the game in an intimate way and are even hoping that they will come in contact with some projectile from the field (in the form of a souvenir baseball). See, e.g., *Rudnick, supra* at 802, 202 Cal.Rptr. 900 ("the chance to apprehend a misdirected baseball is as much a part of the game as the seventh inning stretch or peanuts and Cracker Jack"). In other words, spectators know about the risk of being in the stands and, in fact, welcome that risk to a certain extent. On the other hand, the area behind home plate is especially dangerous and spectators who want protected seats should be able to find them in this area. Balancing all of these concerns, courts generally have adopted the limited duty doctrine that prevents liability if there are a sufficient number of protected seats behind home plate to meet the ordinary demand for that kind of seating. If that seating is provided, the baseball stadium owner has fulfilled its duty and there can be no liability for spectators who are injured by a projectile from the field.

An oft-cited precedent, *Akins v. Glens Falls City School Dist.*, 53 N.Y.2d 325, 441 N.Y.S.2d 644, 424 N.E.2d 531 (1981), provides a good illustration of the reasoning employed. There, a spectator at a baseball game was permanently and seriously injured when a sharply hit foul ball struck her in the eye. *Id.* at 327, 441 N.Y.S.2d 644, 424 N.E.2d 531. As is the case in Michigan,[8] New York has disavowed the "assumption of risk" doctrine and thus the *Akins* court analyzed the situation anew, without reliance on that doctrine. *Id.* at 329, 441 N.Y.S.2d 644, 424 N.E.2d 531. In doing so, the court reasoned that an owner of a baseball field is not an insurer of the safety of its spectators. Rather, like any

continued

other owner or occupier of land, it is only under a duty to exercise 'reasonable care under the circumstances' to prevent injury to those who come to watch the games played on its field. [*Id.* (citations omitted).]

The court noted that "many spectators prefer to sit where their view of the game is unobstructed by fences or protective netting and the proprietor of a ball park has a legitimate interest in catering to these desires." *Id.* at 330, 441 N.Y.S.2d 644, 424 N.E.2d 531. Balancing the interests involved, the court adopted what it considered to be the "majority rule"—"the owner must screen the most dangerous section of the field—the area behind home ***653** plate—and the screening that is provided must be sufficient for those spectators who may be reasonably anticipated to desire protected seats on an ordinary occasion." *Id.* The *Akins* court reasoned that this rule appropriately recognizes the "practical realities of this sporting event." *Id.* at 331, 441 N.Y.S.2d 644, 424 N.E.2d 531.

[2] We find *Akins* and similar precedents to be well-reasoned and persuasive. It seems axiomatic that baseball fans attend games knowing that, as a natural result of play, objects may leave the field with the potential of causing injury in the stands. It is equally clear that most spectators, nonetheless, prefer to be as "close to the play" as possible, without an insulating and obstructive screen between them and the action. In contrast, a smaller number of spectators prefer the protection offered by screening. The most dangerous part of the spectator stands is the area in the lower deck behind home plate and along each of the baselines. Certainly home plate is the center of the most activity on the field. Most notably, it is there that pitched balls, traveling at great speeds in a line that would extend into the stands, are often deflected or squarely hit into those stands. Quite logically, the limited duty rule protects a stadium owner that provides screening for this most dangerous area and, in so doing, accommodates baseball patrons who seek protected seating. Because the limited duty rule is based on the desires of spectators, it further makes sense to define the extent of screening that should be provided behind home plate on the basis of consumer demand.

[3] Plaintiffs do nothing to argue substantively against the limited duty rule, but merely argue that baseball stadium cases should be governed by usual invitor-invitee principles, not any special "baseball rule." Thus, plaintiffs argue that the jury properly determined that defendant failed to exercise "ordinary care" and failed to provide "reasonably safe" premises. However, the limited duty rule does not ignore or abrogate usual premises liability principles. Instead, it identifies the duty of baseball stadium proprietors with greater specificity than the usual "ordinary care/reasonably safe" standard provides. The limited duty precedents "do not eliminate the stadium owner's duty to exercise reasonable care under the circumstances to protect patrons against injury." *Friedman, supra* at 574, quoting *McNiel v. Ft. Worth Baseball Club,* 268 S.W.2d 244, 246 (Tex.Civ.App. 1954). Rather, these precedents "define that duty so that once the stadium owner has provided 'adequately screened seats' for *all* those desiring them, the stadium owner has fulfilled its duty of care as a matter of law." *Id.* The limited duty doctrine establishes the "outer limits" of liability and "thereby prevent[s] a jury from requiring [a stadium owner] to take precautions that are clearly unreasonable." *Bellezzo, supra* at 554, 851 P.2d 847. By providing greater specificity with regard to the duty imposed on stadium owners, the rule prevents burgeoning litigation that might signal the demise or substantial alteration of the game of baseball as a spectator sport.

We also note that the precedents applying the limited duty rule are consistent with the reasoning of the closest Michigan case available, *Ritchie-Gamester v. City of Berkley,* 461 Mich. 73, 597 N.W.2d 517 (1999). *Ritchie* is not directly on point because it did not involve a spectator at a sporting event but, instead, considered a person injured while participating in recreational ice skating. See *id.* at 75, 597 N.W.2d 517. Nonetheless, the analysis in *Ritchie* is similar to the analysis employed by courts in other jurisdictions as they have developed the limited duty rule with respect to spectator injuries. *Ritchie* considered whether ordinary principles of negligence should be used to determine whether there was liability for an injury resulting from a collision between skaters or, instead, whether the higher recklessness standard should be used. *Id.* at 76, 597 N.W.2d 517. In answering this question, the Court first recognized "the everyday reality of participation in recreational activities," most notably, that "[w]hen people engage in a recreational activity, they have voluntarily subjected themselves to certain risks inherent in that activity." *Id.*

at 86–87, 597 N.W.2d 517. With this recognition in mind, the Court concluded that a recklessness standard "most nearly comports with the expectations of participants in recreational activities." *Id.* at 90, 597 N.W.2d 517. In reaching this conclusion, the Court reasoned:

> When a player steps on the field, she must recognize that an injury may occur, but she does not know whether she will be injured, or whether she will inadvertently injure another player. We do not believe that a player expects an injury, even if it results from a rule violation, to give rise to liability. Instead, we think it more likely that players participate with the expectation that no liability will arise unless a participant's actions exceed the normal bounds of conduct associated with the activity.
>
> * * *
>
> Consequently, we believe that the line of liability for recreational activities should be drawn at recklessness. [*Id.* at 94, 597 N.W.2d 517.]

The Court further reasoned that an ordinary negligence standard would unduly restrict people in the enjoyment of recreational skating by promoting a potentially debilitating threat of litigation. *Id.* at 92–93, n. 13, 597 N.W.2d 517.

The Court's reasoning in *Ritchie* is similar to that employed by the limited duty precedents described above. For most fans, the everyday reality of attending a baseball game includes voluntarily subjecting oneself to the risk that a ball or bat might leave the field and cause injury. The limited duty rule comports more nearly with that everyday reality than would usual invitor- invitee principles of liability. While requiring that protected seats be provided for those who want them, the limited duty rule leaves the baseball stadium owner free, without fear of liability, to accommodate the majority of fans who prefer unobstructed and uninsulated contact with the game. Under usual invitor-invitee principles of liability, fear of litigation would likely require screening far in excess of that required to meet the desires of baseball fans.

This case, tried under usual invitor-invitee principles of liability, provides a good example. Plaintiff's expert testified that, on the basis of his review of accidents occurring over time in the spectator stands between first base and third base, reasonable safety precautions would include screening in that entire area. In another

case, where an injury occurred farther down the baseline, testimony and argument would likely be adduced to support a further extension as "reasonably necessary" to protect fans. The logical result of having these cases governed by usual invitor-invitee principles of liability would be that warned against in *Akins, supra* at 331, 441 N.Y.S.2d 644, 424 N.E.2d 531: "[E]very spectator injured by a foul ball, no matter where he is seated or standing in the ball park, would have an absolute right to go to the jury on every claim of negligence."

Both because the limited duty doctrine represents a good accommodation of the interests that must be balanced in this case and because it is consistent with the reasoning employed in *Ritchie*, we adopt that doctrine as a matter of Michigan law.[9] Specifically, we hold that a baseball stadium owner that provides screening behind home plate sufficient to meet ordinary demand for protected seating has fulfilled its duty with respect to screening and cannot be subjected to liability for injuries resulting to a spectator by an object leaving the playing field.[10] We do not today hold that a baseball stadium operator that does not provide this level of protection can be held liable. For reasons previously noted, there may be an argument that would prevent the imposition of liability in that situation as well.[11] In any event, that is not the situation presented on this appeal and we express no opinion regarding the merits of any such argument.

Applying the limited duty rule here, we conclude that plaintiffs have failed to provide any proof sufficient to find that liability could be imposed. Clearly, there was a screen behind home plate and there was no proof whatsoever that persons wanting seats protected by the screen could not be accommodated. To the contrary, uncontested testimony by Tigers ticket personnel established that protected seating is generally open and available to fans who want it. Accordingly, we conclude that the screening provided by defendant was sufficient under the limited duty doctrine applicable in this case.

DUTY TO WARN

Plaintiffs also argue that defendant failed to provide an adequate warning regarding the possibility that some object might come flying off the field and cause injury in the stands. However, we conclude that defendant did not have any duty to warn regarding this well-known risk.

Plaintiffs rely primarily on *Falkner v. John E. Fetzer, Inc.*, 113 Mich.App. 500, 317 N.W.2d 337 (1982). While

continued

acknowledging the "generally accepted proposition that there is no duty to warn of the risk of being hit by batted balls when attending a baseball game, because the risk is obvious," the *Falkner* panel nonetheless reasoned that "plaintiffs presented an apparently unique record in an attempt to demonstrate that the magnitude of the risk involved is much greater than commonly believed" and, therefore, reasoned that it was "proper to submit to the jury the question whether it would be reasonable to require defendant to warn spectators of the unexpectedly high degree of risk." *Id.* at 502–503, 317 N.W.2d 337. The opinion does not indicate why the record before the panel was "unique." In any event, we conclude that *Falkner* cannot reasonably be understood as suggesting that, in all cases, baseball stadiums have a duty to warn spectators of the risk that objects from the field might cause injury.

[4] As discussed above, one of the premises of the universally adopted limited duty rule for protective screening is the fact that baseball spectators generally know that attending a game involves risks from off-field projectiles. Accordingly, precedents from other jurisdictions conclude that there is no duty to warn regarding this risk. See, e.g., *City of Milton v. Broxson*, 514 So.2d 1116, 1118–1119 (Fla.App., 1987); *Friedman*, *supra* at 575; *Stradtner v. Cincinnati Reds, Inc.*, 39 Ohio App.2d 199, 316 N.E.2d 924 (1972); *Baker v. Topping*, 15 A.D.2d 193, 196, 222 N.Y.S.2d 658 (1961); *Anderson v. Kansas City Baseball Club*, 231 S.W.2d 170 (Mo., 1950); *Hunt v. Thomasville Baseball Co.*, 80 Ga.App. 572, 573, 56 S.E.2d 828 (1949). See also, generally, *Neinstein v. Los Angeles Dodgers, Inc.*, 185 Cal.App.3d 176, 184, 229 Cal.Rptr. 612 (1986). As noted by one court, "[i]t would have been absurd, and no doubt would have been resented by many patrons, if the ticket seller, or other employees, had warned each person entering the park that he or she would be imperiled by vagrant baseballs . . . ." *Keys v. Alamo City Baseball Co.*, 150 S.W.2d 368, 371 (Tex.Civ.App.1941).

We find these precedents to be compelling and persuasive. Further, having concluded that the limited duty rule should be adopted in Michigan partly on the premise that spectators know about the dangers of objects leaving the field, it would be inconsistent to impose a duty to warn of those dangers. Finally, to impose such a duty would be contrary to the many Michigan precedents decided since *Falkner*, regarding "open and obvious dangers," with respect to which

there is no duty to warn. See, e.g., *Riddle v. McLouth Steel Products Corp.*, 440 Mich. 85, 96, 485 N.W.2d 676 (1992); *Arias v. Talon Development Group, Inc.*, 239 Mich.App. 265, 267, 608 N.W.2d 484 (2000); *Hughes v. PMG Bldg., Inc.*, 227 Mich.App. 1, 10, 574 N.W.2d 691 (1997); *Novotney v. Burger King Corp. (On Remand)*, 198 Mich.App. 470, 472–473, 499 N.W.2d 379 (1993).

Falkner has been described as the lone case that supports a duty to warn in this context. *Friedman, supra* at 575. To the extent that it might be read as stating a general rule requiring a duty to warn in all cases, rather than a limited rule applicable only to the "unique record" presented, we decline to follow *Falkner*. We conclude that defendant had no duty to warn plaintiffs regarding the well-known risk that some object might leave the playing field and cause injury.[12]

Having concluded that, under the facts of this case, defendant did not breach any duty to provide screening and was under no duty to provide a warning to plaintiffs regarding the risk of injury from objects leaving the field, we reverse the jury verdict and remand this matter for entry of an order finding no cause of action against defendant. We need not consider other arguments advanced by defendant in support of that result.[13]

We reverse and remand. We do not retain jurisdiction.

635 N.W.2d 219, 246 Mich.App. 645

FOOTNOTES

1. Most of the evidence at trial suggested that the bat fragment curved around the net, although it may have traveled in a straight line and bounced off a nearby seat before striking Alyssia.

2. In addition, plaintiffs elicited evidence at trial that the Tigers' home plate was too close to the spectator stands (about sixteen inches less than the sixty feet required by a league rule). However, there was no evidence that the league rule was for safety purposes (rather than to define the playing field), nor to suggest how this discrepancy materially increased the risk of injury to Alyssia. Nonetheless, plaintiffs did not include the issue in their "theory of the case" presentation to the jury and do not argue this matter on appeal.

3. Plaintiffs also sued the maker of the bat, Hillerich and Bradsby, but settled that claim before trial.

4. However, dictum comments in Michigan precedents are consistent with the limited duty rule that defendant advocates. See *Ritchie-Gamester v. City of Berkley*, 461 Mich. 73, 87, 597 N.W.2d 517 (1999) (quoting with approval Justice Cardozo's observation that a baseball spectator accepts the danger of possibly being hit by a ball); *Felgner v. Anderson*, 375 Mich. 23, 45, n. 6, 133 N.W.2d 136 (1965) ("[a] spectator's suit is barred . . . by a lack of negligence on the part of the park owner . . . in the ordinary instance of a batted ball flying into unscreened stands"); *Blakeley v. White Star Line*, 154 Mich. 635, 638, 118 N.W. 482 (1908) ("It is knowledge common to all that in these [baseball] games hard balls are thrown and batted with great swiftness; that they are liable to be muffed or batted or thrown outside the lines of the diamond, and visitors standing in position that may be reached by such balls have voluntarily placed themselves there with knowledge of the situation, and may be held to assume the risk.").

5. Plaintiffs argue that two Illinois cases, *Yates v. Chicago Nat'l League Ball Club, Inc.*, 230 Ill.App.3d 472, 172 Ill.Dec. 209, 595 N.E.2d 570 (1992), and *Coronel v. Chicago White Sox, Ltd.*, 230 Ill.App.3d 734, 171 Ill.Dec. 917, 595 N.E.2d 45 (1992), have rejected the limited duty rule. However, those cases have been superseded by more recent legislation granting baseball owners limited immunity from liability for spectator injuries.

6. Although we have concentrated our analysis on foreign precedents decided during the last twenty years, courts in other states had previously indicated support for the limited duty rule as well. See, generally, *Perry v. Seattle School Dist. No. 1*, 66 Wash.2d 800, 405 P.2d 589 (1965); *McFatridge v. Harlem Globe Trotters*, 69 N.M. 271, 365 P.2d 918 (1961); *Schentzel v. Philadelphia Nat'l League Club*, 173 Pa.Super. 179, 96 A.2d 181 (1953); *Erickson v. Lexington Baseball Club*, 233 N.C. 627, 65 S.E.2d 140 (1951); *Cincinnati Baseball Club Co. v. Eno*, 112 Ohio St. 175, 147 N.E. 86 (1925); *Anderson v. Kansas City Baseball Club*, 231 S.W.2d 170 (Mo., 1950); *Lorino v. New Orleans Baseball & Amusement Co.*, 16 La.App. 95, 133 So. 408 (1931). The limited duty rule was apparently first recognized almost ninety years ago in *Edling v. Kansas City Baseball & Exhibition Co.*, 181 Mo.App. 327, 168 S.W. 908 (1914).

7. Although many of the cases relied on considered baseballs and other objects that left the field of play and caused injury, we see no difference analytically between those situations and the bat fragment at issue here.

8. In Michigan, the assumption of risk doctrine has been disavowed for all nonemployment cases since *Felgner v. Anderson*, 375 Mich. 23, 55-56, 133 N.W.2d 136 (1965).

9. Although the concurring opinion in *Ritchie*, *supra*, is not binding precedent, we note that our decision in this case seems consistent with its analysis. The concurring justices reasoned that the majority had inappropriately employed an "assumption of risk" analysis, even though that doctrine has long been abrogated by Michigan precedents. *Id.* at 102, 597 N.W.2d 517 (Brickley, J., concurring). Nonetheless, the concurring justices noted that assumption of risk has been recognized as surviving in the sense of the "primary assumption of risk." *Id.* at 103–104, 597 N.W.2d 517. Although the concurring justices found this concept to be inapplicable to the facts in *Ritchie*, see *id.* at 104, 597 N.W.2d 517, it would apparently apply to the facts of this case. As authority for the "primary assumption of risk" doctrine, the concurring justices quoted Prosser and Keeton's treatise on Torts. *Id.* at 103, 597 N.W.2d 517. This authority states:

A second situation is where the plaintiff voluntarily enters into some relation with the defendant, with knowledge that the defendant will not protect him against one or more future risks that may arise from the relation. He may then be regarded as tacitly or *impliedly* consenting to the negligence, and agreeing to take his chances. Thus, . . . *he may enter a baseball park, sit in an unscreened seat, and so consent that the players may proceed with the game without taking any precautions to protect him from being hit by the ball.* Again, the legal result is that the defendant is simply relieved of the duty which would otherwise exist. [Prosser & Keeton, Torts (5th ed.), § 68, p. 481. (First emphasis in original; second emphasis added).]

Similarly, *Felgner, supra*, while generally abrogating the assumption of risk doctrine as an affirmative defense available to a negligent defendant, also

continued

recognized that because "certain risks of accident attend all outdoor sports," *id.* at 45, n. 6, 133 N.W.2d 136, quoting *Williams v. Wood*, 260 Mich. 322, 327, 244 N.W. 490 (1932), there is no breach of duty giving rise to liability when those inherent risks become reality as in "the ordinary instance of a batted ball flying into unscreened stands." *Felgner, supra.*

10. This assumes, of course, that the screening provided is not in a state of disrepair or otherwise in a condition whereby projectiles can permeate it and allow injuries to occur in the protected area of the stands.

11. See n. 9, *supra.*

12. We further note that plaintiffs presented little if any evidence regarding how the language of the warnings actually given (a general announcement over the loudspeaker, a notice on the center field video board, and small print language on the back of the ticket) were inadequate. Nor was there any evidence concerning the warning systems used at other ball parks or whether some more effective warning would have made any difference in this case (Alyssia's friend's mother, who chose the seating behind the protective netting, testified that she knew of the risks of balls and bats entering the stands). Accordingly, even if we were to recognize a duty to warn in this context we would conclude that plaintiffs did not present sufficient evidence to support a finding of liability on this basis. See, e.g., *Nichols v. Clare Community Hosp.*, 190 Mich.App. 679, 684, 476 N.W.2d 493 (1991) (observing that when proceeding under a theory of liability based on a negligent failure to warn, proximate cause cannot be established unless it is shown that an adequate warning would have prevented the plaintiff's injury by altering the conduct involved).

13. Most notably, we do not consider defendant's argument that, considering the "freak" nature of the bat's flight path here, the injury that Alyssia suffered was not foreseeable. We understand this to be a "proximate cause" argument and, having concluded that defendant did not breach any duty, we need not consider whether any alleged breach of duty proximately caused the injury. We note, however, that in similar cases, similar arguments have been accepted. See, e.g., *Curtis v. Portland Baseball Club*, 130 Or. 93, 96–97, 279 P. 277 (1929) (where "the injury sustained was due to a foul ball which performed the remarkable feat of taking a sharp inshoot around the end of the screen and striking plaintiff" the accident "was one which could not reasonably have been anticipated" and the judgment in favor of plaintiff was reversed).

athlete continue to participate in an event because it is in the team's best interest rather than the athlete's? To whom does the medical practitioner owe a duty of care, the athlete or the team? Sometimes this decision is not clear cut. An allegation of negligence on behalf of a sports medical practitioner is referred to as **malpractice**. Malpractice is a broad category that could involve anything from an improper diagnosis to the prescription of an inappropriate medication.

Whenever the alleged malpractice of a team doctor, physician, or trainer is at issue, courts usually use the "locality rule" and compare the alleged negligence of the physician to other physicians in the same geographic area or practice specialty.

malpractice   negligence by a professional person, such as a lawyer or physician

■ Sports Officials

Another area of sports torts involves the officials of sports contests. It is a generally held principle that officials in sports can greatly affect the outcome of the sports contest. Professional sports such as football, basketball, and hockey have often incorporated the use of the television replay to ensure that the often subjective regulation of the sports contest remains as objective as possible.

Sports officials, however, are often subject to harassment, intimidation, and sometimes violent, physical displays of abuse from fans, players, and coaches. Whether at the professional or amateur level, sports officials are often targets of hostile emotions due to the extreme competitiveness in the sports arena.

Due to numerous lawsuits against sports officials for alleged intentional improprieties while judging a sports contest, states have been forced to enact laws that protect officials and provide immunity from such lawsuits. Immunity from civil suits only applies to unintentional, negligent acts by the officials. This affords the sports official some protection against the sports litigant. Such protection is not absolute, however. For intentional or grossly negligent acts by officials, the law generally provides no protection. Sports officials, of course, may sue fans, athletic participants, and others for torts suffered by them.

■ Workers Compensation

In professional sports that involve a players association or union, compensation for injuries to an athlete is a prime subject for any collective bargaining agreement. When players are injured from an activity arising out of and in the course of their employment, the private agreement between the players, team, and league often avoid any necessity of filing a claim under the state's workers compensation statute. **Workers compensation** is a form of insurance required by the state to provide benefits to employees who are injured on the job. Independent contractors are generally not covered under workers compensation statutes.

Since being an employee is a prerequisite to filing a claim under workers compensation, usually only professional athletes or athletes paid for their professional services may consider filing a claim. What about amateur and recreational athletes and the workers compensation law? Are student-athletes who receive athletic scholarships, for example, entitled to compensation if they suffer a temporary or permanent injury while participating in their sport for their school, college, or university? It seems clear that the student-athlete has not yet been

---

workers compensation   system designed to compensate employees injured on the job in the course of their employment

afforded the opportunity to claim workers compensation since student-athletes are not yet recognized as employees. However, the NCAA has established a Catastrophic Insurance Plan covering every student who participates in college sports, including managers, trainers, and cheerleaders. One can learn more about this plan by visiting the NCAA website (www.ncaa.org).

■ Insurance

Since any sports activity involves a degree of risk or injury, it is generally recognized that events and participants should purchase **insurance** to protect against a claim of negligence arising from that activity. Sports insurance policies do not relieve an individual or event from liability from negligent behavior. However, having insurance does ensure that if a judge or jury believes that damages should be awarded for an injury arising from the activity, the insurance company stands in the shoes of the defendant and must therefore pay in accordance with terms of the insurance policy. This is often referred to as *indemnification* or *subrogation* in the insurance industry.

Exceptional student-athletes, professional athletes, sporting events, and organizations are wise to purchase a policy—if possible—that covers their own participation in the activity if an underwriter will provide such coverage. Such insurance for the professional athlete may be referred to as "career-ending injury" insurance and usually requires large premiums to maintain because of the potential for great financial loss, especially at the professional level. One may also purchase insurance for organized amateur recreational activities such as a local road race.

■ Torts and Waivers

Courts do not favor a form of contract called a *waiver*. Sometimes waivers are called *releases*, *disclaimers*, or even *exculpatory clauses*. The ultimate purpose of the waiver is to relieve a party from liability and/or relinquishing the right of an injured party to pursue legal action in the event of an injury. Sports that involve high risks, including bungee jumping, scuba diving, and parasailing, often require the signing of a waiver as a prerequisite to participation.

Though courts do not favor upholding these private agreements, most courts will do so as long as the agreement waived ordinary negligence as opposed to gross negligence or recklessness. Waivers found to have been an attempt to contract out

---

insurance   contract in which a company agrees to compensate the insured for loss due to perils or other liability

of liability for gross negligence will likely be unenforceable, though a few states recognize waivers against gross negligence.[4] Such agreements, if enforced, would have virtually encouraged carelessness on the part of parties by offering them unlimited lack of liability for their actions. Also, courts are likely to find that waivers signed by minors are void or voidable.

Ticket Stubs and Waivers

Many waivers are found on the backside of ticket stubs for sporting and entertainment events. Most fans or customers do not read these waivers (many are not even aware of the existence of the waiver on the back). Defendants will often raise as a defense to a negligence claim that such language should relieve them from liability. Generally speaking, though, these waivers are virtually unenforceable since there was no intent on the part of the fan to agree to such terms. Also at issue is the lack of "informed consent" and courts' refusal to impose such waivers on fans as a matter of public policy.

Minors and Waivers

Whether one analyzes Little League sports or amusement park rides, waivers are often signed by parents of a minor to avoid liability or give up the right to sue in the event of an accident that causes injuries. The law remains unclear as to whether parents who sign waivers on behalf of their children will release a potential defendant from liability to the minor.

Though the trend is to enforce such waiver arrangements signed by parents on behalf of a child, it is quite possible that a court could refuse to enforce such a waiver, especially for gross negligence or recklessness. Still, a court does have the option of not enforcing a waiver signed by the minor or parent. The best view is to analyze such cases on a case-by-case basis, paying particular attention to the particular state's common law interpretations of waivers.

■ Statutes of Limitation

Though the statutes vary, it is important to recognize that claims for personal injury have **statutes of limitation** that force a plaintiff to sue within a particular time frame. If the potential plaintiff fails to bring suit within that time frame, the claim will be time-barred and forever lost under that particular legal theory. The clock usually begins to run for only one year beginning from the time of the injury or when the injury was discovered (whichever is later) in many torts. Plaintiffs are well

---

statute of limitations   amount of time a plaintiff has to file a lawsuit

advised to research a particular jurisdiction's statute of limitations before filing suit under a particular legal theory.

■ Intentional Torts

When an individual intends to bring about an injury to another, such injury is categorized as an intentional tort. The major intentional torts in the sports context include assault, battery, and defamation. Intentional torts differ from negligence in that a person's motivation may be considered, similar to the intent or *mens rea* element of criminal law (for further discussion see Chapter 4).

It is perplexing to the courts, however, to view most sports as arenas for awarding damages to plaintiffs since the element of personal injury is usually obvious to the participants. Additionally, in sports such as football, hockey, and boxing, participants are usually encouraged to hurt the opponent. However, there are some instances in which the sports tort is so outside the scope of a game or contest that courts have awarded damages to participants for intentional injuries.

Head-butting referees, kicking camera operators, and strangling or spitting on coaches or players often result in prime intentional tort claims. However, most athletes, coaches, and referees seem reluctant to bring suit for these sorts of potential claims.

Defamation of Character

Professional athletes certainly live in the limelight of society. As such, they are often subject to a public life rife with criticism. Public opinions can often turn into slanderous and libelous statements made by journalists and others.[5] Since many professional athletes would likely be considered to be "public figures," suits by athletes for **defamation of character** are often unsuccessful on the ground that the media is merely expressing a statement of opinion rather than a statement of fact.

When a journalist publishes a statement of opinion, such speech is generally regarded as protected speech under constitutional standards. The athlete litigant will only be successful if he or she can prove that the statement by the defendant was knowingly false or made with reckless disregard of whether it was true or false.[6] This standard is referred to as *actual malice*. However, even if such a statement is found to be false and therefore defamatory, if the sports participant cannot prove damages, then the journalist[7] defendant may successfully survive the suit.

---

defamation of character   intentional tort whereby a false statement is published (libel) or spoken (slander) about the plaintiff

intentional infliction of emotional distress   intentional tort in which the defendant causes emotional distress by extreme or outrageous conduct

Intentional Infliction of Emotional Distress

Virtually all states now recognize the tort of **intentional infliction of emotional distress**. This tort used to require some measurable degree of physical illness due to extreme and outrageous conduct on the part of the defendant. However, it is now common for litigants to offer proof and recover for purely mental and emotional injuries for such egregious conduct on the part of members of our society.

Intentional Interference with Contractual Relations

An intentional tort that often rears its head in sports is when one team attempts to lure a player from another team even though the player is clearly under contract with the other team or league. In the sports industry this is called *tampering*. This tort emerged from the old English case of *Lumley v. Gye*, 118 Eng. Rep. 749 (1853). The elements of the tort of **intentional interference with contractual relations** are

1. existence of a contract
2. intentional interference with that contract by a nonparty
3. causation
4. damages to a club or organization as a result of the interference

Commercial Misappropriation

Though athletes may find that a successful suit under defamation standards is extremely difficult, an area that proves worthy of a lawsuit involves the use of the athlete's name, image, or likeness without the athlete's consent in order to make a profit or sale. Such nonapproved use of an athlete's persona is referred to as **commercial misappropriation**.

Since manufacturers and other sellers of products and services commonly use an athlete in marketing in the form of an endorsement contract, athletes must be cognizant to protect from the unauthorized misuse of their image. Establishing a trademark (including an Internet domain name) for one's name or image may be necessary for professional athletes (and certainly professional and amateur leagues and organizations) to prevent improper use of a name for profit.

■ Products Liability

Products liability in sports represents an area of negligence involving a sporting good. When plaintiffs sue a manufacturer of sporting goods, the claimants allege

intentional interference with contractual relations   intentional tort of interfering with a known contractual relationship with the intent to induce one of the parties to breach

commercial misappropriation   tort of intentionally using a person's name, image, or likeness without permission for personal gain and profit

that they suffered an injury due to the use of a product that was defective. Bats, gloves, shoes, helmets, pads and other goods used in a sport are subject to a lawsuit if there is a defect in the design or manufacturing process. This may be referred to as a *manufacturing defect* or *design defect.*

Manufacturers of goods may also be sued for failing to warn the user of potential dangers involving use of the product. Since goods are involved, the **Uniform Commercial Code (UCC)** is often called into play, and the user of the product alleges that there was a **breach of the warranty of merchantability** or a **breach of the implied warranty of fitness for a particular purpose.**[8] UCC article 2 governs the sales of goods and has been adopted in whole or in part by every state.

■ Strict Liability in Torts

Strict liability rarely applies in sports. Under a strict (or absolute) liability theory, a seller of sporting goods is liable for any harm that is caused to a plaintiff due to a "defective condition unreasonably dangerous to the user or consumer."[9] Though many sporting goods may be deemed potentially harmful or unsafe, to hold a manufacturer to the standard of strict liability is virtually nonexistent in the sports arena. Most claims would fall under the negligence theories of breach of warranty, defect in design, defect in manufacture, or failure to warn.

■ Summary

Tort law allows an injured party to sue for damages. The burden of proof in any tort case is preponderance of the evidence. Some torts are also crimes. Torts can generally be divided into four major categories: negligence, intentional torts, strict liability, and products liability. Debate continues as to whether a sports participant should be able to sue another competitor for injuries suffered during a sports contest. As long as the injury suffered by one party was clearly outside the scope of the game, a personal injury claim may be brought.

Negligence is the failure to act as a "reasonable person." Most states recognize the comparative negligence standard. Gross negligence and recklessness are higher

---

Uniform Commercial Code (UCC)   model act drafted to provide certainty in governing the sale of goods, commercial paper, secured transactions, etc.

breach of warranty of merchantability   implied promise that a product will be merchantable and fit for its ordinary use

breach of the implied warranty of fitness for a particular purpose   implied warranty that arises when a seller of goods knows the particular purpose for which the purchaser needs the goods.

forms of negligence where injury occurs due to intentional misconduct on the part of a defendant. If proof of recklessness is shown, punitive damages might be appropriate. A wrongful death action may be brought in the event a death occurs as the result of negligent conduct.

Insurance issues are important for owners, managers, athletic directors, and others involved in the sports industry. Other tort issues include defamation, intentional infliction of emotional distress, intentional interference with contractual relations, and commercial misappropriation. Though waivers and releases are not favored by the courts, such private contracts will be enforced as long as they are reasonable. A study of tort law is important for all of the participants in a sporting event, including players, coaches, trainers, and owners.

■ Key Terms

breach of the implied warranty of
    fitness for a particular purpose
breach of the warranty of
    merchantability
commercial misappropriation
comparative fault
contributory negligence
defamation of character
gross negligence
insurance
intent
intentional infliction of emotional
    distress
intentional interference with
    contractual relations

intentional tort
malpractice
negligence
no fly zones
preponderance of the evidence
products liability
recklessness
reasonable person standard
statute of limitation
strict (absolute) liability
tort
Uniform Commercial Code
    (UCC)
workers compensation
wrongful death

■ Additional Cases

Abdul-Jabbar v. General Motors Corp., 85 F. 3d 407 (9th Cir. 1996)
Adams v. Roark, 686 S.W.2d 73 (Tenn. 1985)
Banfield v. Louis, 589 So.2d 441 (Fla. App. 1991)
Bourque v. Duplechin, 331 So. 2d 40 (La. Ct. App. 1976)
Boll v. Chicago Park District, 620 N.E. 2d 1082 (Ill. 1991)
Dilallo v. Riding Safely Inc., 687 So. 2d 353 (Fla. 4th Dist. 1997)
Dudley Sports Co. v. Schmitt, 279 N.E. 2d 266 (Ind. App. 1972)
Friedman v. Houston Sports Ass'n, 731 S.W. 2d 572 (Tex. App. 1987)
Gauvin v. Clark, 537 N.E.2d 94 (Mass. 1989)
Georgia High School Ass'n v. Waddell, 285 S.E. 2d 7 (Ga. 1981)
Gertz v. Robert Welch, Inc., 418 U.S. 323 (1974)

Georgia High School Ass'n v. Waddell, 285 S.E. 2d 7 (Ga. 1981)

Gertz v. Robert Welch, Inc., 418 U.S. 323 (1974)

Hackbart v. Cincinnati Bengals, Inc. [Hackbart I], 435 F. Supp. 352 (D. Colo. 1977)

Hackbart v. Cincinnati Bengals, Inc. [Hackbart II], 601 F. 2d 516 (10th Cir. 1979)

Handwerker v. T.K.D. Kid, Inc., 924 S.W. 2d 621 (Mo. Ct. App. 1996)

Hunt v. Portland Baseball Club, 296 P. 2d 495 (Or. 1956)

Jones v. Three Rivers Management Corp., 394 A.2d 546 (Pa. 1978)

McCormick v. Lowe & Campbell Athletic Goods Co., 144 S.W. 2d 866 (Mo. Ct. App. 1940)

Montana v. San Jose Mercury News, Inc., 34 Cal. App. 4th 790, 40 Cal. Rptr. 2d 639 (1995)

Nabozny v. Barnhill, 334 N.E. 2d 258 (Ill. 1975)

Namath v. Sports Illustrated, 48 A.D. 2d 487, 371 N.Y.S. 2d 10 (1975)

New York Times Co. v. Sullivan, 376 U.S. 254 (1964)

Ordway v. Casella, 198 Cal. App. 3d 98 (1988)

Rensing v. Indiana St. Univ. Bd. Of Trustees, 444 N.E. 2d 1170 (Ind. 1983)

Sanders v. Kuna Joint. Sch. Dist., 876 P. 2d 154 (Idaho Ct. App. 1994)

Sewell v. Dixie Region Sports Car Club of America, Inc., 451 S.E. 2d 489 (Ga. Ct. App. 1994).

Spahn v. Julian Messner, Inc., 43 Misc. 2d 219, 250 N.Y.S. 2d 529 (1964)

Waldrep v. Texas Employers Ins. Ass'n, (Tex. Ct. App. 2000)

World Football League v. Dallas Cowboys Football Club, Inc., 513 S.W. 2d 102 (Tex. Civ. App. 1974)

■ Review Questions

1. Why is negligence so commonly considered in sports litigation?
2. Discuss the differences between ordinary negligence, gross negligence, and recklessness.
3. How important a role do insurance policies play in mitigating financial loss involving sports?
4. Why are waivers so important for directors of sporting events?
5. Discuss the relationship between tort (civil) law and criminal law.
6. Do high-profile coaches and athletes voluntarily expose themselves to personal attacks in the media that would otherwise be considered defamation to a more private citizen?

■ Endnotes

1 Assault and battery are also crimes in most jurisdictions and are defined by that jurisdiction's statutes.
2 Only the states of North Carolina, Maryland, Alabama, and Virginia currently use this standard. All other states use forms of comparative fault/negligence.
3 There have been numerous instances of deaths at minor league hockey games in North America, however. Additionally, spectators have been killed at baseball

games due to flying bats and balls and at motor sports contests. There appear to be no deaths at basketball or football games, however.

4 Florida and Kentucky, for example.

5 Slander is spoken defamation while libel is its written counterpart.

6 *New York Times Co. v. Sullivan*, 376 U.S. 254 (1964), *Curtis Publishing Co. v. Butts*, 388 U.S. 130 (1967), *Gertz v. Robert Welch, Inc.*, 418 U.S. 323 (1974)

7 Sports journalists are known for inciting the emotions of their readers, cutting a fine line between statements of fact and statements of opinions. Journalists includes writers, interviewers, and broadcasters in television, radio, and internet media.

8 *See* UCC sec. 2-314 and 2-315.

9 *See* Restatement of Torts sec. 402A.

CHAPTER FOUR

Sports Crimes

■ Introduction

Criminal law is based on state or federal statutes defining specific actions that are unacceptable within that jurisdiction and are subject to punishment, including jail time and/or fines. A person is charged with a crime by the state or federal government, which may be acting on behalf of an individual victim or on behalf of society as a whole.

Crimes are generally divided into four major categories: **crimes against the person**, **crimes injurious to personal and real property**, **crimes affecting the public health and welfare**, and **crimes against the government**. Most sports crimes involve crimes against the person, such as assault and battery (which are also torts in most jurisdictions). Other crimes in sports involve governmental and public welfare issues.

There has been debate as to whether or not a sports participant may or should be charged with a crime for activity that occurs during a sports contest. Many jurists believe that occurrences in sports should remain separate from society's rules. Very few cases involving sports crimes have ever gone to court. While the criminal justice system is designed to deal with perpetrators of crimes in the real world, should athletes be subject to such criminal charges during a sports contest for their misconduct or is this better left up to the sports leagues and organizations themselves?

Clearly, high-profile athletes lead a life in the public spotlight and may often be held to higher scrutiny for their behaviors both on and off the field than the general public. However, should such financial and social status affect whether a prosecutor brings a charge against sports participants for intentionally injurious conduct during a sports event?

crimes against the person   including assault, battery, robbery, hazing, murder, rape, and kidnapping

crimes injurious to property   including arson, trespass, vandalism, and theft

crimes affecting the public health and welfare   including blackmail, illegal gambling, and prostitution

crimes against the government   including tax evasion, treason, RICO violations, and terrorism

This chapter examines the role of criminal law in sports, though it appears to have a diminished role during the actual sports contest, particularly in contact sports. Violent and aggressive contact among sports participants provides a vicarious thrill for the crowd, and tenacious behavior is generally perceived to be a legitimate part of the game, not a matter for criminal courts. Still, violence in the sport of hockey seems to have a mild litigious history in Canadian courts.

■ Variety of Crimes

Criminal law and sports are certainly related. For example, numerous federal and state laws outlaw the use of certain performance-enhancing drugs, **sports gambling (gaming)**, **ticket scalping**, **sports bribery**, and the influence of organized crime in sports. Additionally, sports agents who fail to register with the appropriate state agency or those who offer financial inducements to a student-athlete may be subject to criminal and civil penalties for such action or omissions.

Much of the violence found in sports would constitute crimes against the person if it occurred outside the sports contest. Players hit, punch, check, trip, and commit other aggressive and violent acts during the course of a sporting event. Such conduct is usually considered part of the game, but occasionally the conduct is so outrageous that a criminal charge might be warranted. Some states are adopting legislation to address intentional injuries to sports participants, particularly sports officials.

Relationship to Torts

Similar to intentional torts and the concepts of gross negligence and recklessness, the criminal law is designed to deter deviant and unlawful behavior and punish the wrongdoer for transgressing society's statutory rules and morals. Unlike torts, however, a guilty criminal is subject to incarceration and a fine rather than merely monetary damages.

Contact Sports

Athletes in contact sports are trained to be aggressive and are often encouraged to make violent plays even as children. In the sports of football, hockey, and boxing, for example, participants are encouraged from a young age to hurt the opponent. Clearly, this is the ultimate goal of boxing. However, are boxers

---

sports gambling (gaming)   illegal in most states and of particular interest to professional and amateur sports leagues

ticket scalping   buying tickets to sports events and then reselling them for a profit, usually well in excess of face value

sports bribery   illegal influence over an athlete, coach, referee, or other participant to affect the outcome of a sports event

encouraged to bite off an opponent's ear as boxer Mike Tyson did to Evander Holyfield in 1997? Are hockey players encouraged to use their sticks as potentially deadly weapons? Are football players taught to hit each other by leading with their head and hitting a vulnerable opponent?[1] Should the aggressive and sometimes out-of-control behaviors by athletes during a sports contest be subject to criminal law, or would fear of punishment in the criminal justice system deter aggressive competition?

Crimes Unrelated to Sports Conduct

Many athletes are involved in crimes outside the sports arena. Such activity (including domestic violence, rape, disorderly conduct, DUI, and tax evasion, for example) would not necessarily have any relationship to activities that occur during a sports contest and thus will not be addressed in this chapter.

■ General Criminal Law Principles

Burden of Proof

Prosecutors who believe that illegal behavior has occurred during a sports contest (or affecting it in some way) must prove their criminal case **beyond a reasonable doubt**. This is more difficult than the preponderance of evidence test in tort law. It is more difficult to prove that a defendant is guilty of a crime than liable in tort. If the defendant is found guilty of a crime, the judge must then render a sentence. Most criminal laws dictate a minimum and maximum sentence, and the judge must consider mitigating factors that might reduce a sentence or enhancement factors that might increase the sentence. Immoral behavior bears no direct connection to criminal law. One commits a crime by violating a criminal statute, not by engaging in conduct that appears to be unethical or immoral.

Defenses to Crimes

The **defenses to crimes** of consent to contact, self-defense, and a general reluctance by the federal and state government to prosecute alleged crimes have limited the exposure of criminal law in the sports context. Additionally, if a player reasonably fears imminent harm by an opposing player, the defense of self-defense can often overcome the prosecution's attempt to show intent to injure by the same individual.

---

beyond a reasonable doubt   the test the government (state) must prove in a criminal case

defenses to crimes   category in which the criminal defendant alleges lack of intent to commit a crime, self-defense, or another reason to plead not guilty to a criminal charge

Criminal Intent

Societal influences of competitive and aggressive behavior have generally sidelined criminal law in the game of regulating sports violence. Many fans expect violent behavior in sports, and it often becomes a selling point (literally) for a sport or league, both in the sports stadium and via television.

The essence of criminal law is that the perpetrator has formed the intent to commit a crime and then carried out that intent. Such intent is referred to as the **mens rea,** and the act itself is called the **actus reus.** Both elements are necessary for most criminal convictions.

Though one cannot be punished for having criminal thoughts alone, the crime of conspiracy does punish wrongdoers for agreeing to commit a future crime. Additionally, if an individual attempts to commit a crime and fails, he or she may be punished; the theory of attempted murder is one example. In other words, the attempt was a crime even though it failed.

Vital to the essence of a criminal conviction, however, is that the criminal defendant had the intent to commit an unlawful act. Since even violent acts in sports are not normally considered unlawful, charges are rarely filed against athletes or between athletes.

Felony versus Misdemeanor

Crimes can be divided into two major violations: felonies and misdemeanors. **Felonies** are generally regarded as more serious in nature. Such crimes allow for a penalty of more than one year in state or federal prison. **Misdemeanors,** though still serious, do not allow for incarceration for more than one year in county jail. State and federal laws both fall into misdemeanor and felony categories.

Assault and Battery

The crimes of assault and battery would likely be the most prevalent crimes in sports. An **assault** is a willful attempt or willful threat to inflict injury upon another person. It is also defined as intentionally placing someone in fear of imminent bodily harm. A **battery** is the actual intentional physical contact. It is sometimes referred to as a successful assault. When an assault and/or battery involves a weapon, serious bodily injury, deadly force, or when the assault or battery is committed in conjunction with another crime, the term **aggravated** is often used.

---

mens rea   Criminal intent to commit a crime; literally, the "mind thing"

actus reus   Criminal act; literally, the "act thing"

felony   crime punishable by more than one year in prison

misdemeanor   crime punishable by up to one year in county jail

assault   willful attempt or threat to inflict injury; usually associated with battery

battery   crime involving unlawful physical contact with another person

aggravated crime   crime involving the use of a weapon and/or causing serious bodily injury

■ Sports Violence

Governmental Legislation

While certain individual or collective behaviors during a sports contest would likely be prime targets for criminal charges if they occurred outside the arena, prosecutors rarely charge athletes for acts committed during a game. Most people believe that leagues themselves should regulate violence in sports. There have been several attempts at the federal level to regulate sports violence, such as proposal of The Sports Violence Act of 1980.[2] This act would have imposed up to one year in prison for professional athletes who knowingly used excessive force during a game. However, it failed to gain enough votes. Another proposed act, the Sports Violence Arbitration Act of 1983, failed to create a sports court for excessive violence.[3]

Internal League Controls

Violence in sports has become so prevalent that professional sports leagues and other governing bodies and commissions have had to police such activity themselves and provide punishment (i.e., penalties) for misdeeds. In some sports, a stick or ball could conceivably be used as a deadly weapon to seriously hurt an opponent. Most spectators and prosecutors believe that such activity is just part of the game. Some scuffles and plays are so violent, however, that professional and amateur sports leagues have had to form rules that penalize players with fines and suspensions.

Hockey, for example, recognizes a variety of penalties and even a "penalty box" for transgressors. A player may be penalized for numerous violations, including boarding, butt-ending, charging, clipping, cross-checking, elbowing, fighting, high-sticking, holding, hooking, kneeing, roughing, slashing, spearing, and tripping. Baseball endures bench-clearing brawls and pitches intended to "bean" the batter, and players and managers may be thrown out of a game for confrontations with the umpire. Football imposes penalties for roughing the passer and kicker, unnecessary roughness, holding, spearing, and tripping. These acts would constitute criminal and civil assaults and batteries but for their occurrence during a sports contest.

One of the major objections to leagues controlling violent behavior is that their actions have not gone far enough. When fines or suspensions are handed down, they often have little impact to athletes who make millions for their sports prowess.

■ Crimes Against the Person

Illegitimate Sports Violence

In contact sports players often suffer competitive injuries. However, at what point—if any—does an injury as the result of honest play turn into an injury due to intentional and excessive use of force by a player that might subject him or her to criminal liability? Few cases involving athletes during a sports contest have actually proceeded to trial. Much of the analysis of the criminal law in sports context stems from hockey and the Canadian courts. Currently only a few major cases appear to set a standard for prosecuting athletes for violence in sports. Where the line is drawn between acceptable (within the rules) and unacceptable (outside the rules) violence remains unclear.

Regina v. Green and Regina v. Maki [4]

In 1969, Wayne Maki of the St. Louis Blues hockey team swung his stick at Boston Bruins player Ted Green and fractured his skull in a preseason exhibition game in Canada's capital of Ottawa. Both players were involved in two fights in the same game, and both were thereafter charged with different forms of assault. Maki's case was dismissed under the theory of self-defense, but the court refused to differentiate between sports contests and real-world violence. In the *Green* case, Green was found not guilty because it was held that his actions were an "involuntary reflex" to be part of the roughness of the game. No conviction resulted in either case, but the court noted that sports were not immune from criminal prosecution.

State v. Forbes [5]

In 1975, Dave Forbes of the Boston Bruins swung his stick and his fist at Henry Boucha of the Minnesota North Stars. After Forbes hit Boucha with his stick in the head near the eye, Forbes jumped on Boucha and began to pound him repeatedly into the ice. Boucha suffered a fractured eye socket and needed more than 25 stitches. Forbes was charged with aggravated assault by use of a dangerous weapon under Minnesota law and was indicted for his actions. The defense stated that "hockey, not Dave Forbes, should be on trial." The case ended in a hung jury, the judge declared a mistrial, and the prosecution decided not to pursue its case. This marked the first serious attempt to prosecute a professional athlete for a crime in the United States. Boucha later filed a $3.5 million civil lawsuit, and the case was settled out of court.

Hackbart v. Cincinnati Bengals, Inc. [6]

In *Hackbart*, though not a criminal case, the court demonstrated the "involuntary reflex" defense to aggressive contact during a sports contest. Cincinnati Bengals football player Charles Clark hit Denver Broncos player Dale Hackbart on the back of the head out of frustration after an interception. The play was over, and Hackbart was not looking when he was hit from behind. He broke three vertebrae in his neck and suffered several muscular injuries as a result. The district court stated, "The violence of professional football is carefully orchestrated. Both offensive and defensive players must be extremely aggressive in their actions, and they must play with reckless abandonment of self-protective instincts."[7] The 10th Circuit Court of Appeals reversed the trial court by holding that even a football player may be held responsible for injuring an opponent if he acts with the reckless disregard for the opponent's safety.

The Case of Dino Ciccarelli[8]

In another hockey case, Dino Ciccarelli, the captain and all-time leading scorer for the Minnesota North Stars, pounded Luke Richardson in the mouth repeatedly. In 1988, a Canadian court held that Ciccarelli was guilty of criminal assault and had to serve one day in jail and pay a $1,000 fine as an example to others that such violence in hockey is not acceptable. This was the first-ever jail sentence for a professional athlete for violence that occurred during a sports event.

Numerous other cases have been prosecuted, but they have been limited to hockey and have been tried mostly in Canadian courts.[9]

Fans and Spectators

Sometimes sports **fans** may have to be controlled when watching a sports contest. It is quite common for fans during the heat of a contest to become violent in the stands among each other and, unfortunately, against sports officials and even athletes. This phenomenon is not unique to the United States. In fact, it is generally accepted that the most violent fans in the world are at soccer matches. Numerous fans have died during pre- and post-game soccer celebrations.

In the city of Philadelphia, fans have become so disruptive that when the Philadelphia Eagles football team plays home games at Veterans Stadium, a roving municipal court is located literally underneath the playing field. A local municipal judge hears cases involving disorderly conduct, public intoxication, and other offenses.

Sports Officials and Crimes

Numerous examples of players, parents, and other spectators attacking referees and umpires have forced states to enact legislation to protect **sports officials** from violence. Many states have tort laws related to the protection of sports officials.

Though fans and spectators may commit crimes against each other and against the officials of the games, prosecutors are often hesitant to pursue a criminal charge since it is generally held that crimes against the person involving a sports contest may be immune from suit. Still, sports officials are gaining respectable status among professional leagues and state criminal and civil statutes that continue to provide remedies both criminally and civilly for crimes committed against them. A model act has been proposed by the National Association of Sports Officials (NASO). An excerpt follows.

> **Criminal Offense to Physically Assault Sports Officials**
> **Section 1:** Any person who physically assaults any sports official at any level of competition, within the confines or immediate vicinity of the athletic facility at which the athletic contest in which a sports official was an active participant shall

---

fan   person passionate about a favorite player, team, or league; short for "fanatic"

sports official   individual who referees a professional or amateur sports contest

be guilty of a crime (misdemeanor, felony, etc.) which shall be punishable by a fine of $10,000 and/or imprisonment to a maximum of three (3) years.

Section 2: This law shall take effect immediately.

Limited Civil Liability for Sports Officials

Section 1: Sports officials who officiate athletic contests at any level of competition in this State shall not be liable to any person or entity in any civil action for injuries or damages claimed to have arisen by virtue of actions or inactions related in any manner to officiating duties within the confines of the athletic facility at which the athletic contest is played.

Section 2: Sports officials are defined as those individuals who serve as referees, umpires, linesmen, and those who serve in similar capacities but may be known by other titles and are duly registered or members of a local, state, regional, or national organization which is engaged in part in providing education and training to sports officials.

Section 3: Nothing in this law shall be deemed to grant the protection set forth to sports officials who cause injury or damage to a person or entity by actions or inactions which are intentional, willful, wanton, reckless, malicious or grossly negligent.

Section 4: This law shall take effect immediately, and shall apply to all lawsuits filed after the effective date of this law, including those which allege actions or inactions of sports officials which occurred prior to the effective date of this law.

Oklahoma became the first state to adopt state laws to protect sports officials from assaults, and states continue to address this issue through legislation.[10] Currently more than 10 states have enacted legislation to protect sports officials. Some laws have even extended to protect to other personnel, including coaches, trainers, and administrators.

Sports Agent Crimes

No current federal law regulates sports agents generally, either criminally or civilly. Though numerous states have adopted criminal legislation against sports agents for failing to register with the state while recruiting student-athletes as potential clients, one federal case exemplifies the most egregious acts involving sports agents, **RICO**, and other laws.[11]

Clearly the conduct by Norby Walters and Lloyd Bloom (see Case 1) constituted criminal activity both at the federal and state levels. The available adoption of the Uniform Athlete Agents Act addresses such egregious criminal conduct and its sanctions. Additionally, sports leagues and sports associations have created their own internal controls to regulate unethical and illegal conduct by sports agents. A much more detailed discussion of sports agents and their potential criminal and civil liability is found in Chapter 1.

RICO Racketeer Influenced and Corrupt Organizations Act, which spells out laws against organized crime

■ Crimes Affecting the Public Health and Welfare

Ticket Scalping

Ticket scalping is the process of legitimately purchasing a ticket (or large numbers of tickets) from a primary seller such as an off-site box office, the arena or venue, or the team or league office and then reselling the tickets on the street for more money. The intent is to profit from the difference in price.

States that have adopted laws regulating ticket scalpers claim that such activity negatively affects a public interest and allows for civil and criminal penalties for violators. Currently few states and cities either regulate or outlaw ticket scalping; however, this number seems to change annually.[12]

Scalping can be a highly profitable business, particularly when the event is in high demand. Though many spectators recognize that ticket scalpers are simply part of the pre-event pageantry of a sporting event, many others argue that ticket scalpers are mere scavengers who serve as a nuisance to honest spectators.

The regulation of ticket scalping has been a part of society since 1918.[13] In many cities and states regulation of spectator ticket prices is viewed as serving the public interest, while other states, such as Alabama, hold that there is no compelling reason to regulate the resale of tickets.[14] The U.S. Supreme Court ruled in 1927 that a New York City provision to limit the resale of a ticket beyond 50 cents higher than the stated price constituted an unconstitutional restraint of trade since the government thereby regulated prices.[15] However, in 1965 the U.S. Supreme Court held that anti-scalping legislation was a permissible use of a state's police power.[16]

In one sense, the purpose of prohibiting ticket scalping is to prevent the general public from being squeezed out by scalpers who purchase large blocks of tickets and then resell them at higher prices to the general public who are victimized by opportunistic middlemen. On the other hand, scalpers run the risk of poor demand for certain events and then are forced to either take a loss on a "no-sale" of a ticket or, once the event begins, sell the ticket at a price less than face value. This benefits the general public. Unfortunately, certain box offices or other ticket allocation locations have contributed to price gouging (increases) by hiring persons to stand in line and order the best seats or large blocks of tickets for the sole purpose of reselling them for a profit thereafter.

Generally speaking, ticket scalping today is a controversial issue that continually evolves in response to states or municipalities that contend the public is better served by maintaining controls over ticket-scalping activities. The driving force behind scalping and regulation is the profit motive, of course, and to charge the highest price possible for a seat in a limited-seating event.

While some states, such as Tennessee, have repealed their statutes and do not regulate ticket scalping at the state level, states that do have laws governing scalpers usually limit scalpers' activities by one or more of the following:

1. Requiring a license, fee, or other tax to work as a scalper
2. Limiting the amount that a scalper (or "broker") may resell the ticket in terms of actual dollar increase, maximum, or percentage of stated ticket price

3. Establishing a ceiling on the number of tickets an individual scalper may sell for a profit
4. Limiting the resale to no higher than the actual price stated on the ticket
5. Restricting the geographic location of a sale of a scalped ticket in terms of distance away from an event[17]

   Most ticket-scalping laws are misdemeanors and are often difficult to enforce. Additionally, inherent hypocrisy in disallowing ticket scalping for sports while allowing such practices for travel agents and other ticket brokers has not favored such regulation. With the advent of online auction companies and "cyber scalping," enforcement of ticket-scalping laws in those states that have such anti-scalping statutes has become virtually pointless.[18] Ticket scalping must be differentiated from ticket counterfeiting, of course, which is a form of fraud.

Sports Gambling

Though most persons recognize Nevada as the only state that permits gambling, gambling of some form is legal in 48 states and Washington, D.C. For example, 37 states have state lotteries, 44 allow pari-mutuel betting, 47 permit bingo, and 22 license casinos.[19] Gambling on sports is also referred to as *sports wagering, sports betting, sports bookmaking,* or *sports gaming.* While betting on horse races and dog races is legal in many states, in 1992 Congress enacted the Professional and Amateur Sports Protection Act that prevents states from sponsoring sports-based betting other than in Nevada, Oregon, Delaware, and Montana.[20] Since gambling often involves interstate commerce, Article I § 8 of the U.S. Constitution allows the federal government to regulate such activity.

   Sports gambling involves professional and amateur contests. Gambling can be addictive, a danger to the emotional and financial well-being of the gambler. Sports gambling is a major concern on college campuses. The NCAA has amended its own rules 10.3 and 10.4 to address the problems and issues related to sports betting.

   Access to information via sports programming on network, cable, and satellite providers in addition to instantaneous information via the Internet has certainly played a role in growing interest in gambling. Newspapers and numerous Internet sites publish daily odds of sports contests for no other purpose than to promote gambling. Several attempts to regulate and enforce violations of Internet or "cyber" gambling at the federal level have failed, including the Internet Gambling Prohibition Act of 1997.[21] The Justice Department recently rendered all Internet gambling illegal and several credit card issuers have established policies to curb Internet gambling.

Sports Bribery and Game Fixing

At the heart of sports gambling is the concern that games "fixed" by players, coaches, trainers, or others defeat the ideal that the outcome of a sporting event is left to chance and skill. A disturbing issue in professional and amateur sports is the role that the athletes, coaches, and even sports officials themselves might play in altering the outcome of a game in order to profit from betting on a loss, victory, or point spread.

Federal legislation and numerous state laws have addressed the issues of game fixing and "point-shaving," especially after the gambling scandals involving student-athletes in the 1990s.[22] Fixing a game is often associated with the game of basketball since only five players per team are on the court at any given point in time and there is a greater likelihood that one player can affect the game. Federal and state legislation guards against bribery in sports contests by providing for fines and/or imprisonment for such influential conspiracy and clear conflict of interest in the outcome of a game.[23]

Professional Sports Gambling Incidents

In 1919, eight Chicago White Sox baseball players were involved in a scenario that fixed the World Series, and all the players were banned for life. The White Sox players, including "Shoeless Joe" Jackson, became known as the Black Sox. In 1982, the Baltimore Colts football team selected Art Schlichter as the fourth overall pick in the NFL draft. Little did the Colts know that Schlichter had a compulsive gambling addiction, and he was ultimately suspended by the NFL for betting on sports. He has been in jail frequently for his misconduct. Another notable victim of gambling impropriety is baseball player Pete Rose. Rose's alleged gambling problem led Major League Baseball to ban him for life from eligibility to baseball's Hall of Fame.

Amateur Sports

College student-athletes have become targets for illegal gambling activities, particularly since student-athletes presently are not paid for their services and a small financial enticement might be enough to tempt the student-athlete. Additionally, there have been numerous recent attempts to outlaw all betting on any Olympic, college, or other amateur sports nationwide.[24] More than $500 million is wagered on intercollegiate sports each year in Nevada. Such wagering has had its unfortunate consequences as college games have been manipulated for illegal financial gain.

College Incidents[25]

In October 1951, three University of Kentucky players were arrested for taking bribes to shave points in a game in New York's Madison Square Garden two years earlier. In November 1981, Rick Kuhn and four others were found guilty and sentenced to jail for game fixing. Kuhn was a member of the Boston College basketball team. In 1995, Kevin Pendergast, a placekicker from Notre Dame placed a bet of $20,185 in Las Vegas that Northwestern University's basketball team would lose to the University of Michigan by 25.5 points. Pendergast and co-conspirators Dewey Williams and Dion Lee (both Northwestern players) agreed to shave points in exchange for money. All three were found guilty and sentenced to prison; the FBI and the NCAA influenced the court to use the three as examples to warn other student-athletes of the pitfalls in engaging in such activity by having them engage in public discussions over sports gambling.

Nevada's New Rules

On January 25, 2001, the Nevada Gaming Commission adopted new regulations to alter policies regarding sports gambling in that state. The new regulations:

- eliminate all gambling on high school and Olympic sporting events.
- allow gambling on Nevada's college sports teams (previously not allowed).
- create a "black book" of individuals who would be barred from betting on college sporting events.
- prohibit betting by student-athletes and coaches on games in which they are participants.[26]

Such changes, however, did not go far enough in the eyes of the NCAA which claimed that Nevada's rules actually promoted more wagering on college sports. The NCAA remains firm in outlawing all gambling on college sports.

■ Crimes Against the Government

RICO

The Racketeer Influenced and Corrupt Organizations Act (RICO) was enacted in 1970 to prevent illegitimate organizations from engaging in a mock business enterprise to profit through the use of bribery and extortion.[27] This federal law has been used to prosecute attempts by mobsters and other criminals to affect the outcome of otherwise legitimate sports events. Racketeering, according to the Act, is defined as:

A) Any act or threat involving murder, kidnapping, gambling, arson, robbery, bribery, extortion, dealing in an obscene manner . . . or
B) Any act which is indictable under any of the . . . provisions of Title 18, U.S.C.A. § 224 (. . . sports bribery) and § 1084 (. . . transmission of gambling information).

Illegal Drugs

An athlete's use of performance-enhancing drugs or other substances may constitute a violation of a criminal statute if the drug is classified as a controlled substance. On the other hand, many athletes use legal performance-enhancing drugs to increase their performance. Though many of these substances are not illegal, collective bargaining agreements, NCAA regulations, and Olympic rules may prohibit their use. Drug use will be discussed further in Chapter 7.

■ Summary

Criminal law has limited application in the sports world. The state brings a charge against the perpetrator in a criminal case. The burden of proof in a criminal case is beyond a reasonable doubt. Though athletes are usually not prosecuted for crimes that might occur during a sports contest, they are not immune from civil suit. Crimes can be divided into four general categories: crimes against persons, crimes against property, crimes against the public health, safety, and welfare, and crimes against the government. Crimes are either felonies or misdemeanors. The government has an interest in maintaining the integrity of sports contests both on the playing field and in the stands.

Specific types of sports crimes include sports gambling, ticket scalping, and sports bribery. RICO statutes have deterred the influence of organized crime in the sports world. Numerous attempts to regulate criminal activity related to sports, particularly gambling and sports agents, have failed but momentum is gaining ground, particularly in the context of sports gambling over the Internet. Ticket scalping is an ever evolving subject for legislatures to address. Criminal law is now a legitimate issue involving fans and sports officials as well.

■ Key Terms

actus reus
aggravated crime
assault
battery
beyond a reasonable doubt
crimes against the government
crimes against the person
crimes against property
crimes affecting the public health and
    welfare
defenses to crimes

fan
felony
intent
mens rea
misdemeanor
RICO
sports bribery
sports gambling (gaming)
sports official
ticket scalping

■ Additional Cases

Baugh v. Redmond, 565 So.2d 953 (La. Ct. App. 1990)
Crawn v. Campo, 630 A.2d 368 (N.J. Ct. App. 1993)

Nabozny v. Barnhill, 334 N.E.2d 258 (Ill. Ct. App. 1975)

Nebbia v. New York, 291 U.S. 502 (1934)

People v. Shepherd, 141 Cal. Rptr. 379 (1977), cert. denied 436 U.S. 917 (1978)

U.S. v. Gray, 96 F.3d 769 (5th Cir. 1996)

U.S. v. Walters, 704 F. Supp. 844 (N.D. Ill. 1989) motion to dismiss denied, 711 F. Supp. 1435 (N.D. Ill. 1989), rev'd on other grounds, 913 F. 2d 388 (7th Cir. 1990), 775 F. Supp. 1173 (N.D. Ill. 1991), and 997 F. 2d 1219 (7th Cir. 1993)

▣ Review Questions

1. Should violations of criminal law be exempt from consideration during a sports contest due to the inherent violent nature of certain sports?
2. How is the burden of proof in a civil case different from that in a criminal case?
3. Why has there been so much legislation to protect sport officials from criminal violence from fans and sport participants?
4. Should scalping laws be repealed altogether?
5. Why is sport gambling such a "dangerous" issue for fans, participants, and others?
6. Is the use of illegal drugs more common in sports than in society at large?

▣ Endnotes

1 Defensive back Jack Tatum of the Oakland Raiders paralyzed receiver Darryl Stingly of the New England Patriots during a play in a professional football game in 1979. No penalty was called.

2 H.R. 7903, 96th Cong., 2nd Sess.

3 H.R. 4495, 98th Cong., 1st Sess.

4 *Regina v. Green,* 16 D.L.R. 3rd 137 (Ont. Prov. Civ. 1970); *Regina v. Maki,* 3 O.R. 780 (1970).

5 *State v. Forbes,* No. 63280 (Hennepin Co. Minn. Dist. Ct. dismissed Aug. 12, 1975).

6 *Hackbart v. Cincinnati Bengals, Inc.* 435 F. Supp. 352 (D. Co. 1977), rev'd 601 F.2d 516 (10th Cir. 1979), cert. denied 444 U.S. 931 (1979).

7 435 F. Supp. 352, 355 (D. Co. 1977), rev'd 601 F.2d 516 (10th Cir. 1979).

8 *It's 3 Swings and Out For Northstars' Ciccarelli,* THE SPORTING NEWS, Jan. 18, 1988, at 35, col. 3.

9 *See Regina v. Maloney,* 28 C.C.C.2d 323, 326 (Ont. G.S.P. 1976), *Regina v. Leyte,* 13 C.C.C.2d 458, 462 (Ont. Cty. Ct. 1973), and *Regina v. Green,* 2 N.B.R.2d 903 (1970).

10 *See* Okla. Stat. Ann. tit. 21 § 650.1 (West 1995), which specifically refers to assault and battery against a sports official. Other states with similar statutes include Arkansas, California, Delaware, Louisiana, Montana, New Jersey, North Carolina, Pennsylvania, and West Virginia.

11 *U.S. v. Walters*, 711 F. Supp. 1435 (N.D. Ill. 1989), 913 F.2d 388 (7th Cir. Ill.).

12 *See* Stephen K. Happel and Marianne M. Jennings, *The Folly of Anti-Scalping Laws*, THE CATO JOURNAL, 15, 1.

13 *People ex rel. Cort Theater Co. v. Thompson*, 119 N.E. 41 (Ill. 1918).

14 *Estell v. City of Birmingham*, 286 So.2d 872 (Ala. 1973).

15 *Tyson & Brother v. Banton*, 273 U.S. 418 (1927).

16 *Gold v. DiCarlo*, 235 F. Supp. 817 (S.D. N.Y. 1964), aff'd 380 U.S. 520 (1965).

17 Though ever changing, states (or cities within those states) that have anti-scalping statutes and/or states that regulate scalping to some degree include Alabama, Arkansas, California, Connecticut, Delaware, Florida, Georgia, Illinois, Indiana, Kentucky, Maryland, Massachusetts, Michigan, Minnesota, Mississippi, Missouri, New Jersey, New Mexico, New York, North Carolina, Pennsylvania, South Carolina, South Dakota, Virginia, and Wisconsin.

18 Internet sites such as e-Bay provide a market for tickets in which it is difficult, if not impossible, to enforce anti-scalping statutes.

19 *See* Ante Z. Udovicic, *Special Report: Sports and Gambling a Good Mix? I Wouldn't Bet On It*. MARQUETTE SPORTS LAW JOURNAL, Spring 1998.

20 28 U.S.C.A. § 3701 et seq. Those states were grandfathered, since sports wagering was already permitted.

21 Originally introduced by Senator John Kyl of Arizona.

22 Boston College, Northwestern University, Arizona State, and Notre Dame had infamous point-shaving or other scandals in the 1990s.

23 *See* 18 U.S.C.A. § 224.

24 In 2000, a federal bill, the High School and College Sports Gambling Prohibition Act, was proposed. The NCAA has highly supported such a federal ban on betting on college sports.

25 There are over 30 incidents involving college athletes and game fixing.

26 *See* http://sportsillustrated.cnn.com/basketball/college/news/2001/01/25/nevada_betting_ap/

27 18 U.S.C.A. §§ 1961, 1962.

CHAPTER FIVE

Title IX and Other Women's Issues

▓ Introduction

Title IX is a controversial law involving amateur sports.[1] In 1972, President Richard Nixon signed into law a bill that has affected generations of young men and women who desire to compete in sports at the high school and collegiate levels. The law went into effect on July 21, 1975. The number and quality of female high school and college athletes have increased tremendously as a direct result of this federal law that applies to elementary, secondary, and post-secondary schools that receive federal funds.

Title IX is often referred to as the **gender equity** statute. Some equate Title IX as the necessary equivalent of affirmative action for women in sports. Others argue that Title IX is an unjust quota system that punishes male athletes and programs.

▓ Born from the Civil Rights Movement

Title IX actually evolved from and amended Title VII of the Civil Rights Act of 1964.[2] Title VII provides that an employer may not discriminate on the basis of race, color, religion, sex, or national origin. Title IX extends that same philosophy to any program that receives funding from the federal government: It must not discriminate on the basis of gender when it comes to applying the funds to sports programs.[3] Title IX states:

Title IX of the Education Amendments of 1972   federal law prohibiting gender discrimination in athletic programs at institutions that receive federal funds

gender equity   concept associated with Title IX, evaluating whether equal opportunities to participate in intercollegiate athletics are available to both men and women

> No person in the United States shall, on the basis of sex, be excluded from participation in, be denied the benefits of, or be subjected to discrimination under any education program or activity receiving Federal financial assistance.

As a result of such legislation, women have directly benefited from the creation of new programs and new opportunities to showcase athletic talent at the highest amateur level. Additionally, professional leagues in several sports such as the Women's National Basketball Association (WNBA) and the Women's United Soccer Association (WUSA) continue to expand and create even more possibilities for women as professional athletes.[4] Many observers credit Title IX for opening the door to women athletes at both the amateur and professional levels.

■ College Sports

There is no doubt that Title IX has led to an increase in female participation in sports at both the high school and collegiate levels. Collegiate athletic departments and universities that do not comply with Title IX may be subject to severe penalties by the federal government, including termination of federal funds. Such a penalty could crumble or significantly damage college or university sports programs. Still, no such penalty has ever been handed down.

Pursuant to Title VI of the 1964 Civil Rights Act, each federal department and agency that disburses federal funds is required to establish procedures for determining that grant recipients do not discriminate. In 1979, Congress split the **Department of Health, Education and Welfare (HEW)** into the Department of Health and Human Services (HHS) and the Department of Education (DOE), transferring all the education and enforcement functions of the former HEW to DOE. Title IX administration, too, was assigned to DOE's Office of Civil Rights (OCR). The DOE's office is headed by the Assistant Secretary of Education for Civil Rights; HHS's office is headed by the Director of the Office for Civil Rights.

In 1979, the **Office of Civil Rights (OCR)** promulgated an Intercollegiate Athletics Policy Interpretation of Title IX that considered comparison of numerous program areas of financial assistance and other funding categories for both men's and women's sports programs.

Based on the OCR's interpretation, these factors must be taken into account when comparing Title IX compliance between men's and women's programs: (1) equipment and supplies; (2) scheduling of games and practice time; (3) travel and per diem allowances; (4) tutoring; (5) coaching; (6) locker rooms, practice, and competitive facilities; (7) medical and training facilities and services; (8) housing and dining facilities and services; (9) publicity; (10) support services; and (11) recruitment of student-athletes.

Department of Health, Education and Welfare (HEW)   former federal agency originally charged with enforcing Title IX provisions

Office of Civil Rights (OCR)   federal agency that enforces Title IX provisions

Title IX ultimately analyzes whether or not money is being allocated equitably between men's and women's programs based on the number of students attending such schools. Fiscal responsibility is left in the hands of the colleges and universities themselves. The key component in all Title IX cases is whether the institution developed a plan and carried out its mission to expand and accommodate the interests of female student-athletes, coaches, and administrators. Developing a plan is not enough: Carrying out its mission is vital.

NCAA's Role in Promoting Compliance

The NCAA formed the Gender Equity Task Force in 1992 to address concerns and evaluate Title IX in intercollegiate athletics. Athletic directors, coaches, trainers, and others must be continually cognizant of the purposes and effects of Title IX when administering college sports. The NCAA has been a major factor in promoting equitable support of men's and women's sports programs.

■ Title IX Criticism

While the fundamental purpose of Title IX is pure and designed to help prevent gender discrimination, the practical application of this law has generated violent debate. Many opponents of Title IX believe the law has turned into a **quota** system and has contributed to the systematic destruction of male sports programs throughout the United States.

Numerous male swimming, wrestling, football, water polo, baseball, and other programs have been eliminated in the name of Title IX compliance. Almost all of these programs that are eliminated are classified as non–revenue-producing sports according to the NCAA. Proponents of the law argue that Title IX continues to benefit women socially, economically, and even emotionally. Much of the criticism of this law involves the interpretation of how it is applied. Recently, the Department of Education formed the Commission on Opportunity in Athletics to collect information, analyze issues, and obtain public information and feedback on Title IX as to whether its interpretation and application should be revised.[5]

Grove City College v. Bell

In 1984 the U.S. Supreme Court granted a major victory for many collegiate athletic departments by holding that Title IX did not apply to collegiate athletic programs in the case of *Grove City College v. Bell,* 465 U.S. 555 (1984). The Supreme Court held that Title IX only applied to the specific programs that received federal (taxpayer) funds and not the athletic departments themselves (none of whom

---

quota   mandated proportional share often associated with Title IX analysis

received direct federal financial assistance). This victory, however, was short lived. In 1988 Congress enacted the Civil Rights Restoration Act of 1987 that legislatively reversed this decision.[7] As such, Title IX mandates that college athletic departments are no longer immune from its interpretation, and athletic departments are forced to comply with its regulations.

■ Title IX Tests and Fundamentals

In order to comply with Title IX according to the U.S. Department of Education, a school must meet one of three tests. Currently the OCR oversees compliance in this area and in 1996 offered a clarification of what Title IX compliance "really" means. If a school passes any one of the three tests, then theoretically there is compliance. However, courts have rarely viewed compliance with Title IX other than looking at a comparison of the numbers of participants. Passing these tests is often referred to as the "safe harbor" interpretations of the statute.

Test 1: Substantial Proportionality

Question: Is an institution providing participation opportunities for women and men that are substantially proportionate to their respective rates of enrollment as full-time undergraduate students?

The **substantial proportionality** test is the one that is most often used by plaintiffs and courts to determine whether an institution is in compliance with Title IX. It is usually the easiest method to assess compliance because it is based on numbers. If, for example, 50 percent of women are full-time undergraduates enrolled at a particular college, then 50 percent of the participants in sports programs there must be women.

There has been considerable debate as to what the substantial proportionality test means in terms of a specific statistical ratio that athletic departments must adhere to in order to be in compliance. While ideally the ratio would be 50–50, such a ratio has been difficult for athletic departments and universities to achieve. What, then, is "substantial proportionality?" In *Roberts v. Colorado State Board of Agriculture*, the court held that a disparity of 10.5% did not meet the substantial proportionality test.[6]

Test 2: History of Expansion of Women's Programs

Question: Has an institution demonstrated a history and continuing practice of program expansion for the underrepresented sex?

---

substantial proportionality   test under Title IX that reviews whether intercollegiate level participation for male and female students is provided in numbers substantially proportionate to respective enrollments

If an institution can demonstrate a **history of expansion** of women's sports programs, then the institution is likely to survive a claim against it charging noncompliance. However, virtually no court and no institution was able to address this issue extensively or successfully until Syracuse University demonstrated compliance in this area with a potentially major legal victory in 1999 (see Case 5).

Test 3: Full and Effective Accommodation of Women's Interests

Question: Has an institution fully and effectively accommodated the interests and abilities of the underrepresented sex?

How one proves that women (or men) are having their interests **effectively accommodated** is virtually impossible. Recommendations have included conducting on-campus surveys. This is the area of least emphasis when an analysis of compliance occurs since the easiest method of determining compliance tends to focus on the first area, substantial proportionality.

■ Evolution of Title IX

The interpretation of Title IX and its effect on student-athletes and institutions has had its greatest impact in the legal system via cases brought by individuals suing their own institution for failing to comply with the federal law. The case of *Franklin v. Gwinnett County Public Schools*, 503 U.S. 60 (1992) allows for individuals to sue and recover monetary damages for violations of Title IX.

Cohen v. Brown University, 101 F.3d 155 (1st Cir. 1996)[8]

This is generally regarded as the most influential Title IX case ever to be decided. In 1991, Brown University announced that it was going to eliminate four sports: women's volleyball, women's gymnastics, men's golf, and men's water polo. Brown University said the teams could still compete as club sports, but it was not going to provide university funding due to financial pitfalls. At that time, Brown's student body was comprised of 52 percent male and 48 percent female students, though 63 percent of its student-athletes were male. Amy Cohen, a member of the gymnastics team, sued Brown, and the trial court held that Brown failed all three tests under Title IX. The case was appealed to the United States Supreme Court, which subsequently declined to hear the case.

---

history of expansion   test under Title IX on whether a collegiate institution can show a history of continuing practice of program expansion for the underrepresented gender

effective accommodation   test under Title IX that determines whether the interests and abilities of the underrepresented gender have been fully and effectively accommodated by the present state of the athletic program

■ CASE 5　*Boucher v. Syracuse University*

UNITED STATES COURT OF APPEALS,
SECOND CIRCUIT.

Jennifer L. **BOUCHER**, Alexis Snader, Cathryn M.
Ungerman, Rexanne Johannes,
Talya Anter, Catherine S. Biuso, Maggie Rozycki,
Meghan Delehanty, Individually
and on Behalf of all Others Similarly Situated,
Plaintiffs-Appellants,

v.

SYRACUSE UNIVERSITY, Kenneth Shaw,
Chancellor of **Syracuse** University, and John J.
Crouthamel, Athletic Director of **Syracuse** University,
Defendants-Appellees.

Docket No. 98-7678
Argued Dec. 15, 1998.
Decided Jan. 06, 1999.

Female students brought action against university, alleging discrimination against female athletes in university's allocation of participation opportunities and alleging that female athletes did not receive benefits equal to those received by male athletes. The United States District Court for the Northern District of New York, Frederick J. Scullin, Jr., J., 1996 WL 328444, granted summary judgment for university on equal treatment claims, and, 1996 WL 328444, certified class of present and future female lacrosse players for remaining claims. Subsequently, the District Court, 1998 WL 167296, granted summary judgment for university on students' accommodation claims. Students appealed. The Court of Appeals, Calabresi, Circuit Judge, held that: (1) accommodation claim was moot to extent that it sought implementation of varsity women's lacrosse team; (2) district court should have certified present and future female softball players as subclass of plaintiffs, rather than merely excluding them from certified class; (3) district court erred in raising and resolving claim not, asserted by students; and (4) students did not raise broader claim on behalf of all current and future female students interested in varsity athletics at university generally.

Affirmed in part, dismissed in part, and vacated and remanded in part.

Faith A. Seidenberg, Seidenberg and Strunk, Syracuse, NY, for Plaintiffs-Appellants.

Edward R. Conan, Bond Schoeneck & King, LLP, Syracuse, NY, for Defendants-Appellees.

Before: FEINBERG, CALABRESI, and SOTOMAYOR, Circuit Judges.

CALABRESI, Circuit Judge:

Former female club athletes at Syracuse University ("Syracuse" or "the University") appeal from an April 3, 1998 judgment of the United States District Court for the Northern District of New York (Frederick J. Scullin, Jr., *J.*) granting summary judgment to Syracuse on a Title IX accommodation claim. Plaintiffs also appeal two orders of June 12, 1996. The first such order dismissed their Title IX equal treatment claims, and the second conditionally certified a class.

We affirm in part, dismiss the appeal in part, and vacate and remand in part.

FACTS AND PROCEDURAL HISTORY

Plaintiff students "individually and on behalf of all others similarly situated" filed suit in May of 1995 against Syracuse University, alleging numerous violations of Title IX of the Education Amendments of 1972, 20 U.S.C.A. §§ 1681–1688, and its governing regulations. Seven of the eight named plaintiffs were at that time members of Syracuse's club lacrosse team and the eighth was a member of the University's club softball team. All plaintiffs have since graduated from the University.

The plaintiffs argued that Syracuse discriminated against female athletes in its allocation of participation opportunities (which includes decisions regarding which varsity teams to field as well as how many opportunities for participation by female varsity athletes are thereby created as a result of those decisions).[1] Plaintiffs also alleged that Syracuse provided unequal benefits to varsity female athletes as compared to varsity male athletes, and provided unequal scholarship funding to varsity female athletes as compared to varsity male athletes.[2]

Plaintiffs sought class certification in view of the fact that college students are a fluid group and that without such certification, mootness issues would likely arise. See, e.g., Cook v. Colgate Univ., 992 F.2d

17, 19-20 (2d Cir. 1993) (holding a Title IX appeal moot, once plaintiffs, seeking injunctive relief, had graduated). In their equal treatment claims, plaintiffs asked for declaratory and injunctive relief ordering the University to provide equal benefits and scholarships to varsity male and female athletes. In their accommodation claim, plaintiffs sought the establishment of varsity lacrosse and softball teams for women.

Just over 50% of the Syracuse's student population is female, yet, when this complaint was filed, women made up only 32.4% of its athletes. In its 1993–94 National Collegiate Athletic Association submission, Syracuse stated that of its 681 varsity student-athletes, 217 were women, while 464 were men. These numbers reflected a 19% disparity between the percentage of varsity athletes who were female and the percentage of the University's students who were female.[3]

[1] At the time that this suit was begun in May of 1995, the University funded eleven men's varsity teams and nine women's varsity teams. Just prior to the filing of the complaint, Syracuse announced a plan to add two new varsity women's teams to its athletic program—women's varsity soccer and women's varsity lacrosse. These teams began to play, respectively, in the 1996–97 and the 1997–98 academic years, thus bringing the number of varsity teams funded by the school to eleven men's and eleven women's.[4]

The University established five of its nine women's varsity teams in 1971[5]—when it first funded women's varsity sports. It dropped one of these sports (fencing) in 1972, and replaced it with field hockey. Crew was added as a women's varsity team in 1977. Three additional women's sports were added to the varsity roster in 1981. [FN6] After 1981, no new women's varsity team was created by the University until the addition of the varsity soccer team in 1997. Thus, until the filing of this complaint in 1995, fourteen years passed by without the University creating any new women's varsity teams. In the course of this litigation, Syracuse announced plans to institute a varsity women's softball team which, according to the University's representations at oral argument, will begin play in the 1999–2000 academic year.

* * * *

On June 12, 1996, the district court granted summary judgment to the University on plaintiffs' equal treatment claims—those that challenged the alleged unequal allocation of benefits and scholarships between varsity men's and women's teams (brought under 34 C.F.R. § 106.41(c)(2)–(8), (10) and 34 C.F.R. § 106.37). The court held that since none of the named plaintiffs were varsity athletes, they did not have standing to assert the equal treatment claims. Its ruling on this issue was proper and we affirm the dismissal of plaintiffs' equal treatment claims substantially for the reasons the district court gave. *See Boucher v. Syracuse Univ.*, No. 95-CV-620, 1996 WL 328444 (N.D.N.Y. June 12, 1996). At the same time, the court ruled that plaintiffs could go forward with their accommodation claim and additionally deemed that the plaintiffs could pursue an equal treatment claim challenging the allocation of funds between male and female *club* teams—an action that the plaintiffs had not brought and never litigated. *See id.* at *4.

In a separate order issued the same day, the district court held that the plaintiffs' proposed class included members with conflicting interests. *See Boucher v. Syracuse Univ.*, No. 95-CV620, 1996 WL 328441, at *2 & n. 2 (N.D.N.Y. June 12, 1996). Finding that "the factual allegations [of plaintiffs' complaint] only address the need for women's varsity lacrosse and women's varsity softball," the court defined two possible classes: present and future lacrosse players who desire to play varsity lacrosse, and present and future softball players who want to play varsity softball. *Id.* at *2.

The district court reached its conclusion as to appropriate classes by analyzing whether lacrosse and softball players could exist together as one class under Rule 23. That rule requires that: (1) questions of law or fact are common to the class; (2) claims or defenses of the representative parties are typical of those of the class; (3) class representatives are members of the class who possess the same interests and suffered the same injuries as class members; and (4) members of the class are so numerous that joinder would be impracticable. *See* Fed.R.Civ.P. 23(a). Although it found that commonality and typicality existed, the court determined that the two classes were in conflict because "'in an era

continued

of static enrollment and increasing financial demands on institutions of higher learning, the resources available for intercollegiate athletic programs are finite'" and hence that compliance might well be achieved by the elevation of one sport and not the other. *Boucher,* 1996 WL 328441, at *4 (quoting *Bryant v. Colgate Univ.,* 93-CV-1029, 1996 WL 328446, at *15 (N.D.N.Y. June 11, 1996)).

Since the majority of plaintiffs were lacrosse players, the court decided to certify only the current and future "would be" varsity lacrosse players. This certification was made conditional on a demonstration by plaintiffs that joinder of all relevant members of the class would be impractical.[7] *See id.* at *5. The district court did not certify a class of women, current and future, who wished to play varsity softball "because of the potential conflict of interest discussed above." *Id.* at *4 n. 4.

After a period of limited discovery, the district court granted summary judgment to the University on plaintiffs' accommodation claim. It found that although opportunities to participate in varsity athletics at **Syracuse** were not allocated equally between the sexes, the University nevertheless fell within one of the safe harbors set forth in the governing regulations of Title IX. *See Boucher v. Syracuse Univ.,* No. 95-CV-620, 1998 WL 167296, at *4 (N.D.N.Y. Apr.3, 1998). Under the implementing regulations, there are three safe harbor defenses to a claim of unequal accommodation of student interest in varsity athletics. *See* 34 C.F.R. § 106.41(c)(1); 44 Fed.Reg. 71413 (1979). The district court held that Syracuse met the requirements of the second safe harbor because it had "continued a practice of program expansion which is responsive to the abilities and interests of its student body." 1998 WL 167296, at *4.[8]

Specifically, the district court found that (1) Syracuse had a "strong history of adding women's sports programs"; (2) although between 1982 and 1995, the University had added no new varsity women's teams, it did fund additional scholarships and provide enhanced facilities, coaching, and support services for its women varsity athletes; (3) between 1982 and 1995, the absolute number of female participants in varsity sports had increased from 148 to 217; and (4) Syracuse had established two new varsity women's teams since 1995 and planned to add a third in 1999–2000. *Id.*

Finally, the district court noted that in conducting the safe harbor analysis, a court "may consider whether there are any formal policies in place which might indicate that the institution is monitoring the pulse of its students' interests in anticipation of expansion." *Id.* Despite recognizing that the school had not established that it had any formal policy to allow students to voice their interests, the court concluded that "the best evidence of continued expansion is expansion itself." *Id.* Accordingly, it granted summary judgment to the University.

DISCUSSION

A. Lacrosse.

[2] Syracuse argues that this appeal is moot because it has already implemented a varsity women's lacrosse team and that there is, therefore, nothing left for the certified class to pursue. The plaintiffs counter that the appeal is not moot for two reasons. First, they state that they sought to amend their complaint in the district court to add a claim for damages and that the court improperly denied their motion. Second, they argue that their suit did not merely seek class certification of current and future students interested in playing varsity lacrosse, but that they also sought class certification of current and numerous future students interested in playing varsity softball, itself not yet a varsity sport.

[3] It may well be that mootness would have been avoided had plaintiffs originally requested damages in their complaint. *See Cook,* 992 F.2d at 19–20 (noting that "a viable claim for damages generally avoids mootness of the action," but finding a Title IX appeal moot where plaintiffs had graduated, had sought relief solely on their own behalf, and had not appealed the district court's denial of their request for damages); *see also id.* at 19 (holding that an interest in preserving an award of attorneys' fees "is insufficient, standing alone, to sustain jurisdiction"). A request for damages, however, will not avoid mootness if it was "inserted after the complaint was filed in an attempt to breathe life into a moribund dispute." *McCabe v. Nassau County Med. Ctr.,* 453 F.2d 698, 702 (2d Cir.1971).

[4] In the case before us, plaintiffs did not seek to amend their complaint to add a damages claim until three months after the University filed its motion for summary judgment and six months after the district

court granted the University leave to file that motion. Moreover, in their papers in opposition to the University's motion, plaintiffs' counsel represented that if the district court were to enter an order binding the University to its promise to establish varsity women's lacrosse and softball teams, then "plaintiffs shall submit an application for attorney's fees as *there is no longer a controversy between the parties*" (emphasis added). And on appeal, plaintiffs' counsel, despite being asked numerous times at oral argument to specify precisely what relief plaintiffs sought, failed ever to mention damages. *See Perrucci v. Gaffey*, 450 F.2d 356, 358 (2d Cir.1971) (dismissing appeal as moot where *pro se* plaintiff indicated at oral argument that he was not concerned with damages allegations). Under the circumstances, we are satisfied that the district court did not err in denying plaintiffs leave to amend their complaint to add a damages claim.[9]

We, therefore, hold that insofar as plaintiffs' complaint sought a varsity lacrosse team, the claim is now moot, given that the team has been created and is already participating in intercollegiate play *See County of Los Angeles v. Davis*, 440 U.S. 625, 631–32, 99 S.Ct. 1379, 59 L.Ed.2d 642 (1979) (finding case moot where there was no reasonable expectation that the alleged violation would recur). Accordingly, we take no position on whether the safe harbor defense made by Syracuse and granted by the district court was valid.

B. Softball.

Plaintiffs also contest the district court's failure to certify a sub-class of current and future women interested in playing varsity softball. They argue that this issue is not moot because such a team has not yet begun play. We agree with both contentions.

[5] [6] [7] District judges have broad discretion over class definition.[10] But under Rule 23(c)(1), courts are "required to reassess their class rulings as the case develops." *Barnes v. The American Tobacco Co.*, 161 F.3d 127, 140 (3d Cir.1998) (citing *Kuehner v. Heckler*, 778 F.2d 152, 163 (3d Cir. 1985)); *see also Marisol A. v. Giuliani*, 126 F.3d 372, 378–79 (2d Cir.1997) (affirming class certification but ordering a district court to divide the certified class into subclasses); *Richardson v. Byrd*, 709 F.2d 1016, 1019 (5th Cir.1983) ("Under Rule 23 . . . [t]he district judge must define, redefine, subclass, and decertify as appropriate in response to the progression of the case from assertion to facts."). And we agree with the Fifth Circuit that "[o]rdinarily, if a court discerns a conflict . . . the proper solution is to create subclasses of persons whose interests are in accord." *Payne v. Travenol Labs., Inc.*, 673 F.2d 798, 812 (5th Cir.1982). We conclude that although the district court correctly found potential conflicts between members of a class that included both women interested in playing varsity lacrosse and women who wished to play varsity softball, it should have certified two sub-classes—one for each sport—rather than certifying only one class and excluding from that class members of the second.

[8] That being said, the University represented both to the district court and to this Court that a varsity women's softball team is in the process of being established, and that the team will begin play during the 1999–2000 academic year. Because full implementation of a varsity women's softball team would render the remaining live aspect of this case moot, we again choose not to reach the merits of the University's safe harbor defense, and prefer instead to remand the case to the district court with instructions to dismiss the case if the University completes its plan to institute a varsity women's softball team by the date indicated. Should the University not live up to its representations, the district court is ordered to certify a class of current and future women students interested in playing varsity softball and to revisit the merits of the case at that time.[11]

C. Club Athletes.

[9] Although nowhere in their complaint did plaintiffs challenge the allocation of funding between female and male club sports at Syracuse, the district court certified a class of female club athletes to prosecute such a claim. The plaintiffs did not pursue discovery or take any action on this claim—which was essentially created by the district court. Nonetheless, the court granted summary judgment to Syracuse. This was error. A court cannot create a cause of action that a party did not raise (and has no intention of pursuing) and then decide the issue against that party. Beyond the fact that the court is without the power to do so, any ruling on such unargued claims makes law and may bind parties on issues not adequately presented. Such results are to be rigorously avoided. We therefore vacate the district court's ruling on this claim.

continued

D. A Broader Claim.

[10] From time to time, appellants have suggested that their real claim in this suit is to represent all women, present and future, who wish to be varsity athletes at Syracuse—regardless of sport. And in this respect they suggest that "[i]nterest and ability rarely develop in a vacuum; they evolve as a function of opportunity and experience." *Cohen v. Brown Univ.,* 101 F.3d 155, 179 (1st Cir.1996) ("*Cohen II*"), *cert. denied,* 520 U.S. 1186, 117 S.Ct. 1469, 137 L.Ed.2d 682 (1997). They add that it was to ensure such opportunities that Congress passed Title IX. For this reason, they further contend that the importance of Title IX cannot be overstated.[12]

We are inclined to agree. But just as the district court cannot establish a claim for equal treatment for club athletes when that is not presented, so also we cannot create a class of those women who are interested in varsity athletics at Syracuse generally when that issue was never clearly presented in the complaint nor during the prosecution of this case. Too often, both in their briefs, and at oral argument, plaintiffs in this case have made clear that their interests are more specific: equal treatment among varsity athletes, and varsity status for women's lacrosse and softball.[13] Accordingly, we take no position on the merits of such a broader suit. *Cf. Cohen II*, 101 F.3d 155 (upholding suit brought by a similar class against Brown University); *Cohen I*, 991 F.2d 888. It, and the applicability or not of the safe harbor provisions of Title IX as defenses to it, are simply not before us.

* * * *

We affirm the district court's dismissal of the plaintiffs' equal treatment claims with respect to varsity athletes for lack of standing. We dismiss the plaintiffs' appeal as to varsity lacrosse as moot. We vacate the district court's class certification order and its order granting summary judgment to the defendant University on plaintiffs' equal treatment claim with respect to club athletes. We remand the case to the district court for further proceedings consistent with this opinion with respect to the plaintiffs' claim as to varsity softball.

AFFIRMED in part, DISMISSED in part, VACATED and REMANDED in part.

164 F.3d 113, 42 Fed.R.Serv.3d 659, 131 Ed. Law Rep. 635

FOOTNOTES

1. This kind of Title IX claim is commonly referred to as an "accommodation" claim because it derives from the Title IX implementing regulations, which provide that in determining whether equal athletic opportunities for members of both sexes are available, the Office of Civil Rights of the Department of Education (the office charged with enforcement of Title IX) will consider, among other factors, "[w]hether the selection of sports and levels of competition effectively accommodate the interests and abilities of members of both sexes." 34 C.F.R. § 106.41(c)(1); *see also Cohen v. Brown Univ.,* 991 F.2d 888, 897 (1st Cir.1993) ("*Cohen I*") (noting three major areas of regulatory compliance under Title IX: athletic financial assistance (scholarships), equivalence in other athletic benefits and opportunities, and effective accommodation of student interests and abilities).

2. These types of Title IX claims are generally referred to as "equal treatment" claims because they derive from the Title IX regulations found at 34 C.F.R. § 106.37(c) and 106.41(c)(2)-(10), which call for equal provision of athletic scholarships as well as equal provision of other athletic benefits and opportunities among the sexes.

3. Between 1990 and the time of the filing of this suit, the disparity between the percentage of varsity athletes who are female as compared to the percentage of the University's students who are female ranged from 19 to 22%.

4. It is the case, however, that for Title IX accommodation purposes, it is the aggregate number of opportunities provided for each sex, and not the number of teams funded for each sex, that matters. *Cf. Cohen I*, 991 F.2d at 897.

5. These were basketball, fencing, swimming, tennis, and volleyball.

6. These were indoor track, outdoor track, and cross country.

7. The court also certified a class of club athletes to challenge the allocation of funds among male and female club sports teams, but, as noted earlier, the plaintiffs did not pursue this claim because it was not part of their complaint.

8. The court observed:

Where a university has a practice of expanding its athletic program, approaching proportionality and meeting the needs of the under-represented gender; and continues to expand in response to its student body's interest and abilities, as well as that of secondary feeder schools; symmetry in athletic programs is not required under Title IX, and liability may be avoided. Under this "safe harbor" of a continuing practice of program expansion, courts look to the institution's past and continuing remedial efforts to provide nondiscriminatory participation opportunities through program expansion. 1998 WL 167296, at *3 (citing *Cohen I*, 991 F.2d at 898; *Bryant*, 1996 WL 328446, at *10; 44 Fed.Reg. 71,413).

9. We therefore need not and do not reach the issue of whether damages can be recovered under Title IX absent a finding of discriminatory intent. Nor do we address the applicability of the Supreme Court's recent decision in *Gebser v. Lago Vista Indep. Sch. Dist.*, 524 U.S. 274, 118 S.Ct. 1989, 141 L.Ed.2d 277 (1998), in which the Court held, in a Title IX case involving a student who alleged sexual harassment by her teacher, that the plaintiff student could not recover damages from her school district based on principles of respondeat superior or constructive notice. *See id.* 118 S.Ct. at 1997.

10. See Fed.R.Civ.P. 23(c)(4) ("When appropriate (A) an action may be brought or maintained as a class action with respect to particular issues, or (B) a class may be divided into subclasses and each subclass treated as a class, and the provisions of this rule shall then be construed and applied accordingly.").

11. We note additionally that should the district court need to certify a class of current and future women students interested in playing varsity softball at Syracuse, such a class would satisfy the numerosity requirement of Rule 23. Joinder of all relevant parties—when the class includes current female high school students weighing the decision to attend Syracuse based on its athletic offerings—is clearly impracticable.

12. Statistics show that by 1992, in comparison to when Title IX was enacted, the number of young women participating in sports had multiplied six times. *See* Grace-Marie Mowery, Comment & Casenote, *Creating Equal Opportunity for Female Coaches: Affirmative Action Under Title IX*, 66 U. Cin. L.Rev. 283, 283 (1997).

13. For example, in their response to Syracuse's motion for summary judgment on their accommodation claim, plaintiffs stated that if the district court bound Syracuse to its plan to implement varsity women's lacrosse and softball teams, then "plaintiffs shall submit an application for attorney's fees as there is no longer a controversy between the parties."

Reprinted with permission from West Group.

NCAA v. Smith, 525 U.S. 459 (1999)

In this case, Smith was a female volleyball player who attempted to play at two universities in violation of NCAA transfer and eligibility rules. The NCAA did not allow her to play, and Smith sued the NCAA alleging violations of Title IX. Even though the NCAA does not receive federal funds directly, its member institutions do and they pay money to be members of the NCAA. The Supreme Court held that dues payments do not raise the NCAA to the level of a covered program or activity under Title IX, even though its member institutions must still comply. Thus, the NCAA as an organization appears to be safe from Title IX attacks for the time being.

■ Men and Title IX

Male sports programs have become victims of Title IX in the sense that interpretations of Title IX compliance have focused on substantial proportionality. Since historically speaking sports programs for male student-athletes have been larger and more funded than female programs, numerous colleges have cut programs that served the interest of male student-athletes. Are males, therefore, unable to claim reverse discrimination under a Title IX analysis? Probably not. Title IX is gender neutral and applies equally to men and women—at least in theory. A few cases have been brought by male administrators and student-athletes couched in terms of reverse discrimination, but they have usually failed under a Title IX analysis.

Men's Programs Funding Women's Programs

Much of the debate that rages among opponents to Title IX is that men's sports often fund women's sports for survival. Revenue sports such as football and men's basketball serve as the cash cow for women's sports nationwide. Is it fair, then, that men's programs should continue to be cut in order to comply with Title IX while women's programs continue to receive aid from men's programs for their very existence? Though such an argument seems plausible, it is not usually considered a valid one under a Title IX analysis.

Contact Sports Exception

One of the more recent interpretations of Title IX involves the issue of **contact sports**. Though prior decisions had mandated that schools must provide women with the opportunity to compete on male teams when no women's team existed, Title IX regulations governing athletics now exempt contact sports from the traditional purview of Title IX.[9] Sports in this category include boxing, wrestling, rugby, ice hockey, football, basketball, and other sports in which the purpose or major activity involves bodily contact.[10] As with many statutes, the courts have played a significant role in interpreting the statute. The effect of such an interpretation is that women appear to be excluded from participation on all male teams. Once a woman is allowed to compete in that particular sport at that particular institution, however, the woman must not be treated differently than any other person on account of her gender.

Football

Another problem in any Title IX analysis is the sport of football. There are no women's football programs at the intercollegiate level (other than clubs). How does an institution comply with the numerical equivalency in terms of participants and

---

contact sports   sports such as football, wrestling, and lacrosse that inherently involve hostile, even violent physical struggles as part of the game's rules

the financial responsibilities associated with Title IX when 85 scholarships may be awarded by any Division I program for which there is no women's sports equivalent?[11] Such inequity has been easily dealt with by athletic departments by eliminating men's programs and adding women's programs. This balances the numerical imbalance in terms of proportionality. Unfortunately, male athletes in sports such as swimming, wrestling, tennis, and baseball have suffered at the expense of compliance based on numbers even though there is no female equivalent sport as of yet. Many individuals hope that subsequent interpretations of Title IX exclude the sport of football from its purview.

Men's Programs Cut Due to Title IX

Since Title IX has been enforced, numerous men's programs have been eliminated from athletic departments. Some of these programs, such as UCLA's men's swimming program, provided some of the finest amateur, Olympic, and professional athletes in our country's history. Male victims of program termination have sued under Title IX claiming that the fundamental purpose of Title IX was not to eliminate men's programs and such termination amounts to a form of reverse discrimination. However, such claims appear to have no merit under most judicial decisions.

In 1993, the men's swimming team at University of Illinois was cut while the women's was not. The men's fencing team and both diving teams were eliminated as well. As usual, cutbacks were announced due to financial reasons. Members of the men's team sued, claiming discrimination on the basis of sex. Both the trial court and court of appeals held that such decision making by the University of Illinois was acceptable under Title IX analysis, particularly since the men's participation in athletics was 76.6 percent while the overall male enrollment was 56 percent.

A group of former wrestlers sued claiming that Drake University violated Title IX and the Equal Protection Clause of the Constitution by awarding more athletic scholarships to women than men even though men comprised nearly 60 percent of the athletes on campus. In 1993, the district court ruled in favor of Drake University, however, because the Court contended that Drake had provided legitimate, nondiscriminatory reasons for such actions and no wrestler lost his scholarship in order to finish his college degree.

■ General Accounting Office Releases Reports on Title IX

A report on Title IX sponsored by Representative Patsy Mink (D-HI) was released on December 15, 2000. The report examined the impact of Title IX on female participation in higher education (GAO-01–128). The report traced both academic and athletics participation for men and women from 1972 through the school year 1997–98. Highlights of this report included:

■ Women's participation in intercollegiate sports at four-year colleges and universities increased while men's participation has decreased, although men still participate at a higher rate than women.

■ Since Title IX's enactment in 1972, the number of women in intercollegiate sports grew from an estimated 30,000 (1.7 percent of full-time enrolled undergraduate women) to 157,000 (5.5 percent of full-time enrolled undergraduate women). Over the same time period, the number of men participating fell from about 248,000 (10.4 percent of full-time undergraduate men) to about 234,000 (9.5 percent of full-time undergraduate men).

■ During the 1998–99 academic school year, NCAA member institutions spent more per male student athlete than female student athlete in the areas of recruiting, coaches' salaries, and operations. However, institutions spent more on athletic scholarships for women than for men.

■ Men continue to hold the majority of athletics director positions in intercollegiate athletics.

Report on Team Discontinuation

On March 8, the GAO released another report mandated by the Higher Education Act amendments of 1998 on sports team discontinuation (GAO-01–297). The study was adopted as an alternative to legislation that would have required colleges and universities to report to the federal government, up to four years in advance, any teams that would be discontinued or reduced in squad size. The GAO sent a 62-question survey to all NCAA and NAIA institutions asking various questions related to sports team additions and discontinuations at those institutions over the previous eight years. Of the 1,191 institutions that responded with reference to that time period, the findings included:

■ 1,919 teams were added for women, and 702 were added for men; 386 men's teams were discontinued, while 150 women's teams were discontinued.

■ From academic years 1981–82 to 1998–99, women's participation in athletics increased from 90,000 to 163,000. During the same time, men's participation increased from 220,000 to 232,000.

■ The total number of women's teams increased from 5,695 to 9,479 (+ 3,784). The total number of men's teams increased from 9,113 to 9,149 (+ 36).

■ For women, the largest net decrease in teams and participants was in the sport of gymnastics (−100/−683). For men, the largest net decrease in teams and participants was in the sport of wrestling (−171/−2,648).

■ For women, the largest net increase in teams and participation was in the sport of soccer (+ 846/+ 18,132). For men, the largest net increase in participation was in the sport of football (7,199), but there was a reduction in number of teams (−37).

Among Division I institutions, meeting "gender equity goals and requirements" was the primary reason given in adding women's sports teams and discontinuing men's sports teams. Among all Divisions I, II, and III respondents, most indicated that they added both men's and women's teams primarily "to satisfy student interest." The second most common response among all levels of institutions as to why women's teams were added was "to meet gender equity goals and requirements."

■ Other Women's Issues

Women Competing on Male Teams

According to the guidelines issued by the OCR, if a college has a men's team but no women's team in a given sport, female athletes must be allowed to try out for the team unless it is a contact sport.

Recently, Duke University allowed Heather Sue Mercer to try out for the football team as a placekicker. Mercer was listed on the spring roster but was not allowed to attend a summer training camp or dress for the games. Mercer was later cut from the team, and she sued Duke University alleging that once she was allowed on the team that to treat her differently was a form of sex discrimination under Title IX even with the recognition of the contact sports exception. In October 2000, a federal jury ordered Duke to pay $1 in actual damages and $2 million in punitive damages (see case 6).

Men Competing on Women's Teams

Though it may seem awkward, some men attempt to compete on women's teams, especially when a comparable male sport is not offered by the college or university. Such exclusions, however, are usually upheld by the courts to this day under the view that Title IX was meant to help the historically underrepresented sex.[12] Still, one recent case may provide hope for those males desiring to try out for women's teams. In *Williams v. School Dist. of Bethlehem*, 799 F. Supp. 513 (E.D. Pa. 1992), the court ruled that a boy may compete on a woman's field hockey team because it violated his equal protection rights.

Equity in Athletics Disclosure Act[13]

The **Equity in Athletics Disclosure Act (EADA)** requires coeducational colleges and universities that receive federal funds and maintain an intercollegiate athletic program to prepare an annual report to the Department of Education on athletic participation, staffing, and revenues and expenses, by men's and women's teams. This act was first adopted in 1994 to provide Congress and the public with a snapshot of collegiate athletics participation by gender. The Department of Education uses this information in preparing its required report to Congress on gender equity in intercollegiate athletics. Such reports provide a valuable tool for assessing compliance with Title IX. Each university must complete numerous forms that provide public access to certain items.

Equity in Athletics Disclosure Act (EADA)   federal law requiring public disclosure of financial records of college and university records related to athletic expenditures

■ **CASE 6** *Mercer v. Duke University*

UNITED STATES COURT OF APPEALS,
Fourth Circuit

HEATHER SUE **MERCER**,
Plaintiff-Appellant,
v.
No. 99-1014
DUKE UNIVERSITY; FRED GOLDSMITH,
Defendants-Appellees.
Appeal from the United States District Court
for the Middle District of North Carolina, at Durham.
N. Carlton Tilley, Jr., District Judge. (CA-97-959-1)
Argued: June 10, 1999
Decided: July 12, 1999
Before LUTTIG and KING, Circuit Judges, and
BUTZNER, Senior, Circuit Judge.

Student brought claim against university and football coach alleging, inter alia, sex discrimination in violation of Title IX of Education Amendments of 1972 in refusing to allow her to be member of team. Motion to dismiss for failure to state claim was granted by the United States District Court for the Middle District of North Carolina, N. Carlton Tilley, Jr., J., *32 F.Supp.2d 836,* and student appealed. The Court of Appeals, Luttig, Circuit Judge, held that: (1) university was prohibited from discriminating against student on the basis of her sex, once it allowed her to try out for its football team, and (2) student stated a claim under Title IX.

Reversed and remanded.

LUTTIG, Circuit Judge:

Appellant Heather Sue Mercer challenges the federal district court's holding that Title IX provides a blanket exemption for contact sports and the court's consequent dismissal of her claim that Duke University discriminated against her during her participation in Duke's intercollegiate football program. For the reasons that follow, we hold that where a university has allowed a member of the opposite sex to try out for a single-sex team in a contact sport, the university is, contrary to the holding of the district court, subject to Title IX and therefore prohibited from discriminating against that individual on the basis of his or her sex.

I.

Appellee Duke University operates a Division I college football team. During the period relevant to this appeal (1994–98), appellee Fred Goldsmith was head coach of the Duke football team and appellant Heather Sue Mercer was a student at the school. Before attending Duke, Mercer was an all-state kicker at Yorktown Heights High School in Yorktown Heights, New York. Upon enrolling at Duke in the fall of 1994, Mercer tried out for the Duke football team as a walk-on kicker. Mercer was the first—and to date, only—woman to try out for the team. Mercer did not initially make the team, and instead served as a manager during the 1994 season; however, she regularly attended practices in the fall of 1994 and participated in conditioning drills the following spring. In April 1995, the seniors on the team selected Mercer to participate in the Blue-White Game, an intrasquad scrimmage played each spring. In that game, Mercer kicked the winning 28-yard field goal, giving the Blue team a 24–22 victory. The kick was subsequently shown on ESPN, the cable television sports network. Soon after the game, Goldsmith told the news media that Mercer was on the Duke football team, and Fred Chatham, the Duke kicking coach, told Mercer herself that she had made the team. Also, Mike Cragg, the Duke sports information director, asked Mercer to participate in a number of interviews with newspaper, radio, and television reporters, including one with representatives from "The Tonight Show."

Although Mercer did not play in any games during the 1995 season, she again regularly attended practices in the fall and participated in conditioning drills the following spring. Mercer was also officially listed by Duke as a member of the Duke football team on the team roster filed with the NCAA and was pictured in the Duke football yearbook. During this latter period, Mercer alleges that she was the subject of discriminatory treatment by Duke. Specifically, she claims that Goldsmith did not permit her to attend summer camp, refused to allow her to dress for games or sit on the sidelines during games, and gave her fewer opportunities to participate in practices than other walk-on kickers. In addition, Mercer claims that Goldsmith made a number of offensive comments to her, including asking her why she was interested in football, wondering why she did not prefer to participate in beauty pageants rather than football, and suggesting that she sit in the stands with her boyfriend rather than on the sidelines. At the beginning of the 1996 season, Goldsmith informed Mercer that he was dropping her from the team. Mercer alleges that Goldsmith's decision to exclude her from the team was on the basis of her sex because Goldsmith allowed other, less qualified walk-on kickers to remain on the team. Mercer attempted to participate in conditioning drills the following spring, but Goldsmith asked her to leave because the drills were only for members of the team. Goldsmith told Mercer, however, that she could try out for the team again in the fall.

On September 16, 1997, rather than try out for the team again, Mercer filed suit against Duke and Goldsmith, alleging sex discrimination in violation of Title IX of the Education Amendments of 1972, *20 U.S.C.A. §§ 1681–1688*, and negligent misrepresentation and breach of contract in violation of North Carolina law. Duke and Goldsmith filed a motion to dismiss for failure to state a claim under Title IX, and, after discovery was completed, Duke and Goldsmith filed additional motions for summary judgment and a motion to dismiss for lack of subject-matter jurisdiction. On November 9, 1998, the district court granted the motion to dismiss for failure to state a claim under Title IX, and dismissed the state-law claims without prejudice, refusing to exercise supplemental jurisdiction over those claims. The district court declined to rule on any of the other outstanding motions. The district court subsequently denied Mercer's motion to alter judgment. From the district court's order dismissing her Title IX claim for failure to state a claim upon which relief can be granted and its order denying the motion to alter judgment, Mercer appeals.

II.

Title IX prohibits discrimination on the basis of sex by educational institutions receiving federal funding. See 20 U.S.C.A. § 1681(a) ("No person in the United States shall, on the basis of sex, be excluded from participation in, be denied the benefits of, or be subjected to discrimination under any education program or activity receiving Federal financial assistance . . . . "). Soon after enacting Title IX, Congress charged the Department of Health, Education, and Welfare (HEW) with responsibility for developing regulations regarding the applicability of Title IX to athletic programs. *See Pub.L. No. 93–380, § 844*, 88 Stat. 484 (1974). Acting upon that charge, HEW duly promulgated *34 C.F.R. § 106.41*, which reads in relevant part as follows:

Athletics.

(a) General. No person shall, on the basis of sex, be excluded from participation in, be denied the benefits

of, be treated differently from another person or otherwise be discriminated against in any interscholastic, intercollegiate, club or intramural athletics offered by a recipient, and no recipient shall provide any such athletics separately on such basis.

(b) Separate teams. Notwithstanding the requirements of paragraph (a) of this §, a recipient may operate or sponsor separate teams for members of each sex where selection for such teams is based upon competitive skill or the activity involved is a contact sport. However, where a recipient operates or sponsors a team in a particular sport for members of one sex but operates or sponsors no such team for members of the other sex, and athletic opportunities for members of that sex have previously been limited, members of the excluded sex must be allowed to try out for the team offered unless the sport involved is a contact sport. For the purposes of this part, contact sports include boxing, wrestling, rugby, ice hockey, football, basketball and other sports the purpose or major activity of which involves bodily contact. *34 C.F.R. § 106.41 (a)–(b)*[1] The district court held, and appellees contend on appeal, that, under this regulation, "contact sports, such as football, are specifically excluded from Title IX coverage." We disagree.

Subsections (a) and (b) of *§ 106.41* stand in a symbiotic relationship to one another. Subsection (a) establishes a baseline prohibition against sex discrimination in intercollegiate athletics, tracking almost identically the language in the parallel statutory provision prohibiting discrimination by federally funded educational institutions. In addition to generally barring discrimination on the basis of sex in intercollegiate athletics, subsection (a) specifically prohibits any covered institution from "provid[ing] any such athletics separately on such basis."

Standing alone, then, subsection (a) would require covered institutions to integrate all of their sports teams. In order to avoid such a result—which would have radically altered the face of intercollegiate athletics—HEW provided an explicit exception to the rule of subsection (a) in the first sentence of subsection (b), allowing covered institutions to "operate or sponsor separate teams for members of each sex where selection for such teams is based upon competitive skill or the activity involved is a contact sport." By its terms, this sentence permits covered institutions to operate

continued

separate teams for men and women in many sports, including contact sports such as football, rather than integrating those teams.

The first sentence of subsection (b), however, leaves unanswered the question of what, if any, restrictions apply to sports in which a covered institution operates a team for one sex, but operates no corresponding team for the other sex. HEW addressed this question in the second sentence of subsection (b).

This second sentence is applicable only when two predicate criteria are met: first, that the institution in question "operates or sponsors a team in a particular sport for members of one sex but operates or sponsors no such team for members of the other sex," and second, that "athletic opportunities for members of that sex have previously been limited." In this case, appellees do not dispute that athletic opportunities for women at Duke have previously been limited, and thus we assume that the second condition has been met. Further, we assume, without deciding, that Duke operated its football team "for members of one sex"—that is, for only men—but did not operate a separate team "for members of the other sex," and therefore that the first condition has also been satisfied.[2] Thus, insofar as the present appeal is concerned, we consider the predicate conditions to application of the sentence to have been met.

Provided that both of the conditions in the protasis of the second sentence of subsection (b) have been met, the apodosis of the sentence requires that "members of the excluded sex must be allowed to try out for the team offered unless the sport involved is a contact sport." The text of this clause, on its face, is incomplete: it affirmatively specifies that members of the excluded sex must be allowed to try out for single-sex teams where no team is provided for their sex except in the case of contact sports, but is silent regarding what requirements, if any, apply to single-sex teams in contact sports. As to contact sports, this clause is susceptible of two interpretations. First, it could be read to mean that "members of the excluded sex must be allowed to try out for the team offered unless the sport involved is a contact sport, *in which case the anti-discrimination provision of subsection (a) does not apply at all.*" Second, it could be interpreted to mean that "members of the excluded sex must be allowed to try out for the team offered unless the sport involved is a contact sport, *in which case members of the excluded sex need not be allowed to try out.*"

Appellees advocate the former reading, arguing that HEW intended through this clause to exempt contact sports entirely from the coverage of Title IX. We believe, however, that the latter reading is the more natural and intended meaning. The second sentence of subsection (b) does not purport in any way to state an exemption, whether for contact sports or for any other subcategory, from the general antidiscrimination rule stated in subsection (a). And HEW certainly knew how to provide for a complete exemption had it wished, Congress itself having provided a number of such exemptions in the very statute implemented by the regulation. Rather, the sentence says, and says only, that covered institutions must allow members of an excluded sex to try out for single-sex teams in non-contact sports. Therefore, the "unless" phrase at the end of the second clause of the sentence cannot (logically or grammatically) do anything more than except contact sports from the tryout requirement that the beginning of the second clause of the sentence imposes on all other sports.

Contrary to appellees' assertion, this reading of the regulation is perfectly consistent with the evident congressional intent not to require the sexual integration of intercollegiate contact sports. If a university chooses not to permit members of the opposite sex to tryout for a single-sex contact-sports team, this interpretation respects that choice. At the same time, however, the reading of the regulation we adopt today, unlike the one advanced by appellees, ensures that the likewise indisputable congressional intent to prohibit discrimination in all circumstances where such discrimination is unreasonable—for example, where the university itself has voluntarily opened the team in question to members of both sexes—is not frustrated.

We therefore construe the second sentence of subsection (b) as providing that in non-contact sports, but not in contact sports, covered institutions must allow members of an excluded sex to try out for single-sex teams. Once an institution has allowed a member of one sex to try out for a team operated by the institution for the other sex in a contact sport, subsection (b) is simply no longer applicable, and the institution is subject to the general antidiscrimination provision of subsection (a). To the extent that the Third Circuit intended to hold otherwise in *Williams v. School Dist. of Bethlehem, Pa., 998 F.2d 168, 174 (3d Cir. 1993)*, with its lone unexplained statement that, "[i]f it is determined that [a particular sport] is a contact sport, no other inquiry is necessary because that will be dispositive of the title IX claim," we reject such a conclusion as inconsistent with the language of the regulation.

Accordingly, because appellant has alleged that Duke allowed her to try out for its football team (and actually made her a member of the team), then discriminated against her and ultimately excluded her from participation in the sport on the basis of her sex, we conclude that she has stated a claim under the applicable regulation, and therefore under Title IX. We take to heart appellees' cautionary observation that, in so holding, we thereby become "the first Court in United States history to recognize such a cause of action." Br. of Appellees at 20. Where, as here, however, the university invites women into what appellees characterize as the "traditionally all-male bastion of collegiate football," *id.* at 20 n. 10, we are convinced that this reading of the regulation is the only one permissible under law.

The district court's order granting appellees' motion to dismiss for failure to state a claim is hereby reversed, and the case remanded for further proceedings. *REVERSED AND REMANDED*

FOOTNOTES

1. *See also 45 C.F.R. § 86.41 (a)–(b)* (same).

2. At various points in the record, Duke appears to concede that its football team was open to women during the relevant time period. *See, e.g.,* J.A. at 70–72, 91, 99–100. What is unclear, however, is whether the Duke football team was "for" only men, with women allowed to try out, or was "for" both men and women. If the football team was "for" both men and women, then subsection (b) is simply inapplicable, and Duke was subject to the general antidiscrimination rule in subsection (a). It may well be, on the facts as we understand them, that, at the summary-judgment or trial stage of the litigation, appellant can conclusively establish that Duke operated its football team "for" both men and women; however, appellant does not allege in her complaint that Duke operated such a team and therefore we proceed to address the possibility that Duke operated its football team "for" only men.

Reprinted with permission from West Group.

Federal regulations require that the information, based on the previous reporting year, is available for inspection by students, prospective students, and the public by October 30 of each year. A table must be completed that lists sports participants (including walk-ons), operating expenses for mens and women's programs, recruiting expenses, scholarships awarded, revenues, and all coaches salaries.

Once the data is received by the Department of Education, this federal agency must provide a report to Congress on gender trends in intercollegiate athletics based on the reports submitted by individual institutions and make institutional specific reports available to the public through the Internet.

Equal Pay Act of 1963

Women coaches, trainers, and administrators have increasingly sued colleges and universities for gender discrimination under the **Equal Pay Act (EPA)**.[14] This act

---

Equal Pay Act of 1963   federal law mandating, with some exceptions, that all who perform substantially the same work must be paid equally

requires all employers subject to the Fair Labor Standards Act (FLSA) to provide equal pay for men and women performing similar work.

If a female employee sues under the EPA, she must prove that her employer paid her less than a male for "substantially equal" work. Crucial to this analysis, however, is that exceptions are made for differences in pay based upon an established seniority system, a merit system, a system that measures earnings by quantity or quality of production, or any other differential based upon a legitimate factor.

Sexual Harassment

Sexual harassment is unwelcome conduct of a sexual nature. A significant number of claims by students and student-athletes, both male and female, have made this issue very important in the intercollegiate sports and educational setting. Sexual harassment is considered to be a form of sex (gender) discrimination prohibited by Title IX. Sexual harassment might interfere with a student's academic performance and emotional and physical well-being if not addressed properly and timely.

Employees of colleges and universities, such as trainers, professors, counselors, and coaches, are also protected from discrimination under Title IX and on the basis of sex, including sexual harassment, by Title VII of the Civil Rights Act of 1964. Sexual harassment by other employees (or student-athletes) may also interfere with a coach's, trainer's or administrator's job performance and his or her emotional well-being.

Sexual harassment can include unwelcome sexual advances, requests for sexual favors, and other verbal, nonverbal, or physical conduct of a sexual nature. Since many college sports programs employ both male and female trainers and coaches, sexual harassment may be a prime area for litigation, particularly when it comes to locker room and training room behavior.

Sexual Harassment and Title IX

In *Gebser v. Lago Vista Independent School Dist.*, 118 S.Ct. 1989 (1998), the Supreme Court limited the liability of school districts to include only those cases in which "an official who . . . has authority to address the alleged discrimination and to institute corrective measures on the [school's] behalf has actual knowledge of discrimination in the [school's] programs and fails adequately to respond."

Duty to Investigate

Once a college or university becomes aware of a possible sexual harassment violation of Title IX, the institution must conduct a prompt investigation into the situation. An institution may expose itself to liability if the plaintiff shows that official's response shows "deliberate indifference" to "actual knowledge" of dis-

---

sexual harassment　form of employment discrimination that consists of images or verbal or physical abuse sexual in nature and unwelcome

crimination. Instances in which a school administrator had the constructive knowledge to have inferred that an administrator harassed a coach or a coach harassed a student athlete are not sufficient to trigger liability.

Interestingly, the Supreme Court extended the liability of Title IX to include "student-on-student" sexual harassment, *Davis v. Monroe County Bd. of Educ.*, 119 S.Ct. 1661 (1999). A school's "deliberate indifference" to "known acts of harassment" is itself misconduct prohibited by Title IX, which can trigger a private damage action by the plaintiff. A school's misconduct causes the plaintiff to be subject to discrimination when the school exercises "substantial control over the harasser" and the context in which the known harassment occurs.'[15] Whether a school's response to student-on-student actions rises to the level of misconduct prohibited by Title IX is to be judged by the totality of the circumstances.

For example, a report to an administrator indicating that a high school coach had engaged in inappropriate physical conduct of a sexual nature in several instances with different students might suggest a pattern of conduct. This pattern should trigger an inquiry as to whether other students have been sexually harassed by that coach.[16]

False accusations of sexual harassment have no recourse under Title IX or Title VII. However, a victim of false accusations may claim slander, libel, intentional interference with contractual relations, intentional infliction of emotional distress, or other tort claims. Claims of sexual harassment can be fierce, and false claims may attempt to ruin a victim's reputation. However, there are numerous instances of "he said-she said" in which coaches or administrators have retained their jobs or rehabilitated their reputations subsequent to a thorough investigation.

Family and Medical Leave Act

The **Family and Medical Leave Act (FMLA)** was enacted in 1993 and is different from most employment discrimination statutes. Employees are entitled to 12 work weeks of leave (which may be unpaid leave) in a 12-month period for certain family situations or for the employee's own medical problems. Generally speaking, the FMLA applies to businesses that employ 50 or more persons. The FMLA also applies to public agencies and public and private schools.

To be eligible, one must satisfy three basic conditions:

1. One must be an "eligible employee."
2. One must have a family or medical situation that is covered by the act.
3. The FMLA must apply to the employer.

An eligible employee is someone who has been employed for at least 12 months by the employer and who has at least 1,250 hours of service with the employer during the previous 12-month period. In addition, the employee must

---

Family and Medical Leave Act (FMLA)   1993 federal law that guarantees employees unpaid time off from work for childbirth, adoption, and medically related emergencies

work at a location where the employer employs 50 or more persons (or within a 75-mile radius of that work site).[17]

An eligible employee can take *family leave* for: (1) the birth of a child; (2) the adoption of a child; (3) the placement of a child with the employee for foster care; or (3) the care of a child, spouse, or parent who has a serious health condition (29 U.S.C.A. § 2612). A "serious health condition" of an employee or an employee's family member is a physical or mental condition that requires:

1. inpatient care in a hospital, hospice, or residential medical care facility, or
2. continuing treatment by a health care provider (29 U.S.C.A. § 2611(11)).

Substance abuse problems may qualify as serious health conditions, but FMLA leave must be taken for *treatment* of these problems. An employee returning from family or medical leave is entitled:

1. to be restored to the position held when the leave commenced, or
2. to be restored to an equivalent position (29 U.S.C.A. § 2614(a)(1)).

Obviously, it will be interesting to see how the FMLA impacts athletes, coaches, and administrators at all levels of sports.

Clubs for Women Only

Whether or not health clubs for women only constitutes a violation of anti-discrimination laws is still unclear. Some states have specifically excluded women-only health clubs from discrimination laws due to the important privacy issues related to restrooms and showers.

■ Summary

There is no doubt that Title IX has had a positive influence on women's sports in the United States. Such federal legislation has mandated that opportunities for women in athletics must not be hindered by traditional views of sports participants. Title IX grew out of Title VII of the Civil Rights Act of 1964. Title IX's original intent has been challenged on numerous occasions due to the effect of the nationwide reduction of men's athletic programs and simultaneous increase in women's programs. Three tests are used to determine whether an educational institution is in compliance with Title IX: the substantial proportionality, history of expansion, and effective accommodation tests. College coaches, administrators, and student-athletes must remain cognizant of this law and abide by its rules.

Numerous other laws have had an impact in the arena of women and sports. Acts such as the Equal Pay Act, the Equity in Athletics Disclosure Act, and the Family and Medical Leave Act will continue to affect the evolving issues surrounding women in the sports context.

■ Key Terms

contact sports
Department of Health, Education and
  Welfare (HEW)
effective accommodation
Equity in Athletics Disclosure Act
  (EADA)
Equal Pay Act of 1963
Family and Medical Leave Act (FMLA)

gender equity
history of expansion
Office of Civil Rights (OCR)
quota
sexual harassment
substantial proportionality
Title VII of the Education
  Amendments of 1964

■ Additional Cases

Bowers v. Baylor Univ., 862 F. Supp. 142 (W.D. Tex. 1994)
Cannon v. Univ. of Chicago, 441 U.S. 677 (1979)
Cohen v. Brown Univ., 991 F.2d 888 (1st Cir. 1993), cert. denied 520 U.S. 1186 (1997)
Communities for Equity v. Michigan High School Athletic Ass'n, 98-CV-479, (W.D. Mich.), 2002
  U.S. Dist. LEXIS 14220
Franklin v. Gwinnett County Public Schools, 503 U.S. 60 (1992)
Gonyo v. Drake Univ., 837 F. Supp. 989 (S.D. Iowa 1993)
Kelley v. Board of Trustees of the Univ. of Illinois, 832 F.Supp. 237 (C.D. Ill. 1993)
Lowrey v. Texas A&M Univ., 11 F. Supp.2d 895 (S.D. Tex. 1998)
Pederson v. Louisiana State Univ., 912 F. Supp. 892 (M.D. La. 1996), aff'd in part, reversed in
  part, 201 F.3d 388 (5th Cir. 2000)
Roberts v. Colorado State Board of Agriculture, 998 F.2d 824 (10th Cir. 1993)
Stanley v. Univ. of Southern California, 13 F.3d 1313 (9th Cir. 1994)
Tyler v. Howard Univ., No. 91-CA11239 (D.C. June 28, 1993)

■ Review Questions

1. Why was Title IX enacted?
2. Have the goals of Title IX been met?
3. Is it fair to terminate male sports programs to meet the requirements of Title IX?
4. If women can participate on men's teams, should men be allowed to compete on
   women's teams?
5. Does the Equity in Athletics Disclosure Act provide a valuable service to the public?
6. How might the Family and Medical Leave Act affect women sports participants
   and women coaches?

■ Endnotes

1 20 U.S.C.A. § 1681–1688.
2 42 U.S.C.A. §§ 2000e-17.

3 Some claims are brought under both Title IX and the Equal Protection clause of the 14th Amendment, but Title IX is specific to athletics.

4 In 1998 Women's Hockey became an Olympic sport; the U.S. women's soccer team won the World Cup in 1999; the Women's United Soccer Association began play in 2001; and the Women's Professional Football League began in 2000.

5 http://www.ed.gov/inits/commissionsboards/athetics/index.html

6 998 F.2d 824 (10th Cir. 1993).

7 20 U.S.C.A. § 1687.

8 Cert. denied, 520 U.S. 1186 (1997).

9 *See Saint v. Nebraska Sch. Activities Ass'n*, 684 F. Supp. 626 (D.C. Neb. 1988) for example.

10 34 C.F.R. 106.41(b) 1998. Field hockey may also be considered a contact sport, though it is primarily a women's game in the United States.

11 Though there is no current sport for women's football at the collegiate level, there are numerous touch football club leagues. Additionally, there is now an eight-on-eight Women's Professional Football League.

12 *See Kleczek v. Rhode Island Interscholastic League, Inc.*, 768 F. Supp. 951 (D.R.I. 1991).

13 20 U.S.C.A. § 1092.

14 This act applies to both men and women.

15 *Id.* at 1672.

16 *See also Doe v. School Administrative Dist. No. 19*, 66 F. Supp.2d 57, 63–64 and n.6 (D.Me. 1999).

17 *See* 29 U.S.C.A. § 2611(2).

CHAPTER SIX

Disabilities and Sports

■ Introduction

Persons with disabilities are able to compete in sports with much more acceptance and frequency than ever before. The enactment of several federal laws that affected the manner in which society deals with people with disabilities in the sports context. Federal laws also encourage persons with disabilities to overcome those physical challenges.[1]

What constitutes a disability, however, is not entirely clear, and interpretation of that term continues to evolve. How such disabilities affect the eligibility of student-athletes and professionals in sports is an area of continued interpretation and uncertainty. Though physical disabilities may be more easily seen, mental and learning disabilities are addressed under current disability laws as well. Historically, there has not been much litigation involving persons with disabilities and sports until recently.

■ Relevant Statutes

There are three relevant statutes related to persons involved in sports who have disabilities:

1. The Rehabilitation Act of 1973
2. The Americans with Disabilities Act
3. Individuals with Disabilities Education Act[2]

Often these laws and their respective terms overlap. They are largely the same and are often used simultaneously to deal with a person who claims disability status.

High Schools

High school athletic associations within the United States consistently maintain strict eligibility and transfer rules. Enforcement of these rules is of paramount concern to high school athletic directors and student-athletes in order to maintain an honest and competitive balance among public and private schools sports programs. Still, there has been a significant amount of litigation involving disabilities and eligibility rules in high school sports.

Public high school athletic associations have consistently been found to be indirect recipients of federal funds. Therefore, just as public colleges and universities, these associations are subject to a § 504 claim under the Rehabilitation Act, the Americans with Disabilities Act (ADA), or **Individuals with Disabilities Education Act (IDEA)**. When the rules are modified for a person with a disability, such modification is referred to as a "waiver" and should be done on a case-by-case basis. The decision to offer a waiver usually considers whether the waiver places an undue burden on the athletic program or association.

NCAA

The NCAA is the most significant organization in terms of regulating the academic standards of student-athletes at the post-secondary (intercollegiate) athletic level. The NCAA makes it clear that the word *student* is of vital importance in its role as administrator of collegiate sports eligibility for student-athletes. The NCAA has numerous eligibility rules in terms of acquiring and maintaining the eligibility of the student athlete in order to maintain the privilege of participation in college sports. The NCAA has been subject to numerous lawsuits regarding initial eligibility standards for its student-athletes, who may claim that such academic standards are too rigid for persons with disabilities.

■ The Rehabilitation Act of 1973

The **Rehabilitation Act of 1973** (§ 504) applies to public institutions that receive federal funding, such as colleges, universities, and other public school systems.

> Section 504 states:
>
> No otherwise qualified individual with a disability in the United States . . . shall, solely by reason of his or her disability be excluded from participation in, be denied the benefit of, or be subject to discrimination under any program or activity receiving federal financial assistance . . . 29 U.S.C.A. § 794(a).

Individuals with Disabilities Education Act (IDEA)   federal law mandating that all children with disabilities have available to them a free, appropriate public education that emphasizes special education and related services designed to meet their unique needs

Rehabilitation Act of 1973   precursor to the American Disabilities Act stating that "no otherwise qualified handicapped individual in the United States . . . shall, solely by reason of . . . handicap, be excluded from participation in, be denied the benefits of, or be subjected to discrimination under any program or activity receiving federal financial assistance"

A person is considered "disabled" under § 504 if he or she:

1. has a physical or mental impairment that substantially limits one or more major life activities;
2. has a record or history of such an impairment;
3. is regarded as having such impairment if he or she:
   a. has a physical or mental impairment that does not substantially limit a major life activity but is treated by the appropriate institution as having such a limitation (e.g., a student who walks with a limp);
   b. has a physical or mental impairment that substantially limits a major life activity only as result of the attitudes of others towards such impairment; or
   c. has no physical or mental impairment but is treated by the appropriate institution or governing body as having such impairment (e.g., a student who tests positive with the disease but has no physical effects from it).[3]

"Substantially limits" and "major life activities" are terms of art under the Act. "Substantially limits" is difficult to define, but in the Supreme Court's words, "'[s]ubstantially' in the phrase 'substantially limits' suggests 'considerable' or to a large degree'."[4] Major life activities are "activities that are of central importance to daily life." There is no exhaustive list of major life activities, but the Supreme Court cited with approval the regulations promulgated under the Rehabilitation Act defining major life activities to include "functions such as caring for one's self, performing manual tasks, walking, seeing, hearing, speaking, breathing, learning, and working." See *45 C.F.R.§ 84.3(j)(2)(ii)*.

Though instituted with good intentions, the Rehabilitation Act of 1973 nowhere defines what a reasonable accommodation is.

Proof of Discrimination under § 504

To recover damages under a § 504 claim, the student athlete must show:

1. a disability exists;
2. that the student is "otherwise qualified to participate in interscholastic sports";
3. that the exclusion from participation in the sport is solely due to the disability; and
4. that the defendant receives federal financial assistance.

■ The Americans with Disabilities Act[5]

The ADA is recognized as a powerful nondiscrimination law for individuals with disabilities. According to the Act, some 43 million Americans are disabled. Though the ADA is usually applied in the employer-employee relationship, it also applies to public facilities like public schools and other government entities and to privately owned businesses and services that provide public accommodations. student-athletes attending public and private institutions are covered under the ADA.

The **Americans with Disabilities Act (ADA)** extends the provisions of the Rehabilitation Act to state and local governments, and *private* organizations, regardless of the receipt of federal funding. The ADA addresses issues such as physical and programmatic access

> . . . to provide a clear and comprehensive national mandate for the elimination of discrimination against individuals with disabilities.[6]

The ADA also requires that government entities, such as public schools, provide "effective communication" for people with disabilities. It requires those entities to consult, when possible, with people as to their preferred means of communication. For example, a deaf student may prefer a sign language interpreter over closed captioning on television.

Four Major ADA Categories

The ADA is divided into four general sections. Titles II and III appear to be the most relevant to sports and the law.

Title I–Employment

Title II–Public Services (applies to public institutions)

Title III–Public Accommodations and Services Operated by Private Entities (applies to private institutions)

Title IV–Telecommunications and Common Carriers

Reasonable Accommodation

Just as in § 504 of the Rehabilitation Act, the ADA requires employers and others to make **reasonable accommodations** for a qualified individual with a known physical or mental disability. The ADA does not require employers and others to make accommodations that pose an **undue hardship**, defined as significantly difficult or expensive. Accommodations include stadium viewing and seating, access ramps, and restroom areas as well. The ADA protects not only students with disabilities, but any individual with a disability who is employed by the institution or may visit the school.

Americans with Disabilities Act (ADA) of 1990   federal law imposing obligations on employers and other providers of public transport, telecommunications, and public accommodations to accommodate those persons with disabilities

reasonable accommodations   adaptations or adjustments employers must make to accommodate the interests of a person with disabilities without undue hardship

undue hardship   analysis under ADA that would provide a defense for an employer that must pay excessive costs to accommodate a person's disability

What Is Impairment?

Physical **impairments** are defined as

> any physiological disorder or condition, cosmetic disfigurements, or anatomical loss affecting one or more of the following systems: neurological; musculoskeletal; special sense organs; respiratory, including speech organs; cardiovascular; reproductive; digestive; genitourinary; hemic and lymphatic; skin; and endocrine; . . .[7]

Undue Hardship

If a reasonable accommodation poses an undue hardship to an employer, it need not be implemented. Undue hardship is evaluated by assessing various factors, including the nature and cost of the accommodation, the overall financial resources of the facility and of the business, and the impact the accommodation places on the operation of the facility or program.

Not Covered

The following are not considered disabilities under the ADA: homosexuality and bisexuality, transsexualism, voyeurism, kleptomania, transvestitism, pedophilia, exhibitionism, compulsive gambling, pyromania, and psychoactive substance use disorders resulting from current illegal use of drugs.

Rehabilitated drug users or people who are currently participating in a drug rehabilitation program are protected under the ADA because they are regarded as "having such an impairment." Recovering alcoholics and drug users also fall into this category. However, current drug users are not protected under the ADA. An employer may refuse to hire an applicant or may fire an employee because that person is currently using illegal drugs.

Proof of Discrimination under the ADA

To recover damages under an ADA claim, the student athlete must show:

1. a disability exists;
2. that the student is otherwise qualified to participate in interscholastic sports;
3. that the exclusion from participation in the sport is solely due to the disability; and
4. that the defendant falls under Title II or Title III of the act.

Risks to Self and Other Participants

One of the more controversial areas for courts is how to deal with situations in which student-athletes may expose themselves or others to risks of harm by instituting a waiver for the disability and allowing disabled athletes to compete.

---

impairment   diminishment of physical or mental capabilities

Though the federal acts are designed to prevent discrimination against persons with disabilities, what if allowing an individual with a disability to compete presents potential injury problems with other competitors? For example, what if a student is allowed to participate with a special wheelchair that accommodates that individual's interests, but the chair itself poses a danger to other competitors?

Role of EEOC

The **Equal Employment Opportunity Commission (EEOC)** has interpreted the ADA and § 504 of the Rehabilitation Act to provide a defense to a discrimination claim if the accommodation would expose the disabled individual or others to a "significant risk of substantial harm." If there may be a risk to other competitors, a waiver may be considered unreasonable and unenforceable.[8]

■ Alcohol and other Drugs

Alcoholism and drug addiction are considered disabilities under the ADA. However, if such persons affect others during the employment relationship, then they are likely not covered under the act. This could present serious conflicts and considerations for professional sports leagues and the NCAA when use of certain drugs is a violation of a condition of participation in sports. There has not been any reported litigation involving drug users or alcoholic student-athletes, but in *Maddox v. Univ. of Tennessee,* the issue of alcoholism did emerge in the context of the coaching profession (See Case 7).

Also, "[I]ndividuals with a disability" does not include any individual who is an alcoholic whose current use of alcohol prevents such individual from performing the duties of the job in question or whose employment, by reason of such current alcohol abuse, would constitute a direct threat to property or the safety of others.[9]

■ Golfers and other Professional Sports

In 1998, golfer Casey Martin sued the Professional Golfers Association (PGA) for disallowing him to use a cart when traveling from hole to hole during his rounds of golf.[10] Though Martin was not suing a particular golf course, he was asking the court for an injunction to allow him to have the special use of a golf cart when traveling between holes during a round of golf due to Klippel-Trenaunay-Weber syndrome, a disease that impairs his ability to walk. Such an injunction were counter to the rules promulgated by the PGA (See Case 8).

Equal Employment Opportunity Commission (EEOC)   Federal agency responsible for enforcing federal antidiscrimination laws

■ CASE 7 *Maddox v. University of Tennesseee*

UNITED STATES COURT OF APPEALS,
Sixth Circuit

Robert E. **Maddox**, III,
Plaintiff-Appellant,
v.
University of Tennessee;
University of Tennessee
Board of Trustees; Doug A.
Dickey,
Defendants-Appellees.
No. 94–5820

BAILEY BROWN, Circuit Judge. The plaintiff-appellant, Robert Maddox, a former assistant football coach at the University of Tennessee, brought suit against the school, its Board of Trustees, and its athletic director, Doug Dickey (collectively "UT"), under § 504 of the Rehabilitation Act of 1973, as amended, 29 U.S.C. § 701, et seq., and the Americans with Disabilities Act of 1990 ("ADA"), 42 U.S.C. § 12101, et seq., alleging discriminatory discharge on the basis of his disability, alcoholism. The district court granted UT's motion for summary judgment, concluding that Maddox was not terminated solely by reason of, or because of, his handicap, but rather, because of a well-publicized incident in which Maddox was arrested for driving under the influence of alcohol. Maddox appealed. We AFFIRM.

I. FACTS

On February 17, 1992, Doug Dickey, acting as UT's athletic director, extended to Maddox an offer of employment as an assistant football coach. The position did not carry tenure and was terminable at will in accordance with the policies of the Personnel Manual. As part of the hiring process, Maddox completed an application. On the line after "Describe any health problems or physical limitations, which . . . would limit your ability to perform the duties of the position for which you are applying," Maddox wrote "None." In response to the question "have you ever been arrested for a criminal offense of any kind?" Maddox replied "No." These responses were not accurate. According to what Maddox alleges in this lawsuit, he suffers from the disability of alcoholism. Also, Maddox was arrested

three times before 1992, once for possession of a controlled substance, and twice for driving a motor vehicle under the influence of alcohol. As to the first answer, Maddox claims that it is in fact correct because "it has never affected my coaching ability . . . I never drank on the job." As to the second question, Maddox claims that another university employee, Bill Higdon, advised him not to include the information concerning his prior arrests on the application.

On May 26, 1992, after Maddox began working at UT, a Knoxville police officer arrested Maddox and charged him with driving under the influence of alcohol and public intoxication. According to newspaper reports, the accuracy of which is not contested, Maddox backed his car across a major public road at a high rate of speed, almost striking another vehicle. When stopped by the officer, Maddox was combative, his pants were unzipped, and he refused to take a breathalyzer. He also lied to the arresting officer, stating that he was unemployed. This incident was highly publicized, and UT was obviously embarrassed by the public exposure surrounding the event.

Maddox entered an alcohol rehabilitation program at a UT hospital after his arrest. UT first placed Maddox on paid administrative leave. In June 1992, however, Dickey and then Head Coach Johnny Majors determined that the allegations were accurate and jointly issued a letter notifying Maddox that his employment was being terminated. They testified that termination was necessary because of: 1) the criminal acts and misconduct of Maddox; 2) the bad publicity surrounding the arrest; and 3) the fact that Maddox was no longer qualified, in their minds, for the responsibilities associated with being an assistant coach.[1]

Both Dickey and Majors deny that they were aware that Maddox was an alcoholic or that Maddox's alcoholism played any part in the decision to discharge him. Nevertheless, Maddox brought this action alleging that the termination was discriminatory on the basis of his alcoholism in violation of his rights under the Rehabilitation Act and the ADA. UT responded by filing a motion for summary judgment which the district court granted. The court recognized that, under both statutes, a plaintiff must show that he was fired by reason of his disability. In the court's view, summary

continued

judgment was appropriate because Maddox could not establish the existence of a genuine issue of material fact with respect to whether he had been fired by reason of his status as an alcoholic rather than by reason of his criminal misconduct. Maddox now appeals.

II. ANALYSIS

1. Standard of Review

Review of a grant of summary judgment is de novo, utilizing the same test used by the district court to determine whether summary judgment is appropriate. Deaton v. Montgomery County, Ohio, 989 F.2d 885, 887 (6th Cir.1993). A court shall render summary judgment when there is no genuine issue as to any material fact, the moving party is entitled to judgment as a matter of law, and reasonable minds could come to but one conclusion, and that conclusion is adverse to the party against whom the motion is made. See LaPointe v. UAW, Local 600, 8 F.3d 376, 378 (6th Cir.1993); United States v. TRW, Inc., 4 F.3d 417, 423 (6th Cir.1993).

2. Maddox was not terminated because of his disability.

Maddox raises a number of issues on appeal which he contends show that the district court erred in granting summary judgment to the defendants. Maddox first alleges that the district court erred in analyzing his claim under the Rehabilitation Act. Section 504 of the Act provides, "[n]o otherwise qualified individual with a disability . . . shall, solely by reason of her or his disability, be excluded from the participation in, be denied the benefits of, or be subject to discrimination under any program or activity receiving Federal financial assistance." 29 U.S.C. § 794(a). [2] Thus, in order to establish a violation of the Rehabilitation Act, a plaintiff must show: (1) The plaintiff is a "handicapped person" under the Act; (2) The plaintiff is "otherwise qualified" for participation in the program; (3) The plaintiff is being excluded from participation in, being denied the benefits of, or being subjected to discrimination under the program solely by reason of his handicap; and (4) The relevant program or activity is receiving Federal financial assistance.

Doherty v. Southern College of Optometry, 862 F.2d 570, 573 (6th Cir.1988), cert. denied, 493 U.S. 810, (1989). It is not disputed in this case that UT constitutes a program receiving Federal financial assistance under the Act.

Likewise, we assume, without deciding, that alcoholics may be "individuals with a disability" for purposes of the Act. See Tinch v. Walters, 765 F.2d 599, 603 (6th Cir.1985); Fuller v. Frank, 916 F.2d 558, 560 (9th Cir.1990). Thus, our analysis focuses on whether Maddox is "otherwise qualified" under the Act and whether he was discharged "solely by reason of" his disability. The burden of making these showings rests with Maddox. Chandler v. City of Dallas, 2 F.3d 1385, 1390 (5th Cir.1993), cert. denied, 114 S.Ct. 1386, (1994).

In support of its motion for summary judgment, UT contended that both factors weighed in its favor. First, Dickey and Majors contended that they did not even know that Maddox was considered an alcoholic in making both the decision to hire and fire him. Moreover, they contended that Maddox was discharged, not because he was an alcoholic, but because of his criminal conduct and behavior and the significant amount of bad publicity surrounding him and the school. UT alternatively contended that Maddox is nevertheless not "otherwise qualified" to continue in the position of assistant football coach.

The district court granted UT's motion for summary judgment, specifically holding that UT did not discharge Maddox solely by reason of his disability. The court found it beyond dispute that Maddox's discharge resulted from his misconduct rather than his disability of alcoholism. The court noted, "It cannot be denied in this case, Mr. Maddox was charged with . . . [driving while under the influence and public intoxication] which would not be considered socially acceptable by any objective standard. The affidavit testimony of Mr. Dickey and Mr. Majors is clear on the point that it was this specific conduct, not any condition to which it might be related, which provoked the termination of Mr. Maddox's employment.

As a result, the court found it unnecessary to decide the alternative ground of whether Maddox was "otherwise qualified." Maddox contends that the district court erred in distinguishing between discharge for misconduct and discharge solely by reason of his disability of alcoholism. Maddox claims that he has difficulty operating a motor vehicle while under the influence of alcohol and therefore he characterizes drunk driving as a causally connected manifestation of the disability of alcoholism. Thus, Maddox contends that because alcoholism caused the incident upon which UT claims to have based its decision to discharge him, UT in essence discharged him because of his disability of alcoholism. In support, Maddox relies on *Teahan v. Metro-North Commuter R.R. Co.*, 951 F.2d 511, 516–17 (2d Cir.1991), cert. denied, 113 S. Ct. 54, (1992), in which the Second Circuit held that a Rehabilitation Act plaintiff can show that he was fired "solely by reason of" his disability, or at least create a genuine issue of material fact, if he can show that he was fired for conduct that is "causally related" to his disability. In Teahan, the defendant company discharged the plaintiff because of his excessive absenteeism. The plaintiff responded by claiming that his absenteeism was caused by his alcoholism and therefore protected under the Rehabilitation Act. The district court disagreed and granted summary judgment for the employer because, the court found, Teahan was fired for his absenteeism and not because of his alcoholism. The Second Circuit reversed the district court's grant of summary judgment on appeal, however, rejecting the court's distinction between misconduct (absenteeism), and the disabling condition of alcoholism. The court presumed that Teahan's absenteeism resulted from his alcoholism and held that one's disability should not be distinguished from its consequences in determining whether he was fired "solely by reason" of his disability. *Id.* Thus, Maddox argues that, in the instant case, when UT acted on the basis of the conduct allegedly caused by the alcoholism, it was the same as if UT acted on the basis of alcoholism itself.

We disagree and hold that the district court correctly focused on the distinction between discharging someone for unacceptable misconduct and discharging someone because of the disability. As the district court noted, to hold otherwise, an employer would be forced to accommodate all behavior of an alcoholic which could in any way be related to the alcoholic's use of intoxicating beverages; behavior that would be intolerable if engaged in by a sober employee or, for that matter, an intoxicated but non-alcoholic employee. Despite Teahan, a number of cases have considered the issue of misconduct as distinct from the status of the disability. In *Taub v. Frank*, 957 F.2d 8 (1st Cir.1992), the plaintiff Taub, a heroin addict, brought suit against his former employer, the United States Postal Service, alleging discriminatory discharge under

the Rehabilitation Act. The Post Office discharged Taub after he was arrested for possession of heroin for distribution. The district court granted the Post Office's motion for summary judgment and Taub appealed. The First Circuit affirmed and held that Taub could not prevail on his Rehabilitation Act claim because his discharge resulted from his misconduct, possession of heroin for distribution, rather than his disability of heroin addiction. The court reasoned that addiction-related criminal conduct is simply too attenuated to extend the Act's protection to Taub.

The conduct/disability distinction was also recognized by the *Fourth Circuit in Little v. F.B.I.*, 1 F.3d 255 (4th Cir.1993). In Little, the F.B.I. discharged the plaintiff, known by his supervisors to be an alcoholic, after an incident in which he was intoxicated on duty. The district court granted summary judgment in favor of the F.B.I. on the basis that the plaintiff was no longer "otherwise qualified" to serve as an F.B.I. agent. The Fourth Circuit affirmed, noting as an additional basis that the plaintiff's employment was not terminated because of his handicap. *Id.* at 259. The court noted, "based on no less authority than common sense, it is clear that an employer subject to the . . . [Rehabilitation] Act must be permitted to terminate its employees on account of egregious misconduct, irrespective of whether the employee is handicapped." *Id.*; see also *Landefeld v. Marion Gen. Hosp., Inc.*, 994 F.2d 1178, 1183 (6th Cir.1993) (Nelson, J., concurring) ("The plaintiff was clearly suspended because of his intolerable conduct, and not solely because of his mental condition.").

Moreover, language within the respective statutes makes clear that such a distinction is warranted. Section 706(8)(c) of the Rehabilitation Act states:

> "[I]ndividuals with a disability" does not include any individual who is an alcoholic whose current use of alcohol prevents such individual from performing the duties of the job in question or whose employment, by reason of such current alcohol abuse, would constitute a direct threat to property or the safety of others.

29 U.S.C. § 706(8)(c)(v) (emphasis added). Likewise, the ADA specifically provides that an employer may hold an alcoholic employee to the same performance

continued

and behavior standards to which the employer holds other employees "even if any unsatisfactory performance is related to the alcoholism of such employee." 42 U.S.C. § 12114(c)(4). These provisions clearly contemplate distinguishing the issue of misconduct from one's status as an alcoholic.

At bottom, we conclude that the analysis of the district court is more in keeping with the purposes and limitations of the respective Acts, and therefore, we decline to adopt the Second Circuit's reasoning in Teahan. Employers subject to the Rehabilitation Act and ADA must be permitted to take appropriate action with respect to an employee on account of egregious or criminal conduct, regardless of whether the employee is disabled. In the instant case, for example, while alcoholism might compel Maddox to drink, it did not compel him to operate a motor vehicle or engage in the other inappropriate conduct reported. Likewise, suppose an alcoholic becomes intoxicated and sexually assaults a coworker? We believe that it strains logic to conclude that such action could be protected under the Rehabilitation Act or the ADA merely because the actor has been diagnosed as an alcoholic and claims that such action was caused by his disability.

3. Pretext

Maddox alternatively contends that even if UT has successfully disclaimed reliance on his disability in making the employment decision, the district court nevertheless erred in determining that Maddox had produced no evidence that the reasons articulated by UT were a pretext for discrimination. A Rehabilitation Act plaintiff may demonstrate pretext by showing that the asserted reasons had no basis in fact; the reasons did not in fact motivate the discharge, or, if they were factors in the decision, they were jointly insufficient to motivate the discharge. *Chappell v. GTE Products Corp.*, 803 F.2d 261, 266 (6th Cir.1986), cert. denied, 480 U.S. 919 (1987).

Maddox first alleges that Dickey and Majors knew that Maddox was an alcoholic. Setting aside for a moment the legal significance of this statement, it is not supported factually in the record. Dickey and Majors, the district court found, had no knowledge of Maddox's previous criminal history prior to the DUI arrest involved here. In fact, Dickey states that if he had

known of the prior arrests, he would not have hired him. More importantly, however, assuming that Dickey and Majors did know of Maddox's alcoholism, as we must do on a summary judgment motion, that knowledge does not translate into evidence that alcoholism was the basis for the termination. To the contrary, the university stated that the criminal conduct and the bad publicity surrounding it formed the basis of the termination, which we conclude is sufficient to motivate the discharge.

Maddox also claims that he knew of other coaches in the football program who drank alcohol in public and who were arrested for DUI but who were not discharged. This point is also irrelevant. Whether Maddox had such knowledge is immaterial. There is no evidence in the record establishing that Majors or Dickey had knowledge of the public intoxication of any other coach, or failed to reprimand or terminate any coach who they knew to have engaged in such behavior.

Maddox finally contends that UT's conclusion that he is no longer qualified to be an assistant coach at UT is without merit. Maddox claims that his misconduct did not affect his "coaching" responsibilities because an assistant coach's duties are limited to the practice and playing fields, and do not comprise of serving as a counselor or mentor to the players or serving as a representative of the school. Maddox relies on the fact that none of these functions were explained to him in his formal job description.

We first note that this allegation seems more appropriate for determining whether he was "otherwise qualified" rather than whether he was discharged because of his disability. Nevertheless, Maddox's position is simply unrealistic. It is obvious that as a member of the football coaching staff, Maddox would be representing not only the team but also the university. As in the instant case, UT received full media coverage because of this "embarrassing" incident. The school falls out of favor with the public, and the reputation of the football program suffers. Likewise, to argue that football coaches today, with all the emphasis on the misuse of drugs and alcohol by athletes, are not "role models" and "mentors" simply ignores reality. The district court's grant of summary judgment in favor of the defendants is AFFIRMED.

The PGA is a private tour and receives no funds from the state or federal governments. However, many of its matches are played on golf courses that are characterized as a "public course." PGA rules prevent the use of a golf cart as part of the game of golf on its tour to force the golfers to add physical endurance of walking as part of the game. Should the ADA apply to this circumstance and Mr. Martin be allowed to use a cart when others may not? If so, argued the PGA, the fundamental rules of the game of golf would change, and this could open the floodgates of litigation to all professional sports that use public facilities.

Possible Unfair Advantage

Nowhere in the ADA does it mention its applicability to private sports organizations and associations. This is unique in the sense that sports leagues and organizations very existence centers on the notion of fair competition without any inherent advantage on either side. It is one concern that the facilities that are used by the sports participants and fans are able to accommodate the interests of all parties in compliance with the ADA. It is another issue, however, that changing the competitive rules of a private sports league in order to comply with the vague definitions of the ADA could change the sport itself.

Title III was the most relevant portion of the ADA that required an interpretation for the Ninth Circuit in the *Martin* case. Title III defines "public accommodation" to include restaurants, stadiums, auditoriums, bakeries, laundromats, museums, parks, schools, gymnasiums, and golf courses.[11] Additionally, the ADA requires that any private entity must make reasonable modifications "unless the entity can demonstrate that making such modifications would fundamentally alter the nature of the good, service, facility, privilege, advantage, or accommodation being offered or would result in an undue burden.[12] This was the heart of the issue in the *Martin* case: whether the request for the use of the cart was a reasonable modification.

Martin's Supreme Court Decision

In May 2001, the United States Supreme Court issued an opinion in *PGA Tour, Inc., v. Martin*, 532 U.S. 661 (2001) (See Case 8). In *Martin*, the Court affirmed the United States Court of Appeals for the Ninth Circuit's decision allowing Martin to use a cart. More specifically, the Court stated that the PGA Tour was subject to the mandates of Title III of the ADA, and Martin was a member of the protected class of persons. Also, the Court stated that a cart would not fundamentally alter the nature of competitive golf tournaments. Although the Court's opinion ended Martin's case, it did not resolve a larger controversy surrounding the integration of disabled athletes into competitive athletics.

The Olinger Case

In another golf case, the court ruled just the opposite of *Martin*. In *Olinger v. United States Golf Ass'n*, golfer Ford Olinger sued the USGA for not allowing the use of golf carts during play at the U.S. Open.[13] Olinger suffered from bilateral avascular necrosis and was unable to walk due to the pain. However, the court sided with the USGA, holding that to alter the USGA rule would fundamentally alter the game of golf.

■ The Individuals with Disabilities Education Act

The **Individuals with Disabilities Education Act (IDEA)**[14] is a federal law that governs special education through the high school level. It does not apply to colleges and universities. IDEA requires schools to provide a free and appropriate public education to students who meet certain eligibility criteria. If a student qualifies for special education under IDEA, he or she is protected and guaranteed certain rights to education. To determine eligibility for Special Education, the student must first be evaluated. A formal, written Individual Education Plan (IEP) should be established for each student in order to afford possible recovery under this act.

On June 4, 1997, President Bill Clinton signed a bill into law that modified the 1990 version of the IDEA. The new law also amended the original act to include new sections that deal with disciplining students with disabilities. In addition, the power to determine whether a child should be removed from schools for certain actions is now given to an administrative hearing officer rather than a judge. The newer law seeks to protect the rights of students with disabilities against arbitrary exclusion from schools based upon traditional stereotypes.

Individuals with Disabilities Education Act (IDEA)   federal law mandating that all children with disabilities have available to them a free, appropriate public education that emphasizes special education and related services designed to meet their unique needs

■ CASE 8   *PGA Tour v. Martin*

SUPREME COURT OF THE UNITED STATES

PGA TOUR, INC., Petitioner,

v.

Casey MARTIN.

No. 00–24.

Argued Jan. 17, 2001.

Decided May 29, 2001.

Professional golfer suffering from circulatory disorder resulting in malformation of his right leg sued non-profit professional golf association, alleging that association's rule banning use of golf carts in certain of its tournaments violated Americans with Disabilities Act (ADA). The United States District Court for the District of Oregon, Thomas M. Coffin, United States Magistrate Judge, entered partial summary judgment for golfer, 984 F.Supp. 1320, and, following bench trial, entered permanent injunction requiring association to permit golfer to use cart, 994 F.Supp. 1242. Association appealed. The United States Court of Appeals for the Ninth Circuit, 204 F.3d 994, affirmed. Certiorari was granted. The Supreme Court, Justice Stevens, held that: (1) even if the protected class under Title III of the ADA is limited to "clients or customers," it would be entirely appropriate to classify the golfers who paid the association $3,000 for the chance to compete in its qualifying tournaments and, if successful, in the subsequent tour events, as association's "clients or customers," and (2) allowing disabled golfer to use a golf cart, despite the walking requirement that applied to the association's tours, was not a modification that would "fundamentally alter the nature" of those events, and was required by Title III of the ADA.

Affirmed.

Justice Scalia, with whom Justice Thomas joined, filed a dissenting opinion.

Petitioner sponsors professional golf tournaments conducted on three annual tours. A player may gain entry into the tours in various ways, most commonly through successfully competing in a three-stage qualifying tournament known as the "Q-School." Any member of the public may enter the Q-School by submitting two letters of recommendation and paying a $3,000 entry fee to cover greens fees and the cost of golf carts, which are permitted during the first two stages, but have been prohibited during the third stage since 1997. The rules governing competition in tour events include the "Rules of Golf," which apply at all levels of amateur and professional golf and do not prohibit the use of golf carts, and the "hard card," which applies specifically to petitioner's professional tours and requires players to walk the golf course during tournaments, except in "open" qualifying events for each tournament and on petitioner's senior tour. Respondent Martin is a talented golfer afflicted with a degenerative circulatory disorder that prevents him from walking golf courses. His disorder constitutes a disability under the Americans with Disabilities Act of 1990(ADA), 42 U.S.C. § 12101 *et seq.* When Martin turned pro and entered the Q-School, he made a request, supported by detailed medical records, for permission to use a golf cart during the third stage. Petitioner refused, and Martin filed this action under Title III of the ADA, which, among other things, requires an entity operating "public accommodations" to make "reasonable modifications" in its policies "when . . . necessary to afford such . . . accommodations to individuals with disabilities, *unless the entity can demonstrate that making such modifications would fundamentally alter the nature of such . . .* accommodations," § 12182(b)(2)(A)(ii) (emphasis added). In denying petitioner summary judgment, the Magistrate Judge rejected its contention, among others, that the play areas of its tour competitions are not places of "public accommodation" within Title III's scope. After trial, the District Court entered a permanent injunction requiring petitioner to permit Martin to use a cart. Among its rulings, that court found that the walking rule's purpose was to inject fatigue into the skill of shot-making, but that the fatigue injected by walking a golf course cannot be deemed significant under normal circumstances; determined that even with the use of a cart, the fatigue Martin suffers from coping with his disability is greater than the fatigue his able-bodied competitors endure from walking the course; and concluded that it would not fundamentally alter the nature of petitioner's game to accommodate Martin. The Ninth Circuit affirmed, concluding, *inter alia,* that golf courses, including play areas, are places of public accommodation during professional tournaments and that permitting Martin to use a cart would not "fundamentally alter" the nature of those tournaments.

continued

Held:

1. Title III of the ADA, by its plain terms, prohibits petitioner from denying Martin equal access to its tours on the basis of his disability. *Cf. Pennsylvania Dept. of Corrections v. Yeskey*, 524 U.S. 206, 209, 118 S.Ct. 1952, 141 L.Ed.2d 215. That Title provides, as a general rule, that "[n]o individual shall be discriminated against on the basis of a disability in the full and equal enjoyment of the . . . privileges . . . of any place of public accommodation." § 12182(a). The phrase "public accommodation" is defined in terms of 12 extensive categories, § 12181(7), which the legislative history indicates should be construed liberally to afford people with disabilities equal access to the wide variety of establishments available to the nondisabled. Given the general rule and the comprehensive definition of "public accommodation," it is apparent that petitioner's golf tours and their qualifying rounds fit comfortably within Title III's coverage, and Martin within its protection. The events occur on "golf course[s]," a type of place specifically identified as a public accommodation. § 12181(7)(L). And, at all relevant times, petitioner "leases" and "operates" golf courses to conduct its Q-School and tours. § 12182(a). As a lessor and operator, petitioner must not discriminate against any "individual" in the "full and equal enjoyment of the . . . privileges" of those courses. *Ibid.* Among those "privileges" are competing in the Q-School and playing in the tours; indeed, the former is a privilege for which thousands of individuals from the general public pay, and the latter is one for which they vie. Martin is one of those individuals. The Court rejects petitioner's argument that competing golfers are not members of the class protected by Title III–*i.e.*, "clients or customers of the covered public accommodation," § 12182(b)(1)(A)(iv)–but are providers of the entertainment petitioner sells, so that their "job-related" discrimination claims may only be brought under Title I. Even if Title III's protected class were so limited, it would be entirely appropriate to classify the golfers who pay petitioner $3,000 for the chance to compete in the Q-School and, if successful, in the subsequent tour events, as petitioner's clients or customers. This conclusion is consistent with case law in the analogous context of Title II of the Civil Rights Act of 1964. See, e.g., Daniel v. Paul, 395 U.S. 298, 306, 89 S.Ct. 1697, 23 L.Ed.2d 318. Pp. 1889–1893.

2. Allowing Martin to use a golf cart, despite petitioner's walking requirement, is not a modification that would "fundamentally alter the nature" of petitioner's tours or the third stage of the Q-School. In theory, a modification of the tournaments might constitute a fundamental alteration in these ways: (1) It might alter such an essential aspect of golf, *e.g.*, the diameter of the hole, that it would be unacceptable even if it affected all competitors equally; or (2) a less significant change that has only a peripheral impact on the game itself might nevertheless give a disabled player, in addition to access to the competition as required by Title III, an advantage over others and therefore fundamentally alter the character of the competition. The Court is not persuaded that a waiver of the walking rule for Martin would work a fundamental alteration in either sense. The use of carts is not inconsistent with the fundamental character of golf, the essence of which has always been shot-making. The walking rule contained in petitioner's hard cards is neither an essential attribute of the game itself nor an indispensable feature of tournament golf. The Court rejects petitioner's attempt to distinguish golf as it is generally played from the game at the highest level, where, petitioner claims, the waiver of an "outcome-affecting" rule such as the walking rule would violate the governing principle that competitors must be subject to identical substantive rules, thereby fundamentally altering the nature of tournament events. That argument's force is mitigated by the fact that it is impossible to guarantee that all golfers will play under exactly the same conditions or that an individual's ability will be the sole determinant of the outcome. Further, the factual basis of petitioner's argument–that the walking rule is "outcome affecting" because fatigue may adversely affect performance–is undermined by the District Court's finding that the fatigue from walking during a tournament cannot be deemed significant. Even if petitioner's factual predicate is accepted, its legal position is fatally flawed because its refusal to consider Martin's personal circumstances in deciding whether to accommodate his disability runs counter to the ADA's requirement that an individualized inquiry be conducted. Cf. *Sutton v. United Air Lines, Inc.*, 527 U.S. 471, 483, 119 S.Ct. 2139, 144 L.Ed.2d 450. There is no doubt that allowing Martin to use a cart would not fundamentally alter the nature of petitioner's tournaments, given the District

Court's uncontested finding that Martin endures greater fatigue with a cart than his able-bodied competitors do by walking. The waiver of a peripheral tournament rule that does not impair its purpose cannot be said to fundamentally alter the nature of the athletic event. Pp. 1893–1898.

204 F.3d 994, affirmed.

STEVENS, J., delivered the opinion of the Court, in which REHNQUIST, C. J., and O'CONNOR, KENNEDY, SOUTER, GINSBURG, and BREYER, JJ., joined. SCALIA, J., filed a dissenting opinion, in which THOMAS, J., joined.

H. Bartow Farr, III, Washington, DC, for petitioner.

Roy L. Reardon, New York City, for respondent.

Barbara D. Underwood, Washington, DC, for United States as amicus curiae, by special leave of the Court, supporting respondent.

Justice STEVENS delivered the opinion of the Court.

This case raises two questions concerning the application of the Americans with Disabilities Act of 1990, 104 Stat. 328, 42 U.S.C. § 12101 *et seq.,* to a gifted athlete: first, whether the Act protects access to professional golf tournaments by a qualified entrant with a disability; and second, whether a disabled contestant may be denied the use of a golf cart because it would "fundamentally alter the nature" of the tournaments, § 12182(b)(2) (A)(ii), to allow him to ride when all other contestants must walk.

I.

Petitioner PGA TOUR, Inc., a nonprofit entity formed in 1968, sponsors and cosponsors professional golf tournaments conducted on three annual tours. About 200 golfers participate in the PGA TOUR; about 170 in the NIKE TOUR[1]; and about 100 in the SENIOR PGA TOUR. PGA TOUR and NIKE TOUR tournaments typically are 4-day events, played on courses leased and operated by petitioner. The entire field usually competes in two 18-hole rounds played on Thursday and Friday; those who survive the "cut" play on Saturday and Sunday and receive prize money in amounts determined by their aggregate scores for all four rounds. The revenues generated by television, admissions, concessions, and contributions from cosponsors amount to about $300 million a year, much of which is distributed in prize money.

There are various ways of gaining entry into particular tours. For example, a player who wins three NIKE TOUR events in the same year, or is among the top-15 money winners on that tour, earns the right to play in the PGA TOUR. Additionally, a golfer may obtain a spot in an official tournament through successfully competing in "open" qualifying rounds, which are conducted the week before each tournament. Most participants, however, earn playing privileges in the PGA TOUR or NIKE TOUR by way of a three-stage qualifying tournament known as the "Q-School."

Any member of the public may enter the Q-School by paying a $3,000 entry fee and submitting two letters of reference from, among others, PGA TOUR or NIKE TOUR members. The $3,000 entry fee covers the players' greens fees and the cost of golf carts, which are permitted during the first two stages, but which have been prohibited during the third stage since 1997. Each year, over a thousand contestants compete in the first stage, which consists of four 18-hole rounds at different locations. Approximately half of them make it to the second stage, which also includes 72 holes. Around 168 players survive the second stage and advance to the final one, where they compete over 108 holes. Of those finalists, about a fourth qualify for membership in the PGA TOUR, and the rest gain membership in the NIKE TOUR. The significance of making it into either tour is illuminated by the fact that there are about 25 million golfers in the country.[2]

Three sets of rules govern competition in tour events. First, the "Rules of Golf," jointly written by the United States Golf Association (USGA) and the Royal and Ancient Golf Club of Scotland, apply to the game as it is played, not only by millions of amateurs on public courses and in private country clubs throughout the United States and worldwide, but also by the professionals in the tournaments conducted by petitioner, the USGA, the Ladies' Professional Golf Association, and the Senior Women's Golf Association. Those rules do not prohibit the use of golf carts at any time.[3]

Second, the "Conditions of Competition and Local Rules," often described as the "hard card," apply specifically to petitioner's professional tours. The hard cards for the PGA TOUR and NIKE TOUR require players to walk the golf course during tournaments, but not during open qualifying rounds.[4] ON THE SENIOR PGA tour, WHICH IS LIMITED to golfers age 50 and older,

continued

the contestants may use golf carts. Most seniors, however, prefer to walk.[5]

Third, "Notices to Competitors" are issued for particular tournaments and cover conditions for that specific event. Such a notice may, for example, explain how the Rules of Golf should be applied to a particular water hazard or man-made obstruction. It might also authorize the use of carts to speed up play when there is an unusual distance between one green and the next tee.[6]

The basic Rules of Golf, the hard cards, and the weekly notices apply equally to all players in tour competitions. As one of petitioner's witnesses explained with reference to "the Masters Tournament, which is golf at its very highest level . . . the key is to have everyone tee off on the first hole under exactly the same conditions and all of them be tested over that 72-hole event under the conditions that exist during those four days of the event." App. 192.

II.

Casey Martin is a talented golfer. As an amateur, he won 17 Oregon Golf Association junior events before he was 15, and won the state championship as a high school senior. He played on the Stanford University golf team that won the 1994 National Collegiate Athletic Association (NCAA) championship. As a professional, Martin qualified for the NIKE TOUR in 1998 and 1999, and based on his 1999 performance, qualified for the PGA TOUR in 2000. In the 1999 season, he entered 24 events, made the cut 13 times, and had 6 top-10 finishes, coming in second twice and third once.

Martin is also an individual with a disability as defined in the Americans with Disabilities Act of 1990 (ADA or Act).[7] Since birth he has been afflicted with Klippel-Trenaunay-Weber Syndrome, a degenerative circulatory disorder that obstructs the flow of blood from his right leg back to his heart. The disease is progressive; it causes severe pain and has atrophied his right leg. During the latter part of his college career, because of the progress of the disease, Martin could no longer walk an 18-hole golf course.[8] Walking not only caused him pain, fatigue, and anxiety, but also created a significant risk of hemorrhaging, developing blood clots, and fracturing his tibia so badly that an amputation might be required. For these reasons, Stanford made written requests to the Pacific 10 Conference and the NCAA to waive for Martin their rules requiring players to walk and carry their own clubs. The requests were granted.[9]

When Martin turned pro and entered petitioner's Q-School, the hard card permitted him to use a cart during his successful progress through the first two stages. He made a request, supported by detailed medical records, for permission to use a golf cart during the third stage. Petitioner refused to review those records or to waive its walking rule for the third stage. Martin therefore filed this action. A preliminary injunction entered by the District Court made it possible for him to use a cart in the final stage of the Q-School and as a competitor in the NIKE TOUR and PGA TOUR. Although not bound by the injunction, and despite its support for petitioner's position in this litigation, the USGA voluntarily granted Martin a similar waiver in events that it sponsors, including the U.S. Open.

III.

In the District Court, petitioner moved for summary judgment on the ground that it is exempt from coverage under Title III of the ADA as a "private clu[b] or establishmen[t],"[10] or alternatively, that the play areas of its tour competitions do not constitute places of "public accommodation" within the scope of that Title.[11] The Magistrate Judge concluded that petitioner should be viewed as a commercial enterprise operating in the entertainment industry for the economic benefit of its members rather than as a private club. Furthermore, after noting that the statutory definition of public accommodation included a "golf course,"[12] he rejected petitioner's argument that its competitions are only places of public accommodation in the areas open to spectators. The operator of a public accommodation could not, in his view, "create private enclaves within the facility . . . and thus relegate the ADA to hop-scotch areas." 984 F.Supp. 1320, 1326–1327 (D.Or.1998). Accordingly, he denied petitioner's motion for summary judgment.

At trial, petitioner did not contest the conclusion that Martin has a disability covered by the ADA, or the fact "that his disability prevents him from walking the course during a round of golf." 994 F.Supp. 1242, 1244 (D.Or.1998). Rather, petitioner asserted that the condition of walking is a substantive rule of competition, and that waiving it as to any individual for any reason would fundamentally alter the nature of the competition.

Petitioner's evidence included the testimony of a number of experts, among them some of the greatest golfers in history. Arnold Palmer,[13] Jack Nicklaus,[14] and Ken Venturi[15] explained that fatigue can be a critical factor in a tournament, particularly on the last day when psychological pressure is at a maximum. Their testimony makes it clear that, in their view, permission to use a cart might well give some players a competitive advantage over other players who must walk. They did not, however, express any opinion on whether a cart would give Martin such an advantage.[16]

Rejecting petitioner's argument that an individualized inquiry into the necessity of the walking rule in Martin's case would be inappropriate, the District Court stated that it had "the independent duty to inquire into the purpose of the rule at issue, and to ascertain whether there can be a reasonable modification made to accommodate plaintiff without frustrating the purpose of the rule" and thereby fundamentally altering the nature of petitioner's tournaments. Id., at 1246. The judge found that the purpose of the rule was to inject fatigue into the skill of shot-making, but that the fatigue injected "by walking the course cannot be deemed significant under normal circumstances." Id., at 1250. Furthermore, Martin presented evidence, and the judge found, that even with the use of a cart, Martin must walk over a mile during an 18-hole round,[17] and that the fatigue he suffers from coping with his disability is "undeniably greater" than the fatigue his able-bodied competitors endure from walking the course. Id., at 1251. As the judge observed:

"[P]laintiff is in significant pain when he walks, and even when he is getting in and out of the cart. With each step, he is at risk of fracturing his tibia and hemorrhaging. The other golfers have to endure the psychological stress of competition as part of their fatigue; Martin has the same stress plus the added stress of pain and risk of serious injury. As he put it, he would gladly trade the cart for a good leg. To perceive that the cart puts him–with his condition–at a competitive advantage is a gross distortion of reality." Id., at 1251–1252.

As a result, the judge concluded that it would "not fundamentally alter the nature of the PGA Tour's game to accommodate him with a cart." Id., at 1252. The judge accordingly entered a permanent injunction requiring petitioner to permit Martin to use a cart in tour and qualifying events.

On appeal to the Ninth Circuit, petitioner did not challenge the District Court's rejection of its claim that it was exempt as a "private club," but it renewed the contention that during a tournament the portion of the golf course "'behind the ropes' is not a public accommodation because the public has no right to enter it." 204 F.3d 994, 997 (2000). The Court of Appeals viewed that contention as resting on the incorrect assumption that the competition among participants was not itself public. The court first pointed out that, as with a private university, "the fact that users of a facility are highly selected does not mean that the facility cannot be a public accommodation." Id., at 998.[18] In its opinion, the competition to enter the select circle of PGA TOUR and NIKE TOUR golfers was comparable because "[a]ny member of the public who pays a $3000 entry fee and supplies two letters of recommendation may try out in the qualifying school." Id., at 999. The court saw "no justification in reason or in the statute to draw a line beyond which the performance of athletes becomes so excellent that a competition restricted to their level deprives its situs of the character of a public accommodation." Ibid. Nor did it find a basis for distinguishing between "use of a place of public accommodation for pleasure and use in the pursuit of a living." Ibid. Consequently, the Court of Appeals concluded that golf courses remain places of public accommodation during PGA tournaments. Ibid.

On the merits, because there was no serious dispute about the fact that permitting Martin to use a golf cart was both a reasonable and a necessary solution to the problem of providing him access to the tournaments, the Court of Appeals regarded the central dispute as whether such permission would "fundamentally alter" the nature of the PGA TOUR or NIKE TOUR. Like the District Court, the Court of Appeals viewed the issue not as "whether use of carts generally would fundamentally alter the competition, but whether the use of a cart by Martin would do so." Id., at 1001. That issue turned on "an intensively fact-based inquiry," and, the court concluded, had been correctly resolved by the trial judge. In its words, "[a]ll that the cart does is permit Martin access to a type of competition in which he otherwise could not engage because of his disability." Id., at 1000.

The day after the Ninth Circuit ruled in Martin's favor, the Seventh Circuit came to a contrary conclusion in a case brought against the USGA by a disabled golfer who

continued

failed to qualify for "America's greatest–and most democratic–golf tournament, the United States Open." *Olinger v. United States Golf Assn.*, 205 F.3d 1001 (C.A.7 2000).[19] The Seventh Circuit endorsed the conclusion of the District Court in that case that "the nature of the competition would be fundamentally altered if the walking rule were eliminated because it would remove stamina (at least a particular type of stamina) from the set of qualities designed to be tested in this competition." *Id.*, at 1006 (internal quotation marks omitted). In the Seventh Circuit's opinion, the physical ordeals endured by Ken Venturi and Ben Hogan when they walked to their Open victories in 1964 and 1950 amply demonstrated the importance of stamina in such a tournament.[20] As an alternative basis for its holding, the court also concluded that the ADA does not require the USGA to bear "the administrative burdens of evaluating requests to waive the walking rule and permit the use of a golf cart." *Id.*, at 1007.

Although the Seventh Circuit merely assumed that the ADA applies to professional golf tournaments, and therefore did not disagree with the Ninth on the threshold coverage issue, our grant of certiorari, 530 U.S. 1306, 121 S.Ct. 30, 147 L.Ed.2d 1052 (2000), encompasses that question as well as the conflict between those courts.

IV.

Congress enacted the ADA in 1990 to remedy widespread discrimination against disabled individuals. In studying the need for such legislation, Congress found that "historically, society has tended to isolate and segregate individuals with disabilities, and, despite some improvements, such forms of discrimination against individuals with disabilities continue to be a serious and pervasive social problem." 42 U.S.C. § 12101(a)(2); see § 12101(a)(3) ("[D]iscrimination against individuals with disabilities persists in such critical areas as employment, housing, public accommodations, education, transportation, communication, recreation, institutionalization, health services, voting, and access to public services"). Congress noted that the many forms such discrimination takes include "outright intentional exclusion" as well as the "failure to make modifications to existing facilities and practices." § 12101(a)(5). After thoroughly investigating the problem, Congress concluded that there was a "compelling need" for a

"clear and comprehensive national mandate" to eliminate discrimination against disabled individuals, and to integrate them "into the economic and social mainstream of American life." S.Rep. No. 101–116, p. 20 (1989); H.R.Rep. No. 101–485, pt. 2, p. 50 (1990), U.S.Code Cong. & Admin.News 1990, pt. 2, pp. 303, 332.

In the ADA, Congress provided that broad mandate. See 42 U.S.C. § 12101(b). In fact, one of the Act's "most impressive strengths" has been identified as its "comprehensive character," Hearings on S. 933 before the Senate Committee on Labor and Human Resources and the Subcommittee on the Handicapped, 101st Cong., 1st Sess., 197 (1989) (statement of Attorney General Thornburgh), and accordingly the Act has been described as "a milestone on the path to a more decent, tolerant, progressive society," *Board of Trustees of Univ. of Ala. v. Garrett*, 531 U.S. 356, 375, 121 S.Ct. 955, 148 L.Ed.2d 866 (2001) (KENNEDY, J., concurring). To effectuate its sweeping purpose, the ADA forbids discrimination against disabled individuals in major areas of public life, among them employment (Title I of the Act),[21] public services (Title II),[22] and public accommodations (Title III).[23] At issue now, as a threshold matter, is the applicability of Title III to petitioner's golf tours and qualifying rounds, in particular to petitioner's treatment of a qualified disabled golfer wishing to compete in those events.

Title III of the ADA prescribes, as a "[g]eneral rule":

> "No individual shall be discriminated against on the basis of disability in the full and equal enjoyment of the goods, services, facilities, privileges, advantages, or accommodations of any place of public accommodation by any person who owns, leases (or leases to), or operates a place of public accommodation." 42 U.S.C. § 12182(a).

The phrase "public accommodation" is defined in terms of 12 extensive categories,[24] which the legislative history indicates "should be construed liberally" to afford people with disabilities "equal access" to the wide variety of establishments available to the nondisabled.[25]

[1] It seems apparent, from both the general rule and the comprehensive definition of "public accommodation," that petitioner's golf tours and their qualifying rounds fit comfortably within the coverage of Title III, and Martin within its protection. The events occur on

"golf course[s]," a type of place specifically identified by the Act as a public accommodation. § 12181(7)(L). In addition, at all relevant times, petitioner "leases" and "operates" golf courses to conduct its Q-School and tours. § 12182(a). As a lessor and operator of golf courses, then, petitioner must not discriminate against any "individual" in the "full and equal enjoyment of the goods, services, facilities, privileges, advantages, or accommodations" of those courses. Ibid. Certainly, among the "privileges" offered by petitioner on the courses are those of competing in the Q-School and playing in the tours; indeed, the former is a privilege for which thousands of individuals from the general public pay, and the latter is one for which they vie. Martin, of course, is one of those individuals. It would therefore appear that Title III of the ADA, by its plain terms, prohibits petitioner from denying Martin equal access to its tours on the basis of his disability. Cf. *Pennsylvania Dept. of Corrections v. Yeskey*, 524 U.S. 206, 209, 118 S.Ct. 1952, 141 L.Ed.2d 215 (1998) (holding that text of Title II's prohibition of discrimination by "public entities" against disabled individuals "unmistakably includes State prisons and prisoners within its coverage").

[2] Petitioner argues otherwise. To be clear about its position, it does not assert (as it did in the District Court) that it is a private club altogether exempt from Title III's coverage. In fact, petitioner admits that its tournaments are conducted at places of public accommodation.[26] Nor does petitioner contend (as it did in both the District Court and the Court of Appeals) that the competitors' area "behind the ropes" is not a public accommodation, notwithstanding the status of the rest of the golf course. Rather, petitioner reframes the coverage issue by arguing that the competing golfers are not members of the class protected by Title III of the ADA.[27]

[3] According to petitioner, Title III is concerned with discrimination against "clients and customers" seeking to obtain "goods and services" at places of public accommodation, whereas it is Title I that protects persons who work at such places.[28] As the argument goes, petitioner operates not a "golf course" during its tournaments but a "place of exhibition or entertainment," 42 U.S.C. § 12181(7)(C), and a professional golfer such as Martin, like an actor in a theater production, is a provider rather than a consumer of the entertainment that petitioner sells to the public. Martin therefore cannot bring a claim under Title III because he is not one of the "'*clients or customers* of the covered public accommodation.'"[29] Rather, Martin's claim of discrimination is "job-related"[30] and could only be brought under Title I–but that Title does not apply because he is an independent contractor (as the District Court found) rather than an employee.

[4] The reference to "clients or customers" that petitioner quotes appears in 42 U.S.C. § 12182(b)(1)(A)(iv), which states: "For purposes of clauses (i) through (iii) of this subparagraph, the term 'individual or class of individuals' refers to the clients or customers of the covered public accommodation that enters into the contractual, licensing or other arrangement." Clauses (i) through (iii) of the subparagraph prohibit public accommodations from discriminating against a disabled "individual or class of individuals" in certain ways[31] either directly or indirectly through contractual arrangements with other entities. Those clauses make clear on the one hand that their prohibitions cannot be avoided by means of contract, while clause (iv) makes clear on the other hand that contractual relationships will not expand a public accommodation's obligations under the subparagraph beyond its own clients or customers.

As petitioner recognizes, clause (iv) is not literally applicable to Title III's general rule prohibiting discrimination against disabled individuals.[32] Title III's broad general rule contains no express "clients or customers" limitation, § 12182(a), and § 12182(b)(1)(A)(iv) provides that its limitation is only "[f]or purposes of" the clauses in that separate subparagraph. Nevertheless, petitioner contends that clause (iv)'s restriction of the subparagraph's coverage to the clients or customers of public accommodations fairly describes the scope of Title III's protection as a whole.

We need not decide whether petitioner's construction of the statute is correct, because petitioner's argument falters even on its own terms. If Title III's protected class were limited to "clients or customers," it would be entirely appropriate to classify the golfers who pay petitioner $3,000 for the chance to compete in the Q-School and, if successful, in the subsequent tour events, as petitioner's clients or customers. In our view, petitioner's tournaments (whether situated at a "golf course" or at a "place of exhibition or entertainment") simultaneously offer at least two "privileges" to the public–that of watching the golf competition and

continued

that of competing in it. Although the latter is more difficult and more expensive to obtain than the former, it is nonetheless a privilege that petitioner makes available to members of the general public. In consideration of the entry fee, any golfer with the requisite letters of recommendation acquires the opportunity to qualify for and compete in petitioner's tours. Additionally, any golfer who succeeds in the open qualifying rounds for a tournament may play in the event. That petitioner identifies one set of clients or customers that it serves (spectators at tournaments) does not preclude it from having another set (players in tournaments) against whom it may not discriminate. It would be inconsistent with the literal text of the statute as well as its expansive purpose to read Title III's coverage, even given petitioner's suggested limitation, any less broadly.[33]

[5] Our conclusion is consistent with case law in the analogous context of Title II of the Civil Rights Act of 1964, 78 Stat. 243, 42 U.S.C. § 2000a *et seq.* Title II of that Act prohibits public accommodations from discriminating on the basis of race, color, religion, or national origin. § 2000a(a). In *Daniel v. Paul,* 395 U.S. 298, 306, 89 S.Ct. 1697, 23 L.Ed.2d 318 (1969), applying Title II to the Lake Nixon Club in Little Rock, Arkansas, we held that the definition of a "place of exhibition or entertainment," as a public accommodation, covered participants "in some sport or activity" as well as "spectators or listeners." We find equally persuasive two lower court opinions applying Title II specifically to golfers and golf tournaments. In *Evans v. Laurel Links, Inc.,* 261 F.Supp. 474, 477 (E.D.Va.1966), a class action brought to require a commercial golf establishment to permit black golfers to play on its course, the District Court held that Title II "is not limited to spectators if the place of exhibition or entertainment provides facilities for the public to participate in the entertainment."[34] And in *Wesley v. Savannah,* 294 F.Supp. 698 (S.D.Ga.1969), the District Court found that a private association violated Title II when it limited entry in a golf tournament on a municipal course to its own members but permitted all (and only) white golfers who paid the membership and entry fees to compete.[35] These cases support our conclusion that, as a public accommodation during its tours and qualifying rounds, petitioner may not discriminate against either spectators or competitors on the basis of disability.

V.

[6] As we have noted, 42 U.S.C. § 12182(a) sets forth Title III's general rule prohibiting public accommodations from discriminating against individuals because of their disabilities. The question whether petitioner has violated that rule depends on a proper construction of the term "discrimination," which is defined by Title III to include:

> "a failure to make reasonable modifications in policies, practices, or procedures, when such modifications are necessary to afford such goods, services, facilities, privileges, advantages, or accommodations to individuals with disabilities, *unless the entity can demonstrate that making such modifications would fundamentally alter the nature* of such goods, services, facilities, privileges, advantages, or accommodations." § 12182(b)(2)(A)(ii) (emphasis added).

Petitioner does not contest that a golf cart is a reasonable modification that is necessary if Martin is to play in its tournaments. Martin's claim thus differs from one that might be asserted by players with less serious afflictions that make walking the course uncomfortable or difficult, but not beyond their capacity. In such cases, an accommodation might be reasonable but not necessary. In this case, however, the narrow dispute is whether allowing Martin to use a golf cart, despite the walking requirement that applies to the PGA TOUR, the NIKE TOUR, and the third stage of the Q-School, is a modification that would "fundamentally alter the nature" of those events.

[7] In theory, a modification of petitioner's golf tournaments might constitute a fundamental alteration in two different ways. It might alter such an essential aspect of the game of golf that it would be unacceptable even if it affected all competitors equally; changing the diameter of the hole from three to six inches might be such a modification.[36] Alternatively, a less significant change that has only a peripheral impact on the game itself might nevertheless give a disabled player, in addition to access to the competition as required by Title III, an advantage over others and, for that reason, fundamentally alter the character of the competition.[37] We are not persuaded that a waiver of the walking rule for Martin would work a fundamental alteration in either sense.[38]

As an initial matter, we observe that the use of carts is not itself inconsistent with the fundamental character of the game of golf. From early on, the essence of the game has been shot-making–using clubs to cause a ball to progress from the teeing ground to a hole some distance away with as few strokes as possible.[39] That essential aspect of the game is still reflected in the very first of the Rules of Golf, which declares: "The Game of Golf consists in playing a ball from the *teeing ground* into the hole by a *stroke* or successive strokes in accordance with the rules." Rule 1–1, Rules of Golf, App. 104 (italics in original). Over the years, there have been many changes in the players' equipment, in golf course design, in the Rules of Golf, and in the method of transporting clubs from hole to hole.[40] Originally, so few clubs were used that each player could carry them without a bag. Then came golf bags, caddies, carts that were pulled by hand, and eventually motorized carts that carried players as well as clubs. "Golf carts started appearing with increasing regularity on American golf courses in the 1950's. Today they are everywhere. And they are encouraged. For one thing, they often speed up play, and for another, they are great revenue producers."[41] There is nothing in the Rules of Golf that either forbids the use of carts, or penalizes a player for using a cart. That set of rules, as we have observed, is widely accepted in both the amateur and professional golf world as the rules of the game.[42] The walking rule that is contained in petitioner's hard cards, based on an optional condition buried in an appendix to the Rules of Golf,[43] is not an essential attribute of the game itself.

Indeed, the walking rule is not an indispensable feature of tournament golf either. As already mentioned, petitioner permits golf carts to be used in the SENIOR PGA TOUR, the open qualifying events for petitioner's tournaments, the first two stages of the Q-School, and, until 1997, the third stage of the Q- School as well. See *supra*, at 1884–1885. Moreover, petitioner allows the use of carts during certain tournament rounds in both the PGA TOUR and the NIKE TOUR. See *supra*, at 1885, and n. 6. In addition, although the USGA enforces a walking rule in most of the tournaments that it sponsors, it permits carts in the Senior Amateur and the Senior Women's Amateur championships.[44]

Petitioner, however, distinguishes the game of golf as it is generally played from the game that it sponsors in the PGA TOUR, NIKE TOUR, and (at least recently)

the last stage of the Q-School–golf at the "highest level." According to petitioner, "[t]he goal of the highest-level competitive athletics is to assess and compare the performance of different competitors, a task that is meaningful only if the competitors are subject to identical substantive rules."[45] The waiver of any possibly "outcome-affecting" rule for a contestant would violate this principle and therefore, in petitioner's view, fundamentally alter the nature of the highest level athletic event.[46] The walking rule is one such rule, petitioner submits, because its purpose is "to inject the element of fatigue into the skill of shot-making,"[47] and thus its effect may be the critical loss of a stroke. As a consequence, the reasonable modification Martin seeks would fundamentally alter the nature of petitioner's highest level tournaments even if he were the only person in the world who has both the talent to compete in those elite events and a disability sufficiently serious that he cannot do so without using a cart.

The force of petitioner's argument is, first of all, mitigated by the fact that golf is a game in which it is impossible to guarantee that all competitors will play under exactly the same conditions or that an individual's ability will be the sole determinant of the outcome. For example, changes in the weather may produce harder greens and more head winds for the tournament leader than for his closest pursuers. A lucky bounce may save a shot or two.[48] Whether such happenstance events are more or less probable than the likelihood that a golfer afflicted with Klippel-Trenaunay-Weber Syndrome would one day qualify for the NIKE TOUR and PGA TOUR, they at least demonstrate that pure chance may have a greater impact on the outcome of elite golf tournaments than the fatigue resulting from the enforcement of the walking rule.

Further, the factual basis of petitioner's argument is undermined by the District Court's finding that the fatigue from walking during one of petitioner's 4-day tournaments cannot be deemed significant. The District Court credited the testimony of a professor in physiology and expert on fatigue, who calculated the calories expended in walking a golf course (about five miles) to be approximately 500 calories–"nutritionally . . . less than a Big Mac." 994 F.Supp., at 1250. What is more, that energy is expended over a 5-hour period, during which golfers have numerous intervals for rest and

continued

refreshment. In fact, the expert concluded, because golf is a low intensity activity, fatigue from the game is primarily a psychological phenomenon in which stress and motivation are the key ingredients. And even under conditions of severe heat and humidity, the critical factor in fatigue is fluid loss rather than exercise from walking.

Moreover, when given the option of using a cart, the majority of golfers in petitioner's tournaments have chosen to walk, often to relieve stress or for other strategic reasons.[49] As NIKE TOUR member Eric Johnson testified, walking allows him to keep in rhythm, stay warmer when it is chilly, and develop a better sense of the elements and the course than riding a cart.[50]

[8] Even if we accept the factual predicate for petitioner's argument–that the walking rule is "outcome affecting" because fatigue may adversely affect performance–its legal position is fatally flawed. Petitioner's refusal to consider Martin's personal circumstances in deciding whether to accommodate his disability runs counter to the clear language and purpose of the ADA. As previously stated, the ADA was enacted to eliminate discrimination against "individuals" with disabilities, 42 U.S.C. § 12101(b)(1), and to that end Title III of the Act requires without exception that any "policies, practices, or procedures" of a public accommodation be reasonably modified for disabled "individuals" as necessary to afford access unless doing so would fundamentally alter what is offered, § 12182(b)(2)(A)(ii). To comply with this command, an individualized inquiry must be made to determine whether a specific modification for a particular person's disability would be reasonable under the circumstances as well as necessary for that person, and yet at the same time not work a fundamental alteration. See S.Rep. No. 101–116, at 61; H.R.Rep. No. 101–485, pt. 2, at 102, U.S.Code Cong. & Admin.News 1990, pt. 2, at pp. 303, 385 (public accommodations "are required to make decisions based on facts applicable to individuals"). Cf. *Sutton v. United Air Lines, Inc.,* 527 U.S. 471, 483, 119 S.Ct. 2139, 144 L.Ed.2d 450 (1999) ("[W]hether a person has a disability under the ADA is an individualized inquiry").

[9][10] To be sure, the waiver of an essential rule of competition for anyone would fundamentally alter the nature of petitioner's tournaments. As we have demonstrated, however, the walking rule is at best

peripheral to the nature of petitioner's athletic events, and thus it might be waived in individual cases without working a fundamental alteration. Therefore, petitioner's claim that all the substantive rules for its "highest-level" competitions are sacrosanct and cannot be modified under any circumstances is effectively a contention that it is exempt from Title III's reasonable modification requirement. But that provision carves out no exemption for elite athletics, and given Title III's coverage not only of places of "exhibition or entertainment" but also of "golf course[s]," 42 U.S.C. §§ 12181(7)(C), (L), its application to petitioner's tournaments cannot be said to be unintended or unexpected, see §§ 12101 (a)(1), (5). Even if it were, "the fact that a statute can be applied in situations not expressly anticipated by Congress does not demonstrate ambiguity. It demonstrates breadth." *Pennsylvania Dept. of Corrections v. Yeskey,* 524 U.S., at 212, 118 S.Ct. 1952 (internal quotation marks omitted).[51]

Under the ADA's basic requirement that the need of a disabled person be evaluated on an individual basis, we have no doubt that allowing Martin to use a golf cart would not fundamentally alter the nature of petitioner's tournaments. As we have discussed, the purpose of the walking rule is to subject players to fatigue, which in turn may influence the outcome of tournaments. Even if the rule does serve that purpose, it is an uncontested finding of the District Court that Martin "easily endures greater fatigue even with a cart than his able-bodied competitors do by walking." 994 F.Supp., at 1252. The purpose of the walking rule is therefore not compromised in the slightest by allowing Martin to use a cart. A modification that provides an exception to a peripheral tournament rule without impairing its purpose cannot be said to "fundamentally alter" the tournament. What it can be said to do, on the other hand, is to allow Martin the chance to qualify for and compete in the athletic events petitioner offers to those members of the public who have the skill and desire to enter. That is exactly what the ADA requires.[52] As a result, Martin's request for a waiver of the walking rule should have been granted.

[11] The ADA admittedly imposes some administrative burdens on the operators of places of public accommodation that could be avoided by strictly adhering to general rules and policies that are entirely

fair with respect to the able-bodied but that may indiscriminately preclude access by qualified persons with disabilities.[53] But surely, in a case of this kind, Congress intended that an entity like the PGA not only give individualized attention to the handful of requests that it might receive from talented but disabled athletes for a modification or waiver of a rule to allow them access to the competition, but also carefully weigh the purpose, as well as the letter, of the rule before determining that no accommodation would be tolerable.

The judgment of the Court of Appeals is affirmed.

It is so ordered.

Justice SCALIA, with whom Justice THOMAS joins, dissenting.

In my view today's opinion exercises a benevolent compassion that the law does not place it within our power to impose. The judgment distorts the text of Title III, the structure of the ADA, and common sense. I respectfully dissent.

I.

The Court holds that a professional sport is a place of public accommodation and that respondent is a "custome[r]" of "competition" when he practices his profession. *Ante,* at 1891–1892. It finds, *ante,* at 1892, that this strange conclusion is compelled by the "literal text" of Title III of the Americans with Disabilities Act of 1990(ADA), 42 U.S.C. § 12101 *et seq.,* by the "expansive purpose" of the ADA, and by the fact that Title II of the Civil Rights Act of 1964, 42 U.S.C. § 2000a(a), has been applied to an amusement park and public golf courses. I disagree.

The ADA has three separate titles: Title I covers employment discrimination, Title II covers discrimination by government entities, and Title III covers discrimination by places of public accommodation. Title II is irrelevant to this case. Title I protects only "employees" of employers who have 15 or more employees, §§ 12112(a), 12111(5)(A). It does not protect independent contractors. See, *e.g., Birchem v. Knights of Columbus,* 116 F.3d 310, 312–313 (C.A.8 1997); cf. *Nationwide Mut. Ins. Co. v. Darden,* 503 U.S. 318, 322–323, 112 S.Ct. 1344, 117 L.Ed.2d 581 (1992). Respondent claimed employment discrimination under Title I, but the District Court found him to be an independent contractor rather than an employee.

Respondent also claimed protection under § 12182 of Title III. That section applies only to particular places and persons. The place must be a "place of public accommodation," and the person must be an "individual" seeking "enjoyment of the goods, services, facilities, privileges, advantages, or accommodations" of the covered place. § 12182(a). Of course a court indiscriminately invoking the "sweeping" and "expansive" purposes of the ADA, *ante,* at 1889–1890, 1892, could argue that when a place of public accommodation denied *any* "individual," on the basis of his disability, *anything* that might be called a "privileg[e]," the individual has a valid Title III claim. Cf. *ante,* at 1890. On such an interpretation, the employees and independent contractors of every place of public accommodation come within Title III: The employee enjoys the "privilege" of employment, the contractor the "privilege" of the contract.

For many reasons, Title III will not bear such an interpretation. The provision of Title III at issue here (§ 12182, its principal provision) is a public-accommodation law, and it is the traditional understanding of public-accommodation laws that they provide rights for customers. "At common law, innkeepers, smiths, and others who made profession of a public employment, were prohibited from refusing, without good reason, to serve a customer." *Hurley v. Irish-American Gay, Lesbian and Bisexual Group of Boston, Inc.,*.515 U.S. 557, 571, 115 S.Ct. 2338, 132 L.Ed.2d 487 (1995) (internal quotation marks omitted). See also *Heart of Atlanta Motel, Inc. v. United States,* 379 U.S. 241, 85 S.Ct. 348, 13 L.Ed.2d 258 (1964). This understanding is clearly reflected in the text of Title III itself. Section 12181(7) lists 12 specific types of entities that qualify as "public accommodations," with a follow-on expansion that makes it clear what the "enjoyment of the goods, services, etc." of those entities consists of–and it plainly envisions that the person "enjoying" the "public accommodation" will be a *customer.* For example, Title III is said to cover an "auditorium" or "other place of public gathering," § 12181(7)(D). Thus, "gathering" is the distinctive enjoyment derived from an auditorium; the persons "gathering" at an auditorium are presumably covered by Title III, but those contracting to clean the auditorium are not. Title III is said to cover a "zoo" or "other place of recreation," § 12181(7)(I). The persons "recreat[ing]" at a "zoo" are presumably covered, but the animal handlers bringing in the latest panda are not. The one place where Title

continued

III specifically addresses discrimination by places of public accommodation through "contractual" arrangements, it makes clear that discrimination against the other party to the contract is not covered, but only discrimination against "clients or customers of the covered public accommodation that enters into the contractual, licensing or other arrangement." § 12182(b)(1)(A)(iv). And finally, the regulations promulgated by the Department of Justice reinforce the conclusion that Title III's protections extend only to customers. "The purpose of the ADA's public accommodations requirements," they say, "is to ensure accessibility to the goods offered by a public accommodation." 28 CFR, Ch. 1, pt. 36, App. B, p. 650 (2000). Surely this has nothing to do with employees and independent contractors.

If there were any doubt left that § 12182 covers only clients and customers of places of public accommodation, it is eliminated by the fact that a contrary interpretation would make a muddle of the ADA as a whole. The words of Title III must be read "in their context and with a view to their place in the overall statutory scheme." *Davis v. Michigan Dept. of Treasury,* 489 U.S. 803, 809, 109 S.Ct. 1500, 103 L.Ed.2d 891 (1989). Congress expressly excluded employers of fewer than 15 employees from Title I. The mom-and-pop grocery store or laundromat need not worry about altering the nonpublic areas of its place of business to accommodate handicapped employees—or about the litigation that failure to do so will invite. Similarly, since independent contractors are not covered by Title I, the small business (or the large one, for that matter) need not worry about making special accommodations for the painters, electricians, and other independent workers whose services are contracted for from time to time. It is an entirely unreasonable interpretation of the statute to say that these exemptions so carefully crafted in Title I are entirely eliminated by Title III (for the many businesses that are places of public accommodation) because employees and independent contractors "enjoy" the employment and contracting that such places provide. The only distinctive feature of places of public accommodation is that they accommodate the public, and Congress could have no conceivable reason for according the employees and independent contractors of such businesses protections that employees

and independent contractors of other businesses do not enjoy.

The United States apparently agrees that employee claims are not cognizable under Title III, see Brief for United States as *Amicus Curiae* 18- 19, n. 17, but despite the implications of its own regulations, see 28 CFR, Ch. 1, pt. 36, App. B, p. 650 (2000), appears to believe (though it does not explicitly state) that claims of independent contractors are cognizable. In a discussion littered with entirely vague statements from the legislative history, cf. *ante,* at 1889, the United States argues that Congress presumably wanted independent contractors with private entities covered under Title III because independent contractors with governmental entities are covered by Title II, see Brief for United States as *Amicus Curiae* 18, and n. 17–a line of reasoning that does not commend itself to the untutored intellect. But since the United States does not provide (and I cannot conceive of) any possible construction of the *terms* of Title III that will exclude employees while simultaneously covering independent contractors, its concession regarding employees effectively concedes independent contractors as well. Title III applies only to customers.

The Court, for its part, assumes that conclusion for the sake of argument, *ante,* at 1891–1892, but pronounces respondent to be a "customer" of the PGA TOUR or of the golf courses on which it is played. That seems to me quite incredible. The PGA TOUR is a professional sporting event, staged for the entertainment of a live and TV audience, the receipts from whom (the TV audience's admission price is paid by advertisers) pay the expenses of the tour, including the cash prizes for the winning golfers. The professional golfers on the tour are no more "enjoying" (the statutory term) the entertainment that the tour provides, or the facilities of the golf courses on which it is held, than professional baseball players "enjoy" the baseball games in which they play or the facilities of Yankee Stadium. To be sure, professional ballplayers *participate* in the games, and *use* the ballfields, but no one in his right mind would think that they are *customers* of the American League or of Yankee Stadium. They are themselves the entertainment that the customers pay to watch. And professional golfers are no different. It makes not a bit of difference, insofar as their "customer" status is concerned, that the remuneration for their performance (unlike most of the remuneration for ballplayers) is not fixed but contingent–viz., the purses for the winners in the various events, and the compensation from product endorsements that consistent winners are assured. The compensation of *many* independent contractors is contingent upon their success–real estate brokers, for example, or insurance salesmen.

As the Court points out, the ADA specifically identifies golf courses as one of the covered places of public accommodation. See § 12181(7)(L) ("a gymnasium, health spa, bowling alley, golf course, or other place of exercise or recreation"); and the distinctive "goo[d], servic[e], facilit[y], privileg[e], advantag[e], or accommodatio[n]" identified by that provision as distinctive to that category of place of public accommodation is "exercise or recreation." Respondent did not seek to "exercise" or "recreate" at the PGA TOUR events; he sought to make money (which is why he is called a *professional* golfer). He was not a customer *buying* recreation or entertainment; he was a professional athlete selling it. That is the reason (among others) the Court's reliance upon Civil Rights Act cases like *Daniel v. Paul*, 395 U.S. 298, 89 S.Ct. 1697, 23 L.Ed.2d 318 (1969), see *ante*, at 1892–1893, is misplaced. A professional golfer's practicing his profession is not comparable to John Q. Public's frequenting "a 232-acre amusement area with swimming, boating, sun bathing, picnicking, miniature golf, dancing facilities, and a snack bar." *Daniel, supra*, at 301, 89 S.Ct. 1697.

The Court relies heavily upon the Q-School. It says that petitioner offers the golfing public the "privilege" of "competing in the Q-School and playing in the tours; indeed, the former is a privilege for which thousands of individuals from the general public pay, and the latter is one for which they vie." *Ante*, at 1890–1891. But the Q-School is no more a "privilege" offered for the general public's "enjoyment" than is the California Bar Exam.[1] It is a competition for entry into the PGA TOUR–an open tryout, no different in principle from open casting for a movie or stage production, or walk-on tryouts for other professional sports, such as baseball. See, *e.g.*, Amateurs Join Pros for New Season of HBO's "Sopranos," Detroit News, Dec. 22, 2000, p. 2 (20,000 attend open casting for "The Sopranos"); Bill Zack, Atlanta Braves, Sporting News, Feb. 6, 1995 (1,300 would-be players attended an open tryout for the Atlanta Braves). It may well be that some amateur golfers enjoy trying to make the grade, just as some

amateur actors may enjoy auditions, and amateur baseball players may enjoy open tryouts (I hesitate to say that amateur lawyers may enjoy taking the California Bar Exam). But the purpose of holding those tryouts is not to provide entertainment; it is to hire. At bottom, open tryouts for performances to be held at a place of public accommodation are no different from open bidding on contracts to cut the grass at a place of public accommodation, or open applications for any job at a place of public accommodation. Those bidding, those applying–and those trying out–are not converted into customers. By the Court's reasoning, a business exists not only to sell goods and services to the public, but to provide the "privilege" of employment to the public; wherefore it follows, like night the day, that everyone who seeks a job is a customer.[2]

II.

Having erroneously held that Title III applies to the "customers" of professional golf who consist of its practitioners, the Court then erroneously answers–or to be accurate simply ignores–a second question. The ADA requires covered businesses to make such reasonable modifications of "policies, practices, or procedures" as are necessary to "afford" goods, services, and privileges to individuals with disabilities; but it explicitly does not require "modifications [that] would fundamentally alter the nature" of the goods, services, and privileges. § 12182(b)(2)(A)(ii). In other words, disabled individuals must be given access to the same goods, services, and privileges that others enjoy. The regulations state that Title III "does not require a public accommodation to alter its inventory to include accessible or special goods with accessibility features that are designed for, or facilitate use by, individuals with disabilities." 28 CFR § 36.307 (2000); see also 28 CFR, ch. 1, pt. 36, App. B, p. 650 (2000). As one Court of Appeals has explained:

> "The common sense of the statute is that the content of the goods or services offered by a place of public accommodation is not regulated. A camera store may not refuse to sell cameras to a disabled person, but it is not required to stock cameras specially designed for such persons. Had Congress purposed to impose so enormous a burden on the retail sector of the economy and so vast a supervisory responsibility on the federal courts, we think it would have made its intention clearer and would at least have imposed some standards. It is hardly a

continued

feasible judicial function to decide whether shoestores should sell single shoes to one-legged persons and if so at what price, or how many Braille books the Borders or Barnes and Noble bookstore chains should stock in each of their stores." *Doe v. Mutual of Omaha Ins. Co.,* 179 F.3d 557, 560 (C.A.7 1999).

Since this is so, even if respondent here is a consumer of the "privilege" of the PGA TOUR competition, see *ante,* at 1890, I see no basis for considering whether the rules of that competition must be altered. It is as irrelevant to the PGA TOUR's compliance with the statute whether walking is essential to the game of golf as it is to the shoe store's compliance whether "pairness" is essential to the nature of shoes. If a shoe store wishes to sell shoes only in pairs it may; and if a golf tour (or a golf course) wishes to provide only walk-around golf, it may. The PGA TOUR cannot deny respondent *access* to that game because of his disability, but it need not provide him a game different (whether in its essentials or in its details) from that offered to everyone else.

Since it has held (or assumed) professional golfers to be customers "enjoying" the "privilege" that consists of PGA TOUR golf; and since it inexplicably regards the rules of PGA TOUR golf as merely "policies, practices, or procedures" by which access to PGA TOUR golf is provided, the Court must then confront the question whether respondent's requested modification of the supposed policy, practice, or procedure of walking would "fundamentally alter the nature" of the PGA TOUR game, § 12182(b)(2)(A)(ii). The Court attacks this "fundamental alteration" analysis by asking two questions: first, whether the "essence" or an "essential aspect" of the sport of golf has been altered; and second, whether the change, even if not essential to the game, would give the disabled player an advantage over others and thereby "fundamentally alter the character of the competition." *Ante,* at 1893–1894. It answers no to both.

Before considering the Court's answer to the first question, it is worth pointing out that the assumption which underlies that question is false. Nowhere is it writ that PGA TOUR golf must be classic "essential" golf. Why cannot the PGA TOUR, if it wishes, promote a new game, with distinctive rules (much as the American League promotes a game of baseball in which the pitcher's turn at the plate can be taken by a "designated hitter")? If members of the public do not like the new rules–if they feel that these rules do not truly test the individual's skill at "real golf" (or the team's skill at "real baseball") they can withdraw their patronage. But the rules are the rules. They are (as in all games) entirely arbitrary, and there is no basis on which anyone–not even the Supreme Court of the United States–can pronounce one or another of them to be "nonessential" if the rulemaker (here the PGA TOUR) deems it to be essential.

If one assumes, however, that the PGA TOUR has some legal obligation to play classic, Platonic golf–and if one assumes the correctness of all the other wrong turns the Court has made to get to this point–then we Justices must confront what is indeed an awesome responsibility. It has been rendered the solemn duty of the Supreme Court of the United States, laid upon it by Congress in pursuance of the Federal Government's power "[t]o regulate Commerce with foreign Nations, and among the several States," U.S. Const., Art. I, § 8, cl. 3, to decide What Is Golf. I am sure that the Framers of the Constitution, aware of the 1457 edict of King James II of Scotland prohibiting golf because it interfered with the practice of archery, fully expected that sooner or later the paths of golf and government, the law and the links, would once again cross, and that the judges of this august Court would some day have to wrestle with that age-old jurisprudential question, for which their years of study in the law have so well prepared them: Is someone riding around a golf course from shot to shot *really* a golfer? The answer, we learn, is yes. The Court ultimately concludes, and it will henceforth be the Law of the Land, that walking is not a "fundamental" aspect of golf.

Either out of humility or out of self-respect (one or the other) the Court should decline to answer this incredibly difficult and incredibly silly question. To say that something is "essential" is ordinarily to say that it is necessary to the achievement of a certain object. But since it is the very nature of a game to have no object except amusement (that is what distinguishes games from productive activity), it is quite impossible to say that any of a game's arbitrary rules is "essential." Eighteen-hole golf courses, 10-foot-high basketball hoops, 90-foot baselines, 100-yard football fields–all are arbitrary and none is essential. The only support for any of them is tradition and (in more modern times) insistence by what has come to be regarded as the ruling body of the sport–both of which factors support the PGA TOUR's position in the present case. (Many, indeed, consider walking to be *the central feature* of the game of golf–hence Mark Twain's classic criticism of the sport: "a good walk spoiled.") I suppose there is some point at which the rules of a well-known game are changed to such a degree that no reasonable person would call it the same game. If the PGA TOUR competitors were required to dribble a large, inflated ball and put it through a round hoop, the game could no longer reasonably be called golf. But this criterion–destroying recognizability as the same generic game–is surely not the test of "essentialness" or "fundamentalness" that the Court applies, since it apparently thinks that merely changing the diameter of the *cup* might "fundamentally alter" the game of golf, *ante,* at 1893.

Having concluded that dispensing with the walking rule would not violate federal-Platonic "golf" (and, implicitly, that it is federal-Platonic golf, and no other, that the PGA TOUR can insist upon) the Court moves on to the second part of its test: the competitive effects of waiving this nonessential rule. In this part of its analysis, the Court first finds that the effects of the change are "mitigated" by the fact that in the game of golf weather, a "lucky bounce," and "pure chance" provide different conditions for each competitor and individual ability may not "be the sole determinant of the outcome." *Ante,* at 1895. I guess that is why those who follow professional golfing consider Jack Nicklaus the *luckiest* golfer of all time, only to be challenged of late by the phenomenal *luck* of Tiger Woods. The Court's empiricism is unpersuasive. "Pure chance" is randomly distributed among the players, but allowing respondent to use a cart gives him a "lucky" break every time he plays. Pure chance also only matters at the margin–a stroke here or there; the cart substantially improves this respondent's competitive prospects beyond a couple of strokes. But even granting that there are significant nonhuman variables affecting competition, that fact does not justify adding another variable that always favors one player.

In an apparent effort to make its opinion as narrow as possible, the Court relies upon the District Court's finding that even with a cart, respondent will be at least as fatigued as everyone else. *Ante,* at 1897. This, the Court says, *proves* that competition will not be affected. Far from thinking that reliance on this finding cabins the effect of today's opinion, I think it will prove to be its most expansive and destructive feature. Because step one of the Court's two-part inquiry into whether a requested change in a sport will "fundamentally alter [its] nature," § 12182(b)(2)(A)(ii), consists of an utterly unprincipled ontology of sports (pursuant to which the Court is not even sure whether golf's "essence" requires a 3-inch hole), there is every reason to think that in future cases involving requests for special treatment by would-be athletes the second step of the analysis will be determinative. In resolving that second step–determining whether waiver of the "nonessential" rule will have an impermissible "competitive effect"–by measuring the athletic capacity of the requesting individual, and asking whether the special dispensation would do no more than place him on a par (so to speak) with other competitors, the Court guarantees that future cases of this sort will have to be decided on the basis of individualized factual findings. Which means that future cases of this sort will be numerous, and a rich source of lucrative litigation. One can envision the parents of a Little League player with attention deficit disorder trying to convince a judge that their son's disability makes it at least 25% more difficult to hit a pitched ball. (If they are successful, the only thing that could prevent a court order giving the kid four strikes would be a judicial determination that, in baseball, three strikes are metaphysically necessary, which is quite absurd.)

The statute, of course, provides no basis for this individualized analysis that is the Court's last step on a long and misguided journey. The statute seeks to assure that a disabled person's disability will not deny him *equal access* to (among other things) competitive sporting events–not that his disability will not deny him an *equal chance to win* competitive sporting events. The latter is quite impossible, since the very *nature* of competitive sport is the measurement, by uniform rules, of unevenly distributed excellence. This unequal distribution is precisely what determines the winners and losers–and artificially to "even out" that distribution, by giving one or another player exemption from a rule that emphasizes his particular weakness, is to destroy the game. That is why the "handicaps" that are customary in social games of

continued

golf–which, by adding strokes to the scores of the good players and subtracting them from scores of the bad ones, "even out" the varying abilities–are *not* used in professional golf. In the Court's world, there is one set of rules that is "fair with respect to the able-bodied" but "individualized" rules, mandated by the ADA, for "talented but disabled athletes." *Ante,* at 1897–1898. The ADA mandates no such ridiculous thing. Agility, strength, speed, balance, quickness of mind, steadiness of nerves, intensity of concentration–these talents are not evenly distributed. No wild-eyed dreamer has ever suggested that the managing bodies of the competitive sports that test precisely these qualities should try to take account of the uneven distribution of God-given gifts when writing and enforcing the rules of competition. And I have no doubt Congress did not authorize misty-eyed judicial supervision of such a revolution.

My belief that today's judgment is clearly in error should not be mistaken for a belief that the PGA TOUR clearly *ought not* allow respondent to use a golf cart. *That* is a close question, on which even those who compete in the PGA TOUR are apparently divided; but it is a *different* question from the one before the Court. Just as it is a different question whether the Little League *ought* to give disabled youngsters a fourth strike, or some other waiver from the rules that makes up for their disabilities. In both cases, whether they *ought* to do so depends upon (1) how central to the game that they have organized (and over whose rules they are the master) they deem the waived provision to be, and (2) how competitive–how strict a test of raw athletic ability in all aspects of the competition–they want their game to be. But whether Congress has said they must do so depends upon the answers to the legal questions I have discussed above–not upon what this Court sententiously decrees to be "decent, tolerant, [and] progressive," *ante,* at 1889–1890 (quoting *Board of Trustees* of *Univ. of Ala. v. Garrett,* 531 U.S. 356, 375, 121 S.Ct. 955, 148 L.Ed.2d 866 (2001) (KENNEDY, J., concurring)).

And it should not be assumed that today's decent, tolerant, and progressive judgment will, in the long run, accrue to the benefit of sports competitors with disabilities. Now that it is clear courts will review the rules of sports for "fundamentalness," organizations that value their autonomy have every incentive to defend vigorously the necessity of every regulation.

They may still be second-guessed in the end as to the Platonic requirements of the sport, but they will *assuredly* lose if they have at all wavered in their enforcement. The lesson the PGA TOUR and other sports organizations should take from this case is to make sure that the same written rules are set forth for all levels of play, and never voluntarily to grant any modifications. The second lesson is to end open tryouts. I doubt that, in the long run, even disabled athletes will be well served by these incentives that the Court has created.

Complaints about this case are not "properly directed to Congress," *ante,* at 1896–1897, n. 51. They are properly directed to this Court's Kafkaesque determination that professional sports organizations, and the fields they rent for their exhibitions, are "places of public accommodation" to the competing athletes, and the athletes themselves "customers" of the organization that pays them; its Alice in Wonderland determination that there are such things as judicially determinable "essential" and "nonessential" rules of a made-up game; and its Animal Farm determination that fairness and the ADA mean that everyone gets to play by individualized rules which will assure that no one's lack of ability (or at least no one's lack of ability so pronounced that it amounts to a disability) will be a handicap. The year was 2001, and "everybody was finally equal." K. Vonnegut, Harrison Bergeron, in Animal Farm and Related Readings 129 (1997).

FOOTNOTES

1. After the trial of the case, the name of the NIKE TOUR was changed to the Buy.com TOUR.

2. Generally, to maintain membership in a tour for the succeeding year, rather than go through the Q-School again, a player must perform at a certain level.

3. Instead, Appendix I to the Rules of Golf lists a number of "optional" conditions, among them one related to transportation: If it is desired to require players to walk in a competition, the following condition is suggested: "Players shall walk at all times during a stipulated round." App. 125.

4. The PGA TOUR hard card provides: "Players shall walk at all times during a stipulated round unless permitted to ride by the PGA TOUR Rules

Committee." *Id.*, at 127. The NIKE TOUR hard card similarly requires walking unless otherwise permitted. *Id.*, at 129. Additionally, as noted, golf carts have not been permitted during the third stage of the Q-School since 1997. Petitioner added this recent prohibition in order to "approximat[e] a PGA TOUR event as closely as possible." *Id.*, at 152.

5. 994 F.Supp. 1242, 1251 (D.Or.1998).

6. See, *e.g.*, App. 156–160 (Notices to Competitors for 1997 Bob Hope Chrysler Classic, 1997 AT & T Pebble Beach National Pro-Am, and 1997 Quad City Classic).

7. 42 U.S.C. § 12102 provides, in part: "The term 'disability' means, with respect to an individual–

"(A) a physical or mental impairment that substantially limits one or more of the major life activities of such individual . . . "

8. Before then, even when Martin was in extreme pain, and was offered a cart, he declined. Tr. 564–565.

9. When asked about the other teams' reaction to Martin's use of a cart, the Stanford coach testified:

"Q. Was there any complaint ever made to you by the coaches when he was allowed a cart that that gave a competitive advantage over the–

"A. Any complaints? No sir, there were exactly–exactly the opposite. Everybody recognized Casey for the person he was, and what he was doing with his life, and every coach, to my knowledge, and every player wanted Casey in the tournament and they welcomed him there.

"Q. Did anyone contend that that constituted an alteration of the competition to the extent that it didn't constitute the game to your level, the college level?

"A. Not at all, sir." App. 208.

10. Title 42 U.S.C. § 12187 provides: "The provisions of this subchapter shall not apply to private clubs or establishments exempted from coverage under Title II of the Civil Rights Act of 1964 (42 U.S.C. § 2000-a(e)) or to religious organizations or entities controlled by religious organizations, including places of worship."

11. See § 12181(7).

12. § 12181(7)(L).

13. "Q. And fatigue is one of the factors that can cause a golfer at the PGA Tour level to lose one stroke or more?

"A. Oh, it is. And it has happened.

"Q. And can one stroke be the difference between winning and not winning a tournament at the PGA Tour level?

"A. As I said, I've lost a few national opens by one stroke." App. 177.

14. "Q. Mr. Nicklaus, what is your understanding of the reason why in these competitive events . . . that competitors are required to walk the course?

"A. Well, in my opinion, physical fitness and fatigue are part of the game of golf." *Id.*, at 190.

15. "Q. So are you telling the court that this fatigue factor tends to accumulate over the course of the four days of the tournament?

"A. Oh definitely. There's no doubt.

"Q. Does this fatigue factor that you've talked about, Mr. Venturi, affect the manner in which you–you perform as a professional out on the golf course?

"A. Oh, there's no doubt, again, but that, that fatigue does play a big part. It will influence your game. It will influence your shot-making. It will influence your decisions." *Id.*, at 236–237.

16. "Q. Based on your experience, do you believe that it would fundamentally alter the nature of the competition on the PGA Tour and the Nike Tour if competitors in those events were permitted to use golf carts?

"A. Yes, absolutely.

"Q. Why do you say so, sir?

"A. It would–it would take away the fatigue factor in many ways. It would–it would change the game.

"Q. Now, when you say that the use of carts takes away the fatigue factor, it would be an aid, et cetera, again, as I understand it, you are not testifying now about the plaintiff. You are just talking in general terms?

"A. Yes, sir." *Id.*, at 238. See also *id.*, at 177–178 (Palmer); *id.*, at 191 (Nicklaus).

17. "In the first place, he does walk while on the course–even with a cart, he must move from cart to

continued

shot and back to the cart. In essence, he still must walk approximately 25% of the course. On a course roughly five miles in length, Martin will walk 1 1/4 miles." 994 F.Supp., at 1251.

18. It explained: "For example, Title III includes in its definition 'secondary, undergraduate, or post-graduate private school [s].' 42 U.S.C. § 12181(7)(J). The competition to enter the most elite private universities is intense, and a relatively select few are admitted. That fact clearly does not remove the universities from the statute's definition as places of public accommodation." 204 F.3d, at 998.

19. The golfer in the Seventh Circuit case, Ford Olinger, suffers from bilateral avascular necrosis, a degenerative condition that significantly hinders his ability to walk.

20. For a description of the conditions under which they played, see *Olinger v. United States Golf Assn.*, 205 F.3d, at 1006–1007.

21. 42 U.S.C. §§ 12111–12117.

22. §§ 12131–12165.

23. §§ 12181–12189.

24. "(A) an inn, hotel, motel, or other place of lodging, except for an establishment located within a building that contains not more than five rooms for rent or hire and that is actually occupied by the proprietor of such establishment as the residence of such proprietor;

"(B) a restaurant, bar, or other establishment serving food or drink;

"(C) a motion picture house, theater, concert hall, stadium, or other place of exhibition or entertainment;

"(D) an auditorium, convention center, lecture hall, or other place of public gathering;

"(E) a bakery, grocery store, clothing store, hardware store, shopping center, or other sales or rental establishment;

"(F) a laundromat, dry-cleaner, bank, barber shop, beauty shop, travel service, shoe repair service, funeral parlor, gas station, office of an accountant or lawyer, pharmacy, insurance office, professional office of a health care provider, hospital, or other service establishment;

"(G) a terminal, depot, or other station used for specified public transportation;

"(H) a museum, library, gallery, or other place of display or collection;

"(I) a park, zoo, amusement park, or other place of recreation;

"(J) a nursery, elementary, secondary, undergraduate, or postgraduate private school, or other place of education;

"(K) a day care center, senior citizen center, homeless shelter, food bank, adoption agency, or other social service center establishment; and

"(L) a gymnasium, health spa, bowling alley, *golf course,* or other place of exercise or recreation." § 12181(7) (emphasis added).

25. S.Rep. No. 101–116, at 59; H.R. No. 101–485, pt. 2, at 100, U.S.Code Cong. & Admin.News 1990, pt. 2, at pp. 303, 382–383.

26. Reply Brief for Petitioner 1–2.

27. Martin complains that petitioner's failure to make this exact argument below precludes its assertion here. However, the Title III coverage issue was raised in the lower courts, petitioner advanced this particular argument in support of its position on the issue in its petition for certiorari, and the argument was fully briefed on the merits by both parties. Given the importance of the issue, we exercise our discretion to consider it. See *Harris Trust and Sav. Bank v. Salomon Smith Barney Inc.,* 530 U.S. 238, 245–246, n. 2, 120 S.Ct. 2180, 147 L.Ed.2d 187 (2000); *Carlson v. Green,* 446 U.S. 14, 17, n. 2, 100 S.Ct. 1468, 64 L.Ed.2d 15 (1980).

28. Brief for Petitioner 10, 11.

29. *Id.,* at 19 (quoting 42 U.S.C. § 12182(b)(1) (A)(iv)).

30. Brief for Petitioner 15; see also *id.,* at 16 (Martin's claim "is nothing more than a straightforward discrimination-in-the- workplace complaint").

31. Clause (i) prohibits the denial of participation, clause (ii) participation in unequal benefits, and clause (iii) the provision of separate benefits.

32. Brief for Petitioner 20 (clause (iv) "applies directly just to subsection 12182(b)"); Reply Brief

for Petitioner 4, n. 1 (clause (iv) "does not apply directly to the general provision prohibiting discrimination").

33. Contrary to the dissent's suggestion, our view of the Q-School does not make "everyone who seeks a job" at a public accommodation, through "an open tryout" or otherwise, "a customer." *Post,* at 1901 (opinion of SCALIA, J.). Unlike those who successfully apply for a job at a place of public accommodation, or those who successfully bid for a contract, the golfers who qualify for petitioner's tours play at their own pleasure (perhaps, but not necessarily, for prize money), and although they commit to playing in at least 15 tournaments, they are not bound by any obligations typically associated with employment. See, *e.g.,* App. 260 (trial testimony of PGA commissioner Timothy Finchem) (petitioner lacks control over when and where tour members compete, and over their manner of performance outside the rules of competition). Furthermore, unlike athletes in "other professional sports, such as baseball," *post,* at 1901, in which players are employed by their clubs, the golfers on tour are not employed by petitioner or any related organizations. The record does not support the proposition that the purpose of the Q-School "is to hire," *ibid.,* rather than to narrow the field of participants in the sporting events that petitioner sponsors at places of public accommodation.

34. Title II of the Civil Rights Act of 1964 includes in its definition of "public accommodation" a "place of exhibition or entertainment" but does not specifically list a "golf course" as an example. See 42 U.S.C. § 2000a(b).

35. Under petitioner's theory, Title II would not preclude it from discriminating against golfers on racial grounds. App. 197; Tr. of Oral Arg. 11–12.

36. Cf. *post,* at 1903 (SCALIA, J., dissenting) ("I suppose there is some point at which the rules of a well-known game are changed to such a degree that no reasonable person would call it the same game").

37. Accord, *post,* at 1904 (SCALIA, J., dissenting) ("The statute seeks to assure that a disabled person's disability will not deny him equal access to (among other things) competitive sporting events–not that his disability will not deny him an *equal chance to win* competitive sporting events").

38. As we have noted, the statute contemplates three inquiries: whether the requested modification is "reasonable," whether it is "necessary" for the disabled individual, and whether it would "fundamentally alter the nature of" the competition. 42 U.S.C. § 12182(b)(2)(A)(ii). Whether one question should be decided before the others likely will vary from case to case, for in logic there seems to be no necessary priority among the three. In routine cases, the fundamental alteration inquiry may end with the question whether a rule is essential. Alternatively, the specifics of the claimed disability might be examined within the context of what is a reasonable or necessary modification. Given the concession by petitioner that the modification sought is reasonable and necessary, and given petitioner's reliance on the fundamental alteration provision, we have no occasion to consider the alternatives in this case.

39. Golf is an ancient game, tracing its ancestry to Scotland, and played by such notables as Mary Queen of Scots and her son James. That shot-making has been the essence of golf since early in its history is reflected in the first recorded rules of golf, published in 1744 for a tournament on the Leith Links in Edinburgh:

"Articles & Laws in Playing at Golf

"1. You must Tee your Ball, within a Club's length of the [previous] Hole.

"2. Your Tee must be upon the Ground.

"3. You are not to change the Ball which you Strike off the Tee.

"4. You are not to remove, Stones, Bones or any Break Club for the sake of playing your Ball, Except upon the fair Green/ & that only/ within a Club's length of your Ball.

"5. If your Ball comes among Water, or any Watery Filth, you are at liberty to take out your Ball & bringing it behind the hazard and Teeing it, you may play it with any Club and allow your Adversary a Stroke for so getting out your Ball.

"6. If your Balls be found anywhere touching one another, You are to lift the first Ball, till you play the last.

"7. At Holling, you are to play your Ball honestly for the Hole, and, not to play upon your

continued

Adversary's Ball, not lying in your way to the Hole.

"8. If you should lose your Ball, by its being taken up, or any other way, you are to go back to the Spot, where you struck last & drop another Ball, And allow your Adversary a Stroke for the misfortune.

"9. No man at Holling his Ball, is to be allowed, to mark his way to the Hole with his Club or, any thing else.

"10. If a Ball be stopp'd by any person, Horse, Dog, or any thing else, The Ball so stop'd must be play'd where it lyes.

"11. If you draw your Club, in order to Strike & proceed so far in the Stroke, as to be bringing down your Club; If then, your Club shall break, in, any way, it is to be Accounted a Stroke.

"12. He, whose Ball lyes farthest from the Hole is obliged to play first.

"13. Neither Trench, Ditch, or Dyke, made for the preservation of the Links, nor the Scholar's Holes or the Soldier's Lines, Shall be accounted a Hazard; But the Ball is to be taken out/Teed/and play'd with any Iron Club." K. Chapman, Rules of the Green 14–15 (1997).

40. See generally M. Campbell, The Random House International Encyclopedia of Golf 9–57 (1991); Golf Magazine's Encyclopedia of Golf 1- 17 (2d ed.1993).

41. *Olinger v. United States Golf Assn.,* 205 F.3d 1001, 1003 (C.A.7 2000).

42. On this point, the testimony of the immediate past president of the USGA (and one of petitioner's witnesses at trial) is illuminating:
"Tell the court, if you would, Ms. Bell, who it is that plays under these Rules of Golf . . . ?
"A. Well, these are the rules of the game, so all golfers. These are for all people who play the game.
"Q. So the two amateurs that go out on the weekend to play golf together would–would play by the Rules of Golf?
"A. We certainly hope so.
"Q. Or a tournament that is conducted at a private country club for its members, is it your under-

standing that that would typically be conducted under the Rules of Golf?
"A. Well, that's–that's right. If you want to play golf, you need to play by these rules." App. 239.

43. See n. 3, *supra.*

44. Furthermore, the USGA's handicap system, used by over 4 million amateur golfers playing on courses rated by the USGA, does not consider whether a player walks or rides in a cart, or whether she uses a caddy or carries her own clubs. Rather, a player's handicap is determined by a formula that takes into account the average score in the 10 best of her 20 most recent rounds, the difficulty of the different courses played, and whether or not a round was a "tournament" event.

45. Brief for Petitioner 13.

46. *Id.,* at 37.

47. 994 F.Supp., at 1250.

48. A drive by Andrew Magee earlier this year produced a result that he neither intended nor expected. While the foursome ahead of him was still on the green, he teed off on a 322-yard par four. To his surprise, the ball not only reached the green, but also bounced off Tom Byrum's putter and into the hole. Davis, Magee Gets Ace on Par-4, Ariz. Republic, Jan. 26 2001, p. C16, 2001 WL 8510792.

49. That has been so not only in the SENIOR PGA TOUR and the first two stages of the Q-School, but also, as Martin himself noticed, in the third stage of the Q-School after petitioner permitted everyone to ride rather than just waiving the walking rule for Martin as required by the District Court's injunction.

50. App. 201. See also *id.,* at 179–180 (deposition testimony of Gerry Norquist); *id.,* at 225–226 (trial testimony of Harry Toscano).

51. Hence, petitioner's questioning of the ability of courts to apply the reasonable modification requirement to athletic competition is a complaint more properly directed to Congress, which drafted the ADA's coverage broadly, than to us. Even more misguided is Justice SCALIA's suggestion that Congress did not place that inquiry into the hands of the courts at all. According to the

dissent, the game of golf as sponsored by petitioner is, like all sports games, the sum of its "arbitrary rules," and no one, including courts, "can pronounce one or another of them to be 'nonessential' if the rulemaker (here the PGA TOUR) deems it to be essential." *Post*, at 1902–1903. Whatever the merit of Justice SCALIA's postmodern view of "What Is [Sport]," *post*, at 1902, it is clear that Congress did not enshrine it in Title III of the ADA. While Congress expressly exempted "private clubs or establishments" and "religious organizations or entities" from Title III's coverage, 42 U.S.C. § 12187, Congress made no such exception for athletic competitions, much less did it give sports organizations carte-blanche authority to exempt themselves from the fundamental alteration inquiry by deeming any rule, no matter how peripheral to the competition, to be essential. In short, Justice SCALIA's reading of the statute renders the word "fundamentally" largely superfluous, because it treats the alteration of any rule governing an event at a public accommodation to be a fundamental alteration.

52. On this fundamental point, the dissent agrees. See *post*, at 1902 ("The PGA TOUR cannot deny respondent *access* to that game because of his disability").

53. However, we think petitioner's contention that the task of assessing requests for modifications will amount to a substantial burden is overstated. As Martin indicates, in the three years since he requested the use of a cart, no one else has sued the PGA, and only two other golfers (one of whom is Olinger) have sued the USGA for a waiver of the walking rule. In addition, we believe petitioner's point is misplaced, as nowhere in § 12182(b)(2)(A)(ii) does Congress limit the reasonable modification requirement only to requests that are easy to evaluate.

1 The California Bar Exam is covered by the ADA, by the way, because a separate provision of Title III applies to "examinations ... related to applications, licensing, certification, or credentialing for secondary or post-secondary education, professional, or trade purposes." 42 U.S.C. § 12189. If open tryouts were "privileges" under § 12182, and participants in the tryouts "customers," § 12189 would have been unnecessary.

2 The Court suggests that respondent is not an independent contractor because he "play[s] at [his] own pleasure," and is not subject to PGA TOUR control "over [his] manner of performance," *ante*, at 1892 n. 33. But many independent contractors–composers of movie music, portrait artists, script writers, and even (some would say) plumbers–retain at least as much control over when and how they work as does respondent, who agrees to play in a minimum of 15 of the designated PGA TOUR events, and to play by the rules that the PGA TOUR specifies. Cf. *Community for Creative Non-Violence v. Reid*, 490 U.S. 730, 751–753, 109 S.Ct. 2166, 104 L.Ed.2d 811 (1989) (discussing independent contractor status of a sculptor). Moreover, although, as the Court suggests in the same footnote, in rare cases a PGA TOUR winner will choose to forgo the prize money (in order, for example, to preserve amateur status necessary for continuing participation in college play) he is contractually entitled to the prize money if he demands it, which is all that a contractual relationship requires.

Specific Disabilities

Section 504 is much broader than the IDEA. The IDEA is specific and includes mental retardation, blindness, and deafness.[15] Other potential disabilities, covered under § 504 if they substantially limit a major life activity, are not typically covered under the IDEA. They include:

1. communicable diseases, including AIDS, AIDS related complex (ARC), asymptomatic carriers of the AIDS virus (HIV), and tuberculosis;

2. temporary disabilities: students injured in accidents or suffering short-term illnesses;
3. chronic asthma and severe allergies;
4. physical disabilities such as spina bifida, hemophilia, and conditions requiring children to use crutches; and
5. diabetes.

Note that some of these conditions, such as tuberculosis, diabetes, and hemophilia, may be severe enough to affect educational performance and therefore fall under the IDEA.

Age Limits and Eligibility

Age is not usually considered to be a disability but rather a potential form of discrimination. Every state high school athletic association has an age limit to prevent older students and high schools from having an unfair physical advantage when it comes to competition in sports. What happens, however, when a student with a disability takes longer to graduate than nondisabled students, and his or her age exceeds the state high school athletic association's cut-off date for eligible competition?

■ Age Discrimination in Employment Act

The **Age Discrimination in Employment Act (ADEA)**[16] protects individuals who are 40 years of age or older from employment discrimination based on their age. The ADEA's protections apply to both employees and applicants of jobs and prohibit employers of 25 or more persons from discriminating against persons 40 to 65 years old in any area of employment because of age.

Under the ADEA, it is unlawful to discriminate against people age 40 or older because of their age with respect to any term, condition, or privilege of employment, including, but not limited to, hiring, firing, promotion, layoff, compensation, benefits, job assignments, and training. It is also unlawful to retaliate against an individual for opposing employment practices that discriminate based on age or for filing an age discrimination charge, testifying, or participating in any way in an investigation, proceeding, or litigation under the ADEA.

The ADEA applies to employment agencies, labor organizations, and the federal government:

(a) It shall be unlawful for an employer—(1) to fail or refuse to hire or to discharge any individual or otherwise discriminate against any individual with respect to his compensation, terms, conditions, or privileges of employment, because of such

Age Discrimination in Employment Act (ADEA)   1967 law that prohibits job discrimination against people age 40 and older based on age

individual's age; (2) to limit, segregate, or classify his employees in any way which would deprive or tend to deprive any individual of employment opportunities or otherwise adversely affect his status as an employee, because of such individual's age; or (3) to reduce the wage rate of any employee in order to comply with this chapter.[17]

Exceptions to the act's provisions are provided where age is a bona fide occupational qualification (BFOQ) or the institution of a bona fide seniority system or employee benefit plan. Exemptions are provided for the mandatory retirement of bona fide executive and high policy-making employees 65 years of age and older who are entitled to at least $44,000 a year from a retirement plan. Some maximum hiring ages and mandatory retirement are permitted for police and firefighters. The EEOC may establish such reasonable exemptions as it may find necessary and proper in the public interest.

The ADEA could certainly present a challenge for legal scholars in the context and application in sports.

■ Summary

Persons with disabilities in sports present interesting contemporary issues for amateur and professional athletes, including coaches and school administrators. The three federal acts of the Rehabilitation Act of 1973, the Americans with Disabilities Act, and the Individuals with Disabilities Education Act have afforded disabled persons with more consideration when competing in sports than ever before. The Age Discrimination in Employment Act and the FMLA must also be considered. All of the federal laws have noteworthy exceptions and have been the subject of interpretation by the courts. The Supreme Court's decision in Casey Martin's case will hopefully provide more guidance for lower courts when interpreting rules related to disabled persons and the rules governing sports.

■ Key Terms

Age Discrimination in Employment Act (ADEA)

Americans with Disabilities Act (ADA) of 1990

Equal Employment Opportunity Commission (EEOC)

impairment

Individuals with Disabilities Education Act (IDEA)

reasonable accommodation

Rehabilitation Act of 1973

undue hardship

■ Additional Cases

Austin v. Cornell Univ., 891 F. Supp. 740 (N.D. N.Y. 1995)
Baisden v. West Virginia Secondary Schools Activities Comm'n, 568 S.F.2d 32 (W. Va. 2002)
Bombrys v. City of Toledo, 849 F. Supp. 1210 (N.D. Ohio 1993)
Jones v. Southeast Alabama Baseball Umpires Ass'n, 864 F. Supp. 1135 (M.D. Ala. 1994)
Stoutenborough v. NFL, 59 F.3d 580 (6th Cir. 1995)
Western Airlines v. Criswell, 472 U.S. 400 (1985)

■ Review Questions

1. How has the Americans with Disabilities Act affected sports?
2. Should alcoholism be considered a disability under the act?
3. How might sports rules change if *reasonable accommodations* are given to certain sports participants with disabilities and not others?
4. Should the NCAA rewrite or modify its rules with regard to college entrance exams for persons who have learning disabilities?
5. How might the Age Discrimination in Employment Act be used by a plaintiff involved in sports to show that he or she was terminated for age rather than ability?
6. Should someone with a communicable disease be disallowed from playing in a sport that involves physical contact?

■ Endnotes

1 The word *disability* is often used instead of handicap. Some use the phrase "physically challenged" or just "challenged athletes."
2 Formerly called the "Education for All Handicapped Children Act of 1975."
3 34 C.F.R. § 104.3 (j).
4 *Toyota Motor Mfg., Kentucky, Inc. v. Williams*, 534 U.S. 184 (2002).
5 42 U.S.C.A. § 12101 et seq.
6 § 12101(b)(1) of the ADA.
7 42 U.S.C.A. § 12102(2)(A)(1994).
8 29 C.F.R. § 1630 (1997).
9 29 U.S.C.A. § 706(8)(c)(v)(emphasis added).
10 *Martin v. PGA Tour*, 984 F. Supp. 1320 (D. Or. 1998); 994 F. Supp. 1242; 532 U.S. 661 (2001).
11 42 U.S.C.A. § 12181 (7).
12 42 U.S.C.A. § 12182 (2)(A)(iii).
13 *Olinger v. United States Golf Ass'n*, 205 F.3d 1001 (7th Cir. 2000).
14 20 U.S.C.A. § 1400 et seq.
15 20 U.S.C.A. § 1401 (a) (1) (I) (1994).
16 29 U.S.C.A. §§ 621–634 (1990).
17 § 623. [§ 4].

CHAPTER SEVEN

Drugs and Sports

■ Introduction

Drug use by athletes has been a controversial issue for many years. Athletes often use artificial stimulants to give them an unfair competitive physical and mental advantage over their opponents. Other athletes use illegal drugs and are often punished accordingly in the public eye when caught. Only recently has it become generally legally accepted that drug testing in high school, college, and professional sports serves a legitimate and beneficial societal need. The use of performance-enhancing drugs can be traced to the ancient Olympic Games where fame and fortune were rewarded, just as today, for athletic prowess.

While the controversy over drugs and sports focuses primarily on performance-enhancing drugs, there is a heightened awareness that testing for illegal (not necessarily performance-enhancing) drugs in sports at various levels serves a useful governmental purpose in winning the war on illegal drugs in American society. Drug testing issues include the right to privacy and due process protections from illegal searches and seizures, particularly since testing involves an analysis of a sample from a competitor's urine or blood.

■ Performance-Enhancing versus Illegal Drugs

Performance-enhancing drugs are substances athletes inject or consume to increase the human body's ability to perform during training sessions and sports contests. This includes common, over-the-counter muscle-building supplements, recovery products, and endurance-enhancing blood doping. Performance-enhancing drugs might be consumed orally or via needle injection. Illegal drugs do not necessarily increase performance but are outlawed by the federal and/or state governments.

---

performance-enhancing drug   drug or substance ingested, injected, or inhaled by an athlete to increase muscle growth, repair, or development or any substance used to decrease the effects of fatigue

This includes purchasing alcohol (by young athletes), marijuana, cocaine, and other banned or *controlled substances.*

■ Constitutional Framework

When the government or a governmental entity such as a public school or public college desires to test a student-athlete for drugs, this constitutes "state action." There is no state action for private sports leagues, and therefore the fourth, fifth, and fourteenth Amendment issues are generally not applicable in such context unless such testing is established by contract.

Drug testing issues are not solely a concern in sports; President Ronald Reagan issued an executive order for federal agencies to establish programs to test employees in "sensitive" positions.[1] Federal laws that regulate drug use and distribution include the Anabolic Steroid Control Act of 1990.[2] Steroids are artificial and synthetic forms of hormones, such as testosterone, that improve muscle building, growth, and repair.

Since the government (state) desires to invade the privacy of cetain athletes by testing their urine or blood for drugs, athletes have constitutional safeguards that allow a challenge to such a test on the grounds of its constitutionality. Numerous challenges to such policies have failed, and recently courts have given support to the use of mandatory, suspicionless testing. Still, private organizations have their own testing policies that usually require consent to such policies (including appeals) as a condition for participating in that league. Two 1989 federal cases firmly establish the principles surrounding drug testing by the government and the legitimacy of such testing programs.[3]

Fourth Amendment

If a governmental agency tests an athlete for drugs, it must comply with the **Fourth Amendment** of the Constitution. This amendment protects private citizens against unreasonable searches and seizures by the government. Such protection is vital to the privacy protection of all citizens from unacceptable conduct on the part of the government or its officers or agents. The Fourth Amendment provides:

> The right of the people to be secure in their persons, houses, papers and effects, against unreasonable searches and seizures, shall not be violated, and no Warrants shall issue, but upon probable cause, supported by Oath or affirmation, and particularly describing the place to be searched and the persons or things to be seized.

While most athletes now understand that being tested for drugs is part of the nature of competition, numerous cases have reached the trial and appellate courts to determine whether or not an individual athlete has a legitimate expectation of privacy when it comes to drug testing.

Fourth Amendment   amendment to the United States Constitution prohibiting the government from conducting a search of a person's body or home without the individual's consent, a warrant, or a contract; referred to as the "search and seizure" warrant

Vernonia and High School Sports

In a recent decision involving an Oklahoma high school's drug testing policy, the U.S. Supreme Court held in *Vernonia School District 47J v. Acton*, 515 U.S. 646 (1995) that high school athletes have a lower expectation of privacy than the public in general, and that mandatory drug testing policies nationwide are valid as a condition for participating in high school sports. Additionally, though there may not be probable cause *per se* in testing high school athletes, the Supreme Court affirmed that public school districts do have special needs. The Court held that random drug testing was valid since such programs serve a compelling interest in public systems to deter the use of drugs among other justifications.

Fifth Amendment

Another constitutional consideration for drug testing of athletes is the **Fifth Amendment**, which provides:

> No person shall . . . be deprived of life, liberty, or property, without **due process** of law; nor shall private property be taken for public use, without just compensation.

This means that an athlete should be granted a process for a hearing and appealing a positive drug test result.

Fourteenth Amendment

To ensure that no state makes a law that might abridge the rights of a citizen granted to it by the federal government, Congress enacted the **Fourteenth Amendment** that extends all federal rights to individual state constitutions:

> All persons born or naturalized in the United States, and subject to the jurisdiction thereof, are citizens of the United States and of the state wherein they reside. No state shall make or enforce any law which shall abridge the privileges or immunities of citizens of the United States; nor shall any state deprive any person of life, liberty, or property, without due process of law; nor deny to any person within its jurisdiction the **equal protection** of the laws.

Student-athletes' attempts to demonstrate that dismissal from participation in sports due to a positive drug test have not been successful under a Fourth, Fifth, or Fourteenth Amendment argument since courts have refused to recognize participation in sports as a "property right" for the athlete. Case 9 offers one example.

Fifth Amendment   the requirement for a "due process" hearing before a person's life, liberty, or property is taken away; this amendment to the United States Constitution also provides the right against self-incrimination

due process   right to a hearing before a person's life, liberty, or property is taken away

Fourteenth Amendment   prohibition against states abridging the rights guaranteed under the United States Constitution

equal protection   clause in the Fourteenth Amendment that states that the government must treat a person or class of persons the same in similar circumstances

■ **CASE 9**   *Board of Educ. of Indep. Sch. Dist. No. 92 v. Earls*

Supreme Court of the United States
BOARD OF EDUCATION OF INDEPENDENT
SCHOOL DISTRICT NO. 92 OF POTTAWATOMIE
COUNTY, et al., Petitioners,

v.

Lindsay EARLS et al.
No. 01-332
Argued March 19, 2002.
Decided June 27, 2002.

High school students challenged constitutionality of school's suspicionless urinalysis drug testing policy. The United States District Court for the Western District of Oklahoma, David L. Russell, Chief Judge, 115 F.Supp.2d 1281, upheld school's policy, and students appealed. The United States Court of Appeals for the Tenth Circuit, Stephen H. Anderson, Circuit Judge, 242 F.3d 1264, reversed. After granting certiorari, the Supreme Court, Justice Thomas, held that policy requiring all students who participated in competitive extracurricular activities to submit to drug testing was a reasonable means of furthering the school district's important interest in preventing and deterring drug use among its schoolchildren, and therefore did not violate Fourth Amendment.

Reversed.

Justice Breyer, filed concurring opinion.

Justice O'Connor, filed dissenting opinion in which Justice Souter joined.

Justice Ginsburg, filed dissenting opinion in which Justice Stevens, Justice O'Connor, and Justice Souter joined.

Justice THOMAS delivered the opinion of the Court.

The Student Activities Drug Testing Policy implemented by the Board of Education of Independent School District No. 92 of Pottawatomie County (School District) requires all students who participate in competitive extracurricular activities to submit to drug testing. Because this Policy reasonably serves the School District's important interest in detecting and preventing drug use among its students, we hold that it is constitutional.

I.

The city of Tecumseh, Oklahoma, is a rural community located approximately 40 miles southeast of Oklahoma City. The School District administers all Tecumseh public schools. In the fall of 1998, the School District adopted the Student Activities Drug Testing Policy (Policy), which requires all middle and high school students to consent to drug testing in order to participate in any extracurricular activity. In practice, the Policy has been applied only to competitive extracurricular activities sanctioned by the Oklahoma Secondary Schools Activities Association, such as the Academic Team, Future Farmers of America, Future Homemakers of America, band, choir, pom-pom, cheerleading, and athletics. Under the Policy, students are required to take a drug test before participating in an extracurricular activity, must submit to random drug testing while participating in that activity, and must agree to be tested at any time upon reasonable suspicion. The urinalysis tests are designed to detect only the use of illegal drugs, including amphetamines, marijuana, cocaine, opiates, and barbituates, not medical conditions or the presence of authorized prescription medications.

At the time of their suit, both respondents attended Tecumseh High School. Respondent Lindsay Earls was a member of the show choir, the marching band, the Academic Team, and the National Honor Society. Respondent Daniel James sought to participate in the Academic Team.[1] Together with their parents, Earls and James brought a 42 U.S.C. § 1983 action against the School District, challenging the Policy both on its face and as applied to their participation in extracurricular activities.[2] They alleged that the Policy violates the Fourth Amendment as incorporated by the Fourteenth Amendment and requested injunctive and declarative relief. They also argued that the School District failed to identify a special need for testing students who participate in extracurricular activities, and that the "Drug Testing Policy neither addresses a proven problem nor promises to bring any benefit to students or the school." App. 9.

Applying the principles articulated in *Vernonia School Dist. 47J v. Acton,* 515 U.S. 646, 115 S.Ct. 2386, 132 L.Ed.2d 564 (1995), in which we upheld the suspicionless drug testing of school athletes, the United States District Court for the Western District of Oklahoma rejected respondents' claim that the Policy was unconstitutional and granted summary judgment to the School District. The court noted that "special needs" exist in the public school context and that, although the School District did "not show a drug problem of epidemic proportions," there was a history of drug abuse starting in 1970 that presented "legitimate cause for concern." 115 F.Supp.2d 1281, 1287 (2000). The District Court also held that the Policy was effective because "[i]t can scarcely be disputed that the drug problem among the student body is effectively addressed by making sure that the large number of students participating in competitive, extracurricular activities do not use drugs." *Id.*, at 1295.

The United States Court of Appeals for the Tenth Circuit reversed, holding that the Policy violated the Fourth Amendment. The Court of Appeals agreed with the District Court that the Policy must be evaluated in the "unique environment of the school setting," but reached a different conclusion as to the Policy's constitutionality. 242 F.3d 1264, 1270 (2001). Before imposing a suspicionless drug testing program, the Court of Appeals concluded that a school "must demonstrate that there is some identifiable drug abuse problem among a sufficient number of those subject to the testing, such that testing that group of students will actually redress its drug problem." *Id.*, at 1278. The Court of Appeals then held that because the School District failed to demonstrate such a problem existed among Tecumseh students participating in competitive extracurricular activities, the Policy was unconstitutional. We granted certiorari, 534 U.S. 1015, 122 S.Ct. 509, 151 L.Ed.2d 418 (2001), and now reverse.

II.

[1] The Fourth Amendment to the United States Constitution protects "[t]he right of the people to be secure in their persons, houses, papers, and effects, against unreasonable searches and seizures." Searches by public school officials, such as the collection of urine samples, implicate Fourth Amendment interests. See *Vernonia*, supra, at 652, 115 S.Ct. 2386; cf. *New Jersey v. T.L.O.*, 469 U.S. 325, 334, 105 S.Ct. 733, 83 L.Ed.2d 720 (1985). We must therefore review the School District's Policy for "reasonableness," which is the touchstone of the constitutionality of a governmental search.

In the criminal context, reasonableness usually requires a showing of probable cause. See, *e.g.*, *Skinner v. Railway Labor Executives' Assn.*, 489 U.S. 602, 619, 109 S.Ct. 1402, 103 L.Ed.2d 639 (1989). The probable-cause standard,

however, "is peculiarly related to criminal investigations" and may be unsuited to determining the reasonableness of administrative searches where the "Government seeks to *prevent* the development of hazardous conditions." *Treasury Employees v. Von Raab*, 489 U.S. 656, 667–668, 109 S.Ct. 1384, 103 L.Ed.2d 685 (1989) (internal quotation marks and citations omitted) (collecting cases). The Court has also held that a warrant and finding of probable cause are unnecessary in the public school context because such requirements " 'would unduly interfere with the maintenance of the swift and informal disciplinary procedures [that are] needed.' " *Vernonia*, supra, at 653, 115 S.Ct. 2386 (quoting *T.L.O., supra*, at 340–341, 105 S.Ct. 733).

[2][3] Given that the School District's Policy is not in any way related to the conduct of criminal investigations, see Part II-B, *infra*, respondents do not contend that the School District requires probable cause before testing students for drug use. Respondents instead argue that drug testing must be based at least on some level of individualized suspicion. See Brief for Respondents 12-14. It is true that we generally determine the reasonableness of a search by balancing the nature of the intrusion on the individual's privacy against the promotion of legitimate governmental interests. See *Delaware v. Prouse*, 440 U.S. 648, 654, 99 S.Ct. 1391, 59 L.Ed. 2d 660 (1979). But we have long held that "the Fourth Amendment imposes no irreducible requirement of [individualized] suspicion." *United States v. Martinez–Fuerte*, 428 U.S. 543, 561, 96 S.Ct. 3074, 49 L.Ed.2d 1116 (1976). "[I]n certain limited circumstances, the Government's need to discover such latent or hidden conditions, or to prevent their development, is sufficiently compelling to justify the intrusion on privacy entailed by conducting such searches without any measure of individualized suspicion." *Von Raab, supra, at 668,* 109 S.Ct. 1384; see also *Skinner, supra,* at 624, 109 S.Ct. 1402. Therefore, in the context of safety and administrative regulations, a search unsupported by probable cause may be reasonable "when 'special needs, beyond the normal need for law enforcement, make the warrant and probable-cause requirement impracticable.' " *Griffin v. Wisconsin,* 483 U.S. 868, 873, 107 S.Ct. 3164, 97 L.Ed.2d 709 (1987) (quoting *T.L.O., supra,* at 351, 105 S.Ct. 733 (Blackmun, J., concurring in judgment)); see also *Vernonia, supra,* at 653, 115 S.Ct. 2386; *Skinner, supra,* at 619, 109 S.Ct. 1402.

continued

Significantly, this Court has previously held that "special needs" inhere in the public school context. See *Vernonia, supra,* at 653, 115 S.Ct. 2386; T.L.O., supra, at 339–340, 105 S.Ct. 733. While schoolchildren do not shed their constitutional rights when they enter the schoolhouse, see *Tinker v. Des Moines Independent Community School Dist.,* 393 U.S. 503, 506, 89 S.Ct. 733, 21 L.Ed.2d 731 (1969), "Fourth Amendment rights . . . are different in public schools than elsewhere; the 'reasonableness' inquiry cannot disregard the schools' custodial and tutelary responsibility for children." *Vernonia, supra,* at 656, 115 S.Ct. 2386. In particular, a finding of individualized suspicion may not be necessary when a school conducts drug testing.

In *Vernonia,* this Court held that the suspicionless drug testing of athletes was constitutional. The Court, however, did not simply authorize all school drug testing, but rather conducted a fact-specific balancing of the intrusion on the children's Fourth Amendment rights against the promotion of legitimate governmental interests. See 515 U.S., at 652-653, 115 S.Ct. 2386. Applying the principles of *Vernonia* to the somewhat different facts of this case, we conclude that Tecumseh's Policy is also constitutional.

A.

We first consider the nature of the privacy interest allegedly compromised by the drug testing. See *id.,* at 654, 115 S.Ct. 2386. As in *Vernonia,* the context of the public school environment serves as the backdrop for the analysis of the privacy interest at stake and the reasonableness of the drug testing policy in general. See *ibid.* ("Central . . . is the fact that the subjects of the Policy are (1) children, who (2) have been committed to the temporary custody of the State as schoolmaster"); see also *id.,* at 665, 115 S.Ct. 2386 ("The most significant element in this case is the first we discussed: that the Policy was undertaken in furtherance of the government's responsibilities, under a public school system, as guardian and tutor of children entrusted to its care"); *ibid.* ("[W]hen the government acts as guardian and tutor the relevant question is whether the search is one that a reasonable guardian and tutor might undertake").

A student's privacy interest is limited in a public school environment where the State is responsible for maintaining discipline, health, and safety. Schoolchildren are routinely required to submit to physical examinations and vaccinations against disease. See *id.,* at 656, 115 S.Ct. 2386. Securing order in the school environment sometimes requires that students be subjected to greater controls than those appropriate for adults. See *T.L.O., supra,* at 350, 105 S.Ct. 733 (Powell, J., concurring) ("Without first establishing discipline and maintaining order, teachers cannot begin to educate their students. And apart from education, the school has the obligation to protect pupils from mistreatment by other children, and also to protect teachers themselves from violence by the few students whose conduct in recent years has prompted national concern").

Respondents argue that because children participating in nonathletic extracurricular activities are not subject to regular physicals and communal undress, they have a stronger expectation of privacy than the athletes tested in *Vernonia.* See Brief for Respondents 18-20. This distinction, however, was not essential to our decision in *Vernonia,* which depended primarily upon the school's custodial responsibility and authority.[3]

In any event, students who participate in competitive extracurricular activities voluntarily subject themselves to many of the same intrusions on their privacy as do athletes.[4] Some of these clubs and activities require occasional off-campus travel and communal undress. All of them have their own rules and requirements for participating students that do not apply to the student body as a whole. 115 F.Supp.2d, at 1289-1290. For example, each of the competitive extracurricular activities governed by the Policy must abide by the rules of the Oklahoma Secondary Schools Activities Association, and a faculty sponsor monitors the students for compliance with the various rules dictated by the clubs and activities. See *id.,* at 1290. This regulation of extracurricular activities further diminishes the expectation of privacy among schoolchildren. Cf. *Vernonia, supra,* at 657, 115 S.Ct. 2386 ("Somewhat like adults who choose to participate in a closely regulated industry, students who voluntarily participate in school athletics have reason to expect intrusions upon normal rights and privileges, including privacy" (internal quotation marks omitted)). We therefore conclude that the students affected by this Policy have a limited expectation of privacy.

B.

Next, we consider the character of the intrusion imposed by the Policy. See *Vernonia, supra,* at 658, 115 S.Ct. 2386.

Urination is "an excretory function traditionally shielded by great privacy." *Skinner*, 489 U.S., at 626, 109 S.Ct. 1402. But the "degree of intrusion" on one's privacy caused by collecting a urine sample "depends upon the manner in which production of the urine sample is monitored." *Vernonia, supra*, at 658, 115 S.Ct. 2386.

Under the Policy, a faculty monitor waits outside the closed restroom stall for the student to produce a sample and must "listen for the normal sounds of urination in order to guard against tampered specimens and to insure an accurate chain of custody." App. 199. The monitor then pours the sample into two bottles that are sealed and placed into a mailing pouch along with a consent form signed by the student. This procedure is virtually identical to that reviewed in *Vernonia*, except that it additionally protects privacy by allowing male students to produce their samples behind a closed stall. Given that we considered the method of collection in *Vernonia* a "negligible" intrusion, 515 U.S., at 658, 115 S.Ct. 2386, the method here is even less problematic.

In addition, the Policy clearly requires that the test results be kept in confidential files separate from a student's other educational records and released to school personnel only on a "need to know" basis. Respondents nonetheless contend that the intrusion on students' privacy is significant because the Policy fails to protect effectively against the disclosure of confidential information and, specifically, that the school "has been careless in protecting that information: for example, the Choir teacher looked at students' prescription drug lists and left them where other students could see them." Brief for Respondents 24. But the choir teacher is someone with a "need to know," because during off-campus trips she needs to know what medications are taken by her students. Even before the Policy was enacted the choir teacher had access to this information. See App. 132. In any event, there is no allegation that any other student did see such information. This one example of alleged carelessness hardly increases the character of the intrusion.

Moreover, the test results are not turned over to any law enforcement authority. Nor do the test results here lead to the imposition of discipline or have any academic consequences. Cf. *Vernonia, supra*, at 658, and n. 2, 115 S.Ct. 2386. Rather, the only consequence of a failed drug test is to limit the student's privilege of participating in extracurricular activities. Indeed, a student may test positive for drugs twice and still be allowed to participate in extracurricular activities. After the first positive test, the school contacts the student's parent or guardian for a meeting. The student may continue to participate in the activity if within five days of the meeting the student shows proof of receiving drug counseling and submits to a second drug test in two weeks. For the second positive test, the student is suspended from participation in all extracurricular activities for 14 days, must complete four hours of substance abuse counseling, and must submit to monthly drug tests. Only after a third positive test will the student be suspended from participating in any extracurricular activity for the remainder of the school year, or 88 school days, whichever is longer. See App. 201-202.

Given the minimally intrusive nature of the sample collection and the limited uses to which the test results are put, we conclude that the invasion of students' privacy is not significant.

C.

Finally, this Court must consider the nature and immediacy of the government's concerns and the efficacy of the Policy in meeting them. See *Vernonia*, 515 U.S., at 660, 115 S.Ct. 2386. This Court has already articulated in detail the importance of the governmental concern in preventing drug use by schoolchildren. See *id.*, at 661-662, 115 S.Ct. 2386. The drug abuse problem among our Nation's youth has hardly abated since *Vernonia* was decided in 1995. In fact, evidence suggests that it has only grown worse.[5] As in *Vernonia*, "the necessity for the State to act is magnified by the fact that this evil is being visited not just upon individuals at large, but upon children for whom it has undertaken a special responsibility of care and direction." *Id.*, at 662, 115 S.Ct. 2386. The health and safety risks identified in *Vernonia* apply with equal force to Tecumseh's children. Indeed, the nationwide drug epidemic makes the war against drugs a pressing concern in every school.

Additionally, the School District in this case has presented specific evidence of drug use at Tecumseh schools. Teachers testified that they had seen students who appeared to be under the influence of drugs and that they had heard students speaking openly about using drugs. See, *e.g.*, App. 72 (deposition of Dean Rogers); *id.*, at 115 (deposition of Sheila Evans). A drug

continued

dog found marijuana cigarettes near the school parking lot. Police officers once found drugs or drug paraphernalia in a car driven by a Future Farmers of America member. And the school board president reported that people in the community were calling the board to discuss the "drug situation." See 115 F.Supp.2d, at 1285-1286. We decline to second-guess the finding of the District Court that "[v]iewing the evidence as a whole, it cannot be reasonably disputed that the [School District] was faced with a 'drug problem' when it adopted the Policy." *Id.,* at 1287.

Respondents consider the proffered evidence insufficient and argue that there is no "real and immediate interest" to justify a policy of drug testing nonathletes. Brief for Respondents 32. We have recognized, however, that "[a] demonstrated problem of drug abuse . . . [is] not in all cases necessary to the validity of a testing regime," but that some showing does "shore up an assertion of special need for a suspicionless general search program." *Chandler v. Miller,* 520 U.S. 305, 319, 117 S.Ct. 1295, 137 L.Ed.2d 513 (1997). The School District has provided sufficient evidence to shore up the need for its drug testing program.

Furthermore, this Court has not required a particularized or pervasive drug problem before allowing the government to conduct suspicionless drug testing. For instance, in *Von Raab* the Court upheld the drug testing of customs officials on a purely preventive basis, without any documented history of drug use by such officials. See 489 U.S., at 673, 109 S.Ct. 1384. In response to the lack of evidence relating to drug use, the Court noted generally that "drug abuse is one of the most serious problems confronting our society today," and that programs to prevent and detect drug use among customs officials could not be deemed unreasonable. *Id.,* at 674, 109 S.Ct. 1384; cf. *Skinner,* 489 U.S., at 607, and n. 1, 109 S.Ct. 1402 (noting nationwide studies that identified on-the-job alcohol and drug use by railroad employees). Likewise, the need to prevent and deter the substantial harm of childhood drug use provides the necessary immediacy for a school testing policy. Indeed, it would make little sense to require a school district to wait for a substantial portion of its students to begin using drugs before it was allowed to institute a drug testing program designed to deter drug use.

Given the nationwide epidemic of drug use, and the evidence of increased drug use in Tecumseh schools, it was entirely reasonable for the School District to enact this particular drug testing policy. We reject the Court of Appeals' novel test that "any district seeking to impose a random suspicionless drug testing policy as a condition to participation in a school activity must demonstrate that there is some identifiable drug abuse problem among a sufficient number of those subject to the testing, such that testing that group of students will actually redress its drug problem." 242 F.3d, at 1278. Among other problems, it would be difficult to administer such a test. As we cannot articulate a threshold level of drug use that would suffice to justify a drug testing program for schoolchildren, we refuse to fashion what would in effect be a constitutional quantum of drug use necessary to show a "drug problem."

Respondents also argue that the testing of nonathletes does not implicate any safety concerns, and that safety is a "crucial factor" in applying the special needs framework. Brief for Respondents 25-27. They contend that there must be "surpassing safety interests," *Skinner, supra,* at 634, 109 S.Ct. 1402, or "extraordinary safety and national security hazards," *Von Raab,* supra, at 674, 109 S.Ct. 1384, in order to override the usual protections of the Fourth Amendment. See Brief for Respondents 25-26. Respondents are correct that safety factors into the special needs analysis, but the safety interest furthered by drug testing is undoubtedly substantial for all children, athletes and nonathletes alike. We know all too well that drug use carries a variety of health risks for children, including death from overdose.

We also reject respondents' argument that drug testing must presumptively be based upon an individualized reasonable suspicion of wrongdoing because such a testing regime would be less intrusive. See *id.,* at 12–16. In this context, the Fourth Amendment does not require a finding of individualized suspicion, see *supra,* at 2565, and we decline to impose such a requirement on schools attempting to prevent and detect drug use by students. Moreover, we question whether testing based on individualized suspicion in fact would be less intrusive. Such a regime would place an additional burden on public school teachers who are already tasked with the difficult job of maintaining order and discipline. A program of individualized suspicion might unfairly target members of unpopular groups. The fear of lawsuits resulting from such targeted searches may chill enforcement of the program, rendering it ineffective in combating drug use. See *Vernonia*, 515 U.S., at 663-664, 115 S.Ct. 2386 (offering similar reasons for why "testing based on 'suspicion' of drug use would not be better, but worse"). In any case, this Court has repeatedly stated that reasonableness under the Fourth Amendment does not require employing the least intrusive means, because "[t]he logic of such elaborate less-restrictive-alternative arguments could raise insuperable barriers to the exercise of virtually all search-and-seizure powers." *Martinez–Fuerte*, 428 U.S., at 556-557, n. 12, 96 S.Ct. 3074; see also *Skinner, supra,* at 624, 109 S.Ct. 1402 ("[A] showing of individualized suspicion is not a constitutional floor, below which a search must be presumed unreasonable").

Finally, we find that testing students who participate in extracurricular activities is a reasonably effective means of addressing the School District's legitimate concerns in preventing, deterring, and detecting drug use. While in *Vernonia* there might have been a closer fit between the testing of athletes and the trial court's finding that the drug problem was "fueled by the 'role model' effect of athletes' drug use," such a finding was not essential to the holding. 515 U.S., at 663, 115 S.Ct. 2386; cf. *id.,* at 684–685, 115 S.Ct. 2386 (O'CONNOR, J., dissenting) (questioning the extent of the drug problem, especially as applied to athletes). *Vernonia* did not require the school to test the group of students most likely to use drugs, but rather considered the constitutionality of the program in the context of the public school's custodial responsibilities. Evaluating the Policy in this context, we conclude that the drug testing of Tecumseh students who participate in extracurricular activities effectively serves the School District's interest in protecting the safety and health of its students.

III.

Within the limits of the Fourth Amendment, local school boards must assess the desirability of drug testing schoolchildren. In upholding the constitutionality of the Policy, we express no opinion as to its wisdom. Rather, we hold only that Tecumseh's Policy is a reasonable means of furthering the School District's important interest in preventing and deterring drug use among its schoolchildren. Accordingly, we reverse the judgment of the Court of Appeals.

It is so ordered.

Justice BREYER, concurring.

I agree with the Court that *Vernonia School Dist. 47J v. Acton,* 515 U.S. 646, 115 S.Ct. 2386, 132 L.Ed.2d 564 (1995), governs this case and requires reversal of the Tenth Circuit's decision. The school's drug testing program addresses a serious national problem by focusing upon demand, avoiding the use of criminal or disciplinary sanctions, and relying upon professional counseling and treatment. See App. 201-202. In my view, this program does not violate the Fourth Amendment's prohibition of "unreasonable searches and seizures." I reach this conclusion primarily for the reasons given by the Court, but I would emphasize several underlying considerations, which I understand to be consistent with the Court's opinion.

I.

In respect to the school's need for the drug testing program, I would emphasize the following: First, the drug problem in our Nation's schools is serious in terms of size, the kinds of drugs being used, and the consequences of that use both for our children and the rest of us. See, *e.g.,* White House Nat. Drug Control Strategy 25 (Feb. 2002) (drug abuse leads annually to about 20,000 deaths, $160 billion in economic costs); Department of Health and Human Services, L. Johnston et al., Monitoring the Future: National Results on Adolescent Drug Use, Overview of Key Findings 5 (2001) (Monitoring the Future) (more than one-third of all students have used illegal drugs before completing the eighth grade; more than half before completing high school); *ibid.* (about 30% of all students use drugs *other than marijuana* prior to completing high school (emphasis added)); National Center on Addiction and Substance Abuse, Malignant Neglect: Substance Abuse and America's Schools 15 (Sept. 2001) (Malignant Neglect) (early use leads to later drug dependence); Nat. Drug Control Strategy, *supra,* at 2569 (same).

Second, the government's emphasis upon supply side interdiction apparently has not reduced teenage use in recent years. Compare R. Perl, CRS Issue Brief for Congress, Drug Control: International Policy and Options CRS-1 (Dec. 12, 2001) (supply side programs account for 66% of the federal drug control budget), with Partnership for a Drug-Free America, 2001

continued

Partnership Attitude Tracking Study: Key Findings 1 (showing increase in teenage drug use in early 1990's, peak in 1997, holding steady thereafter); 2000–2001 PRIDE National Summary: Alcohol, Tobacco, Illicit Drugs, Violence and Related Behaviors, Grades 6 thru 12 (Apr. 5, 2002), http://www.pridesurveys.com/us00.pdf (slight rise in high school drug use in 2000–2001); Monitoring the Future, Table 1 (lifetime prevalence of drug use increasing over last 10 years).

Third, public school systems must find effective ways to deal with this problem. Today's public expects its schools not simply to teach the fundamentals, but "to shoulder the burden of feeding students breakfast and lunch, offering before and after school child care services, and providing medical and psychological services," all in a school environment that is safe and encourages learning. Brief for National School Boards Association et al. as *Amici Curiae* 3-4. See also *Bethel School Dist. No. 403 v. Fraser,* 478 U.S. 675, 681, 106 S.Ct. 3159, 92 L.Ed.2d 549 (1986) (Schools " 'prepare pupils for citizenship in the Republic [and] inculcate the habits and manners of civility as values in themselves conductive to happiness and as indispensable to the practice of self-government in the community and the nation' ") (quoting C. Beard & M. Beard, New Basic History of the United States 228 (1968)). The law itself recognizes these responsibilities with the phrase *in loco parentis*—a phrase that draws its legal force primarily from the needs of younger students (who here are necessarily grouped together with older high school students) and which reflects, not that a child or adolescent lacks an interest in privacy, but that a child's or adolescent's school-related privacy interest, when compared to the privacy interests of an adult, has different dimensions. Cf. *Vernonia, supra,* at 654–655, 115 S.Ct. 2386. A public school system that fails adequately to carry out its responsibilities may well see parents send their children to private or parochial school instead— with help from the State. See *Zelman v. Simmons-Harris,* U.S. 122 S.Ct. 2460, L.Ed.2d.l.

Fourth, the program at issue here seeks to discourage demand for drugs by changing the school's environment in order to combat the single most important factor leading school children to take drugs, namely, peer pressure. Malignant Neglect 4 (students "whose friends use illicit drugs are more than 10 times likelier to use illicit drugs than those whose friends do not"). It offers the adolescent a nonthreatening reason to decline his friend's drug-use invitations, namely, that he intends to play baseball, participate in debate, join the band, or engage in any one of half a dozen useful, interesting, and important activities.

II.

In respect to the privacy-related burden that the drug testing program imposes upon students, I would emphasize the following: First, not everyone would agree with this Court's characterization of the privacy-related significance of urine sampling as "negligible." *Ante,* at 2566 (quoting *Vernonia,* 515 U.S., at 658, 115 S.Ct. 2386). Some find the procedure no more intrusive than a routine medical examination, but others are seriously embarrassed by the need to provide a urine sample with someone listening "outside the closed rest-room stall," *ante,* at 2566. When trying to resolve this kind of close question involving the interpretation of constitutional values, I believe it important that the school board provided an opportunity for the airing of these differences at public meetings designed to give the entire community "the opportunity to be able to participate" in developing the drug policy. App. 87. The board used this democratic, participatory process to uncover and to resolve differences, giving weight to the fact that the process, in this instance, revealed little, if any, objection to the proposed testing program.

Second, the testing program avoids subjecting the entire school to testing. And it preserves an option for a conscientious objector. He can refuse testing while paying a price (nonparticipation) that is serious, but less severe than expulsion from the school.

Third, a contrary reading of the Constitution, as requiring "individualized suspicion" in this public school context, could well lead schools to push the boundaries of "individualized suspicion" to its outer limits, using subjective criteria that may "unfairly target members of unpopular groups," *ante,* at 2568-2569, or leave those whose behavior is slightly abnormal stigmatized in the minds of others. See Belsky, Random vs. Suspicion-Based Drug Testing in the Public Schools—A Surprising Civil Liberties Dilemma, 27 Okla. City U.L.Rev. 1, 20-21 (forthcoming 2002) (listing court-approved factors justifying suspicion-based drug testing, including tiredness, overactivity, quietness, boisterousness, sloppiness, excessive meticulousness, and tardiness). If so, direct application of the Fourth Amendment's prohibition against "unreasonable searches and seizures" will further that Amendment's liberty-protecting objectives at least to the same extent as application of the mediating "individualized suspicion" test, where, as here, the testing program is neither criminal nor disciplinary in nature.

* * * *

I cannot know whether the school's drug testing program will work. But, in my view, the Constitution does not prohibit the effort. Emphasizing the considerations I have mentioned, along with others to which the Court refers, I conclude that the school's drug testing program, constitutionally speaking, is not "unreasonable." And I join the Court's opinion.

Justice O'CONNOR, with whom Justice SOUTER joins, dissenting.

I dissented in *Vernonia School Dist. 47J v. Acton,* 515 U.S. 646, 115 S.Ct. 2386, 132 L.Ed.2d 564 (1995), and continue to believe that case was wrongly decided. Because *Vernonia* is now this Court's precedent, and because I agree that petitioners' program fails even under the balancing approach adopted in that case, I join Justice GINSBURG's dissent.

Justice GINSBURG, with whom Justice STEVENS, JUSTICE O'CONNOR, and Justice SOUTER join, dissenting.

Seven years ago, in *Vernonia School Dist. 47J v. Acton,* 515 U.S. 646, 115 S.Ct. 2386, 132 L.Ed.2d 564 (1995), this Court determined that a school district's policy of randomly testing the urine of its student-athletes for illicit drugs did not violate the Fourth Amendment. In so ruling, the Court emphasized that drug use "increase[d] the risk of sports-related injury" and that *Vernonia's* athletes were the "leaders" of an aggressive local "drug culture" that had reached " 'epidemic proportions.' " *Id.,* at 649, 115 S.Ct. 2386. Today, the Court relies upon *Vernonia* to permit a school district with a drug problem its superintendent repeatedly described as "not . . . major," see App. 180, 186, 191, to test the urine of an academic team member solely by reason of her participation in a nonathletic, competitive extracurricular activity—participation associated with neither special dangers from, nor particular predilections for, drug use.

"[T]he legality of a search of a student," this Court has instructed, "should depend simply on the reasonableness, under all the circumstances, of the search." *New Jersey v. T.L.O.,* 469 U.S. 325, 341, 105 S.Ct. 733, 83

L.Ed.2d 720 (1985). Although " 'special needs' inhere in the public school context," see *ante,* at 2564 (quoting *Vernonia,* 515 U.S., at 653, 115 S.Ct. 2386), those needs are not so expansive or malleable as to render reasonable any program of student drug testing a school district elects to install. The particular testing program upheld today is not reasonable, it is capricious, even perverse: Petitioners' policy targets for testing a student population least likely to be at risk from illicit drugs and their damaging effects. I therefore dissent.

I.

A.

A search unsupported by probable cause nevertheless may be consistent with the Fourth Amendment "when special needs, beyond the normal need for law enforcement, make the warrant and probable-cause requirement impracticable." *Griffin v. Wisconsin,* 483 U.S. 868, 873, 107 S.Ct. 3164, 97 L.Ed.2d 709 (1987) (internal quotation marks omitted). In *Vernonia,* this Court made clear that "such 'special needs' . . . exist in the public school context." 515 U.S., at 653, 115 S.Ct. 2386 (quoting *Griffin,* 483 U.S., at 873, 107 S.Ct. 3164). The Court observed:

> "[W]hile children assuredly do not 'shed their constitutional rights . . . at the schoolhouse gate,' *Tinker v. Des Moines Independent Community School Dist.,* 393 U.S. 503, 506, 89 S.Ct. 733, 21 L.Ed.2d 731 (1969), the nature of those rights is what is appropriate for children in school . . . . Fourth Amendment rights, no less than First and Fourteenth Amendment rights, are different in public schools than elsewhere; the 'reasonableness' inquiry cannot disregard the schools' custodial and tutelary responsibility for children." 515 U.S., at 655-656, 115 S.Ct. 2386 (other citations omitted).

The *Vernonia* Court concluded that a public school district facing a disruptive and explosive drug abuse problem sparked by members of its athletic teams had "special needs" that justified suspicionless testing of district athletes as a condition of their athletic participation.

This case presents circumstances dispositively different from those of *Vernonia.* True, as the Court stresses, Tecumseh students participating in competitive extracurricular activities other than athletics share two relevant characteristics with the athletes of *Vernonia.*

continued

First, both groups attend public schools. "[O]ur decision in *Vernonia*," the Court states, "depended primarily upon the school's custodial responsibility and authority." *Ante*, at 2565; see also *ante*, at 2570 (BREYER, J., concurring) (school districts act in *loco parentis*). Concern for student health and safety is basic to the school's caretaking, and it is undeniable that "drug use carries a variety of health risks for children, including death from overdose." *Ante*, at 2568 (majority opinion).

Those risks, however, are present for all schoolchildren. *Vernonia* cannot be read to endorse invasive and suspicionless drug testing of all students upon any evidence of drug use, solely because drugs jeopardize the life and health of those who use them. Many children, like many adults, engage in dangerous activities on their own time; that the children are enrolled in school scarcely allows government to monitor all such activities. If a student has a reasonable subjective expectation of privacy in the personal items she brings to school, see *T.L.O.*, 469 U.S., at 338-339, 105 S.Ct. 733, surely she has a similar expectation regarding the chemical composition of her urine. Had the Vernonia Court agreed that public school attendance, in and of itself, permitted the State to test each student's blood or urine for drugs, the opinion in *Vernonia* could have saved many words. See, *e.g.*, 515 U.S., at 662, 115 S.Ct. 2386 ("[I]t must not be lost sight of that [the *Vernonia* School District] program is directed . . . to drug use by school athletes, where the risk of immediate physical harm to the drug user or those with whom he is playing his sport is particularly high.").

The second commonality to which the Court points is the voluntary character of both interscholastic athletics and other competitive extracurricular activities. "By choosing to 'go out for the team,' [school athletes] voluntarily subject themselves to a degree of regulation even higher than that imposed on students generally." *Id.*, at 657, 115 S.Ct. 2386. Comparably, the Court today observes, "students who participate in competitive extracurricular activities voluntarily subject themselves to" additional rules not applicable to other students. *Ante*, at 2565–2566.

The comparison is enlightening. While extracurricular activities are "voluntary" in the sense that they are not required for graduation, they are part of the school's educational program; for that reason, the petitioner (hereinafter School District) is justified in expending public resources to make them available. Participation in such activities is a key component of school life, essential in reality for students applying to college, and, for all participants, a significant contributor to the breadth and quality of the educational experience. See Brief for Respondents 6; Brief for American Academy of Pediatrics et al. as *Amici Curiae* 8-9. Students "volunteer" for extracurricular pursuits in the same way they might volunteer for honors classes: They subject themselves to additional requirements, but they do so in order to take full advantage of the education offered them. Cf. *Lee v. Weisman*, 505 U.S. 577, 595, 112 S.Ct. 2649, 120 L.Ed.2d 467 (1992) ("Attendance may not be required by official decree, yet it is apparent that a student is not free to absent herself from the graduation exercise in any real sense of the term 'voluntary,' for absence would require forfeiture of those intangible benefits which have motivated the student through youth and all her high school years.").

Voluntary participation in athletics has a distinctly different dimension: Schools regulate student-athletes discretely because competitive school sports by their nature require communal undress and, more important, expose students to physical risks that schools have a duty to mitigate. For the very reason that schools cannot offer a program of competitive athletics without intimately affecting the privacy of students, *Vernonia* reasonably analogized school athletes to "adults who choose to participate in a closely regulated industry." 515 U.S., at 657, 115 S.Ct. 2386 (internal quotation marks omitted). Industries fall within the closely regulated category when the nature of their activities requires substantial government oversight. See, *e.g.*, *United States v. Biswell*, 406 U.S. 311, 315–316, 92 S.Ct. 1593, 32 L.Ed.2d 87 (1972). Interscholastic athletics similarly require close safety and health regulation; a school's choir, band, and academic team do not.

In short, *Vernonia* applied, it did not repudiate, the principle that "the legality of a search of a student should depend simply on the reasonableness, *under all the circumstances*, of the search." *T.L.O.*, 469 U.S., at 341, 105 S.Ct. 733 (emphasis added). Enrollment in a public school, and election to participate in school activities beyond the bare minimum that the curriculum requires, are indeed factors relevant to reasonableness, but they do not on their own justify intrusive, suspicionless searches. *Vernonia*, accordingly, did not rest upon these factors; instead, the Court performed what today's majority aptly describes as a "fact-specific balancing," *ante,* at 2565. Balancing of that order, applied to the facts now before the Court, should yield a result other than the one the Court announces today.

B.

Vernonia initially considered "the nature of the privacy interest upon which the search [there] at issue intrude[d]." 515 U.S., at 654, 115 S.Ct. 2386. The Court emphasized that student-athletes' expectations of privacy are necessarily attenuated:

> "Legitimate privacy expectations are even less with regard to student-athletes. School sports are not for the bashful. They require 'suiting up' before each practice or event, and showering and changing afterwards. Public school locker rooms, the usual sites for these activities, are not notable for the privacy they afford. The locker rooms in *Vernonia* are typical: No individual dressing rooms are provided; shower heads are lined up along a wall, unseparated by any sort of partition or curtain; not even all the toilet stalls have doors. . . . [T]here is an element of communal undress inherent in athletic participation." *Id.,* at 657, 115 S.Ct. 2386 (internal quotation marks omitted).

Competitive extracurricular activities other than athletics, however, serve students of all manner: the modest and shy along with the bold and uninhibited. Activities of the kind plaintiff-respondent Lindsay Earls pursued—choir, show choir, marching band, and academic team—afford opportunities to gain self-assurance, to "come to know faculty members in a less formal setting than the typical classroom," and to acquire "positive social supports and networks [that] play a critical role in periods of heightened stress." Brief for American Academy of Pediatrics et al. as *Amici Curiae* 13.

On "occasional out-of-town trips," students like Lindsay Earls "must sleep together in communal settings and use communal bathrooms." 242 F.3d 1264, 1275 (C.A.10 2001). But those situations are hardly equivalent to the routine communal undress associated with athletics; the School District itself admits that when such trips occur, "public-like restroom facilities," which presumably include enclosed stalls, are ordinarily available for changing, and that "more modest students" find other ways to maintain their privacy. Brief for Petitioners 34.[1]

After describing school athletes' reduced expectation of privacy, the *Vernonia* Court turned to "the character of the intrusion . . . complained of." 515 U.S., at 658, 115 S.Ct. 2386. Observing that students produce urine samples in a bathroom stall with a coach or teacher outside, *Vernonia* typed the privacy interests compromised by the process of obtaining samples "negligible." *Ibid.* As to the required pretest disclosure of prescription medications taken, the Court assumed that "the School District would have permitted [a student] to provide the requested information in a confidential manner— for example, in a sealed envelope delivered to the testing lab." *Id.,* at 660, 115 S.Ct. 2386. On that assumption, the Court concluded that *Vernonia*'s athletes faced no significant invasion of privacy.

In this case, however, Lindsay Earls and her parents allege that the School District handled personal information collected under the policy carelessly, with little regard for its confidentiality. Information about students' prescription drug use, they assert, was routinely viewed by Lindsay's choir teacher, who left files containing the information unlocked and unsealed, where others, including students, could see them; and test results were given out to all activity sponsors whether or not they had a clear "need to know." See Brief for Respondents 6, 24; App. 105-106, 131. But see *id.,* at 199 (policy requires that "[t]he medication list shall be submitted to the lab in a sealed and confidential envelope and shall not be viewed by district employees").

In granting summary judgment to the School District, the District Court observed that the District's "Policy expressly provides for confidentiality of test results, and the Court must assume that the confidentiality provisions will be honored." 115 F.Supp.2d 1281, 1293 (W.D.Okla.2000). The assumption is unwarranted. Unlike *Vernonia,* where the District Court held a bench trial before ruling in the School District's favor, this case was decided by the District Court on summary judgment. At that stage, doubtful matters should not have been resolved in favor of the judgment seeker. See *United States v. Diebold, Inc.,* 369 U.S. 654, 655, 82 S.Ct. 993, 8 L.Ed.2d 176 (1962) (*per curiam*) ("On summary judgment the inferences to be drawn from the underlying facts contained in [affidavits, attached exhibits, and depositions] must be viewed in the light most favorable to the party opposing the motion."); see also 10A

continued

Charles Alan Wright, Arthur R. Miller, & Mary Kay Kane, Federal Practice and Procedure § 2716, pp. 274–277 (3d ed.1998).

Finally, the "nature and immediacy of the governmental concern," *Vernonia,* 515 U.S., at 660, 115 S.Ct. 2386, faced by the Vernonia School District dwarfed that confronting Tecumseh administrators. Vernonia initiated its drug testing policy in response to an alarming situation: "[A] large segment of the student body, particularly those involved in interscholastic athletics, was in a state of rebellion . . . fueled by alcohol and drug abuse as well as the student[s'] misperceptions about the drug culture." *Id.,* at 649, 115 S.Ct. 2386 (internal quotation marks omitted). Tecumseh, by contrast, repeatedly reported to the Federal Government during the period leading up to the adoption of the policy that "types of drugs [other than alcohol and tobacco] including controlled dangerous substances, are present [in the schools] but have not identified themselves as major problems at this time." 1998–1999 Tecumseh School's Application for Funds under the Safe and Drug-Free Schools and Communities Program, reprinted at App. 191; accord, 1996–1997 Application, reprinted at App. 186; 1995–1996 Application, reprinted at App. 180.[2] As the Tenth Circuit observed, "without a demonstrated drug abuse problem among the group being tested, the efficacy of the District's solution to its perceived problem is . . . greatly diminished." 242 F.3d, at 1277.

The School District cites *Treasury Employees v. Von Raab,* 489 U.S. 656, 673–674, 109 S.Ct. 1384, 103 L.Ed.2d 685 (1989), in which this Court permitted random drug testing of customs agents absent "any perceived drug problem among Customs employees," given that "drug abuse is one of the most serious problems confronting our society today." See also *Skinner v. Railway Labor Executives' Assn.,* 489 U.S. 602, 607, and n. 1, 109 S.Ct. 1402, 103 L.Ed.2d 639 (1989) (upholding random drug and alcohol testing of railway employees based upon industry-wide, rather than railway-specific, evidence of drug and alcohol problems). The tests in *Von Raab* and *Railway Labor Executives,* however, were installed to avoid enormous risks to the lives and limbs of others, not dominantly in response to the health risks to users invariably present in any case of drug use. See *Von Raab,* 489 U.S., at 674, 109 S.Ct. 1384 (drug use by customs agents involved in drug interdiction creates "extraordinary safety and national security hazards"); *Railway Labor Executives,* 489 U.S., at 628, 109 S.Ct. 1402 (railway operators "discharge duties fraught with such risks of injury to others that even a momentary lapse of attention can have disastrous consequences"); see also *Chandler v. Miller,* 520 U.S. 305, 321, 117 S.Ct. 1295, 137 L.Ed.2d 513 (1997) ("*Von Raab* must be read in its unique context").

Not only did the *Vernonia* and Tecumseh districts confront drug problems of distinctly different magnitudes, they also chose different solutions: *Vernonia* limited its policy to athletes; Tecumseh indiscriminately subjected to testing all participants in competitive extracurricular activities. Urging that "the safety interest furthered by drug testing is undoubtedly substantial for all children, athletes and nonathletes alike," *ante,* at 2568, the Court cuts out an element essential to the *Vernonia* judgment. Citing medical literature on the effects of combining illicit drug use with physical exertion, the *Vernonia* Court emphasized that "the particular drugs screened by [*Vernonia's*] Policy have been demonstrated to pose substantial physical risks to athletes." 515 U.S., at 662, 115 S.Ct. 2386; see also *id.,* at 666, 115 S.Ct. 2386 (GINSBURG, J., concurring) (*Vernonia* limited to "those seeking to engage with others in team sports"). We have since confirmed that these special risks were necessary to our decision in *Vernonia.* See *Chandler,* 520 U.S., at 317, 117 S.Ct. 1295 (*Vernonia* "emphasized the importance of deterring drug use by schoolchildren and the risk of injury a drug-using student-athlete cast on himself and those engaged with him on the playing field"); see also *Ferguson v. Charleston,* 532 U.S. 67, 87, 121 S.Ct. 1281, 149 L.Ed.2d 205 (2001) (KENNEDY, J., concurring) (*Vernonia's* policy had goal of " '[d]eterring drug use by our Nation's schoolchildren,' and particularly by student-athletes, because 'the risk of immediate physical harm to the drug user or those with whom he is playing his sport is particularly high' ") (quoting *Vernonia,* 515 U.S., at 661-662, 115 S.Ct. 2386).

At the margins, of course, no policy of *random* drug testing is perfectly tailored to the harms it seeks to address. The School District cites the dangers faced by members of the band, who must "perform extremely precise routines with heavy equipment and instruments in close proximity to other students," and by Future Farmers of America, who "are required to individually control and restrain animals as large as 1500 pounds." Brief for Petitioners 43. For its part, the United States acknowledges that "the linebacker faces a greater risk of serious injury if he takes the field under the influence of drugs than the drummer in the halftime band," but parries that "the risk of injury to a student who is under the influence of drugs while playing golf, cross country, or volleyball (sports covered by the policy in *Vernonia*) is scarcely any greater than the risk of injury to a student . . . handling a 1500-pound steer (as [Future Farmers of America] members do) or working with cutlery or other sharp instruments (as [Future Homemakers of America] members do)." Brief for United States as *Amicus Curiae* 18. One can demur to the Government's view of the risks drug use poses to golfers, cf. *PGA Tour, Inc. v. Martin*, 532 U.S. 661, 687, 121 S.Ct. 1879, 149 L.Ed.2d 904 (2001) ("golf is a low intensity activity"), for golfers were surely as marginal among the linebackers, sprinters, and basketball players targeted for testing in *Vernonia* as steer-handlers are among the choristers, musicians, and academic-team members subject to urinalysis in Tecumseh.[3] Notwithstanding nightmarish images of out-of-control flatware, livestock run amok, and colliding tubas disturbing the peace and quiet of Tecumseh, the great majority of students the School District seeks to test in truth are engaged in activities that are not safety sensitive to an unusual degree. There is a difference between imperfect tailoring and no tailoring at all.

The *Vernonia* district, in sum, had two good reasons for testing athletes: Sports team members faced special health risks and they "were the leaders of the drug culture." *Vernonia*, 515 U.S., at 649, 115 S.Ct. 2386. No similar reason, and no other tenable justification, explains Tecumseh's decision to target for testing all participants in every competitive extracurricular activity. See *Chandler*, 520 U.S., at 319, 117 S.Ct. 1295 (drug testing candidates for office held incompatible with Fourth Amendment because program was "not well designed to identify candidates who violate antidrug laws").

Nationwide, students who participate in extracurricular activities are significantly less likely to develop substance abuse problems than are their less-involved peers. See, *e.g.*, N. Zill, C. Nord, & L. Loomis, Adolescent Time Use, Risky Behavior, and Outcomes 52 (1995) (tenth graders "who reported spending no time in school-sponsored activities were . . . 49 percent more likely to have used drugs" than those who spent 1–4 hours per week in such activities). Even if students might be deterred from drug use in order to preserve their extracurricular eligibility, it is at least as likely that other students might forgo their

extracurricular involvement in order to avoid detection of their drug use. Tecumseh's policy thus falls short doubly if deterrence is its aim: It invades the privacy of students who need deterrence least, and risks steering students at greatest risk for substance abuse away from extracurricular involvement that potentially may palliate drug problems.[4]

To summarize, this case resembles *Vernonia* only in that the School Districts in both cases conditioned engagement in activities outside the obligatory curriculum on random subjection to urinalysis. The defining characteristics of the two programs, however, are entirely dissimilar. The *Vernonia* district sought to test a subpopulation of students distinguished by their reduced expectation of privacy, their special susceptibility to drug-related injury, and their heavy involvement with drug use. The Tecumseh district seeks to test a much larger population associated with none of these factors. It does so, moreover, without carefully safeguarding student confidentiality and without regard to the program's untoward effects. A program so sweeping is not sheltered by *Vernonia;* its unreasonable reach renders it impermissible under the Fourth Amendment.

II.

In *Chandler*, this Court inspected "Georgia's requirement that candidates for state office pass a drug test"; we held that the requirement "d[id] not fit within the closely guarded category of constitutionally permissible suspicionless searches." 520 U.S., at 309, 117 S.Ct. 1295. Georgia's testing prescription, the record showed, responded to no "concrete danger," *id.*, at 319, 117 S.Ct. 1295, was supported by no evidence of a particular problem, and targeted a group not involved in "high-risk, safety- sensitive tasks," *id.*, at 321-322, 117 S.Ct. 1295. We concluded:

> "What is left, after close review of Georgia's scheme, is the image the State seeks to project. By requiring candidates for public office to submit to drug testing, Georgia displays its commitment to the struggle against drug abuse .... The need revealed, in short, is symbolic, not 'special,' as that term draws meaning from our case law." *Ibid.*

Close review of Tecumseh's policy compels a similar conclusion. That policy was not shown to advance the " 'special needs' [existing] in the public school

continued

context [to maintain] . . . swift and informal disciplinary procedures . . . [and] order in the schools,"
Vernonia, 515 U.S., at 653, 115 S.Ct. 2386 (internal
quotation marks omitted). See *supra,* at 2574, 2575–
2577. What is left is the School District's undoubted
purpose to heighten awareness of its abhorrence of,
and strong stand against, drug abuse. But the desire to
augment communication of this message does not
trump the right of persons—even of children within
the schoolhouse gate—to be "secure in their persons
. . . against unreasonable searches and seizures." U.S.
Const., Amdt. 4.

In *Chandler,* the Court referred to a pathmarking dissenting opinion in which "Justice Brandeis recognized
the importance of teaching by example: 'Our
Government is the potent, the omnipresent teacher. For
good or for ill, it teaches the whole people by its example.' " 520 U.S., at 322, 117 S.Ct. 1295 (quoting *Olmstead
v. United States,* 277 U.S. 438, 485, 48 S.Ct. 564, 72 L.Ed.
944 (1928)). That wisdom should guide decisionmakers
in the instant case: The government is nowhere more a
teacher than when it runs a public school.

It is a sad irony that the petitioning School District seeks
to justify its edict here by trumpeting "the schools'
custodial and tutelary responsibility for children."
Vernonia, 515 U.S., at 656, 115 S.Ct. 2386. In regulating
an athletic program or endeavoring to combat an
exploding drug epidemic, a school's custodial obligations may permit searches that would otherwise unac-
ceptably abridge students' rights. When custodial duties
are not ascendant, however, schools' tutelary obligations
to their students require them to "teach by example" by
avoiding symbolic measures that diminish constitutional
protections. "That [schools] are educating the young
for citizenship is reason for scrupulous protection of
Constitutional freedoms of the individual, if we are not
to strangle the free mind at its source and teach youth
to discount important principles of our government as
mere platitudes." *West Virginia Bd. of Ed. v. Barnette,* 319
U.S. 624, 637, 63 S.Ct. 1178, 87 L.Ed. 1628 (1943).

* * * *

For the reasons stated, I would affirm the judgment of
the Tenth Circuit declaring the testing policy at issue
unconstitutional.

122 S.Ct. 2559, 70 USLW 4737, 166 Ed. Law Rep. 79, 2
Cal. Daily Op. Serv. 5761, 2002 Daily Journal D.A.R.
7275, 15 Fla. L. Weekly Fed. S 483

FOOTNOTES

1.The District Court noted that the School
District's allegations concerning Daniel James
called his standing to sue into question because his
failing grades made him ineligible to participate in
any interscholastic competition. See 115 F.Supp.2d
1281, 1282, n. 1 (W.D.Okla.2000). The court
noted, however, that the dispute need not be
resolved because Lindsay Earls had standing, and
therefore the court was required to address the
constitutionality of the drug testing policy. See *ibid.*
Because we are likewise satisfied that Earls has
standing, we need not address whether James also
has standing.

2.The respondents did not challenge the Policy
either as it applies to athletes or as it provides for
drug testing upon reasonable, individualized
suspicion. See App. 28.

3. Justice GINSBURG argues that *Vernonia School
Dist. 47J v. Acton,* 515 U.S. 646, 115 S.Ct. 2386, 132
L.Ed.2d 564 (1995), depended on the fact that the
drug testing program applied only to student-athletes. But even the passage cited by the dissent
manifests the supplemental nature of this factor, as
the Court in *Vernonia* stated that "[l]egitimate
privacy expectations are *even less* with regard to student-athletes." *See post,* at 2574 (citing *Vernonia,* 515
U.S., at 657, 115 S.Ct. 2386) (emphasis added). In
upholding the drug testing program in *Vernonia,*
we considered the school context "[c]entral" and
"[t]he most significant element." 515 U.S., at 654,
665, 115 S.Ct. 2386. This hefty weight on the side
of the school's balance applies with similar force in
this case even though we undertake a separate balancing with regard to this particular program.

4. Justice GINSBURG's observations with regard to
extracurricular activities apply with equal force to
athletics. See *post,* at 2573 ("Participation in such
[extracurricular] activities is a key component of
school life, essential in reality for students applying
to college, and, for all participants, a significant
contributor to the breadth and quality of the
educational experience").

5. For instance, the number of 12th graders using
any illicit drug increased from 48.4 percent in 1995
to 53.9 percent in 2001. The number of 12th graders
reporting they had used marijuana jumped from

41.7 percent to 49.0 percent during that same period. See Department of Health and Human Services, Monitoring the Future: National Results on Adolescent Drug Use, Overview of Key Findings (2001) (Table 1).

1. According to Tecumseh's choir teacher, choir participants who chose not to wear their choir uniforms to school on the days of competitions could change either in "a rest room in a building" or on the bus, where "[m]any of them have figured out how to [change] without having [anyone] . . . see anything." 2 Appellants' App. in No. 00-6128 (CA10), p. 296.

2. The Court finds it sufficient that there be evidence of *some* drug use in Tecumseh's schools: "As we cannot articulate a threshold level of drug use that would suffice to justify a drug testing program for schoolchildren, we refuse to fashion what would in effect be a constitutional quantum of drug use necessary to show a 'drug problem.' " *Ante,* at 2568. One need not establish a bright-line "constitutional quantum of drug use" to recognize

the relevance of the superintendent's reports characterizing drug use among Tecumseh's students as "not . . . [a] major proble[m]," App. 180, 186, 191.

3. Cross-country runners and volleyball players, by contrast, engage in substantial physical exertion. See *Vernonia School Dist. 47J v. Acton* 515 U.S. 646, 663, 115 S.Ct. 2386, 132 L.Ed.2d 564 (1995) (describing special dangers of combining drug use with athletics generally).

4. The Court notes that programs of individualized suspicion, unlike those using random testing, "might unfairly target members of unpopular groups." *Ante,* at 2570; see also *ante,* at 2568–2569 (BREYER, J., concurring). Assuming, *arguendo,* that this is so, the School District here has not exchanged individualized suspicion for random testing. It has installed random testing in addition to, rather than in lieu of, testing "at any time when there is reasonable suspicion." App. 197.

Reprinted with permission from West Group.

■ NCAA Regulation

Intercollegiate student-athletes must sign a consent form in order to play college sports under the National Collegiate Athletic Association's policies. The NCAA established its own drug testing program in 1986 and comprehensively tests for both illegal "street" drugs and performance-enhancing drugs. Whether the NCAA is a "state actor" is subject to debate, though the answer seems to be that it is not and therefore is characterized as a private actor.[4]

■ Professional Sports

All major professional sports in the United States coordinate their own drug testing and use policies through collective bargaining agreements (CBAs) or consent from the professional athletes via an individual professional contract. The major aim of professional sports and drug testing appears to be treatment for the offender rather than punishment. Such policy is much different than the Olympic Games where punishment and future deterrence appears to be the primary concern.

One of the major concerns with drug testing in professional sports is that there is no uniform standard that applies to the NFL, NBA, NHL, and MLB. Each sport has different testing for a variety of drugs and punishments and treatment are different in each league. Additionally, there is confusion as to what drugs should be banned since the spectators themselves could legally purchase certain performance-enhancing training supplements at the local supermarket while the athletes could be punished for using the same supplements. Drug testing issues in professional sports center on contract and consent issues, not constitutional issues.

National Football League

In the NFL, the illegal use of drugs and the abuse of prescription drugs, over-the-counter drugs, and alcohol are prohibited. This applies to all players who have not yet retired from the league. The NFL's CBA sets the sole and exclusive means of testing for drugs and treating those players who have positive results. The National Football League's program is called the *Intervention Program* and establishes the appropriate levels of discipline. However, NFL players are only tested for cocaine, marijuana, amphetamines, morphine, codeine, and PCP. All players are tested in April and August, during the preseason.

■ The Olympic Games

No other organization in the world has taken a more proactive stance on the prevention of the use of performance-enhancing drugs than the International Olympic Committee (IOC).[5] In 1968 the IOC established the first testing of athletes in Grenoble, France's winter Olympic Games. The most infamous case involving an Olympic athlete was the use of illegal steroids by Canadian track star Ben Johnson in 1988 during the Seoul, Korea, Games. The Olympic Movement sets the standard for both "in competition" drug testing and "out of competition" testing that is the responsibility of each country's national olympic committee (NOC) and the particular national governing body (NGB) for that particular Olympic sport.

International Olympic Committee Policies

The IOC has a Medical Code for testing and disciplinary procedures in the event of a positive drug test. Failure to submit to a drug test is a violation of the IOC Medical Code. An Olympic athlete may appeal an adverse decision to the Court of Arbitration for Sport (CAS) during the Olympic Games competition. While the IOC tests during the Olympic Games, it uses the services of the WADA (World Anti-Doping Agency) for the time between the Pan American games and the Olympic Games. Two samples are taken from an athlete during an announced or unannounced test. These samples are then labeled an "A sample" and a "B sample." The A sample is tested. Then, only upon a positive result is the B sample tested. The athlete is notified of the A sample's positive result, the pending test of the B sample, and his or her right to be present with a witness at the testing of the B sample. The

United States Anti-Doping Agency's rules, for example, then give the suspected athlete access to important documents and provides a preliminary hearing step. Thus, much of the testing process focuses on due process.

After the A sample has been tested, and before the B sample is tested, the athlete is given the laboratory documents from the A sample testing process. These documents could prove valuable to the athlete when preparing to witness the B sample testing. After the B sample has been tested and before any further proceedings, the laboratory documents from the B sample testing are given to the athlete. If the B sample confirms the A sample's positive result, the Anti-Doping Review Board reviews the test results to determine whether there is sufficient evidence of doping to justify a hearing. Currently, blood tests are being experimented with to detect illegal blood doping that enhances performance by increasing an athlete's endurance. See Exhibit 7–1 for the IOC's List of Banned Substances.

Significant Historical Perspectives in Drug Testing

Ancient Greece

Large financial rewards were bestowed to ancient Greek victors during the Olympic Games. Athletes used combinations of plants and fungi such as mushrooms to increase performance.

1886

English cyclist Andrew Linton dies of an overdose of a drug while competing in the Bordeaux-Paris race, becoming the first recorded drug death in sports.

1940s

Testosterone appears on the market as an injectable steroid.

1960s

1960–Denmark's Knut Jensen dies at the 1960 Summer Olympics in Rome after taking amphetamines and nicotinyl tartrate.

1967–British cyclist Tommy Simpson dies while competing in the Tour de France. The Olympics begin drug testing and at the Mexico City games an athlete tests positive for alcohol.

1970s

1972–At the Munich Olympics, urine testing on athletes occurs for first time on a mass scale. Seven athletes test positive for banned drugs.

1975–Anabolic steroids are added to the IOC's banned list.

1980s

1982–Caffeine and testosterone are added to the IOC's banned list.

1983–At the Pan American Games in Caracas, Venezuela, athletes are not given notice of drug testing. The U.S. Olympic Committee immediately institutes testing for the 1984 Games in Los Angeles.

■ **EXHIBIT 7–1**   *International Olympic Committee List of Banned Substances*

LIST OF BANNED SUBSTANCES

INTERNATIONAL OLYMPIC COMMITTEE
MEDICAL CODE

**PROHIBITED CLASSES OF SUBSTANCES AND
PROHIBITED METHODS 31st January 1999**

Doping contravenes the ethics of both sport and medical science. Doping consists of:

1. the administration of substances belonging to prohibited classes of pharmacological agents, and/or

2. the use of various prohibited methods.

Article I:

PROHIBITED CLASSES OF SUBSTANCES

Prohibited substances fall into the following classes of substances:

A. Stimulants

B. Narcotics

C. Anabolic Agents

D. Diuretics

E. Peptide hormones, mimetics and analogues

All substances belonging to the prohibited classes cannot be used even if they are not listed as examples. For this reason, the term **"and related substances"** is introduced. This term describes drugs that are related to the class by their pharmacological action and/or chemical structure.

A. Stimulants: Explanation Text

Prohibited substances in class (A) include the following examples:

> amineptine, amiphenazole, amphetamines, bromantan, caffeine[1], carphedon, cocaine, ephedrines[2], fencamfamine, mesocarb, pentetrazol, pipradrol, salbutamol[3], salmeterol[3], terbutaline[3], . . . and related substances.

1. For caffeine the definition of a positive is a concentration in urine greater than 12 micrograms per millilitre.

2. For ephedrine, cathine and methylephedrine, the definition of a positive is a concentration in urine greater than 5 micrograms per millilitre. For phenylpropanolamine and pseudoephedrine, the definition of a positive is a concentration in urine greater than 10 micrograms per millilitre. If more than one of these substances are present below their respective thresholds, the concentrations should be added. If the sum is greater than 10 micrograms per millilitre, the sample shall be considered positive.

3. Permitted by inhaler only to prevent and/or treat asthma and exercise-induced asthma. Written notification of asthma and/or exercise-induced asthma by a respiratory or team physician is necessary to the relevant medical authority.

NOTE: All imidazole preparations are acceptable for topical use, e.g. oxymetazoline. Vasoconstrictors (e.g. adrenaline) may be administered with local anaesthetic agents. Topical preparations (e.g. nasal, ophthalmological) of phenylephrine are permitted.

B. Narcotics: Explanation Text

Prohibited substances in class (B) include the following examples:

> buprenorphine, dextromoramide, diamorphine (heroin), methadone, morphine, pentazocine, pethidine, . . . and related substances.

NOTE: codeine, dextromethorphan, dextropropoxyphene, dihydrocodeine, diphenoxylate, ethylmorphine, pholcodine, propoxyphene and tramadol are permitted.

C. Anabolic agents: Explanation Text

Prohibited substances in class (C) include the following examples:

1. Anabolic androgenic steroids:

> a/ clostebol, fluoxymesterone, metandienone, metenolone, nandrolone, 19-norandrostenediol, 19-norandrostenedione, oxandrolone, stanozolol, . . . and related substances

> b/ androstenediol, androstenedione, dehydroepiandrosterone (DHEA), dihydrotestosterone, testosterone[1], . . . and related substances

Evidence obtained from metabolic profiles and/or isotopic ratio measurements may be used to draw definitive conclusions.

1. The presence of a testosterone (T) to epitestostrone (E) ratio greater than six (6) to one (1) in the urine of a competitor constitutes an offence unless there is

evidence that this ratio is due to a physiological or pathological condition, e.g. low epitestosterone excretion, androgen producing tumour, enzyme deficiencies.

In the case of T/E greater than 6, it is mandatory that the relevant medical authority conducts an investigation before the sample is declared positive. A full report will be written and will include a review of previous tests, subsequent tests and any results of endocrine investigations. In the event that previous tests are not available, the athlete should be tested unannounced at least once per month for three months. The results of these investigations should be included in the report. Failure to co-operate in the investigations will result in declaring the sample positive.

2. Beta-2 agonists When administered orally or by injection:

bambuterol, clenbuterol, fenoterol, formoterol, reproterol, salbutamol[1], terbutaline[1], . . . and related substances

1. Authorized by inhalation as described in Article (I.A.).

D. Diuretics: Explanation Text

Explanation Text Prohibited substances in class (D) include the following examples:

acetazolamide, bumetanide, chlorthalidone, etacrynic acid, furosemide, hydrochlorothiazide, mannitol[1], mersalyl, spironolactone, triamterene, . . . and related substances

1. Prohibited by intravenous injection.

E. Peptide hormones, mimetics and analogues: Explanation Text

Prohibited substances in class (E) include the following examples and their analogues and mimetics:

1. Chorionic Gonadotrophin (hCG);

2. Pituitary and synthetic gonadotrophins (LH);

3. Corticotrophins (ACTH, tetracosactide);

4. Growth hormone (hGH);

5. Insulin-like Growth Factor (IGF-1) and all the respective releasing factors and their analogues;

6. Erythropoietin (EPO);

7. Insulin permitted only to treat insulin-dependent diabetes. Written notification of insulin-dependent diabetes by an endocrinologist or team physician is necessary.

The presence of an abnormal concentration of an endogenous hormone or its diagnostic marker(s) in the urine of a competitor constitutes an offence unless it has been conclusively documented to be solely due to a physiological or pathological condition.

Article II:

PROHIBITED METHODS

The following procedures are prohibited:

A. Blood doping: Explanation Text

Blood doping is the administration of **blood, red blood cells, artificial oxygen carriers, and related blood products** to an athlete.

B. Pharmacological, chemical and physical manipulation

Pharmacological, chemical and physical manipulation is the use of substances and of methods which alter, attempt to alter, or may reasonably be expected to alter the integrity and validity of samples used in doping controls. These include, without limitation, the administration of diuretics, catheterisation, sample substitution and or tampering, inhibition of renal excretion such as by **probenecid** and related compounds, and alterations of testosterone and epitestosterone measurements such as **epitestosterone**[1] or **bromantan** administration.

1. An epitestosterone concentration in the urine greater than 200 nanograms per millilitre will be investigated by studies as in Article (I..C. Ib) for testosterone.

The success or failure of the use of a prohibited substance or method is not material. It is sufficient that the said substance or procedure was used or attempted for the infraction to be considered as consummated.

Article III:

CLASSES OF DRUGS SUBJECT TO CERTAIN RESTRICTIONS

Alcohol

Where the rules of a responsible authority so provide, tests will be conducted for ethanol.

continued

Cannabinoids

Where the rules of a responsible authority so provide, tests will be conducted for cannabinoids (e.g. Marijuana, Hashish). At the Olympic Games, tests will be conducted for cannabinoids. A concentration in urine of 11-nor-delta 9-tetrahydrocannabinol-9-carboxylic acid (carboxy-THC) greater than 15 nanograms per millilitre is prohibited.

Local anaesthetics

Injectable local anaesthetics are permitted under the following conditions:

a. bupivacaine, lidocaine, mepivacaine, procaine, etc. can be used but not cocaine. Vasoconstrictor agents (e.g. adrenaline) may be used in conjunction with local anaesthetics.

b. only local or intra-articular injections may be administered;

c. only when medically justified.

Where the rules of a responsible authority so provide, notification of administration may be necessary.

Corticosteroids: Explanation Text

The systemic use of corticosteroids is prohibited.

Anal, aural, dermatological, inhalational, nasal and ophthalmological (but not rectal) administration is permitted. Intra-articular and local injections of corticosteroids are permitted. Where the rules of a responsible authority so provide, notification of administration may be necessary.

Beta-blockers: Explanation Text

Some examples of beta-blockers are: acebutolol, alprenolol, atenolol, labetalol, metoprolol, nadolol, oxprenolol, propranolol, sotalol, . . . and related substances

Where the rules of an International Sports Federation so provide, tests will be conducted for beta-blockers.

SUMMARY OF IOC REGULATIONS FOR DRUGS WHICH NEED THE WRITTEN NOTIFICATION OF A PHYSICIAN

SUBSTANCES	PROHIBITED	AUTHORIZED WITH NOTIFICATION	AUTHORIZED WITHOUT NOTIFICATION
Selected beta-agonists*	Oral Systemic injections	Inhalational	
Corticosteroids	Oral Systemic injections Rectal		anal, aural, dermatological, inhalational, nasal, ophthalmological, local and intra-articular injections***
Local anaesthetics**	Systemic injections		local and intra-articular injections***[1]

*salbutamol, salmeterol, terbutaline; all other beta-agonists are prohibited
**except cocaine, which is prohibited
***where the rule of the responsible authority so provide, notification may be necessary

SUMMARY OF URINARY CONCENTRATIONS ABOVE WHICH IOC ACCREDITED LABORATORIES MUST REPORT FINDINGS FOR SPECIFIC SUBSTANCES

Caffeine	> 12 micrograms/millilitre
Carboxy-THC	> 15 nanograms/millilitre
Cathine	> 5 micrograms/millilitre
Ephedrine	> 5 micrograms/millilitre
Epitestosterone	> 200 nanograms/millilitre
Methylephedrine	> 5 micrograms/millilitre
Morphine	> 1 micrograms/millilitre
Phenylpropanolamine	> 10 micrograms/millilitre
Pseudoephedrine	> 10 micrograms/millilitre
T/E ratio	> 6

Article IV:

Except as specifically otherwise provided in the IOC Medical Code, the detected presence of any amount of substances in classes (a), (b), (c), (d) and (e) in respect of a test conducted in connection with a competition shall constitute a definitive case of doping. The quantity of the substance detected is not material to a definitive case of doping.

Article V:

The detected presence of ephedrine, pseudoephedrine, phenylpropanolamine and cathine in respect of a test conducted in connection with a competition shall constitute a prima facie case of doping. The person affected shall have the opportunity to rebut the presumption of doping by providing evidence that the substance was present under circumstances which, on a balance of probabilities, including the quantity of substance detected, would support a conclusion that doping was neither intended, nor the result of gross negligence, willful negligence nor imprudence. In all cases, the onus of rebutting the presumption of doping, when the substance has been detected, shall rest with the person affected.

Article VI:

Out-of-competition testing is directed solely at prohibited substances in class I(c), (d) and (e). The only positive results for purposes of out-of-competition testing and the application of the IOC Medical Code will be in respect of such classes of prohibited substances and pharmacological, chemical and physical manipulation (class II(b)).

Article VII:

LIST OF EXAMPLES OF PROHIBITED SUBSTANCES

CAUTION: This is not an exhaustive list of prohibited substances. Many substances that do not appear on this list are considered prohibited under the term "and related substances"

All athletes are strongly advised only to take medicines which are prescribed by a medical doctor and to ensure that they contain only drugs that are not prohibited by the IOC Medical Commission or the responsible authorities.

Whenever an athlete is required to undergo a doping control all medications and drugs taken or administered in the previous seven days should be declared on the doping control official record.

Stimulants

amineptine	cropropamide	heptaminol
amfepramone	crotethamide	mefenorex
amiphenazole	ephedrine	mephentermine
amphetamine	etamivan	mesocarb
bambuterol	etilamphetamine	methamphetamine
bromantan	etilefrine	methoxyphenamine
caffeine	fencamfamin	methylenedioxy-amphetamine
carphedon	fenetylline	methylephedrine
cathine	fenfluramine	methylphenidate
cocaine	formoterol	nikethamide
prolintane	propylhexedrine	pseudoephedrine
salbutamol	salmeterol	selegiline
terbutaline	norfenfluramine	parahydroxy-amphetamine
pemoline	pentetrazol	phendimetrazine
phentermine	phenylephrine	phenyl-propanolamine
pholedrine	pipradrol	reproterol
strychnine		

continued

Narcotics

buprenorphine	hydrocodone	pentazocine
dextromoramide	methadone	pethidine
diamorphine(heroin)	morphine	

Anabolic Agents

androstenediol	dihydrotestosterone	metenolone
androstenedione	drostanolone	methandriol
bambuterol	fenoterol	methyltestosterone
boldenone	fluoxymesterone	mibolerone
clenbuterol	formebolone	nandrolone
clostebol	formoterol	19-norandrostenediol
danazol	gestrinone	19-norandrostenedione
dehydrochlormethyl-testosterone	mesterolone	norethandrolone
dehydroepiandrosterone (DHEA)	metandienone	oxandrolone
oxymesterone	oxymetholone	reproterol
salbutamol	salmeterol	stanozolol
terbutaline	testosterone	trenbolone

Diuretics

acetazolamide	ethacrynic acid	mannitol
bendroflumethiazide	furosemide	mersalyl
bumetanide	hydrochlorothiazide	spironolactone
canrenone	indapamide	triamterene
chlortalidone		

Masking Agents

bromantan	diuretics (see above)
epitestosterone	probenecid

Peptide Hormones, Mimetics and Analogues		
ACTH	erythropoietin (EPO)	hGH
hCG	insulin	LH

Beta Blockers:			
acebutolol	betaxolol	labetalol	oxprenolol
alprenolol	bisoprolol	metoprolol	propranolol
atenolol	bunolol	nadolol	sotalol

Reprinted with permission from the IOC. Content subject to change.

1984–The U.S. cycling team wins nine medals but use illegal blood transfusions to enhance their performance. Officials say the results were stolen or shredded.

1988–Seoul Olympic gold medal sprinter Ben Johnson of Canada tests positive for stanozolol, a steroid, and is later stripped of his medal. At the same games, Bulgaria is stripped of two weightlifting gold medals for using diuretics that mask steroids.

1990s

1990–American track star and world record-holder Butch Reynolds tests positive for nandrolone and is suspended by the IAAF. He later sues and wins a $27.4 million judgment against the IAAF, which is later overturned by a U.S. court of appeal.

1996–American track star Mary Slaney fails drug test at the U.S. Olympic trials and is later suspended by IAAF. She claims it was due to the use of a birth control pill. During the Summer Olympic Games in Atlanta, several positive drug tests on the last weekend of competition are tossed out by the IOC. The IOC says it was concerned about "technical difficulties" in the drug-testing process.

1998–The Tour de France becomes a haven for positive drug tests, and numerous athletes and teams are ejected from competition while other riders quit in protest. In early 1998, Australian customs agents find 13 vials of HGH (human growth hormone) carried by a Chinese swimmer. Irish swimmer Michelle Smith (winner of three gold medals and a bronze in Atlanta) receives a four-year ban after submitting a tainted urine sample having high levels of whiskey. American shot put competitor Randy Barnes receives a lifetime suspension for his second positive test for a banned Olympic substance.

1999–British track star Linford Christie is suspended by UK athletics after testing positive for nandrolone. Cuban high jumper Javier Sotomayor is stripped of his gold medal at the Pan American Games after testing positive for cocaine. He won the gold medal in 1992 in Barcelona. American sprinter Dennis Mitchell is suspended for testing positive for testosterone. He had won the bronze medal in the 100m in 1992 Olympic Games.

2000–Sydney Olympic Games silver medalist Ivan Ivanov of Bulgaria tests positive for Furosemide, a diuretic. The entire Bulgarian weightlifting team is thrown out of the Olympic Games. Vadim Devyatkovsky of Belarus tests positive for nandrolone. Czech Republic cyclist Jan Hruska tests positive for Nandrolone and is thrown out of the Olympics. American Shot Put competitor C. J. Hunter is unable to compete in Olympics due to injury and positive drug test for banned steroid.

2001–Spain's Txema Del Olmo failed a test for EPO. He was later dropped from the Tour de France and banned from racing in France for three years.

2002–During the Salt Lake City Olympics, a total of 1,960 drug tests—642 in-competition urine tests, 96 out-of-competition urine controls and 1,222 blood screening tests— were conducted during the games, the most comprehensive testing ever. This represented an increase over the 621 tests conducted at the 1998 Winter Games in Nagano, Japan. Three cross-country athletes, all gold medalists, tested positive during the games for darbepoetin. Spain's Johann Muehlegg was stripped of his gold in the 50-kilometer race, one of his three gold medals; Russia's Larissa Lazutina lost her gold in the 30-kilometer race; and Russia's Olga Danilova was disqualified from the 30 K event. However, all three kept medals won in earlier races. French rider Laurent Paumier was kicked out of the Tour de France for failing a drug test. Several other racers were suspended as well, including Italians Gilberto Simoni, Stefano Garzelli and Marco Pantani. 1997 Tour de France winner Jan Ullrich tested positive for amphetamines while recovering from a knee injury. Also, Dutchman Hein Verbruggen, the president of the International Cycling Union (UCI), resigned from the world anti-doping agency (WADA) in protest of WADA procedures.

Recent Drug Concerns: HGH and EPO

Human growth hormone (HGH) and **erythropoietin (EPO)** are of most recent concern to the IOC. Blood tests are considered the best option for eventually identifying EPO and HGH, which cannot be competely detected through urine testing. The IOC and the WADA are making strides in finding a reliable test for such drugs. Until recently, it was impossible to detect EPO, which builds endurance by boosting the production of oxygen-rich red blood cells.

United States

The United States Olympic Committee (USOC) is the National Olympic Committee (NOC) for the United States Olympic Movement. The USOC super-

---

human growth hormone (HGH)   hormone that affects all body systems and plays a major role in muscle growth and development

erythropoietin (EPO)   performance-enhancing hormone affecting red blood cells

vises each particular Olympic sport and its NGB.[4] The USOC has a NAN (no advance notice) out-of-competition drug testing policy. The USOC coordinates all Olympic trials and Pan American Games trials and all activities relevant to those trials. The USOC initiated its first formal drug testing program in 1985.

National Governing Bodies

Each NGB has an MOA (Memorandum of Agreement) with the USOC that recognizes athlete's rights during the drug testing process in accordance with Article IX of the USOC Constitution. Under grievance procedures in accordance with the AAA (American Arbitration Association), an athlete is entitled to a decision within 48 hours.

■ Summary

The legality of drug testing of high school and professional athletes has been established and affirmed by the Supreme Court. Fourth and Fifth Amendment considerations are vital when establishing any governmental or other public drug testing campaign as it serves a legitimate public interest. While illegal and performance-enhancing drugs will continue to be of concern to competitors and administrators, testing has become more accurate. The NCAA, the IOC, and professional sports leagues have different drug testing policies and procedures that can be confusing at times. Numerous athletes have been dismissed from competition due to testing positive for drugs. As the tests become more accurate and prevalent, athletes will continue to be deterred from using drugs, though some will continue to attempt to outsmart the test. It is important for the practitioner to be well versed in the specific rules with regard to supplements and substances when working with the student-athlete or professional.

■ Key Terms

Fourteenth Amendment
due process
erythropoietin (EPO)
equal protection

Fifth Amendment
Fourth Amendment
human growth hormone (HGH)
performance-enhancing drugs

■ Additional Cases

Arlosoroff v. NCAA, 746 F.2d 1019 (4th Cir. 1984)
Foschi v. United States Swimming, Inc. 916 F. Supp. 232 (E.D.N.Y. 1996)
Hill v. NCAA, 865 P.2d 633 (Cal. 1994)
Joye ex rel. Joye v. Hunterdon Central Regional High School Bd. of Educ., 803 A.2d 706 (N.J. 2002)

NCAA v. Tarkanian, 488 U.S. 179 (1988)
Schaill by Kross v. Tippecanoe County School Corp., 679 F. Supp. 833 (N.D. Ind. 1988)
Skinner v. Railway Labor Executives' Ass'n., 489 U.S. 602 (1989)

■ Review Questions

1. Why do athletes continue to use performance-enhancing drugs even though it might affect their eligibility to participate in a sport?
2. Is testing for drugs via urine or blood a violation of constitutional rights? What constitutional amendments are primarily involved?
3. Is participation in high school or college sports a privilege or a right or both?
4. Why are some drugs legal in some sports and not in others?
5. Why is there such a push in recent years for the testing of the use of drugs at the international level?
6. Should the use of performance-enhancing drugs be legalized?

■ Endnotes

1 Exec. Order No. 12,564 51 Fed. Reg. 32,889 (1986).
2 21 U.S.C.A. §13 et seq.
3 *Skinner v. Railway Labor Executives' Ass'n.,* 489 U.S. 602 (1989), and *National Treasury Employees Union v. Von Raab,* 489 U.S. 656 (1989).
4 For example, USA Triathlon, US Swimming, and USA Track and Field.

CHAPTER EIGHT

International Sports Issues

■ Introduction

International sports and the law revolve primarily around the Olympic Games. The international Olympic rules, policies, and procedures have faced controversial national and international legal challenges and other disputes—including outright boycotts—since its inception. The summer and winter Olympic Games often produce modern heroes and legendary triumphs over adversity. However, confusing enforcement of Olympic rules is often considered among the participants surrounding the Olympic landscape.

As exposure of the Olympics has increased, so too has the money involved in the Olympic Games at all levels.[1] Athletes compete for international fame and fortune by winning a medal or having an uplifting story of overcoming obstacles to success. Professional athletes are now commonplace during the Olympics as well. In fact, the United States sent professional basketball players such as Michael Jordan to compete in the summer games in Barcelona, Spain, in 1992. The U.S. Olympic Committee now awards cash prizes to American athletes based on their performance at the Olympics, a practice that other countries have offered for a number of years.

This chapter focuses on the **Olympic Movement's** evolution and its impact on international law related to sport. It is important to understand that the Olympic Games are heavily influenced by political and financial forces, and athletes and other individuals have been victims of these external forces over time.

Olympic Movement term used to describe the underlying goals and themes of the Olympic Games and the International Olympic Committee

■ Competition for and During the Olympic Games

Nations fiercely compete for the ability to hold the Olympic Games within their borders to enhance their economic and social well-being. Such desire to reach economic and monetary rewards by athletes has tempted many Olympic participants to use illegal and unethical means to obtain an unfair advantage over other competitors despite the Olympic system's set of strict guidelines and rules with regard to illegal drugs, for example. Additionally, the IOC has suspended and permanently banned many medal hopefuls (and sometimes winners) for violations of the rules. Recently revealed corruption within the Olympic Movement itself has forced IOC to reevaluate the way it conducts business.

■ American Legal Challenges

Several prominent American athletes have challenged in American courts the Olympic system of eligibility and participation, including the infamous cases of Butch Reynolds and Tonya Harding. Though Olympic athletes may challenge actions of the Olympic system in a more organized and voluntary, private court for resolving such international disputes today, prior inconsistencies and sheer craziness with regard to jurisdiction has led to the formation of the **Court of Arbitration of Sport (CAS)**.

■ The Olympic Movement

The modern Olympic Games began in 1896 in Athens, Greece. At that time, athletes were thought to compete in the Olympic Games in an international setting only as amateurs. In other words, a competitor was seen as someone who competed only for the love of the sport without regard to financial rewards or fame. Today, however, after more than a century in existence, the Olympics are no longer just for amateurs. Professional athletes have been welcomed with open arms into the once pristine amateur world. The Olympics showcase athletic talents at the highest levels at the largest international party lasting several weeks every four years.[2]

Court of Arbitration of Sport (CAS)   body that addresses complaints of athletes, coaches, and federations under the jurisdiction of the Olympic Movement

■ International Political Landscape of the Olympic Games

The Olympic Games have been a combination of athletic competition, corporate promotions, and international politics. With the advent of television, and especially satellite transmission of broadcasts in the 1960s, the games became increasingly commercialized to produce profits and serve as a prestigious showcase for major countries, athletes, and corporations. Such powerful international influence has become part of the political game of the Olympics as well.

While the Olympic Games are supposed to unite the world through sport, international politics has interfered with the Olympics. At the 1936 Berlin Olympics, Adolf Hitler refused to recognize African American Jesse Owens' four gold medals, a wonder at that time. The 1972 Munich (West Germany) Games were marred by tragedy; Arab guerrillas killed Israeli athletes and took nine other hostages. The 1976 Montreal Olympic Games were also marred by the Canadian government's refusal to allow Taiwan's team to carry its flag or have its national anthem played at the games. Also, in Montreal, several African nations demanded that New Zealand be prevented from competing because one of its rugby teams had played in South Africa, at that time a racially segregationist nation. Thirty-one nations withdrew their teams from the 1976 Olympics competition as a result of New Zealand's refusal.

1980 Boycott

The United States boycotted the 1980 Moscow Olympics to protest the Soviet Union's invasion of Afghanistan. More than 60 other nations boycotted this event as well. As a result, the Soviet Union and 15 other nations withdrew from the 1984 Games in Los Angeles.

Recent Politics

The 1992 Olympics in Barcelona, Spain, included the Unified Team (with athletes from 12 former Soviet republics), a reunited Germany, and South Africa, appearing for the first time since 1960. At the 2000 Olympics in Sydney, Australia, North and South Korea entered the games under one flag, although they competed as separate countries. Teams from 199 nations and territories took part in the 2000 Summer Olympics in Sydney, Australia. Three nations—Eritrea, the Federated States of Micronesia, and Palau—competed for the first time, and four athletes from East Timor participated as individual Olympic athletes.

1980 Olympic Boycott   President Jimmy Carter's refusal to send a United States team to the Summer Olympic Games in Moscow

■ Olympic Structural Hierarchy

The Olympic Movement is the general term used to describe the international Olympic system of rules, regulations, policies, and procedures. One must understand how each level of the Olympic Movement works in order to appreciate the web of rules and regulations that can become complicated and sometimes seems extremely unfair and disheartening. The IOC is not a national government, but it is very powerful. It cannot force its rules on national governments, but countries that wish to participate in the Olympics must agree to its procedures in order to promote fair play and jurisprudence when resolving disputes. This includes an understanding of the relationship between the:

- International Olympic Committee (IOC)
- International Federations (IFs)
- National Olympic Committees (NOCs)

The International Olympic Committee

The IOC was established in 1894 for the 1896 Olympics in Athens, Greece. The IOC's headquarters are in Lausanne, Switzerland, and the organization was led by Juan Antonio Samaranch for the last two decades. The current President is Jacques Rogge, elected in 2001. The IOC sets and enforces Olympic policies. As of 2000, the IOC recognized 199 national Olympic committees, including the U.S. Olympic Committee (USOC), founded in 1900 and currently headquartered in Colorado Springs, Colorado. The IOC normally chooses the site of future games at least six years in advance.

The IOC mandates in its own rules that "every person or organization that plays any part whatsoever in the Olympic Movement shall accept the supreme authority of the IOC and shall be bound by its Rules and submit to its jurisdiction." It is the supreme authority in decisions regarding the suspension, expulsion, or disqualification of all athletes. The IOC relies heavily on the IFs governing individual sports. The IOC must also rely heavily on national Olympic committees and governments to enforce its rules and regulations.

IOC Supremacy

Being the supreme authority of the Olympic Movement, the IOC is the final authority on all questions concerning the Olympic Games and the Olympic Movement, including matters of discipline affecting athletes and coaches. Additionally, the IOC is the final arbiter for permanent and temporary penalties of all kinds, the heaviest of which are suspension, expulsion, disqualification, and exclusion. The powers of the IOC are paramount. It delegates to the IFs, however, the technical control of the sports they govern. The IOC has recently emphasized that disputes involving its own rules must be submitted to binding arbitration under the CAS.

International Olympic Committee (IOC)   Organization responsible for managing the Olympic Movement

International Federations

The IOC delegates to individual **international federations (IFs)** the technical control of all aspects of the sport they supervise as well as authority for suspending or disciplining individual athletes who violate the IF's rules or codes of conduct in accordance with the Olympic charter. Table 8–1 offers a list of IFs.

However, sometimes domestic (national) rights of the individual athletes conflict with the rules of the IOC or the IFs. Additionally, it is possible that athletes from one country might be treated differently from athletes from another country. This is inherently unfair and has led to numerous domestic and international lawsuits. The introduction of the International Council of Arbitration for Sport (ICAS) and its supervision over the CAS were designed to deal with ensuring that athletes around the world are treated the same for similar violations of the Olympic Movement.[3]

The National Olympic Committees

The IOC recognizes **national olympic committees (NOCs)** as the sole authorities responsible for representing their respective countries at the Olympic Games as well as at other events held under the patronage of the IOC. For the United States, that NOC is the United States Olympic Committee (USOC), which was originally chartered by Congress as an independent corporation on September 21, 1950.

The USOC exercises exclusive jurisdiction over all matters pertaining to the participation of the United States in the Olympic Games and in the Pan American Games. Further, the USOC is charged with providing for the swift resolution of conflicts and disputes involving amateur athletes, national governing bodies, and amateur sports organizations and with protecting the opportunity of any amateur athlete to participate in amateur athletic competition. Swift resolution of legal disputes, however, has not always been possible.

National Governing Bodies

Within the Olympic system of the United States, the USOC oversees organizations responsible for the administration of individual and team sports. Each of these organizations is called a **national governing body (NGB)**, and authority for their creation is found in the Amateur Sports Act.[4] The authority of the NGBs includes recommending individual athletes to the USOC for participation in the Olympic or Pan American Games as well as establishing internal procedures for determining eligibility standards.[5] The NGBs are responsible both to the USOC (and U.S. courts) and to the IF for their sport. In an eligibility dispute, the first decision to suspend a U.S. athlete is

---

international federation (IF)   sport-specific regulatory body that sets international rules under the jurisdiction of the IOC

national olympic committee (NOC)   designated national organization responsible for managing the affairs of a particular country's Olympic teams, such as the USOC

national governing body (NGB)   sport-specific regulatory body for a particular country, such as United States Swimming

■ **TABLE 8–1**　Olympic National and International Regulating Bodies

Sport	National Governing Body	International Federation
Archery	National Archery Association	Federation Internationale de Tir a l'Arc
Badminton	U.S. Badminton Association	International Badminton Federation
Baseball	USA Baseball	International Baseball Association
Basketball	USA Basketball	Federation Internationale de Basketball
Biathlon	U.S. Biathlon Association	Union Internationale de Pentathlon Moderne et Biathlon
Bobsled	U.S. Bobsled and Skeleton Federation	Federation Internationale de Bobsleigh et de Tobagganing
Boxing	USA Boxing	Association Internationale de Boxe Amateur
Canoe/Kayak	U.S. Canoe and Kayak Team	Federation Internationale de Canoe
Curling	USA Curling	World Curling Federation
Cycling	USA Cycling Inc.	Union Cycliste Internationale
Diving	United States Diving, Inc.	Federation Internationale de Natation Amateur
Equestrian	U.S. Equestrian Team	Federation Equestre Internationale
Fencing	U.S. Fencing Association	Federation International d'Escrime
Field Hockey	U.S. Field Hockey Association	Federation Internationale de Hockey
Figure Skating	U.S. Figure Skating Association	International Skating Union
Gymnastics	USA Gymnastics	Federation Internationale de Gymnastique
Ice Hockey	USA Hockey	International Ice Hockey Federation
Judo	United States Judo, Inc.	International Judo Federation
Luge	U.S. Luge Association	Federation Internationale de Luge de Course
Modern Pentathlon	U.S. Modern Pentathlon Association	Union Internationale de Pentathlon Moderne et Biathlon
Rowing	U.S. Rowing Association	Federation Internationale des Societes d'Aviron
Sailing	United States Sailing Association	International Yacht Racing Union
Shooting	USA Shooting	Union Internationale de Tir
Skiing	U.S. Skiing	Federation Internationale de Ski
Soccer	U.S. Soccer Federation	Federation Internationale de Football Association

■ **TABLE 8-1** Olympic National and International Regulating Bodies

Sport	National Governing Body	International Federation
Softball	Amateur Softball Association	Federation Internationale de Softball
Speed Skating	U.S. Speedskating	International Skating Union
Swimming	U.S. Swimming, Inc.	Federation Internationale de Natation Amateur
Synchronized Swimming	U.S. Synchronized Swimming, Inc.	Federation Internationale de Natation Amateur
Table Tennis	USA Table Tennis	International Table Tennis Federation
Tae kwon do	U.S. Tae kwon do Union	The World Tae kwon do Federation
Team Handball	U.S. Team Handball Federation	Federation Internationale de Handball
Tennis	U.S. Tennis Association	International Tennis Federation
Track and Field	USA Track & Field	International Amateur Athletic Federation
Triathlon	Triathlon Federation USA	International Triathlon Union
Volleyball	USA Volleyball	Federation Internationale de Volleyball
Water Polo	U.S. Water Polo	Federation Internationale de Natation Amateur
Weightlifting	U.S. Weightlifting Federation	International Weightlifting Federation
Wrestling	USA Wrestling	Federation Internationale de Luttes Associees

most likely to come from an NGB, although an IF may declare the athlete ineligible without a prior action by an NGB. This has led to vicious legal battles. However, the addition of the CAS has provided a much needed emphasis for these legal disputes.

■ The Amateur Sports Act of 1978

Congress expanded the powers of the USOC by enacting the **Amateur Sports Act of 1978**,[6] which includes sections dealing with grievance procedures for individual

---

Amateur Sports Act of 1978 American amateur sports act that established guidelines for athletes and the United States Olympic Committee

athletes wishing to contest suspensions. The United States government controls the very existence of the USOC even though the USOC has been held not to be a state actor.[7] In seeking protection from suspension procedures, many athletes have attempted to obtain shelter in the due process provision of the Fifth Amendment to the U.S. Constitution but have failed each time.

Under the 1978 Act, the USOC was granted the exclusive right to use:

1. the name "United States Olympic Committee;"
2. the five interlocking rings of the International Olympic Committee;
3. the USOC's emblem "consisting of an escutcheon having a blue chief and vertically extending red and white bars on the base with 5 interlocking rings displayed on the chief;" and
4. The words "Olympic," "Olympiad," "Citius Altius Fortius," or any combination of those words.[8]

The 1998 Amendments to the Amateur Sports Act of 1978

On October 21, 1998, President Bill Clinton signed into law some modifications of the 1978 Act and renamed it the **Ted Stevens Olympic and Amateur Sports Act (TSOASA).** The 1998 amendments modify the 1978 significantly. Such modifications included the additional supervision over the Paralympics,[9] preventing injunctions against the USOC 21 days prior to the relevant Games,[10] requiring the USOC to hire an "athlete ombudsman" charged with providing free independent advice to athletes about the Act, USOC bylaws, and rules of national governing bodies with respect to the resolution of any opportunity-to-compete dispute arising out of the Olympics, Paralympics, or any other competition covered by the statute,[11] and incorporating athletes with disabilities into the USOC structure.[12]

■ International Legal Cases

1980 U.S. Boycott of the Moscow Olympic Games

As Soviet tanks invaded Afghanistan, President Jimmy Carter threatened to boycott the 1980 Summer Olympics in Moscow unless the Soviets pulled out their troops. The Soviets refused. President Carter threatened to withhold funding and revoke the organization's tax exemption if the USOC would not comply with his request. A few weeks later the USOC voted 2–1 to support the boycott—the first time in U.S. history. More than 60 teams, including Japan and West Germany, joined the United

Ted Stevens Olympic and Amateur Sports Act (TSOASA) of 1998 Amendments to the Amateur Sports Act of 1978 giving amateur athletes more specific competition rights and recognizing the role and needs of athletes with disabilities

States in boycotting the games, leaving the number of participating countries at 80. It was the first Olympic Games held in a communist country. President Carter asked the IOC to move the location or delay the games, to no avail. The Winter Olympics, held later that same year in Lake Placid, New York, ironically did allow the Soviets to compete.

Many American athletes were understanding of the situation. Most were not, however, and a lawsuit ensued prior to the Games to determine whether the USOC had the authority to refuse to send a team. A group of 25 American athletes led by Anita DeFrantz, a member of the rowing team and the spokesperson for the USOC's Athletes Advisory Council, took legal action. However, the case was ruled in favor of the USOC to the athletes' dismay[13] (see Case 10). The plaintiffs alleged that the USOC violated the 1978 Amateur Sports Act, but their position was rejected by the district court. The district court concluded that the USOC was a private organization, and there was no intermingling between government and private functions other than having to submit an annual report to the President and Congress.

Butch Reynolds's Battle Royal

Harry "Butch" Reynolds was a world record holder and American sprinter. Reynolds ran in a meet in Monte Carlo on August 12, 1990, and was randomly tested for drugs by the IAAF, the IF responsible for track and field events. His drug test proved positive for the illegal steroid nandrolone, and the IAAF immediately suspended him for two years. Such a ban automatically disqualified him from the 1992 Olympics in Barcelona, Spain. Reynolds contested the suspension, claiming that he did not take steroids or other illegal drugs. Reynolds brought suit against TAC in the U.S. District Court for the Southern District of Ohio and alleged that the certain information vital for him to properly prepare for the hearing was not provided to him and that the decision with respect to eligibility had been predetermined.[14] The court dismissed Reynolds's due process claim under the Fifth Amendment, finding that TAC and the USOC were not state actors. Reynolds made the U.S. Olympic team as an alternate for the 400-meter relay, but the IAAF refused to let him compete in the 1992 Olympics and forced TAC to remove him from the U.S. Olympic team roster.

On August 10, 1992, the day before Reynolds's two-year ban by the IAAF was to expire, the IAAF extended the suspension until January 1, 1993, as a form of punishment for his participation at the U.S. Olympic Trials. Reynolds then filed a supplemental complaint in the Southern District of Ohio, and on December 3, 1992, the court finally awarded Reynolds $27.4 million in compensatory and treble punitive damages, finding the IAAF acted with revenge and ill will toward Reynolds.

When Reynolds and his attorneys attempted to collect the judgment, an appeal to the Sixth Circuit Court of Appeals was made by the IAAF. This court reversed the $27.4 million judgment, citing lack of personal jurisdiction, and the case ended swiftly thereafter, but not until after a war had been waged.

■ CASE 10 *DeFrantz v. United States Olympic Committee*

United States District Court, District of Columbia.

Anita DeFRANTZ et al., Plaintiffs,

v.

UNITED STATES OLYMPIC COMMITTEE,
Defendant

Civ. A. No. 80–1013.

May 16, 1980.

On motion of 25 athletes and one member of the executive board of the United States Olympic Committee for injunction barring the Committee from carrying out a resolution not to send an American team to participate in the games of the XXIInd Olympiad, the District Court, John H. Pratt, J., held that: (1) under International Olympic Committee rules and the Amateur Sports Act of 1978, the Committee not only had authority to decide not to send an American team to the summer olympics but also could do so for a reason not directly related to sports considerations, and (2) decision of the Committee not to send an American team to the summer olympics was not state action and therefore did not give rise to an actionable claim for infringements of constitutional rights.

Order accordingly.

William H. Allen, Edward R. Mackiewicz, Covington & Burling, Washington, D.C., for plaintiffs.

Patrick H. Sullivan, James S. Morris, Michael S. Press, Whitman & Ransom, Washington, D.C., for defendant.

JOHN H. PRATT, District Judge.

MEMORANDUM OPINION

Plaintiffs, 25 athletes and one member of the Executive Board of defendant United States Olympic Committee (USOC), have moved for an injunction barring defendant USOC from carrying out a resolution, adopted by the USOC House of Delegates on April 12, 1980, not to send an American team to participate in the Games of the XXIInd Olympiad to be held in Moscow in the summer of 1980. Plaintiffs allege that in preventing American athletes from competing in the Summer Olympics, defendant has exceeded its statutory powers and has abridged plaintiffs' constitutional rights.

For the reasons discussed below, we find that plaintiffs have failed to state a claim upon which relief can be granted. Accordingly, we deny plaintiffs' claim for injunctive and declaratory relief and dismiss the action.

THE FACTS

In essence, the action before us involves a dispute between athletes who wish to compete in the Olympic Games to be held in Moscow this summer,[1] and the United States Olympic Committee, which has denied them that opportunity in the wake of the invasion and continued occupation of Afghanistan by Soviet military forces. Because this dispute confronts us with questions concerning the statutory authority of the USOC, its place and appropriate role in the international Olympic movement, and its relationship to the United States Government and with certain United States officials, we begin with a brief discussion of the organizational structure of the Olympic Games and the facts which have brought this action before us. These facts are not in dispute.

According to its Rules and By-laws, the International Olympic Committee (IOC) governs the Olympic movement and owns the rights of the Olympic games.[2] IOC Rules provide that National Olympic Committees (NOC) may be established "as the sole authorities responsible for the representation of the respective countries at the Olympic Games,"[3] so long as the NOC's rules and regulations are approved by the IOC.[4] The USOC is one such National Olympic Committee.

The USOC is a corporation created and granted a federal charter by Congress in 1950. Pub.L. No. 81-805, 64 Stat. 899. This charter was revised by the Amateur Sports Act of 1978, Pub.L. No. 95-606, 92 Stat. 3045, 36 U.S.C. § 371 et seq. Under this statute, defendant USOC has "exclusive jurisdiction" and authority over participation and representation of the United States in the Olympic Games.

The routine procedure initiating the participation of a national team in Olympic competition is the acceptance by the NOC of an invitation from the Olympic Organizing Committee for the particular games.[5] In accordance with this routine procedure under IOC Rules, the Moscow Olympic Organizing Committee extended an invitation to the USOC to participate in the summer games. Recent international and domestic events, however, have made acceptance of this invitation, which must come on or before May 24, 1980, anything but routine.

On December 27, 1979, the Soviet Union launched an invasion of its neighbor, Afghanistan. That country's ruler was deposed and killed and a new government was installed. Fighting has been at times intense, casualties have been high, and hundreds of thousands of Afghan citizens have fled their homeland. At present, an estimated 100,000 Soviet troops remain in Afghanistan, and fighting continues.

President Carter termed the invasion a threat to the security of the Persian Gulf area as well as a threat to world peace and stability and he moved to take direct sanctions against the Soviet Union. These sanctions included a curtailment of agricultural and high technology exports to the Soviet Union, and restrictions on commerce with the Soviets. The Administration also turned its attention to a boycott of the summer Olympic Games as a further sanction against the Soviet Union.

As the affidavit of then Acting Secretary of State Warren Christopher makes clear, the Administration was concerned that "(t)he presence of American competitors would be taken by the Soviets as evidence that their invasion had faded from memory or was not a matter of great consequence or concern to this nation." Affidavit of Acting Secretary of State Warren Christopher, at 3. The Administration's concern was sharpened because "(t)he Soviet Union has made clear that it intends the Games to serve important national political ends. For the U.S.S.R., international sports competition is an instrument of government policy and a means to advance foreign policy goals." *Id.*

With these concerns in mind, the Administration strenuously urged a boycott of the Moscow games. On January 20, 1980, President Carter wrote the President of the United States Olympic Committee to urge that the USOC propose to the IOC that the 1980 summer games be transferred from Moscow, postponed, or cancelled if the Soviet forces were not withdrawn within a month. On January 23, 1980 the President delivered his State of the Union Message, in which he said that he would not support sending American athletes to Moscow while Soviet military forces remained in Afghanistan.

Following these statements, the United States House of Representatives passed, by a vote of 386 to 12, a Concurrent Resolution opposing participation by United States athletes in the Moscow Games unless Soviet troops were withdrawn from Afghanistan by February 20th. The Senate passed a similar resolution by a vote of 88 to 4.

As this was unfolding, the USOC's 86 member Executive Board held a meeting in Colorado Springs on January 26, 1980, inviting White House counsel Lloyd Cutler to address them "because no officer or any member of the Board was knowledgeable about the far-reaching implications of the Soviet invasion." Affidavit of Robert J. Kane, at 3. According to USOC President Kane, in early January some USOC officers became concerned that sending American athletes to Moscow could expose them to danger if hostility erupted at the games, and that acceptance of the invitation could be seen as tacit approval of or at least acceptance of the Soviet invasion. Mr. Culter also met with USOC officers at least twice in February to discuss the matter further. On each occasion, according to the Kane affidavit, Mr. Cutler urged Mr. Kane to convene an emergency meeting of the USOC Executive Board to act on the Moscow problem. However, legal counsel for the USOC advised Mr. Kane that only the House of Delegates and not the USOC Executive Board could decide whether or not to send a team to Moscow.

On March 21, 1980, President Carter told members of the Athletes Advisory Council, an official body of the USOC, that American athletes will not participate in the Moscow summer games. On April 8, 1980, the President sent a telegram to the president and officers of the USOC and to its House of Delegates, urging the USOC vote against sending an American team to Moscow. In an April 10th speech, the President said that "if legal actions are necessary to enforce (my) decision not to send a team to Moscow, then I will take those legal actions." Among the legal measures the President apparently contemplated was invoking the sanctions of the International Emergency Economic Powers Act, 50 U.S.C.A. § 1701 et seq. On April 10 and 11, 1980, the 13 member Administrative Committee of the USOC met in Colorado Springs and voted to support a resolution against sending a team to Moscow. Only Anita DeFrantz, a plaintiff in this action, dissented.

continued

At the President's request and over initial objections by the USOC, Vice President Mondale addressed the assembled House of Delegates prior to their vote on April 12, 1980. The Vice President strongly and vigorously urged the House of Delegates to support a resolution rejecting American participation in the summer games in Moscow.

After what USOC President Kane describes in his affidavit as "full, open, complete and orderly debate by advocates of each motion," the House of Delegates, on a secret ballot, passed by a vote of 1,604 to 798, a resolution which provided in pertinent part:

> RESOLVED that since the President of the United States has advised the United States Olympic Committee that in light of international events the national security of the country is threatened, the USOC has decided not send a team to the 1980 Summer Games in Moscow . . .

> FURTHER RESOLVED, that if the President of the United States advises the United States Olympic Committee, on or before May 20, 1980, that international events have become compatible with the national interest and the national security is no longer threatened, the USOC will enter its athletes in the 1980 Summer Games.

Plaintiffs describe these attempts by the Administration to persuade the USOC to vote not to send an American team to Moscow as "a campaign to coerce defendant USOC into compliance with the President's demand for a boycott of the Olympic Games." Amended Complaint for Declaratory and Injunctive Relief, P 10. In addition, plaintiffs' complaint alleges that the President and other Executive Branch officials threatened to terminate federal funding of the USOC and that they raised the possibility of revoking the federal income tax exemption[6] of the USOC if the USOC did not support the President's decision to boycott the 1980 Games.[7] The complaint also alleges that these officials state that the Federal government would provide increased funding to the USOC if the USOC supported a boycott.

Plaintiffs state three causes of action in their complaint. The first, a statutory claim, is that defendant violated the Amateur Sports Act of 1978, supra, in the following respects:

a. Defendant exercised a power it does not have to decide that no United States amateur athletes shall participate in the 1980 Games.

b. Defendant breached a duty to organize, finance and control participation in the events and competitions of the Olympic Games by United States athletes.

c. Defendant denied to United States amateur athletes the opportunity to compete in these Games on a basis other than their want of athletic merit, or for a sports related reason.

d. Defendant yielded its exclusive jurisdiction over Olympic matters to the political leaders of the nation.

e. Defendant acted in a political manner.

f. Defendant yielded its autonomy and has succumbed to political and economic pressure.

Plaintiffs' second cause of action, a constitutional claim, alleges that defendant's action constituted "governmental action" which abridged plaintiffs' rights of liberty, self-expression, personal autonomy and privacy guaranteed by the First, Fifth and Ninth Amendments to the United States Constitution.

Plaintiffs' third cause of action is that the USOC has violated its Constitution, By-laws and governing statute, injuring the USOC and violating the rights of plaintiff Shaw, a member of the USOC's Executive Board, and that defendant is subject to an action to compel compliance with its Constitution, By-laws and governing statute.

Plaintiffs allege that unredressed, these violations will result in great and irreparable injury to the athletes. "Many would lose a once-in-a- lifetime opportunity to participate in the Olympic Games, and the honor and prestige that such participation affords. Most of the class members are at or near their physical peaks at the present time and will not physically be capable of reaching the same or higher levels at a later period of their lives." Amended Complaint for Declaratory and Injunctive Relief, P 19.

In summary, plaintiffs ask this court to declare the April 12, 1980 resolution of the USOC House of Delegates null and void because it violated statutory authority and constitutional provisions and to permanently enjoin the USOC from carrying out that resolution.

Defendant and the Government have moved to dismiss pursuant to Rule 12(b)(6), Fed.R.Civ.P. and argue for dismissal of this action on several grounds. They contend that the Amateur Sports Act of 1978 has not been violated by defendant, that the Act does not deny the USOC the authority to decide not to send an American team to the Moscow Games, that the Act does not grant plaintiffs a right to compete in the Olympics if the USOC decides not to enter a team, and that plaintiffs lack a cause of action under the Act to maintain this lawsuit. As for the constitutional claims, they argue that the decision of the USOC was not "state action" and therefore, that plaintiffs have no cognizable constitutional claims. They further argue that even if the action of the USOC could be considered "state action," no rights guaranteed to plaintiffs under the Constitution were abridged.

Because of the time constraints involved in this action, this court granted plaintiffs' motion that a trial of the action on the merits be advanced and consolidated with the hearing of the application for a preliminary and permanent injunction.

Oral argument was heard by this court on May 13, 1980. At that time, the court granted the motion of the United States to appear as Amicus Curiae and the court denied the motion of the Washington Legal Foundation to appear as Amicus Curiae.[8]

ANALYSIS

This action presents us with several issues for decision, falling into two distinct categories; one is statutory and the other is constitutional. We turn first to the statutory issues.[9]

1. THE AMATEUR SPORTS ACT OF 1978

Plaintiffs allege in their complaint that by its decision not to send an American team to compete in the summer Olympic Games in Moscow, defendant USOC has violated the Amateur Sports Act of 1978, supra, (The Act) in at least six respects, which we have listed above. We deal with two of the alleged violations here. Reduced to their essentials, these allegations are that the Act does not give, and that Congress intended to deny, the USOC the authority to decide not to enter an American team in the Olympics, except perhaps for sports-related reasons, and that the Act guarantees to certain athletes[10] a right to compete in the Olympic Games which defendant denied them. We consider each allegation in turn.[11]

(a) THE USOC'S AUTHORITY NOT TO SEND A TEAM TO MOSCOW

The United States Olympic Committee was first incorporated and granted a federal charter in 1950. Pub.L. No. 81–805, supra. However, predecessors to the now federally-chartered USOC have existed since 1896, and since that time, they have exercised the authority granted by the International Olympic Committee to represent the United States as its National Olympic Committee in matters pertaining to participation in Olympic games. It is unquestioned by plaintiffs that under the International Olympic Committees Rules and By-laws, the National Olympic Committees have the right to determine their nation's participation in the Olympics. IOC Rule 24B provides that "NOC's shall be the sole authorities responsible for the representation of the respective countries at the Olympic Games . . . " and Chapter 5, paragraph 7 of the By-laws to Rule 24 provides that "(r)epresentation covers the decision to participate . . . . " (emphasis supplied). Nothing in the IOC Charter, Rules or By-laws requires a NOC, such as the USOC, to accept an invitation to participate in any particular Olympic contest and the President of the IOC has said that participation in the Olympic games is entirely voluntary. As defendant has argued, an invitation to participate is just that, an invitation which may be accepted or declined.

(1)(2) Because defendant USOC clearly has the power under IOC Rules to decide not to enter an American team in Olympic competition, the question then becomes whether the Amateur Sports Act of 1978, which rewrote the USOC's charter, denies the USOC that power. Plaintiffs emphatically argue that it does, and defendant and the Government just as emphatically argue that it does not.

Plaintiffs' argument is simple and straightforward: The Act by its terms does not expressly confer on the USOC the power to decline to participate in the Olympic Games, and if any such power can be inferred from the statute, the power must be exercised for sports-related reasons. Defendant and the Government respond that the Act gives the USOC broad powers, including the authority to decide not to accept an invitation to send an American team to the Olympics.

The principal substantive powers of the USOC are found in § 375(a) of the Act.[12] In determining whether the USOC's authority under the Act encompasses the right to decide not to participate in an Olympic contest, we must read these provisions in the context in which they were written. In writing this legislation, Congress did not create a new relationship between the USOC

continued

and the IOC. Rather, it recognized an already long-existing relationship between the two and statutorily legitimized that relationship with a federal charter and federal incorporation.[13] The legislative history demonstrates Congressional awareness that the USOC and its predecessors, as the National Olympic Committee for the United States, have had a continuing relationship with the IOC since 1896.[14] Congress was necessarily aware that a National Olympic Committee is a creation and a creature of the International Olympic Committee, to whose rules and regulations it must conform. The NOC gets its power and its authority from the IOC, the sole proprietor and owner of the Olympic Games.

In view of Congress' obvious awareness of these facts, we would expect that if Congress intended to limit or deny to the USOC powers it already enjoyed as a National Olympic Committee, such limitation or denial would be clear and explicit. No such language appears in the statute. Indeed, far from precluding this authority, the language of the statute appears to embrace it. For example, the "objects and purposes" section of the Act speaks in broad terms, stating that the USOC shall exercise "exclusive jurisdiction" over " . . . all matters pertaining to the participation of the United States in the Olympic Games . . . . " (emphasis supplied). We read this broadly stated purpose in conjunction with the specific power conferred on the USOC by the Act to "represent the United States as its national Olympic committee in relations with the International Olympic Committee," and in conjunction with the IOC Rules and By-laws, which provide that "representation" includes the decision to participate. In doing so, we find a compatibility and not a conflict between the Act and the IOC Rules on the issue of the authority of the USOC to decide whether or not to accept an invitation to field an American team at the Olympics. The language of the statute is broad enough to confer this authority, and we find that Congress must have intended that the USOC exercise that authority in this area, which it already enjoyed because of its long-standing relationship with the IOC. We accordingly conclude that the USOC has the authority to decide not to send an American team to the Olympics.

Plaintiffs next argue that if the USOC does have the authority to decide not to accept an invitation to send an American team to the Moscow Olympics, that decision must be based on "sports-related considerations."

In support of their argument, plaintiffs point to § 392(a)(5) and (b) of the Act, which plaintiffs acknowledge "are not in terms applicable to the USOC,"[15] but rather concern situations in which national governing bodies of various sports,[16] which are subordinate to the USOC, are asked to sanction the holding of international competitions below the level of the Olympic or Pan American Games in the United States or the participation of the United States athletes in such competition abroad. These sections provide that a national governing body may withhold its sanctions only upon clear and convincing evidence that holding or participating in the competition "would be detrimental to the best interests of the sport." Plaintiffs argue by analogy that a similar "sports-related" limitation must attach to any authority the USOC might have to decide not to participate in an Olympic competition. We cannot agree.

The provision on which plaintiffs place reliance by analogy is specifically concerned with eliminating the feuding between various amateur athletic organizations and national governing bodies which for so long characterized amateur athletics.[17] As all parties recognize, this friction, such as the well-publicized power struggles between the NCAA and the AAU, was a major reason for passage of the Act, and the provisions plaintiffs cite, among others, are aimed at eliminating this senseless strife, which the Senate and House Committee reports indicate had dramatically harmed the ability of the United States to compete effectively in international competition.[18] In order to eliminate this internecine squabbling, the Act elevated the USOC to a supervisory role over the various amateur athletic organizations, and provided that the USOC establish procedures for the swift and equitable settlement of these disputes. As indicated above, it also directed that the national governing bodies of the various sports could only withhold their approvals of international competition for sports-related reasons. Previously, many of these bodies had withheld their sanction of certain athletic competitions in order to further their own interests at the expense of other groups and to the detriment of athletes wishing to participate.

In brief, this sports-related limitation is intimately tied to the specific purpose of curbing the arbitrary and unrestrained power of various athletic organizations subordinate to the USOC not to allow athletes to compete in international competition below the level of the

Olympic Games and the Pan American Games. This purpose has nothing to do with a decision by the USOC to exercise authority granted by the IOC to decide not to participate in an Olympic competition.

In an attempt to escape this conclusion, plaintiffs seek to bolster their argument by pointing to an amendment offered by Congressman Drinan during consideration of this legislation by the House Judiciary Committee. That amendment would have prohibited the use of Federal funds[19] in support of United States athletic involvement in countries which engage in gross violations of human rights. Congressman Drinan clearly indicated he considered the Soviet Union as one such country. Plaintiffs argue that the defeat of the amendment by the Committee was an indication that the Congress meant the USOC to act independently of national policy, by implication supporting the view that any decision not to compete in the Olympics must be sports-related rather than related to national policy reasons. We cannot read that much into a single Committee's disposition of an amendment, which did not address the scope of the USOC's power to decide against fielding an American team for the Moscow Games or any other Olympics because of national interest considerations. To the extent we try to divine Congressional intent from its defeat, we find it equally as plausible that the Committee very well may have intended, as the Government has argued, to keep the USOC free of statutory restraints.

We therefore conclude that the USOC not only had the authority to decide not to send an American team to the summer Olympics, but also that it could do so for reasons not directly related to sports considerations.[20]

(b) ATHLETES STATUTORY RIGHT TO COMPETE IN THE OLYMPICS

Plaintiffs argue that the Act provides, "in express terms" an "Athlete's Bill of Rights,"[21] pointing to the following provisions in the Act's "objects and purposes" section, which directs that the USOC shall:

> provide for the swift resolution of conflicts and disputes involving amateur athletes, national governing bodies, and amateur sports organizations, and protect the opportunity of any amateur athlete, coach, trainer, manager, administrator, or official to participate in amateur athletic competition. (emphasis supplied).

36 U.S.C. § 374(8).

A similar provision is contained in § 382b, which provides that:

> The (USOC) shall establish and maintain provisions for the swift and equitable resolution of disputes involving any of its members and relating to the opportunity of an amateur athlete, coach, trainer, manager, administrator, or official to participate in the Olympic Games . . . or other such protected competition as defined in such constitution and bylaws.

(3) Plaintiffs argue that the Report of the President's Commission on Olympic Sports,[22] which was the starting point for the legislation proposed, and the legislative history supports their argument that the statute confers an enforceable right on plaintiffs to compete in Olympic competition. Again, we are compelled to disagree with plaintiffs.

The legislative history and the statute are clear that the "right to compete," which plaintiffs refer to, is in the context of the numerous jurisdictional disputes between various athletic bodies, such as the NCAA and the AAU, which we have just discussed, and which was a major impetus for the Amateur Sports Act of 1978. Plaintiffs recognize that a major purpose of the Act was to eliminate such disputes. However, they go on to argue that the Presidential report, which highlighted the need for strengthening the USOC in order to eliminate this feuding, made a finding that there is little difference between an athlete denied the right to compete because of a boycott and an athlete denied the right to compete because of jurisdictional bickering.

The short answer is that although the Congress may have borrowed heavily from the Report on the President's Commission, it did not enact the Report. Instead, it enacted a statute and that statute relates a "right to compete" to the elimination of jurisdictional disputes between amateur athletic groups, which for petty and groundless reasons have often deprived athletes of the opportunity to enter a particular competition. §§ 382b and 374(8) originated in Senate Bill 2727, and were adopted by the House of Representatives without change. We quote at length from the Senate Report, S.Rep. No. 770, supra, at 5-6, which clarifies beyond doubt the meaning of the language unsuccessfully relied on by plaintiffs:

continued

Athletes' Rights

That section of S. 2727 relating to an athlete's opportunity to participate in amateur athletic competition represents a compromise reached in the amateur sports community and accepted by the Committee. Language contained in the first version of the Amateur Sports Act, S. 2036, would have included a substantive provision on athletes' rights. This provision met with strong resistance by the high school and college communities. Ultimately, the compromise reached was that certain substantive provisions on athletes' rights would be included in the USOC Constitution, and not in the bill.

As reported, § 2727 makes clear that amateur athletes, coaches, trainers, managers, administrators, and other officials have the right, which will be guaranteed in the Olympic Committee Constitution, to take part in the Olympic Games, the Pan-American Games, world championship competition, and other competition designated by the Olympic Committee.

Athletes are to be encouraged that this is a positive step forward. For the first time, their rights to compete in amateur athletic competition are legislatively being recognized. § 2727 acknowledges that athletes must be given an opportunity to decide what is best for their athletic careers . . . . (T)he decision should not be dictated by an arbitrary rule which, in its application, restricts, for no real purpose, an athlete's opportunity to compete.

Further, as differences between amateur sports organizations are settled, athletes will no longer be used as pawns by one organization to gain advantage over another. The Committee feels that § 2727, by establishing guidelines for the amateur sports community, will bring about a resolution of those controversies which have so long plagued amateur sports. With the coordinating efforts of the Olympic Committee, the vertical structure which § 2727 promotes, and a cooperative attitude on the part of amateur sports organizations, athletes should, in the future, realize more opportunities to compete than ever before. (emphasis supplied).

The Senate Report makes clear that the language relied on by plaintiffs is not designed to provide any substantive guarantees, let alone a Bill of Rights. Further, to the extent that any guarantees of a right to compete are included in the USOC Constitution as a result of this provision, they do not include a right that amateur athletes may compete in the Olympic Games despite a decision by the USOC House of Delegates not to accept an invitation to enter an American team in the competition. This provision simply was not designed to extend so far. Rather, it was designed to remedy the jurisdictional disputes among amateur athletic bodies, not disputes between athletes and the USOC itself over the exercise of the USOC's discretion not to participate in the Olympics.

(c) STATUTORY CAUSE OF ACTION

Plaintiffs argue that they have a private cause of action under the Amateur Sports Act of 1978 to maintain an action to enforce their rights under that Act. This argument assumes (1) the existence of a right and (2) the capability of enforcing that right by a private cause of action. As the foregoing discussion establishes, we have found that the statute does not guarantee plaintiffs a right to compete in the Olympics if the USOC decides not to send an American team to the Olympic Games and we have found that defendant has violated no provision of the Act. Thus, the "right" the plaintiffs seek to enforce under the Act simply does not exist. (Plaintiffs have pointed to no express private right of action in the statute, and none exists). Under these circumstances, we cannot find that plaintiffs have an implied private right of action under the Amateur Sports Act to enforce a right which does not exist.

(4)(5)Assuming, arguendo, the existence of some right, such as the right to compete, plaintiffs still have the difficult task of demonstrating the existence of a private cause of action to enforce such right. "The question of the existence of a statutory cause of action is, of course, one of statutory construction . . . . (O)ur task is limited solely to determining whether Congress intended to create the private right of action asserted . . . . " *Touche Ross & Co. v. Redington*, 442 U.S. 560, 568, 99 S.Ct. 2479, 2485, 61 L.Ed.2d 82 (1979). The Supreme Court recently has reaffirmed that the basic inquiry is one of Congressional intent, despite earlier cases indicating several areas of exploration.

It is true that in *Cort v. Ash* (422 U.S. 66, 95 S.Ct. 2080, 45 L.Ed.2d 26), supra, the Court set forth four factors that it considered 'relevant' in determining whether a private remedy is implicit in a statute not expressly providing one. But the Court did not decide that each of (those) factors is entitled to equal weight. The central inquiry remains whether Congress intended to create, either expressly or by implication, a private cause of action.

Transamerica Mortgage Advisors, Inc. v. Lewis, 444 U.S. 11, 23, 100 S.Ct. 242, 249, 62 L.Ed.2d 146 (1979), quoting *Touche Ross & Co. v. Redington, supra,* 442 U.S. at 575, 99 S.Ct. at 2489.

Our discussion of Congressional intent will be exceedingly brief, for we have indicated in the preceding sections that the legislative history of the Act reveals unequivocably that Congress never intended to give plaintiffs a right to compete in the Olympics if the USOC determines not to enter a team. It necessarily follows that Congress therefore did not intend to create an implied private cause of action under the statute allowing plaintiffs to sue to enforce a right to compete in the Olympics. To believe otherwise is to believe that by its silence Congress intended to confer a cause of action to enforce nonexistent rights. This we cannot do. Not only is the legislative history barren of any implication that Congress intended to confer an enforceable right to compete in the Olympics in the face of a decision by the USOC not to compete, but it is also barren of any implication that Congress intended to create a private cause of action in such circumstances.

As noted above, to the extent Congress provided protection for amateur athletes to compete, it did so in terms of eliminating the rivalries between sports organizations. For this reason, § 395 of the Act establishes detailed procedures for the USOC's consideration and resolution of jurisdictional and eligibility issues, subject to review by arbitration under 36 U.S.C.A. § 395(c) (1). Even for disputes covered by § 395, there is therefore no private cause of action.

Because we conclude that the rights plaintiffs seek to enforce do not exist in the Act, and because the legislative history of the Act nowhere allows the implication of a private right of action, we find that plaintiffs have no implied private right of action under the Amateur Sports Act of 1978 to maintain this suit.[23]

2. CONSTITUTIONAL CLAIMS

Plaintiffs have alleged that the decision of the USOC not to enter an American team in the summer Olympics has violated certain rights guaranteed to plaintiffs under the First, Fifth and Ninth Amendments to the United States Constitution. This presents us with two questions: (1) whether the USOC's decision was "governmental action"(state action), and, assuming state action is found, (2) whether the USOC's decision abridged any constitutionally protected rights.

(a) STATE ACTION

(6) Although federally chartered, defendant is a private organization. Because the Due Process Clause of the Fifth Amendment, on which plaintiffs place great reliance, applies only to actions by the federal government,[24] plaintiffs must show that the USOC vote is a "governmental act," i. e., state action. In defining state action, the courts have fashioned two guidelines. The first involves an inquiry into whether the state:

> . . . has so far insinuated itself into a position of interdependence with (the private entity) that it must be recognized as a joint participant in the challenged activity.

Burton v. Wilmington Parking Authority, 365 U.S. 715, 725, 81 S.Ct. 856, 862, 6 L.Ed.2d 45 (1961).

In Burton, the Supreme Court found state action, but it did so on wholly different facts than those existing here. The private entity charged with racially discriminating against plaintiff was a restaurant which was physically and financially an integral part of a public building, built and maintained with public funds, devoted to a public parking service, and owned and operated by an agency of the State of Delaware for public purposes. Noting the obvious and deep enmeshment of defendant and the state, the court found that the state was a joint participant in the operation of the restaurant, and accordingly found state action. Here, there is no such intermingling, and there is no factual justification for finding that the federal government and the USOC enjoyed the "symbiotic relationship" which courts have required to find state action. The USOC has received no federal funding[25] and it exists and operates independently of the federal government. Its chartering statute gives it "exclusive jurisdiction" over "all matters pertaining to the participation of the United States in the Olympic Games . . . . " 36 U.S.C.A. § 374(3). To be sure, the Act does link the USOC and the federal government to the extent it requires the USOC to submit an annual

continued

report to the President and the Congress. But this hardly converts such an independent relationship to a "joint participation."

The second guideline fashioned by the courts involves an inquiry of whether:

> . . . there is a sufficiently close nexus between the state and the challenged action of the regulated entity so that the action of the latter may be fairly treated as that of the state itself.

Jackson v. Metropolitan Edison Co., 419 U.S. 345, 351, 95 S.Ct. 449, 453, 42 L.Ed.2d 477 (1974).

Jackson provides an indication of how close this nexus must be in order to find state action. In that case, the Supreme Court found there was no state action even though the defendant was a utility closely regulated by the state, and even though the action complained of (the procedure for termination of electrical services) had been approved by the state utility commission.[26] In the instant case, there was no requirement that any federal government body approve actions by the USOC before they become effective.

Plaintiffs clearly recognize this, but they argue that by the actions of certain federal officials, the federal government initiated, encouraged, and approved of the result reached (i. e., the vote of the USOC not to send an American team to the summer Olympics). Plaintiffs advance a novel theory. Essentially, their argument is that the campaign of governmental persuasion, personally led by President Carter, crossed the line from "governmental recommendation," which plaintiffs find acceptable and presumably necessary to the operation of our form of government, into the area of "affirmative pressure that effectively places the government's prestige behind the challenged action," and thus, results in state action. We cannot agree.

Plaintiff can point to no case outside the area of discrimination law which in any way supports their theory, and we can find none. Furthermore, this Circuit's Court of Appeals has addressed what level of governmental involvement is necessary to find state action in cases not involving discrimination.

Each party cites numerous cases dealing with the amount of governmental involvement which is necessary before a private entity becomes sufficiently entangled with governmental functions that federal jurisdiction attaches. If any principle emerges from these cases, it would appear

to be that, at least where race is not involved, it is necessary to show that the Government exercises some form of control over the actions of the private party. (emphasis supplied).

Spark v. Catholic University of America, supra, at 1281–82.

Here there is no such control. The USOC is an independent body, and nothing in its chartering statute gives the federal government the right to control that body or its officers. Furthermore, the facts here do not indicate that the federal government was able to exercise any type of "de facto" control over the USOC. The USOC decided by a secret ballot of its House of Delegates. The federal government may have had the power to prevent the athletes from participating in the Olympics even if the USOC had voted to allow them to participate, but it did not have the power to make them vote in a certain way. All it had was the power of persuasion. We cannot equate this with control. To do so in cases of this type would be to open the door and usher the courts into what we believe is a largely nonjusticiable realm, where they would find themselves in the untenable position of determining whether a certain level, intensity, or type of "Presidential" or "Administration" or "political" pressure amounts to sufficient control over a private entity so as to invoke federal jurisdiction.

We accordingly find that the decision of the USOC not to send an American team to the summer Olympics was not state action, and therefore, does not give rise to an actionable claim for the infringements of the constitutional rights alleged.

(b) CONSTITUTIONALLY PROTECTED RIGHTS

(7) Assuming arguendo that the vote of the USOC constituted state action, we turn briefly to plaintiffs' contention that by this action they have been deprived of their constitutional rights to liberty, to self-expression, to travel, and to pursue their chosen occupation of athletic endeavor. Were we to find state action in this case, we would conclude that defendant USOC has violated no constitutionally protected right of plaintiffs.

We note that other courts have considered the right to compete in amateur athletics and have found no deprivation of constitutionally protected rights. As the Government has pointed out in *Parish v. National Collegiate Athletic Association,* 506 F.2d 1028 (5th Cir.

1975), basketball players sought an injunction to prevent the NCAA from enforcing its ruling declaring certain athletes ineligible to compete in tournaments and televised games. The court, quoting *Mitchell v. Louisiana High School Athletics Association*, 430 F.2d 1155, 1158 (5th Cir. 1970), stated that:

... the privilege of participation in interscholastic activities must be deemed to fall ... outside the protection of due process.

Plaintiffs have been unable to draw our attention to any court decision which finds that the rights allegedly violated here enjoy constitutional protection, and we can find none. Plaintiffs would expand the constitutionally-protected scope of liberty and self-expression to include the denial of an amateur athlete's right to compete in an Olympic contest when that denial was the result of a decision by a supervisory athletic organization acting well within the limits of its authority. Defendant has not denied plaintiffs the right to engage in every amateur athletic competition. Defendant has not denied plaintiffs the right to engage in their chosen occupation. Defendant has not even denied plaintiffs the right to travel, only the right to travel for one specific purpose. We can find no justification and no authority for the expansive reading of the Constitution which plaintiffs urge. To find as plaintiffs recommend would be to open the floodgates to a torrent of lawsuits. The courts have correctly recognized that many of life's disappointments, even major ones, do not enjoy constitutional protection. This is one such instance.

At this point, we find it appropriate to note that we have respect and admiration for the discipline, sacrifice, and perseverance which earns young men and women the opportunity to compete in the Olympic Games. Ordinarily, talent alone has determined whether an American would have the privilege of participating in the Olympics. This year, unexpectedly, things are different. We express no view on the merits of the decision made. We do express our understanding of the deep disappointment and frustrations felt by thousands of American athletes. In doing so, we also recognize that the responsibilities of citizenship often fall more heavily on some than on others. Some are called to military duty. Others never serve. Some return from military service unscathed. Others never return. These are the simple, although harsh, facts of life, and they are immutable.

FOOTNOTES

1. Of the 25 athletes who are named plaintiffs in this action, the record now before us indicates that only one has been selected as a member of the 1980 United States Olympic Team. The complaint alleges that most of the other named plaintiffs stand an "excellent chance" of selection as the result of competitive athletic trials being held this Spring. Plaintiffs have moved for certification as a class action pursuant to Rule 23(b)(2), Fed.R.Civ.P. Included in this intended class are athletes who have already been selected for the 1980 United States Olympic Team.

2. International Olympic Committee Olympic Charter, Rule 4.

3. *Id.*, Rule 24B.

4. *Id.*, By-laws Ch. 5(a).

5. *Id.*, Rule 61.

6. Plaintiffs have submitted as Exhibit G an April 9, 1980 Washington Post article which reports that a White House official acknowledged that lifting the USOC's tax exempt status had been discussed by Administration officials with members of Congress but that the idea was not being proposed at that time.

7. Plaintiffs have submitted as Exhibit E an April 10, 1980 New York Times article which reports that a USOC official said 16 corporations were delinquent in pledges to the USOC and that one corporation, Sears, Roebuck & Company, acknowledged it was withholding a contribution because of delays by the USOC on the boycott issue. The article also reported that a Sears official said the action was taken after "the chairman had talked with Anne Wexler, an assistant to President Carter." The report adds that Miss Wexler denied that any pressure had been put on Sears.

8. Defendant consented to the Washington Legal Foundation filing an amicus brief but plaintiffs refused to consent.

9. In response to questioning from the court at oral argument, counsel for plaintiffs indicated

continued

that class action certification in this case is not necessary to insure that appropriate relief would be granted to the envisioned class by any order this court may issue. If we were to rule in favor of the named plaintiffs, the class of athletes envisioned by plaintiffs would receive full benefit of that ruling. Accordingly, we deny plaintiffs' motion for certification as a class pursuant to Rule 23(b)(2), Fed.R.Civ.P.

10. By virtue of their athletic abilities.

11. Plaintiffs raise four other violations of the Act in their complaint: defendant yielded its autonomy and has succumbed to political and economic pressure; defendant acted in a political manner; defendant yielded its exclusive jurisdiction over Olympic matters to the political leaders of the nation; and defendant breached a duty to organize, finance, and control participation in the events and competitions of the Olympic Games by United States athletes. The first three refer to the exercise of "political pressure" on the USOC by the Administration and the USOC's response to the political pressure. At oral argument, counsel for plaintiffs conceded that the significant statutory questions could be decided without reference to whether the Administration exerted political pressure on defendant. We agree with plaintiffs and for this reason, we do not consider these three alleged violations against the plaintiffs. As for the last alleged violation, we deal with this issue below.

12. They are to: "(1) serve as the coordinating body for amateur athletic activity in the United States directly relating to international amateur athletic competition; (2) represent the United States as its national Olympic committee in relations with the International Olympic Committee . . . ; (3) organize, finance, and control the representation of the United States in the competitions and events of the Olympic Games . . . and obtain, either directly or by delegation to the appropriation national governing body, amateur representation for summer games." 36 U.S.C. § 375(a)(1), (2), (3). The "objects and purposes" section of the Act includes the provision, also found in the 1950 Act, that the USOC shall "exercise exclusive jurisdiction . . . over all matters pertaining to the participation of the United

States in the Olympic Games . . . including the representation of the United States in such games . . . ." Id., § 374(3).

13. To the extent the USOC was granted extended power by the 1978 Act, the legislative history makes clear, and the plaintiffs do not dispute the fact, that these powers were primarily designed to give the USOC supervisory authority over United States amateur athletic groups in order to eliminate the numerous and frequent jurisdictional squabbles among schools, athletic groups and various national sports governing bodies.

14. See S.Rep. No. 770, 95th Cong., 2d Sess. 2 (1978); H.R.Rep. No. 95–1627, 95th Cong., 2d Sess. (1978), reprinted in (1978) U.S.Code Cong. & Admin.News, p. 7478.

15. Plaintiffs' Memorandum in Reply to Memoranda of the Defendant and the United States as Amicus Curiae and in Opposition to Defendant's Motion to Dismiss, at 5.

16. A national governing body is a non-profit amateur sports organization which acts as this country's representative in the corresponding international sports federation for that particular sport. It sets goals and directs policy in the sport it governs and has the power to sanction internal competitions held in the United States in their sport.

17. See S.Rep. No. 770, supra, at 2, 5–6; H.R.Rep. No. 95–1627, supra, at 7484–5.

18. See S.Rep. No. 770, supra, at 3; H.R.Rep. No. 95–1627, at 7482–83.

19. Congress authorized federal funding of $16 million "to finance the construction, improvement, and maintenance of facilities for programs of amateur athletic activity and to defray direct operating costs of programs of amateur athletic activity . . . ." 36 U.S.C.A. § 384(a). Although this funding has been authorized, it has never been appropriated. To date, the USOC has received no federal funding.

20. Resolution of this issue also disposes of plaintiffs' allegation that defendant violated the Act by breaching a duty to organize, finance, and control participation in the events and competition of the Olympic Games by United States athletes. Because defendant had the authority to decide not to send

a team to compete in the summer Olympics, it could not have breached this duty, which does not arise and become relevant, when the USOC has decided that an American team will not participate in the Olympics.

21. Plaintiffs Reply Memorandum, supra, at 9.

22. I President's Commission on Olympic Sports, Final Report (1977).

23. Plaintiffs have also alleged as a cause of action that in addition to violating its governing statute, defendant USOC has also violated its Constitution and By-laws, injuring plaintiff Shaw, a member of USOC's Executive Board. In particular, plaintiffs argue in their memorandum, at 33, that the USOC has violated its corporate purpose of coordinating amateur sports so as to obtain the "most competent amateur representation" in the Olympic Games. This corporate purpose appearing in the USOC Constitution is identical to that appearing in the Act, § 374(4), and we have already found that defendant has not violated that statute. Just what other specific violations of the USOC Constitution and By-laws plaintiffs are alleging does not appear in the complaint or in the plaintiffs' memoranda. To the extent they allege violations of provisions also contained in the Act, we have already determined that question. To the extent they involve a yielding to "political pressures," we

note that on April 23, 1980 the IOC Executive Board reviewed the actions of the USOC and concluded that they were not in violation of IOC Rule 24(C), which requires that NOC's "must be autonomous and must resist all pressures of any kind whatsoever, whether of a political, religious or economic nature." To the extent that plaintiffs are alleging that defendant has violated any provision of its Constitution and By-laws requiring it to be autonomous, we adopt the conclusion of the IOC and find that this resolves any such allegations in favor of defendant.

24. *Public Utilities Commission v. Pollak*, 343 U.S. 451, 72 S.Ct. 813, 96 L.Ed. 1068 (1952).

25. Federal funds were authorized under the Amateur Sports Act of 1978 but have never been appropriated. But the mere receipt of federal funds by a private entity, without more, is not enough to convert that entity's activity into state action. Spark v. Catholic University of America, 510 F.2d 1277 (D.C.Cir. 1975).

26. The termination procedure was contained in a general tariff filed with the Public Utility Commission. The Commission approved the tariff without focusing on or specifically approving the termination provision.

Reprinted with permission from West Group.

Tonya Harding's Legal Adventure

Tonya Harding, a talented American Olympic figure skater, was allowed to compete on the 1994 U.S. Olympic figure skating team sent to represent the United States in Lillehammer, Norway, despite a criminal incident involving her prior to the Olympic Trials. Harding admitted that she knew of the plot to physically injure rival skater Nancy Kerrigan so that she could eliminate a top American rival from competing in the Olympics. Kerrigan did compete and earned a silver medal in the Olympics, but the legal events took center stage prior to the Games themselves.

The NGB for figure skating, U.S. Figure Skating Association (USFSA), and the USOC faced a legal dilemma in deciding whether to remove Harding from the team for such misconduct. Harding threatened a multimillion dollar lawsuit if she was not allowed to represent the United States at the Games in Norway. The USFSA formed a five-member panel to review the evidence, which determined that Harding had violated the USFSA's rules of ethics and sportsmanship. Still, the USFSA reserved judgment on any suspension until a disciplinary hearing scheduled after the Olympics on March 10, 1994. At that time, the Butch Reynolds case had not been completely resolved, and there was legal chaos involving the IOC, USOC, and its NGBs.

Despite the USFSA's decision to delay a decision, the USOC scheduled a Games Administrative Board hearing to take place in Oslo, Norway, on February 15 to determine Harding's fate. Harding filed suit in Oregon state court on February 10 seeking a temporary restraining order and preliminary injunction against the USOC hearing along with $25 million in compensatory and punitive damages if she was banned from the Games. On February 13, lawyers met and agreed that Harding would drop her suit and the USOC would let her compete in the Olympics.

Harding competed in the women's figure skating events in Lillehammer on February 23 and 25, but finished a disappointing eighth place. The USFSA planned to hold the disciplinary hearing, scheduled for March 10, 1994, in plenty of time to suspend Harding before the World Championships later that same month. Harding countered with yet another suit, obtained an injunction preventing the USFSA from holding a disciplinary hearing prior to June 27, finding that the USFSA had violated its own rules.[15]

In the end, Tonya Harding pled guilty to criminal conspiracy charges and resigned from the USFSA, the injunction was removed, and the case was dismissed. Later, the USFSA panel met and voided Harding's 1994 national championship title and banned her from the sport for life.

The 2000 Sydney Olympics

The Sydney Olympics represented an attempt to manage Olympic rules at an international level during a competition. More drug tests proved positive than at any other Olympics, and Sydney became known as the "Doping Games" as the IOC fought with a vengeance against the use of illegal drugs in its Olympic Games.

Numerous examples of the supremacy of the IOC and the power of the decisions of the CAS reigned during the Sydney games. Unfortunately, 4-foot-10 gymnast Andreea Raducan of Romania lost her gold medal because she tested positive for the banned stimulant pseudoephedrine, a drug found in over-the-counter cold medicine, after the all-around finals. CAS arbitrators denied the Romanian all-around winner's appeal to have her gold medal restored, upholding a decision by the IOC. The IOC was understanding but still enforced the letter of the law. A Romanian doctor, banished from the Olympics through 2004 for offering the decongestant, appeared to have made a vital error by offering such medicine to Andreea.

Shot put champion Alexander Bagach of the Ukraine was suspended from competition for testing positive for steroids for a third time. Simon Kemboi, a member of the Kenyan 1,600-meter relay team, also was suspended for testing positive for steroids. Neither was allowed to compete in the Sydney Games. The CAS also refused to reconsider the two-year suspension of former Olympic 5,000-meter champion Dieter Baumann of Germany who tested positive for the steroid nandrolone. Baumann contended someone had spiked his toothpaste. The German Athletic Federation had cleared Baumann.

In another Sydney Olympics disgrace, several members of Bulgaria's weightlifting team were stripped of their medals for positive drug tests. In Sydney, the

International Weightlifting Federation (IWF) banned Bulgaria's entire weightlifting team from the Games, but the CAS ruled the IWF lacked a legal basis to ban the whole team and lifted the ban, allowing one Bulgarian weightlifter to win a silver medal.

The 2002 Salt Lake City Olympic Games

The most recent Olympics took place beginning in February, 2002 in Salt Lake City, Utah. Athletes and officials from 80 countries involved in 15 different sports participated in these Winter Olympic Games. New sports and events such as the skeleton, women's bobsleigh, short-track speed skating of 1500 meters for men and women, and a few others represented some of the most exciting Games ever.[16] However, much of the excitement took place prior to and after the Games.

Before the 2002 Games

Much before the Games began, Tom Welch, president of the Salt Lake Olympic Committee (SLOC), and Dave Johnson, vice-president of the SLOC, faced 15 charges of fraud, conspiracy, racketeering, and corruption over what many regard as one of the biggest scandals in Olympic history. The United States Department of Justice charged the two men with attempting to bribe members of the IOC in order to win their votes for Salt Lake City to stage the Games. The scandal led to a series of events which led to the eventual resignation and expulsion of 10 members of the IOC who were found guilty of accepting cash, college scholarships for the family, and free hospital treatment. In 2001, however, U.S. District Court Judge David Sam threw out the racketeering charges. Sam tossed the other fraud and conspiracy charges in November, 2001, and denounced the entire case as federal intrusion into state affairs because it was based upon Utah's commercial bribery law.[17]

During the 2002 Games

Unlike many Olympic sporting events which are based upon objective criteria such as time, height, weight or distance, judging in boxing, wrestling, gymnastics, and figure skating are subjective events. This presented a problem in the skating pairs competition. Russians Elena Berezhnaya and Anton Sikharulidze won the skating pairs gold medal by a vote over Canadians Jamie Sale and David Pelletier in a highly controversial decision. The next day, French judge Marie-Reine Le Gougne apparently told the event's referee that she had been pressured to vote for the Russians. She later recanted her story. Later in the week, the French ice dancing team of Russian native Marina Anissina and Gwendal Peizerat won the gold medal, and Irina Lobacheva and Ilia Averbukh of Russia took the silver. The International Skating Union (ISU) investigated the pairs event and, after a two-month inquiry, suspended Le Gougne and the head of the French skating federation, Didier Gailhaguet. The IOC also stepped in, and the ISU agreed to award a second gold medal to the Canadian pairs.

After the 2002 Games

Examining the positives of the Salt Lake City Games is often difficult, particularly since the continuing examination into judging improprieties. In fact, some have coined the phrase "Skate gate" as being representative of the Games controversy.[18]

Still, in June, 2002, an alleged international mob figure was arrested in Italy on U.S. federal charges that he fixed two of the four events in the Salt Lake's figure skating events. The federal complaint alleged that Alimzhan Tokhtakhounov, identified by the FBI as a member of Russian organized crime, and "unnamed co-conspirators" used their influence with members of the Russian and French skating federations to fix the gold medal outcome of the pairs and ice dancing competitions. Hopefully there will be less controversies involved in the Summer Olympics of 2004 in Athens, Greece.

Olympic Trademarks and the Internet

Perhaps the most intriguing international issue involving the Olympic Games is the use of the word *Olympic* itself. The IOC continues to wage a war to protect its international trademark, the word *Olympic*.

In 2000, the IOC hired a British firm to monitor any Internet sites using the word "Olympic" in their web addresses. About 1,800 sites had been told to cease and desist, and the IOC actually filed suit in federal court in the United States to protect the word *Olympics* and the Olympic symbol of five interlocking rings. The IOC in Sydney forbade Olympic athletes from writing Internet diaries on their own websites or for their hometown newspapers. Many Sydney Olympians who had their own sites were prohibited from selling their diaries to any publication during the Games. The IOC also has deployed brigades of "pin police" who confiscate souvenir pins that carry the word Olympic and the five rings if they are not officially licensed products. The most ferocious battle is being fought, however, for the cyber-future of the Olympic movement. Most agree that the concern focuses on money.

The IOC sells the TV and radio rights to a number of companies worldwide. In the past, sponsor and trademark protection has usually amounted to asking businesses in Olympic cities to rename themselves if they are using the word *Olympic*. Often these are companies that have been started by Greek immigrants, such as an Olympic Diner. So serious is the issue of "Olympic" that several cases involving American courts were forced to decide on litigation involving the use of the word *Olympic*.[19]

San Francisco Arts & Athletics, Inc. v. United States Olympic Committee

Though the Amateur Sports Act was amended in 1998, the act still granted USOC the right to prohibit certain commercial and promotional uses of the word *Olympic* and various Olympic symbols. Despite the act, the San Francisco Arts & Athletics, Inc. (SFAA), a nonprofit California corporation, promoted the "Gay Olympic Games" to be held in 1982 by using "Olympics" on its letterheads and mailings and on various merchandise sold for the planned Games. The USOC informed the SFAA of the existence of the act and requested that it terminate use of the word *Olympic* in its description of the planned Games.

The SFAA did not comply, and the USOC brought suit in federal district court for injunctive relief. The court granted the USOC summary judgment and a permanent injunction. The Ninth Circuit Court of Appeals affirmed, holding that the act granted the USOC exclusive use of the word *Olympic* and that the USOC's property right in the word and its associated symbols and slogans can be protected without violating the First Amendment. The case was appealed to the Supreme Court and it agreed, noting that when a word acquires value as the result of an organization and the expenditure of labor, skill, and money by an entity, that entity constitutionally may obtain a limited property right in the word.[20] The Supreme Court also reaffirmed that the USOC is not a governmental actor for which the Fifth Amendment applies. The USOC's choice of how to enforce its exclusive right to use the word *Olympic* was determined not to be a governmental decision, and the case was affirmed.[21]

■ Summary

The Olympic Games is more than an international event that occurs every few years. The Olympic Games affect and have been affected by wars, protests, and other major international events. The International Olympic Committee oversees each country's National Olympic Committee and respective national governing bodies. At the same time, International Federations set standards for particular Olympic sports. American Olympic athletes were not granted statutory rights until the enactment of the Amateur Sports Act of 1978, which was amended in 1998 by the Ted Stevens Olympic and Amateur Sports Act. With its hierarchy of rules and regulations, including drug testing procedures in and out of competition, challenges to the Olympic system in a court of law have been awkward for American courts. However, the recent emphasis on deferring disputes to the Court of Arbitration of Sport has added balance and an element of fairness to the jurisprudence of the Games.

■ Key Terms

1980 Olympic Boycott
Amateur Sports Act of 1978
Court of Arbitration of Sport (CAS)
International Federation (IF)
International Olympic Committee (IOC)

National Governing Body (NGB)
National Olympic Committee (NOC)
Olympic Movement
Ted Stevens Olympic and Amateur
   Sports Act (TSOASA)

■ Additional Cases

Foschi v. United States Swimming, Inc. 916 F. Supp. 232 (E.D.N.Y. 1996)
Martin v. IOC, 740 F.2d 670 (9th Cir. 1984)
Michels v. USOC, 741 F.2d 1555 (7th Cir. 1984)
Reynolds v. IAAF, 23 F.3d 1110 (6th Cir. 1994)

■ Review Questions

1. What is the Olympic Movement?
2. How have politics played a role in affecting the Olympic Games?
3. Why has the IOC deferred to the International Federations and National Olympic Committees as to defining who is eligible to participate in the Olympic Games (i.e., whether they can be professionals or not)?
4. What was the motivation behind the enactment and then revision of the Amateur Sports Act?
5. How has the Internet affected international issues in sport?
6. What is the Court of Arbitration of Sport and what is its role?

■ Endnotes

1 NBC television paid the sum of $705 million to the IOC for the right to broadcast the 2000 Sydney Games in the USA.
2 In 1994, the Olympic Games changed its standard to every two years by alternating the summer and winter Olympics beginning with the Lillehammer, Norway Games.
3 Also headquartered in Lausanne, Switzerland.
4 United States Swimming, USA Basketball, USA Baseball, USA Hockey, United States Triathlon, and United States Track & Field are some of the more prominent NGBs.
5 Selections are normally made at the Olympic Trials events for each NGB rather than based purely upon world ranking.
6 36 U.S.C.A. § 371.
7 Therefore challenges under the Fifth Amendment's due process clause almost always fail.
8 35 U.S.C.A. § 380(a).
9 36 U.S.C.A. § 220522(a)(14).
10 36 U.S.C.A. § 220509(a).
11 36 U.S.C.A. § 220509(b).
12 36 U.S.C.A. § 220503(3) and (4), 220505(c).

13 *See DeFrantz v. United States Olympic Comm.*, 492 F. Supp. 1181, 1188 (D.D.C.), *aff'd*, 701 F.2d 221 (6th Cir. 1980).

14 *See Reynolds v. International Amateur Athletic Fed'n*, 841 F. Supp. 1444 (S.D. Ohio 1992); See Also *Reynolds v. International Amateur Athletic Fed'n*, 23 F.3d 1110 (6th Cir. 1994), *cert. denied*, 115 S. Ct. 423 (1994).

15 *See Harding v. United States Figure Skating Ass'n*, 851 F. Supp. 1476 (D. Or. 1994).

16 *See* http://english.peopledaily.com.cn/200201/08/eng20020108_88225. shtml

17 *See* http://www.ksl.com/TV/olympics/sloc/appeal_0831.php

18 http://news.bbc.co.uk/winterolympics2002/hi/english/skating/newsid_1861000/1861145.stm

19 *See, e.g., San Francisco Arts & Athletics, Inc. v. United States Olympic Committee*, 483 U.S. 522 (1987).

20 *See Id.* at 532-535.

21 *Id.* at 542-547.

CHAPTER NINE

Antitrust and Labor Issues in Sports

■ Introduction

America is the land of capitalism and free markets. The American dream fosters the spirit of individuals to pursue the best life possible, including the right to pursue an occupation that generates the greatest amount of income for the employee. Fundamental to the American economy are the laws of supply and demand and the theory of freedom of competition. When the industrial revolution and big business created monopolies in industries such as sugar and cotton, a concerned United States Congress enacted **antitrust** laws designed to prevent anticompetitive behavior in business in order to promote competition and ultimately drive down prices for consumers.

Sports in America have faced antitrust and labor issues at both the professional and amateur levels of competition. No labor issues have been so nationally infamous as the strikes and lockouts related to professional sports leagues as the owners of teams and leagues have fought the employee-players in court. Judges have pondered and struggled as to how to apply traditional antitrust and labor laws to the sports industry, all in the public's watchful eye.

To protect the rights of workers, unions were formed to represent workers' employment needs and to negotiate employment contracts "collectively" in order to achieve a collective bargaining agreement (CBA). In the sports industry, the unions that represent the players are called *players associations.* Recently, the Supreme Court has attempted to send the message to players and owners of sports leagues that disputes that arise out of the employment relationship should not be resolved in the courtroom.

This chapter discusses how labor issues have affected sports and how courts have treated the application of antitrust rules to the sports industry, particularly to the situation involving a professional sports union that negotiates with owners of a

---

antitrust   term used to describe any contract, combination, or conspiracy that illegally restrains trade and promotes anticompetitive behavior

league. While the concepts of antitrust and labor law are often considered distinct subjects on their own, in the sports industry these areas of the law are quite often interrelated.

■ The Federal Laws

Labor and antitrust issues are governed primarily by federal statutes.[1] The following acts and statutes are most relevant in the sports context.

Sherman Act

The **Sherman Antitrust Act of 1890** (Sherman Act)[2] is the most fundamental federal law that governs anticompetitive business behavior. Congress enacted the Sherman Act to regulate business practices among competitors affecting interstate commerce. In other words, whenever commerce or trade crosses states lines, antitrust laws apply. The primary purpose of the Sherman Act is to promote competition and to deter monopolistic practices that ultimately hurt consumers.

Section 1 of the Sherman Act forbids contracts, combinations, or conspiracies that may unreasonably restrain trade. Section 2 of the act prohibits monopolization of trade and commerce. The Supreme Court has implemented two separate standards in deciding whether a particular restraint on trade is unreasonable: the "per se" rule and the "rule of reason."

Violations of the Sherman Act may subject the wrongdoer to criminal penalties. Individuals may be fined by the government up to $350,000 per violation while corporations may be fined up to $10 million per violation. The government may also pursue civil damages for violations of the Sherman Act and such damages are automatically trebled (tripled). Additionally, reasonable costs and attorneys fees may be awarded.[3]

Clayton Act

Congress passed the **Clayton Act** in 1914. This act provides that labor unions and labor activities are exempt from the Sherman Act. Section 6 of the Clayton Act states that labor is not to be considered "commerce." This exemption to antitrust laws is known as the *statutory labor exemption*.[4] Section 16 of the Clayton Act allows the government or a private plaintiff to obtain an injunction against anticompetitive behavior if necessary.

Sherman Antitrust Act   1890 federal law that prohibits interference with interstate production and distribution of goods

Clayton Act   1914 federal law that allows the government or a private plaintiff to obtain an injunction against anticompetitive behavior

Norris-LaGuardia Act

The **Norris-LaGuardia Act**, enacted in 1932, allows employees to organize as a collective bargaining unit, which allows the employer to negotiate a contract that governs all covered employees as a unit. Section 17 of the Clayton Act and the Norris-LaGuardia Act exempt labor union activities from antitrust law. The Norris-LaGuardia Act was another attempt to remove the courts from having to become involved in labor matters. It also places restrictions on the power of the federal courts to grant injunctions in labor disputes. This is of particular concern to the sports industry and for players unions that engage in collective bargaining such as the NBPA, NFLPA, NHLPA, or MLBPA.[5]

National Labor Relations Act

The **National Labor Relations Act (NLRA)**[6] was enacted in 1935. It encourages the practice of collective bargaining between employers and employees and requires employers and employees to meet at reasonable times and confer in good faith with respect to wages, hours, and other terms and conditions of employment.

The NLRA supports collective bargaining between management and labor. The Act encourages: "the practice and procedure of collective bargaining and by protecting the exercise by workers of full freedom of association, self-organization, and designation of representatives of their own choosing, for the purpose of negotiating the terms and conditions of their employment or other mutual aid or protection."[7]

The NLRA's collective bargaining requirement is bilateral, protecting both employers and unions. The NLRA requires good faith bargaining. However, it does not compel either party to agree to a proposal or require the making of a concession.

National Labor Relations Board

The **National Labor Relations Board (NLRB)** was established in 1935 under the NLRA. Its purpose is to oversee and referee the process of collective bargaining, leaving the results of the contest to the bargaining strengths of the parties. This administrative body is the most powerful administrative agency with regard to enforcing federal labor laws and rules, particularly preventing and remedying unfair labor practices by employers. The NLRB's five members are appointed by the President of the United States.

Norris-LaGuardia Act   1932 federal law that forbids federal courts from abusing the injunctive process and to prevent employers from abusing the courts to obtain injunctions on union activities

National Labor Relations Act (NLRA)   federal act regulating relations between employers and employees

National Labor Relations Board (NLRB)   federal agency created by the NLRA to regulate employer and employee relations, particularly in the union context

■ Judicial Analysis

Once there has been an allegation of a violation of antitrust laws, the NLRB and the courts often determine whether in fact a violation has occurred. Key to this determination is whether an organization is clearly attempting to monopolize a market by using an unfair labor practice or, if unclear, whether the alleged monopolistic practice is reasonable or unreasonable. The two methods used to analyze such issues have become known as the *per se analysis* and the *rule of reason analysis*.

Per Se Rule Analysis

When a court uses the **per se rule analysis**, any labor practices that are inherently unreasonable restraints of trade will be invalidated. In *Northern Pacific Railway Co. v. United States*, 356 U.S. 1 (1958), the Supreme Court stated that certain agreements or practices, because of their pernicious effect on competition, are conclusively presumed to be unreasonable and therefore illegal.[8] For example, price fixing is a *per se* violation of antitrust laws. Price fixing is anticompetitive and hurts consumers.

Rule of Reason Analysis

Under the **rule of reason analysis**, a court must examine the labor practice at issue and determine whether it is reasonable or unreasonable. Some restraints are necessary as a "legitimate business practice."[9] If a restraint of trade fails the *per se* test, further examination of the labor practice is not necessary under a rule of reason analysis.

Nonstatutory Labor Exemption

The **nonstatutory labor exemption** is a controversial judicial principle that holds that antitrust laws are not applicable when unions (employees) and management (employers) take part in the collective bargaining process of negotiating a working labor contract. Congress favors the process of collective bargaining rather than having to ask the courts to intervene in labor disputes. In *Brown v. Pro Football, Inc.*,[10] the U.S. Supreme Court affirmed the position that courts should become less involved in disputes that arise from the collective bargaining process.

---

per se rule analysis   rule that holds that certain types of trade agreements or arrangements are inherently anticompetitive and therefore illegal

rule of reason analysis   rule that holds that only unreasonable restraints of trade violate Section 1 of the Sherman Act

nonstatutory labor exception   general term describing any union-management agreement that was a product of good faith negotiation and will therefore receive protection from federal antitrust laws

Mandatory Subjects of Collective Bargaining

The **collective bargaining** process must discuss wages, hours, and working conditions.[11] These subjects are the "compulsory" subjects of the collective bargaining process. All other subjects are considered "permissive."

Strikes and Lockouts

The NLRA grants workers the right to **strike** if a CBA cannot be reached. Before a strike can occur, however, a union must have a vote and the members must vote by a majority. The union must give the employer 60 days notice before a strike can occur during what is called the "cooling-off period." Similarly, if a CBA cannot be reached, an employer may prevent its own employees from working by actually locking the employees out—thus, the term **lockout**—when the employer reasonably anticipates a strike.

■ Antitrust in Professional Sports

Part of the uniqueness of application of federal antitrust and labor laws to professional sports is that teams in a sports league are both competitors and joint venturers. Baseball, football, basketball, and hockey have all had legal battles involving the application of the antitrust laws. Players associations, acting as the exclusive bargaining agent for the players, have certainly had an effect on the current labor landscape and league organization of the sports industry.

Single Entity Structure

Even though the individual teams may compete with each other on the court or field, the league itself is solitary, and therefore the question arises as to whether the teams are actually "competing" with each other. Professional sports leagues are usually not considered "single entities" under antitrust law since the teams are separately owned. Recently, start-up leagues such as the Women's National Basketball Association (WNBA), Major League Soccer (MLS), Women's United Soccer Association (WUSA), and Arena Football League (AFL) are examples in which the league owns the teams and is thus considered a single entity. In this league structure, while teams compete with each other for wins and losses, the league is able to keep salaries manageable. One court ruled Major League Soccer (MLS) had not violated

collective bargaining   process of negotiating a contract between management and labor in the union context

strike   cessation of work by union members to obtain benefits or prevent abuses in the workplace

lockout   temporary withholding of work by the employer to resolve a labor dispute

antitrust laws by organizing in the single-entity structure in which the league (rather than the teams) negotiates and owns all players' contracts.[12] Organization as a single entity will likely be the choice of organizational structure for future leagues.

■ Historical Perspectives

Due to the special relationship between owners and players in the professional sports industry, courts have encountered difficulties applying the rule of reason and the *per se* rule to determine whether there has been a violation of antitrust law in the sports context. While CBAs represent the contractual agreements[13] between players and owners, the courts have been uncertain how to apply antitrust laws once a CBA has expired in the sports industry. In fact, numerous cases involving professional leagues have reached different (and sometimes conflicting) results when attempting to apply federal antitrust laws. Discussions of a few major sport-specific cases follow.

Baseball

Baseball has held a unique exemption from antitrust laws in accordance with the interpretation of the Supreme Court in *Federal Baseball Club of Baltimore, Inc. v. National League of Professional Baseball Clubs*, 259 U.S. 200 (1922). The Court held that antitrust laws do not apply to professional baseball. Prior to that, professional baseball had a "reserve system" in which once a player signed with a team, he became the property of that team only until he retired from the team or the team no longer wanted him.

Major League Baseball (MLB) has had eight work stoppages since 1972, with player strikes or owner lockouts causing the cancellation or postponement of games in 1972, 1981, 1985, and 1994, as well as spring training cancellation in 1990. The MLBPA was formed in 1954, and MLB had its first collective bargaining agreement in 1968. To date, the baseball players association has won virtually all of the labor disputes. This accounts for baseball players having the highest salaries among the four major sports leagues. MLB also has the most tenuous relationship between its players and owners.

Federal Baseball

In one of the most controversial opinions of the U.S. Supreme Court, baseball was held to not involve interstate commerce (as required by the Sherman Act) in *Federal Baseball Club of Baltimore, Inc. v. National League of Professional Baseball Clubs*. Even though players traveled across state lines, Justice Oliver Wendell Holmes held that it was only incidental to the game; baseball was "purely a state affair" and held to remain exempt from antitrust laws. Baseball used the "reserve clause," which precluded players from jumping to another baseball league, the Federal Baseball League. Therefore, since the court held that antitrust laws did not apply to baseball, baseball's reserve clause was acceptable.

Flood v. Kuhn[14]

Baseball player Curt Flood challenged the ruling in *Federal Baseball* following the 1969 season when he was traded from the St. Louis Cardinals to the Philadelphia Phillies. Though he lost his case, the Supreme Court noted that the reserve system was illogical and unrealistic. Still, the Court held that Major League Baseball's exemption from antitrust laws could only be challenged and changed by Congress.

Curt Flood Act of 1998[15]

Effective in 1999, Congress modified the antitrust exemption in baseball to allow baseball players the same rights as athletes in other sports and allows players to bring suits against team owners. Numerous attempts to legislatively overturn the *Federal Baseball* case had previously failed. Still, the amateur baseball draft, the relationship between the major and minor leagues, and franchise location and relocation remain exempt under the **Curt Flood Act of 1998**.

Football

NFL players have not been very successful in their attempts to bargain collectively with their team owners. However, in recent years, the relationship between the NFL and the NFLPA seems to be stable. Through a joint effort, the NFL became the first major league to test for ephedrine, a stimulant often found in performance-enhancing supplements. Additionally, the NFLPA has worked hard to enforce its own code of ethics as the exclusive bargaining agent for the NFL players. Enforcing policies governing sports agents such as William "Tank" Black have proven to be successful as Case 11 demonstrates.

Mackey v. NFL[16]

In *Mackey v. NFL*, the court rejected the *per se* rule analysis and laid out a three-prong test applicable to cases involving the professional sports industry. This case involved challenging the validity of the Rozelle Rule, which provided that when a player's contract expired and he signed with a different club, the new club must compensate the previous club. This was professional football's version of baseball's reserve rule. The net effect of the Rozelle Rule was that it kept salaries low. The court held that there was no bona fide arm's length bargaining and concluded that for the nonstatutory labor exemption to apply, collective bargaining resulting from good faith arm's length bargaining must have occurred. The Rozelle Rule was considered an unreasonable restraint of trade under *Mackey*.

Curt Flood Act of 1998   federal law that revokes part of a 1922 U.S. Supreme Court decision exempting baseball owners from antitrust laws

CASE 11   *Black v. NFLPA*

United States District Court,
District of Columbia.
William BLACK and Professional Management, Inc.,
Plaintiffs,
v.
NATIONAL FOOTBALL LEAGUE PLAYERS
ASSOCIATION, Defendant.
No. CIV. A. 99-1649(JR).
Feb. 2, 2000.

Agent for professional football players sued players' union, claiming that unlawful disciplinary proceedings instituted against him affected his livelihood. Union moved for summary judgment. The District Court, Robertson, J., held that: (1) additional discovery would be allowed regarding agent's claim that he was denied equal contracting rights due to race; (2) state law claim that union tortiously interfered with contractual relations between agent and players was preempted by Labor Management Relations Act (LMRA); (3) agent could not compel removal of arbitrator before compulsory arbitration of agent's claims began; (4) agent did not plead defamation on part of union with sufficient particularity; and (5) newspaper article stating that union claimed agent bribed college football coach was insufficient basis for defamation claim.

Motion granted in part, denied in part.

MEMORANDUM

Robertson, District Judge.

William Black claims that the National Football League Players Association (NFLPA) unlawfully initiated disciplinary proceedings against him, affecting his livelihood as a player agent. NFLPA moves for summary judgment.[1] Plaintiff opposes that motion and moves for leave to amend. Plaintiff will be permitted to take discovery on his claim of discrimination under 42 U.S.C.A. § 1981, but defendant is entitled to judgment as a matter of law on the claims of tortious interference and violation of the Federal Arbitration Act. Leave to file new claims of defamation and trade disparagement will de denied. The reasons for those rulings are set forth below.

Background

The following facts are drawn primarily from the parties' LCvR 7.1(h) statements, but are supplemented as needed by subsequent filings. They are undisputed.

NFLPA is the exclusive collective bargaining representative of NFL players pursuant to § 9(a) of the National Labor Relations Act, 29 U.S.C.A. § 159(a). NFLPA nevertheless permits individual agents, or "contract advisors," to represent individual players in negotiations with NFL Clubs. NFLPA "certifies" contract advisors pursuant to a set of regulations. Those regulations set forth a code of conduct for contract advisors, and require that issues regarding the activities of contract advisors be resolved by arbitration.

Mr. Black was first certified as a NFLPA contract advisor in March 1995. He submitted a sworn application to continue his certification on September 9, 1998. The application contained this statement:

> In submitting this Application, I agree to comply with and be bound by these Regulations . . . I agree that if I am denied certification or if subsequent to obtaining certification it is revoked or suspended pursuant to the Regulations, the exclusive method for challenging any such action is through the arbitration procedure set forth in the Regulations. In consideration for the opportunity to obtain certification and in consideration of NFLPA's time and expense incurred in the processing of this application for such certification, I further agree that this Application and the Certification, if one is issued to me, along with the NFLPA Regulations Governing Contract Advisors shall constitute a contract between NFLPA and myself.

In May 1999, Mr. Black received a disciplinary complaint from NFLPA's Disciplinary Committee.[2] He commenced this action a month later, asserting that the disciplinary complaint was the product of an antitrust conspiracy and a secondary boycott, in violation of the Sherman Antitrust Act and the National Labor Relations Act, and that the arbitration system established by the regulations violates the Federal Arbitration Act. Mr. Black's motion for a temporary restraining order was denied on June 22, 1999 by Judge Hogan, and Mr. Black filed an answer to the disciplinary complaint on July 6, 1999.

On July 27, 1999, the Disciplinary Committee issued a proposed ruling revoking Mr. Black's contract advisor certification for a minimum of three years. The regulations provide that Mr. Black may challenge the proposed ruling only by taking the matter to arbitration before an arbitrator selected by NFLPA—in this case, Roger P. Kaplan, Esq.

On July 29, 1999, Mr. Black filed an amended complaint. This first amended complaint jettisons the antitrust and secondary boycott claims and adds two new claims: that NFLPA's initiation of the disciplinary proceedings was based on race discrimination in violation of Section 1981; and that NFLPA tortiously interfered with Mr. Black's business relations (and those of his corporate entity Professional Management, Inc.) by invoking disciplinary action. Mr. Black continues to claim that the arbitration process established by the regulations is illegal under the FAA.

Now before the Court are NFLPA's motion to dismiss or, in the alternative, for summary judgment on all three counts in plaintiffs' first amended complaint, and plaintiffs' motion for leave to file a second amended complaint that would add claims of defamation and trade disparagement.

Analysis

A. Section 1981 Claim

Mr. Black asserts that NFLPA deprived him and his company of full enjoyment of their contractual relationship with NFLPA in violation of 42 U.S.C.A. § 1981. He asserts that three white agents subjected to disciplinary action by the NFLPA—Joel Segal, Jeffrey Irwin and James Ferraro—were treated more favorably than he.

[1] To establish a prima facie case of discrimination under Section 1981, Mr. Black must demonstrate that his non African-American comparators were similarly situated to him in all material respects. *See Coward v. ADT Security Systems*, 140 F.3d 271, 274 (D.C.Cir. 1998). This standard makes it questionable whether Mr. Black's claim can succeed. The timing and gravity of the charges against Mr. Segal appear to be quite different from those against Mr. Black. Mr. Black has not yet had an opportunity for discovery, however, and he has asked in his LCvR 7.1(h) statement for "a chance to obtain affidavits and take depositions and other discovery" pursuant to Fed.R.Civ.P. 56(f). Because Rule 56(f) requests should be "liberally construed," *see* Moore's Federal Practice ¶ 56.10[8][a] (3d ed. 1999), Mr. Black will have a "reasonable opportunity" to justify his opposition. *First*

Chicago Int'l v. United Exchange Co., 836 F.2d 1375, 1380 (D.C.Cir.1988). The same ruling will apply with respect to the other alleged comparators, Messrs. Irwin and Ferraro, as to whom the NFLPA has made no factual response to Mr. Black's section 1981 claims.

B. Tortious Interference

[2] Mr. Black and PMI allege that NFLPA, by means of its racially discriminatory actions and by making defamatory statements, tortiously interfered with their existing and prospective business and contractual relations. NFLPA's motion argues that these state law based claims are preempted by § 301 of the Labor Management Relations Act. It is undisputed that NFLPA is a labor union and that the NFLPA contract advisor regulations were formulated in accordance with the collective bargaining agreement.

In *Allis-Chalmers Corp. v. Lueck*, 471 U.S. 202, 213, 105 S.Ct. 1904, 85 L.Ed.2d 206 (1985), the Supreme Court applied the rule that a tort claim "inextricably intertwined with consideration of the terms of the labor contract" is preempted under § 301. Mr. Black and PMI are not parties to the labor contract, but, as contract advisors, they have agreed to be bound by the regulations promulgated under the collective bargaining agreement. Their license to act as agents for NFL players comes by delegation from the NFLPA, which is a party to the collective bargaining agreement.

[3] State law based claims that depend on construction and application of terms in a collective bargaining agreement are preempted. Those that have a basis wholly independent of the labor contract are not. *Compare United Steelworkers v. Rawson*, 495 U.S. 362, 371, 110 S.Ct. 1904, 109 L.Ed.2d 362 (1990) (state wrongful death claim based on union's negligent inspection of workplace preempted, because duty to inspect was assumed through collective bargaining agreement) *and International Brotherhood of Electrical Workers v. Hechler*, 481 U.S. 851, 862, 107 S.Ct. 2161, 95 L.Ed.2d 791 (1987) (state tort claim alleging employer's failure to train preempted, because not sufficiently independent of collective bargaining agreement) *with Lingle v. Norge Div. of Magic Chef, Inc.*, 486 U.S. 399, 411–12, 108 S.Ct. 1877, 100 L.Ed.2d 410 (1988) (state retaliatory discharge claim *not* preempted, because based on statutory rights separate from the collective bargaining agreement).

continued

The gravamen of Mr. Black's tortious interference claim is that NFLPA engaged in "discriminatory treatment . . . under the pretext of a disciplinary proceeding" and thereby deliberately interfered with his contractual relationships with NFL players. Pls.' Opp'n at 11. He does not assert a violation of a right to contract "owed to every person in society," *Rawson*, 495 U.S. at 370, 110 S.Ct. 1904 or any other generalized statutory right.[3] Mr. Black's complaint is about the way in which NFLPA has conducted and will conduct his disciplinary proceeding. That complaint turns upon the proper application of the regulations to Mr. Black's alleged illegal activities as a contract advisor. Thus, *Rawson*, *Hechler* and their progeny, rather than the *Lingle* line of cases, control. Mr. Black's state law claim "cannot be described as independent of the collective-bargaining agreement." *Id.* at 370.[4]

The validity of PMI's contracts with "various football players relating to certain marketing, promotional and public relations services that PMI was to render for players," Pls.' Opp'n at 9, and PMI's expectancy that those contracts would continue in effect are derivative of Mr. Black's position. Thus, even though PMI's tortious interference claim is in some sense further removed from the regulations than Mr. Black's individual claim, its very existence depends upon interpretation and application of the regulations.

C. Federal Arbitration Act

[4] Mr. Black attacks NFLPA's arbitration system as inherently biased, asserts that Arbitrator Kaplan, who is scheduled to hear the appeal of his disciplinary complaint, is not "neutral" under the terms of the regulations, and demands that Mr. Kaplan be removed. As authority for his demand, Mr. Black invokes Section 10 of the FAA, which empowers a federal court to vacate an arbitration award in limited and specified circumstances, one of which is evident partiality or corruption of the arbitrator.

Mr. Black consented to be bound by NFLPA's contract advisor regulations and agreed that, if his certification should be "suspended or revoked, the exclusive method for challenging any such action is through the arbitration procedure set forth in the Regulations." Section 5.D of the regulations provides: "NFLPA shall select a skilled and experienced person to serve as the outside impartial Arbitrator for all cases arising hereunder."

A written agreement to arbitrate a dispute is "valid, irrevocable, and enforceable" except on grounds that would exist at law or in equity for the revocation of contract. 9 U.S.C.A. § 2. The Supreme Court has observed that "Section 2 is a congressional declaration of a liberal federal policy favoring arbitration agreements." *Perry v. Thomas*, 482 U.S. 483, 489, 107 S.Ct. 2520, 96 L.Ed.2d 426 (1987). Any questions or doubts as to the intentions of the parties "are generously construed as to issues of arbitrability." *Mitsubishi Motors Corp. v. Soler Chrysler-Plymouth, Inc.*, 473 U.S. 614, 626, 105 S.Ct. 3346, 87 L.Ed.2d 444 (1985).

Mr. Black's legal proposition is that a federal court may step in to preempt agreed-upon arbitration methods and appoint a "neutral" arbitrator where "the potential bias of a named arbitrator makes arbitration proceedings a prelude to later judicial proceedings challenging the arbitration award." He relies for that proposition on a single district court decision, *Third National Bank v. WEDGE Group, Inc.*, 749 F.Supp. 851 (M.D.Tenn.1990). That case is factually distinguishable from this one, however, and it has been disavowed by the very court on whose opinions *it* relied. *See Aviall, Inc. v. Ryder System, Inc.*, 110 F.3d 892, 896 (2d Cir.1997).

The *Aviall* decision is more on point. In that case, the court held that a parent company's outside auditor, KPMG Peat Marwick, could not be removed prior to arbitration with a subsidiary because "Aviall was fully aware of KMPG's relationship with Ryder when the [agreement] was executed." Distinguishing *WEDGE*, the *Ryder* court noted that "the touchstone in [cases where arbitrators have been removed] was that the arbitrator's relationship to one party was undisclosed, or unanticipated and unintended, thereby invalidating the contract." *Id.* at 896; *see also NFLPA v. OPEIU*, No. 97-1517 at 5-7 (D.D.C. March 25, 1999).

Mr. Black admits that he was aware of and freely agreed to the arbitration terms contained in the regulations, and he makes no allegation about infirmities in the drafting of the regulations. As *Aviall* makes clear, it is of no moment that Mr. Black did not have a hand in the structuring of the arbitration process. *See Aviall*, 110 F.3d at 896. An NFL-selected arbitrator may have an incentive to appease his or her employer, but "[t]he parties to an arbitration choose their method of dispute resolution, and can ask no more impartiality than inheres in the method they have chosen." *Merit Ins. Co. v. Leatherby Insurance Co.*, 714 F.2d 673, 679 (7th Cir.1983). Mr. Black's peremptory challenge to the neutrality of the NFLPA arbitrator must accordingly be rejected. "He remains free to challenge on the ground of evident partiality any [penalty] ultimately" approved through arbitration. *Aviall*, 110 F.3d at 897.

D. Second Amended Complaint

Mr. Black's proposed second amended complaint sets forth new claims of defamation and trade disparagement. It is well settled that "a liberal, pro- amendment ethos dominates the intent and judicial construction of Rule 15(a)." Moore's Federal Practice § 15.14[1]. It is also true, however, that "[a] motion to amend the [c]omplaint should be denied as 'futile' if the complaint as amended could not survive a motion to dismiss." *FDIC v. Bathgate*, 27 F.3d 850, 874-76 (3d Cir.1994); *Graves v. United States*, 961 F.Supp. 314, 317 (D.D.C.1997) (citing 6 Charles Alan Wright, Arthur R. Miller & Mary Kay Kane, Federal Practice and Procedure § 1487 (2d ed.1990)).

[5] Defamation claims are subject to a "heightened pleading standard." *See Wiggins v. Philip Morris, Inc.*, 853 F.Supp. 458, 466 (D.D.C.1994). To survive a motion to dismiss, "[a]ll averments of defamation must be plead with particularity." *Id.* at 465. Conclusory statements averring defamation "are insufficient to state a claim," *Hoffman v. Hill and Knowlton, Inc.*, 777 F.Supp. 1003, 1005 (D.D.C.1991), and defamation plaintiffs should therefore plead the time, place, content, speaker and listener of the alleged defamatory matter. *See Wiggins v. Equifax*, 848 F.Supp. 213, 223 (D.D.C.1993).

[6] In his second amended complaint, Mr. Black does not set forth his defamation claims with the specificity required to withstand a motion to dismiss. *See Wiggins*, 853 F.Supp. at 465-66 (dismissing plaintiff's defamation claims as too vague and imprecise); *Hoffman*, 777 F.Supp. at 1005 (dismissing plaintiff's defamation claims as "based on inference and conjecture"). Rather, he makes generalized and conclusory allegations about statements made "by NFLPA representatives at [ ] NFLPA Players Representatives meeting[s] . . . to the effect that" Mr. Black was a "bad and corrupt agent" who had engaged in "illegal activities." Second Am. Compl. ¶¶27-28. Mr. Black presents no "factual allegations" that defamatory statements were actually made, let alone what they were and who made them. *See id.*

[7] Mr. Black's one reference to a specific publication does not withstand even modest scrutiny. The charge is that "the NFLPA," in a February 8-14, 1999, edition of *Street & Smith's Sports Business Journal*, stated that "Black tried to bribe an LSU assistant football coach." In fact, the article states that the "Union President . . . wouldn't comment on the Black investigation." *See* Ex. A to Def.'s Opp'n. No reasonable juror could determine that "no comment" is defamatory. Because none of Mr. Black's defamation claims could survive a motion to dismiss, they are "futile" for the purpose of a second Rule 15(a) amendment.

The trade disparagement claim in plaintiffs' proposed second amended complaint, *see* ¶¶63-66, depends for its legal sufficiency on the presence of defamatory statements, so it, too, is futile.[5]

An appropriate order accompanies this memorandum.

ORDER

For the reasons set forth in the accompanying memorandum, it is this 1st day of February 2000,

ORDERED that defendant's motion to dismiss or for summary [# 23] is granted in part and denied in part. And it is

FURTHER ORDERED that plaintiffs' motion for leave to file a second amended complaint [# 25] is denied.

FOOTNOTES

1. Because matters outside the pleadings have been considered, the case has been decided under the rubric of Fed.R.Civ.P. 56.

2. The disciplinary complaint alleged, *inter alia*, that, in violation of the regulations: (1) at various times in 1997 and 1998 Mr. Black provided cash payments to several college players before their eligibility had expired; (2) in late December 1998 Mr. Black arranged the purchase of a Mercedes-Benz automobile for a University of Florida player who was still competing at the college level; (3) in December 1998 Mr. Black met with an assistant coach at Louisiana State University and admitted to purchasing the Mercedes-Benz for the University of Florida football player; (4) in December 1998 an agent identifying himself as Mr. Black's representative

continued

offered a bribe to an assistant coach at LSU to encourage an LSU player to enlist Mr. Black as his agent; (5) at various times in 1996 Mr. Black sold stock in a publicly-traded company to several players; (6) over the past three years Mr. Black has provided a bill paying service for his clients whereby they deposit funds in accounts which Mr. Black's firm jointly controls; (7) on his application for certification as a contract advisor, Mr. Black untruthfully answered "NO" when asked: "Do you manage, invest, or in any other manner handle funds for NFL players?"; and (8) in May 1997 Mr. Black filed suit in South Carolina state court against Brantley Evans, Jr., in contravention of exclusive arbitration procedures in the regulations.

3. This claim is not "based on rights arising out of a statute designed to provide minimum substantive guarantees to individual workers." *Lingle*, 486 U.S. at 411–12, 108 S.Ct. 1877 (citation omitted).

4. The District of Columbia law of tortious interference confirms that Mr. Black's claim is "inextricably intertwined" with the regulations.

To make out a prima facie case of tortious interference, a plaintiff must show: (1) "the existence of a valid business relationship and expectancy, (2) knowledge of the relationship or expectancy on the part of the interferer, (3) intentional interference inducing or causing a breach or termination of the relationship or expectancy, and (4) resultant damage." *Bennett Enterprises, Inc. v. Domino's Pizza, Inc.*, 45 F.3d 493, 498 (D.C.Cir.1995). The NFLPA's regulations in this case establish the parameters of Mr. Black's *expectancy* that his business relationship would continue, in view of his actions.

5. Plaintiffs' claim of "trade disparagement" is virtually identical to a claim for "injurious falsehood." *See Art Metal-U.S.A., Inc. v. United States*, 753 F.2d 1151, 1155–56 (D.C.Cir.1985). Defamation and the tort of "injurious falsehood," are "closely related," and "changes in the law of defamation . . . have further minimized the common law distinctions between the torts." *See id.*

Reprinted with permission from West Group.

The 1987 NFL Strike

The players' strike in 1987 became one of the most publicized labor disputes in history. On September 22, 1987, the NFL players went on strike after unsuccessful negotiations with the owners about, primarily, free agency. During the 1987 strike, NFL owners hired replacement players (referred by some as "scabs") to continue the season. This fielding of replacement players in 1987 has been referred to as the darkest period of labor relations in professional football. Some NFL players crossed the picket lines to play. Television networks broadcast the "scab games" using replacement players. This pitted players against players.

After the 1987 strike demonstrated that traditional collective bargaining practices would probably not obtain a contract with the owners, the NFLPA turned to the courts. For five years after the 1987 strike, NFL players worked with no contract in place, and both sides spent more time in the courtroom than at the collective bargaining table. The resulting successful contract between the owners and players union, especially its salary cap feature, has exerted a great deal of pressure on other sports to follow suit.

Powell v. NFL (1988)[17]

In *Powell*, professional football players brought an antitrust action against the league claiming that the league violated antitrust law when it continued to enforce the terms of the expired CBA. The court concluded that the League and the players should continue to bargain, resort to economic force, or present their claims to the NLRB. The court held that the nonstatutory labor exemption extends beyond impasse, and therefore, the league was not in violation of antitrust law. The effect was that unions were forced to decertify in order to gain leverage during the bargaining relationship.

Brown v. Pro-Football, Inc. (1995)[18]

In 1987, the CBA involving the terms and conditions of employment for all professional football players expired, and the NFL and NFLPA began negotiations for a new collective bargaining agreement. The NFL owners implemented the Developmental Squad Players Program. Brown, a developmental squad player, and others alleged that the NFL owners and the NFL violated the Sherman Act by setting a fixed salary for the Developmental Players Squad. The Supreme Court held that such matters were not for the courts to decide and that the league acted lawfully when it imposed the fixed salary. The *Brown* court, by extending the nonstatutory labor exemption beyond impasse, allows the employer to impose unilateral restraints outside of the collective bargaining process without fear of antitrust violation because the court held that it fell within the scope of the nonstatutory labor exemption.

Basketball

Professional basketball players organized their union, the NBA Players Union, in the 1950s, about the same time baseball players organized collectively. Now known as the NBA Players Association (NBPA), the NBPA has been successful in its advocacy efforts on behalf of professional basketball players and has never participated in a labor strike against NBA team owners. In 1987, following the expiration of its contract, the NBPA filed a broad antitrust lawsuit against the NBA, arguing that labor exemptions granted to the NBA under the previous contract had expired and antitrust laws should apply.

Bridgeman v. NBA (1987)[19]

The plaintiffs in *Bridgeman* brought a suit against the NBA claiming that the enforcement by the league of the college player draft, salary cap, and right of first refusal constituted antitrust violations. The court held that after good faith bargaining, the nonstatutory labor exemption lasts for as long as the employer continues to impose the particular restraint and reasonably believes that the practice or a close variant of it will be incorporated in the next collective bargaining agreement. A restraint that fails the *Mackey* test is subject to antitrust scrutiny.

Wood v. NBA[20]

In *Wood v. National Basketball Association*, the U.S. Court of Appeals for the Second Circuit dismissed a player's antitrust claim challenging certain provisions of a CBA between the NBA and NBPA. Wood, a college senior, challenged the NBA salary cap, the NBA draft, and restricted free agency. The court found that the challenged provisions were mandatory subjects of collective bargaining and therefore were protected by the nonstatutory labor exemption.

Hockey

Hockey has had the fewest antitrust challenges of the four major sports. The NHLPA's existence began in 1967.[21] Still, a few issues have required judicial intervention. Similar to professional basketball in recent years, hockey has enjoyed a surge in popularity and prosperity as the fan base has increased, merchandising revenues have increased, television revenues have increased, and teams have moved to newer and more modern arenas across the country. It is likely that as hockey continues to expand teams in the United States and Canada, antitrust laws will likely be called upon to resolve a dispute.

McCourt v. California Sport[22]

In 1979, in *McCourt v. California Sport*, the Sixth Circuit also addressed whether the nonstatutory labor exemption extended beyond impasse. McCourt, a professional hockey player, claimed that the National Hockey League reserve system was subject to, and in violation of, antitrust laws. The *McCourt* court applied the *Mackey* test to the CBA and found that the reserve system was incorporated into the collective bargaining agreement through bona fide arm's length bargaining. The court held that because the reserve system was a product of good faith bargaining, it was exempt from antitrust laws.

The 1992 NHL Strike

In 1992, the players called their first strike in NHL history through their collective bargaining union, the NHLPA. The 1992 strike proved to be short (only 10 days), and the resulting labor agreement stayed in effect for only one season. While both players and owners won concessions in the 1992 negotiations, the basic agreement remained intact. The players also consented to play the 1994-95 season without a contract, but league owners insisted on negotiations and threatened to postpone the season absent a new contract. The NHL and the union negotiated a contract in early 1995 without a salary cap.

Competitor Leagues

There have been several challenges to the market power of professional sports leagues by rival, upstart leagues. Professional football has had several challenges to its domination of the American marketplace. While newer leagues attempt to form a fan base and gain much needed television contracts for their survival, allegations of antitrust violations are common, particularly if the newer league ultimately folds.

In *American Football League v. National Football League* 323 F.2d 124 (4th Cir. 1963), the AFL claimed the NFL was a monopoly and sued alleging antitrust violations. However, the Fourth Circuit held that the NFL was a "natural monopoly" and did not violate antitrust laws to gain any advantage.

In *United States Football League v. National Football League*, 842 F.2d 1335 (1986), the USFL sought damages of $1.7 billion, alleging that the NFL violated sections 1 and 2 of the Sherman Antitrust Act. A jury found that the NFL intentionally maintained monopoly power over professional football in the United States, but the jury only awarded $1.00 in damages (tripled to $3.00). Thus, the USFL may have won the battle, but to this day the NFL has won the war.

NCAA and Amateur Sports Cases

Amateur sports in America do not have nearly as many queries and legal challenges involving antitrust laws. Courts seem to have afforded amateur athletic organizations more latitude and less scrutiny. Several cases involving antitrust analysis in the amateur sports context have offered some guidance and certainty as to how antitrust laws should apply in the amateur sports context. For example, in *NCAA v. Bd. of Regents of Univ. of Okla.*, 468 U.S. 85 (1984), the NCAA's television broadcast plan was held to be anticompetitive and in violation of the Sherman Act.

In a more recent case, *Law v. NCAA*, 134 F.3d 1010 (10th Cir. 1998), the NCAA was again found to be in violation of federal antitrust laws when it implemented the REC (restricted-earnings coaches) Rule. This rule limited the compensation of assistant coaches in all NCAA Division I sports to a mere $12,000 per year plus a possible $4,000 in the summer months. The rule was enacted as a cost-cutting measure among NCAA institutions that claimed that it also provided for a more competitive balance among member institutions. A group of coaches challenged the rule as being in violation of Section 1 of the Sherman Act, and the federal court found that the rule was anticompetitive and an unlawful restraint of trade. The NCAA was ordered to pay over $22 million in damages that was trebled to $67 million. The case finally settled for $54.5 million. Case 12 presents the appellate court ruling in this lawsuit over sanctions and damages.

As of this writing, NCAA student-athletes are not represented by a players union. Collegiate athletes may compete for no longer than four years[23] and represent a form of free labor, while athletic department coaches and administrators are often paid handsomely. NCAA athletes are not compensated for their services other than a collegiate scholarship ("grant-in-aid"), which can include tuition, room, and books. However, there have been several unsuccesful attempts to organize collectively and to seek payment for services. As more money flows into the pockets of collegiate athletic departments and the NCAA as a whole, there will likely be more challenges to NCAA rules and policies as being violative of antitrust laws.

CASE 12   *Law v. NCAA*

United States Court of Appeals,
Tenth Circuit.

Norman LAW, Andrew Greer, Peter Herrmann,
Michael Jarvis, Jr.; Charles M.
Rieb, Doug Schreiber, Lazaro Collozzo, Robin
Dreizler, Frank Cruz and William
Hall, on behalf of themselves and all others
similarly situated, Plaintiffs-
Appellees,
v.
NATIONAL COLLEGIATE
ATHLETIC ASSOCIATION,
Defendant-Appellant.
No. 96-3340.
Jan. 23, 1998.

College basketball coaches brought action against intercollegiate athletic association, alleging that rule limiting coaches' annual compensation was unlawful restraint of trade. The United States District Court for the District of Kansas, 1997 WL 382040, imposed sanctions on association and its attorneys for failure to obey discovery orders, and they appealed. The Court of Appeals, Logan, Circuit Judge, held that: (1) 25 percent surcharge imposed in addition to costs incurred by coaches in connection with association's failure to permit discovery was criminal in nature and thus was immediately appealable, and (2) neither association nor its counsel received adequate notice of criminal contempt order.

Reversed and remanded.

LOGAN, Circuit Judge.

Defendant National Collegiate Athletic Association (NCAA) and its attorneys William C. Barnard, Gayle A. Reindl, John J. Kitchin, and Linda J. Salfrank, appeal the district court's imposition of sanctions on them for failure to obey discovery orders in plaintiffs' antitrust actions. The district court has not entered a final judgment,[1] but the NCAA and its counsel assert that the sanctions are immediately appealable as a criminal contempt order. They then argue that the district court imposed the criminal contempt sanctions without affording the NCAA and its counsel the required procedural protections and adequate notice that discovery sanctions might be imposed against them.[2]

I

The sanctions order arose out of a discovery dispute over plaintiffs' attempts to obtain damages information and identify additional plaintiffs. Plaintiffs' third set of interrogatories sought information about the salaries and employment benefits that each of the Division I[3] member schools provided to coaches in every sport from 1985–1996. The NCAA sought a protective order on the basis that it had no obligation to collect this data; but the district court denied its motion. The court ordered the NCAA to send a survey to its members, but a dispute arose over the contents of a cover letter to that survey. Ultimately the district court ordered the NCAA to answer the interrogatories by February 26. Asserting that the NCAA did not meet the deadline, plaintiffs moved for discovery sanctions. The district court issued a show cause order, and after a hearing granted plaintiffs' motion and imposed sanctions against both the NCAA and its counsel. The district court order of May 29, 1996, directed Division I NCAA members to answer plaintiffs' interrogatories, and publicly censured and imposed monetary sanctions on the NCAA and its counsel.

The NCAA filed for a writ of mandamus from this court which we denied.[4] Later, however, we granted to state college and university Division I member schools a writ of prohibition, vacating the portion of the district court's order directing them to answer the interrogatories. *University of Texas at Austin v. Vratil*, 96 F.3d 1337 (10th Cir. 1996).

Thereafter the district court vacated its May 29 order and reconsidered plaintiffs' motion for sanctions. The district court rejected the NCAA's argument that the information requested in the interrogatories was not "available" under Fed.R.Civ.P. 33. The court publicly censured the NCAA and its counsel and ordered both "to pay the reasonable expenses and attorneys' fees which plaintiffs incurred on account of their failure to permit discovery, plus a 25 percent surcharge." Appellant's App. 633. The district court further ordered that NCAA and its counsel pay "all expenses and attorneys' fees which plaintiffs reasonably incur in the process of deposing Division I members of the NCAA on the issue of damages," including a "25 percent surcharge." *Id.* The NCAA and its counsel appeal only the portion of that order directing them to pay fees and costs plus twenty-five percent for their failure to permit discovery.[5]

II

[1][2][3] We first address whether we have jurisdiction over this appeal. Sanctions, even if issued as civil contempt orders, generally are not deemed final appealable orders under 28 U.S.C.A. § 1291. *See G.J.B. & Assocs., Inc. v. Singleton*, 913 F.2d 824, 827–29 (10th Cir.1990) (counsel of record may not file interlocutory appeal for imposition of sanctions); *D & H Marketers, Inc. v. Freedom Oil & Gas, Inc.*, 744 F.2d 1443, 1445–46 (10th Cir.1984) (parties may not file interlocutory appeal from imposition of sanctions); *see also Consumers Gas & Oil, Inc., v. Farmland Indus., Inc.*, 84 F.3d 367, 370 (10th Cir.1996) (party to a pending proceeding may appeal civil contempt order only as part of appeal from final judgment). Criminal contempt orders, however, are deemed final orders that are immediately appealable. *Id.* The NCAA and its counsel assert that although the district court's order did not expressly hold the NCAA and its counsel in contempt, it found that they acted in contempt of court. They further argue the court imposed criminal contempt sanctions and thus we have jurisdiction.

The order at issue followed a show cause hearing on plaintiffs' motion for sanctions under Fed.R.Civ.P. 37(b)(2).[6] The court found that the NCAA "affirmatively encouraged its members to *withhold* information for the purpose of defeating plaintiffs' legitimate interrogatories," Appellant's App. 626, and that such conduct was "wilful, in bad faith, and expressly calculated to frustrate the Court's orders with respect to discovery." *Id.; see also id.* at 597. The district court stated that "Rule 37(b)(2) provides that if a party fails to obey an order to provide discovery under Rule 37(a), the Court 'may make such orders in regard to the failure as are just . . . .' Rule 37(b)(2) sets forth possible sanctions, including orders that certain facts be taken as established or evidence excluded, that claims or defenses be unopposed or pleadings struck, that reasonable expenses caused by the recalcitrant party be paid, and that the party be held in contempt." Appellant's App. 627. The court then "publicly censured" the NCAA and its counsel and ordered them to pay 125% of the expenses and attorneys' fees incurred in making the motion. *Id.* at 629-30. The district court reasoned:

A monetary award is also necessary to reimburse plaintiffs the expenses and attorneys' fees which they incurred in making the subject motion to compel. An unenhanced order for compensation would be remedial, and no circumstances of record would render such an award unjust. Such an order would have no meaningful deterrent effect, however, for the NCAA, its counsel or others. As noted elsewhere in this opinion, the NCAA is *already* subject to liability for payment of all costs and fees which plaintiffs have incurred and will incur on account of the NCAA's established violation of federal antitrust law. The Court finds that a 25 percent surcharge is a reasonable sanction and that it is the least severe penalty that will serve to deter future misconduct.

Id. at 630.[7]

The district court clearly intended to impose the sanctions under Rule 37. The language ordering payment of "the reasonable expenses and attorneys' fees which plaintiffs incurred on account of their failure to permit discovery," Appellant's App. 633, tracks the language of the final paragraph of Rule 37(b)(2). This leaves the question of the basis for the twenty-five percent surcharge ordered paid to plaintiffs. The NCAA and its counsel assert that the only monetary sanctions authorized by Rule 37(b)(2), absent contempt, are the compensatory sanctions authorized by its final paragraph. Because the twenty-five percent is not compensatory, they argue that the court must have imposed that sanction based on a contempt finding under Rule 37(b)(2)(D). Plaintiffs counter that a noncompensatory monetary sanction is authorized under the provision that the court "may make such orders in regard to the failure [to comply with discovery orders] as are just." Fed.R.Civ.P. 37(b)(2).

The Second Circuit noted that "[t]here is a split in authority on the question whether a district court can order non-compensatory sanctions under Rule 37 without a finding of contempt." *Satcorp Int'l Group v. China Nat'l Silk Import & Export Corp.*, 101 F.3d 3, 5 (2d Cir.1996). The Fourth Circuit has held "that a Rule 37 fine is effectively a criminal contempt sanction, requiring notice and the opportunity to be heard." *Hathcock v. Navistar Int'l Transp. Corp.*, 53 F.3d 36, 42 (4th Cir.1995) (Rule 37 sanction of $5,000 imposed without prior notice or hearing was effectively criminal

continued

contempt sanction) (citing *Buffington v. Baltimore County*, 913 F.2d 113, 133-35 (4th Cir.1990)). Similarly, the Third Circuit has held that "[a]bsent contempt, the only monetary sanctions Rule 37 authorizes are 'reasonable expenses' resulting from the failure to comply with discovery." *Martin v. Brown*, 63 F.3d 1252, 1263 (3d Cir.1995). Several district courts, however, have imposed a fine under Rule 37 without making a finding of contempt. *See, e.g., Pereira v. Narragansett Fishing Corp.*, 135 F.R.D. 24, 26-28 (D.Mass. 1991) (finding that under Rule 37(b)(2) it could impose a monetary sanction "over and above an award of the opposing party's costs and attorney's fees" without a finding of contempt); *J.M. Cleminshaw Co. v. City of Norwich*, 93 F.R.D. 338, 355-57 (D.Conn. 1981). This position is bolstered by the First Circuit's opinion in *Media Duplication Servs., Ltd. v. HDG Software, Inc.*, 928 F.2d 1228, 1241-42 (1st Cir. 1991), which held that under the Fed.R.Civ.P. 16(f) language that a court "may make such orders . . . as are just" a district court may impose punitive monetary sanctions, seemingly without a finding of contempt.

Federal courts, of course, have power to impose sanctions and adjudicate contempt against parties and counsel on bases other than Rule 37. *See Roadway Express, Inc. v. Piper*, 447 U.S. 752, 100 S.Ct. 2455, 65 L.Ed.2d 488 (1980). We need not attempt to distinguish between a sanction order that is not civil contempt and one that is civil contempt. If the district court's interlocutory sanction order is properly classified as civil, we have no jurisdiction to review whether it was appropriate. Conversely, if it is criminal contempt it is appealable.

[4][5] The distinction between criminal and civil contempt is important because "[c]riminal contempt is a crime in the ordinary sense, and criminal penalties may not be imposed on someone who has not been afforded the protections that the Constitution requires of such criminal proceedings." *International Union, United Mine Workers of America v. Bagwell*, 512 U.S. 821, 826, 114 S.Ct. 2552, 2556, 129 L.Ed.2d 642 (1994) (quotations and citation omitted). Succinctly, "[c]ivil as distinguished from criminal contempt is a sanction to enforce compliance with an order of the court or to compensate for losses or damages sustained by reason of noncompliance." *McComb v. Jacksonville Paper Co.*, 336 U.S. 187, 191, 69 S.Ct. 497, 499, 93 L.Ed. 599 (1949). The NCAA and its

counsel argue that the district court's order constitutes criminal contempt because the twenty-five percent surcharge is a fine. We agree it is a fine even though the court ordered it paid to plaintiffs, not to the court.

[6] *United States v. United Mine Workers of America*, 330 U.S. 258, 67 S.Ct. 677, 91 L.Ed. 884 (1947), states:

> Judicial sanctions in civil contempt proceedings may, in a proper case, be employed for either or both of two purposes: to coerce the defendant into compliance with the court's order, and to compensate the complainant for losses sustained.
>
> Where compensation is intended, a fine is imposed, payable to the complainant. Such fine must of course be based upon evidence of complainant's actual loss, and his right, as a civil litigant, to the compensatory fine is dependent upon the outcome of the basic controversy.

Id. at 303-04, 67 S.Ct. at 701-02 (citation and footnotes omitted). Plaintiffs rely upon the statement in *Hicks v. Feiock*, 485 U.S. 624, 632, 108 S.Ct. 1423, 1429, 99 L.Ed.2d 721 (1988): "If the relief provided is a fine, it is remedial when it is paid to the complainant, and punitive when it is paid to the court." Despite the generalization in *Hicks* we believe the district court could not make a noncompensatory fine civil simply by requiring it to be paid to the complainant instead of to the court.

Plaintiff also cites the following statement from *Bagwell*:

> Certain indirect contempts nevertheless are appropriate for imposition through civil proceedings. Contempts such as *failure to comply with document discovery*, for example, while occurring outside the court's presence, impede the court's ability to adjudicate the proceedings before it and thus touch upon the core justification for the contempt power. Courts traditionally have broad authority through means other than contempt—such as by striking pleadings, assessing costs, excluding evidence, and entering default judgment—to penalize a party's failure to comply with the rules of conduct governing the litigation process. See, *e.g.*, Fed. rules Civ. Proc. 11, 37. Such judicial sanctions never have been considered criminal, and the imposition of *civil, coercive fines* to police the litigation process appears consistent with this authority.

512 U.S. at 833, 114 S.Ct. at 2560 (emphasis added). The *Bagwell* Court held that fines ordered paid to complainants and to the state and counties damaged by unlawful activities were criminal.

[7] A civil fine is by definition either compensatory or coercive. The Supreme Court has made this plain. A fine payable to a complainant "must of course be based upon evidence of complainant's actual loss." *United Mine Workers*, 330 U.S. at 304, 67 S.Ct. at 701. The offending party is punished, but a critical feature of civil contempt is that "the punishment is remedial." *Hicks*, 485 U.S. at 631, 108 S.Ct. at 1429 (quoting *Gompers v. Bucks Stove & Range Co.*, 221 U.S. 418, 441, 31 S.Ct. 492, 498, 55 L.Ed. 797 (1911)). "A fine payable to the complaining party and proportioned to the complainant's loss is compensatory and civil." *Hicks*, 485 U.S. at 646–47, 108 S.Ct. at 1437. One reason given by the Supreme Court in *Bagwell* for finding a fine criminal was that no one "suggested that the challenged fines are compensatory." 512 U.S. at 834, 114 S.Ct. at 2561; *see also Yanish v. Barber*, 232 F.2d 939, 944 (9th Cir. 1956) (civil fine cannot exceed actual loss to complainant).

[8] Courts have upheld as civil fines intended to coerce, as long as the offending party can avoid them by complying with the court's order. *See Hicks*, 485 U.S. at 632, 108 S.Ct. at 1429–30 (fine payable to the court itself may be remedial "when the defendant can avoid paying the fine simply by performing the affirmative act required by the court's order"); *NLRB v. Local 825, Int'l Union of Operating Eng'rs*, 430 F.2d 1225, 1229–30 (3d Cir.1970).[8]

In the instant case the twenty-five percent surcharge above plaintiffs' actual costs was neither compensatory nor, as to the portion of the order appealed here, avoidable by complying with the court's order. Thus it was criminal. When an order is partially civil and partially criminal, the criminal aspect controls for purposes of review. *See Hicks*, 485 U.S. at 638–39 n. 10, 108 S.Ct. at 1433; *Lamar Fin. Corp. v. Adams*, 918 F.2d 564 (5th Cir.1990). We therefore have jurisdiction to review the portion of the district court's order appealed here.

III

[9] The NCAA and its counsel argue that they did not receive the required procedural safeguards for a criminal contempt order.

[T]his Court has found that defendants in criminal contempt proceedings must be presumed innocent, proved guilty beyond a reasonable doubt, and accorded the right to refuse to testify against themselves; must be advised of charges, have a reasonable opportunity to respond to them, and be permitted the assistance of counsel and the right to call witnesses; must be given a public trial before an unbiased judge; and must be afforded a jury trial for serious contempts.

Young v. United States ex rel. Vuitton et Fils S.A., 481 U.S. 787, 798–99, 107 S.Ct. 2124, 2133, 95 L.Ed.2d 740 (1987). "A criminal contempt . . . shall be prosecuted on notice . . . [which shall] state . . . the essential facts constituting the criminal contempt charged and describe it as such." Fed.R.Crim.P. 42(b).

Neither the motion for sanctions nor the show cause order included notice that the NCAA and its attorneys were subject to a criminal contempt charge. Plaintiffs' motion for sanctions did not request monetary sanctions above the reasonable "attorneys' fees and expenses" set out in the last paragraph of Rule 37(b)(2). The district court's show cause order, while it did include the possibility that attorneys Barnard and Reindl might be denied their admission pro hac vice, or that Fed.R.Civ.P. 11 sanctions might be imposed on counsel, did not specifically name attorneys Kitchin and Salfrank. Because neither the NCAA nor its counsel had adequate notice that they might be held in criminal contempt and liable for noncompensatory monetary sanctions, and were not afforded the process required for criminal contempt, we must reverse the district court's sanctions order.

REVERSED and REMANDED.

FOOTNOTES

1. The district court granted summary judgment to plaintiffs on liability on May 24, 1995, ruling that the NCAA violated § 1 of the Sherman Act. On January 8, 1996, the district court granted a permanent injunction against the NCAA enjoining it from enforcing compensation limits against the named plaintiffs, who are "restricted earning coaches." The NCAA appealed that injunction in case number 96–3034. In a separate opinion issued this day this panel has affirmed the district court's order granting that

continued

injunction. *See Law v. NCAA*, 134 F.3d 1010 (10th Cir.1998). Because the issue of damages is still pending the district court has not entered a final order in the cases.

The district court also entered several other orders regarding interim attorneys' fees which are the subject of separate appeals in which we issue opinions this day. *See Law v. NCAA*, 134 F.3d 1025 (10th Cir.1998).

2. Alternatively, the NCAA and its counsel contend that the sanctions must fall because the underlying discovery order was based on an erroneous finding that the information sought by plaintiffs' third interrogatories was "available" to the NCAA within the meaning of Fed.R.Civ.P. 33(a). Because we do not reach the issue of whether the underlying discovery order was erroneous we do not address this argument.

3. Although the third set of interrogatories to defendant requested this information for Division II schools as well, plaintiffs later limited the request to Division I schools.

4. We concluded that the NCAA had an adequate remedy at law because it could appeal the sanctions after entry of final judgment, the monetary amount of sanctions did not impose irreparable injury to the NCAA, and no alleged abuse of discretion by the district court amounted to judicial usurpation of power. *NCAA v. Vratil*, No. 96–3208 (10th Cir. June 27, 1996).

5. Although the full amount of the discovery sanctions has not been set, *see Turnbull v. Wilcken*, 893 F.2d 256, 258 (10th Cir.1990) (appeal from imposition of sanctions may not be taken until amount has been determined), this does not present a jurisdictional problem in addition to that discussed hereafter. Defendant asserts that it paid plaintiffs over $48,000 after the May 29 order, and plaintiffs have not challenged this assertion. Defendant and counsel state they will appeal that portion of the order directing them to pay for attorneys' fees and expenses incurred by plaintiffs in deposing NCAA Division I members when the district court sets an amount.

6. The motion requested sanctions for failing to obey an order to provide discovery, and specifically requested:

1. striking defendant's opposition to plaintiffs' motions for class certification and certifying the plaintiff classes; and

2. striking defendant's answers and rendering final default judgments against defendant in each of these cases in amounts to be proven up by plaintiffs at a hearing to be held for that purpose.

Alternatively, plaintiffs seek an order:

1. allowing plaintiffs to prove class-wide damages by means of sampling and averaging techniques and precluding defendant from offering expert testimony on the issue of damages or otherwise contesting such techniques or the sufficiency of the data used by plaintiffs in calculating damages; and

2. requiring defendant to pay (a) the attorneys' fees and expenses incurred by plaintiffs to date in attempting to obtain information responsive to Plaintiffs' Third Set of Interrogatories, and (b) all future attorneys' fees and expenses incurred by plaintiffs in obtaining such information from NCAA members, to be paid as they are incurred.

Appellant's App. 251.

7. The district court apparently overlooked the possibility that its finding of an antitrust violation might be reversed on appeal. In that event plaintiffs would not be entitled to attorneys' fees as a prevailing party. But defendant and its counsel still would have to pay a properly levied discovery sanction, which could include plaintiffs' attorneys' fees incurred in pursuing the motion to compel.

8. Even coercive fines that may be avoided by obeying the court's orders may be considered criminal if the sanctionable conduct did not occur in the court's presence and elaborate fact finding is required. *See Bagwell*, 512 U.S. 821, 114 S.Ct. 2552; Hostak, *International Union, United Mine Workers v. Bagwell, A Paradigm Shift in the Distinction Between Civil and Criminal Contempt*, 81 Cornell L.Rev. 181 (1995).

■ Summary

Both professional and amateur sports involve labor and federal antitrust and labor issues. Congress enacted several laws to promote commerce and prevent monopolistic behavior by big business in general. The Sherman Act, the Clayton Act, and the Norris-LaGuardia Act are all specific examples of federal laws designed to prevent anticompetitive behavior, and such acts are effective in the sports business. All professional sports are subject to scrutiny by the National Labor Relations Board under the authority of the National Labor Relations Act. Numerous strikes and lockouts have affected professional sports over the years. The NCAA, too, has been the victim of interpretation by federal courts as being in violation of antitrust laws on several occasions. A study of the history of the application of antitrust laws in the sports industry provides a nice summary for the student to appreciate the development of professional leagues over time.

■ Key Terms

antitrust

Clayton Act

collective bargaining

Curt Flood Act of 1998

lockout

National Labor Relations Act
(NLRA)

National Labor Relations Board
(NLRB)

nonstatutory labor exception

Norris-LaGuardia Act

per se analysis

rule of reason

Sherman Antitrust Act

strike

■ Additional Cases

Adidas America, Inc. v. NCAA, 64 F. Supp.2d 1097 (D. Kan. 1999)

Banks v. NCAA, 977 F.2d 1081 (7th Cir. 1992)

Henessey v. NCAA, 564 F.2d 1136 (5th Cir. 1998)

Major League Baseball v. Butterworth, 181 F. Supp.2d 1316 (N.D. Fla. 2001)

Metropolitan Sports Facilities Comm'n v. Minnesota Twins Partnership, 638 N.W.2d 214 (Minn. Ct. App. 2002)

■ Review Questions

1. What does the word *antitrust* mean, and why is it so important in the American landscape of regulation?
2. Why are collective bargaining agreements so important in professional sports?

3. What are the mandatory subjects of collective bargaining?
4. How have strikes and lockouts affected and shaped professional sports today in America?
5. Are players associations too powerful?
6. Should cities and fans have a say in the regulatory framework involving professional sports and athletes?

▪ End notes

1 Most states also have antitrust laws that are modeled after the federal government.
2 15 U.S.C.A. § 1-17 (1997) et seq.
3 Antitrust Amendments Act of 1990.
4 15 U.S.C.A. § 17 (1994).
5 29 U.S.C.A. § 104 (1994).
6 29 U.S.C.A. § 151-169 (1994). The NLRA is sometimes called the Wagner Act.
7 N.L.R.A., § 1, 29 U.S.C.A. § 151 (2001).
8 *Northern Pacific Railway Co. v. United States*, 356 U.S. 1, 5 (1958).
9 *Standard Oil Company of New Jersey v. United States*, 221 U.S. 1 (1911).
10 *Brown v. Pro Football, Inc.*, 116 S.Ct. 2116 (1996).
11 29 U.S.C.A. § 158 (d). *See Also, Amalgamated Meat Cutters v. Jewel Tea Co.*, 381 U.S. 676 (1965).
12 *Fraser v. Major League Soccer L.L.C.*, 284 F.3d 47 (1st Cir. 2002).
13 Baseball's CBA is known as the "Basic Agreement."
14 *Flood v. Kuhn*, 407 U.S. 258 (1972).
15 15 U.S.C.A. § 27.
16 *Mackey v. National Football League*, 543 F.2d 606 (8th Cir. 1976), *cert. dismissed, NFL v. Mackey*, 434 U.S. 801 (1977).
17 *Powell v. National Football League*, 930 F.2d 1293 (8th Cir. 1989).
18 *Brown v. Pro Football, Inc.*, 116 S.Ct. 2116,(1996).
19 *Bridgeman v. National Basketball Ass'n*, 675 F. Supp. 960 (D.N.J. 1987).
20 *Wood v. National Basketball Ass'n*, 809 F.2d 954 (2d Cir. 1987).
21 *See* www.NHLPA.com.
22 *McCourt v. California Sports, Inc.*, 600 F.2d 1193 (6th Cir. 1979).
23 There has been recent discussion of expanding this to five years.

CHAPTER TEN

Intellectual Property Issues in Sports

■ Introduction

This chapter addresses basic, fundamental intellectual property issues in sports. Such subjects certainly present unique challenges to the student of the law because it involves rights related to intangible property. Much of the law in these areas is transient and still evolving as societal values and technology continue to change. The traditional areas of **intellectual property** include copyright, patent, and trademark law. While protection is granted to copyrights and patents under Article 1, § 8, clause 8 of the Constitution, trademarks fall under federal law created by Congrass's ability to regulate interstate commerce under Article 1, § 8, clause 3.

■ History

Copyright Law

Intellectual property is primarily federally regulated. Congress enacted the United States Copyright Act of 1909 to protect the "creative" ideas of individuals against the unauthorized use of copyrighted materials and works. A **copyright** protects original literary and artistic expressions. In 1976, the entire law was revised, and in 1989 the United States became a member of the Berne Convention, which established an international copyright treaty. Copyright law in the United States was again modified in 1990, 1994, and 1999 particularly with the advent of the issues related to

---

intellectual property   category of law pertaining to trademark, copyright, and patent rights

copyright   property right in an original work of authorship such as literary, musical, artistic, or photgraphic work

the Internet. Copyright law in the United States is now governed by the 1976 Copyright Act and the Digital Millennium Copyright Act of 1998. There is no state copyright protection.

Fair Use

In the sports business, the main area of copyright concern appears to be the protection of sports broadcasting media. Unauthorized broadcasts of games is considered an **infringement**. Laws and cases involving attempts to control or provide unauthorized telephone audio video satellite, microwave, and Internet broadcasts related to events and games in progress are contemporary issues being addressed by the legal system.[1] A major exception in copyright law is the concept of **fair use**. The doctrine of fair use developed over the years as courts tried to balance the rights of copyright owners with society's interest in allowing copying in certain circumstances. The fair use doctrine holds that not all copying should be banned, especially in important endeavors such as teaching and research.

Patent Law

Patent laws were enacted in 1870 to promote "science" and the useful arts, such as inventions. The United States recognizes three kinds of **patents**: utility patents (lasts 20 years), design patents (lasts 14 years) and plant patents (lasts 20 years). A patent permits its owner to exclude members of the public from making, using, or selling the claimed invention. Those who use a patent without permission also commit a patent infringement. Obviously patents are relevant to the design and manufacture of all sports equipment.

Trademark Law

Important to the discussion of copyright and patent law is a fundamental understanding of **trademark** law. Trademark law is federal in nature. Trademark law allows an owner of a name or emblem (logo) to prevent someone else from using the trademarked name or symbol without prior permission. This is extremely important for professional and amateur sports leagues and teams that profit from the licensing of their logos. Ownership of a trademark prevents copying, imitating, or simply reproducing a mark without authorization. Trademarks include brand names, **trade dress**,

---

infringement   act that interferes with one of the exclusive rights of a patent, copyright, or trademark owner

fair use   term used in the copyright context that allows reasonable yet limited use of a work without the author's prior permission

patent   federal government's grant for the exclusive right to use, make, or sell an invention if the device is novel, useful, and nonobvious

trademark   word, phrase, logo, slogan or symbol used to distinguish a product from others

trade dress   the total image and appearance of a product or service

service marks, certification marks and **collective marks**. An unregistered mark may use the symbol "TM" for trademark and 'SM' for servicemark. After the mark has been registered at the federal level, the symbol ® may be used.

At issue, of course, is the potential lost revenue that a trademarked name could have generated for the licensor by charging a fee to use the logo to help sell a product. This is applicable in the sports context when consumers purchase officially **licensed** products bearing their favorite team name and logo. This includes shirts, jerseys, caps, trading cards, and other goods. This is often called *sports merchandising*. Failure to prevent the unauthorized use of the trademarked name or logo could dilute its market value.

Lanham Act

In 1946, the federal government enacted the **Lanham Act** to allow owners to seek injunctions and other remedies from individuals who infringe on their protected registered mark. The Lanham Act is the cornerstone of trademark law in the United States. The primary purpose of trademark law is to distinguish goods of one seller from those of another and to protect consumers from being confused over the quality and source of the product. The Lanham Act was revised in 1988 to allow a trademark owner to apply for registration of a mark prior to using it.

Trademarks are registered with the federal Patent and Trademark Office. § 43 (a) of the Lanham Act allows for an individual to bring a civil suit for infringement for the use of a mark if it is likely to cause confusion, mistake, or deception as to the origin of the mark. This is similar to other more recent and general consumer protection statutes.

■ Licensing Trademarks

Colleges and professional sports teams make millions of dollars each year by licensing their names, logos, and colors. A license allows a licensee to pay the licensor a fee or commission (often called *royalty*) to use such names, logos, and colors to manufacture products or provide services that bear such trademarks. Even the color of certain paint is currently licensed and sold in stores as the "official" color of a college or university's sports teams.[2] Additionally, professional sports leagues address licensing issues in their CBAs in order to share revenue among teams and with the players associations.

---

service mark   mark used in sale or advertising of services to distinguish it from others

collective mark   trademark of an association, union, or other group

license   revocable permission to commit an act such as copying a trademark

Lanham Act   1946 federal act that provides for a national system of registration of trademarks

Protecting the Trademark

Licensing issues have become so important to colleges that "licensing police" venture up and down avenues in college towns during sports events to ensure that vendors who sell merchandise bear an officially licensed symbol. Many counterfeit products or services seek to associate themselves with these events even though they are not authorized to do so. Failure to regulate the sales of nonlicensed products can lead to thousands of dollars in lost profits for the licensor.

Atlanta-based Collegiate Licensing Co. (CLC), the NCAA's licensing representative, works in conjunction with the undercover officers, including federal marshals, who disguise themselves as fans to find violators. Royalties are generated by the NCAA from television, radio, Internet, and other contracts related to NCAA tournaments and events. The NCAA has approximately 35 licensees for merchandise, 16 marketing partners, 10 official ball licensees, registered 200 different domain names and holds 40 U.S. trademarks and service marks.[3] For example, phrases such as "the Final Four" and "the Big Dance" have become so important to revenue for the NCAA that it has been forced to apply for trademark protection for these phrases.

Licensing Revenues

Licensing revenues for all four major leagues are shared by their respective teams. Licensing these revenues is shared equally among all teams regardless of how much of the licensing income is generated by a specific team. In college sports, the University of Michigan merchandise sells better than any public college in the nation, according to CLC.[4] The school's longtime success in basketball and football has swelled its reputation. More than 600 items bear Michigan's name or logo. This includes boxers, a door chime that plays the Michigan fight song, and cologne that smells "like 180 years of academic and athletic excellence." In 1999, the University of Michigan made $4.7 million in royalties from the sale of $100 million in licensed products.[5]

Case 13 presents a decision in a trademark infringement lawsuit filed by the Indianapolis Colts against a Canadian Football League team with a similar name.

■ Mascots and Trademarks

In 1999, the Trademark Trial and Appeal Board of the United States Patent and Trademark Office canceled seven of Pro-Football, Inc.'s (i.e., the Washington Redskins' legal name) registered trademarks that had the word *Redskin* in it after validity was challenged under federal law as violating the offensive statutory regulations that prevent disparaging mark registration. This Board held that the mark was disparaging, contemptuous, and scandalous and violated § 2(a) of the Lanham Act.[6]

■ CASE 13 *Indianapolis Colts, Inc. v. Metropolitan Baltimore Football Club*

UNITED STATES COURT OF APPEALS,
Seventh Circuit.

INDIANAPOLIS COLTS, INC.,
National Football League Properties, Inc.,
and National Football League,
Plaintiffs-Appellees,

v.

METROPOLITAN
BALTIMORE FOOTBALL CLUB LIMITED
PARTNERSHIP, James L. Speros, and Canadian
Football League,
Defendants-Appellants.

No. 94-2578.

Argued Aug. 3, 1994.
Decided Aug. 12, 1994.*

Indianapolis Colts and National Football League brought suit for trademark infringement against the Canadian Football League's Baltimore team trying to call itself "Baltimore CFL Colts." The United States District Court for the Southern District of Indiana, Larry J. McKinney, J., granted preliminary injunction against Baltimore football team's use of name "Colts" or "CFL Colts," and Baltimore team appealed. The Court of Appeals, Posner, Chief Judge, held that: (1) Baltimore team was subject to personal jurisdiction in Indiana under Indiana's long-arm statute based on existence of trademark there, and (2) district court did not commit clear error in finding that Baltimore's use of name "Baltimore CFL Colts" was likely to confuse substantial numbers of consumers, warranting preliminary injunction.

Affirmed.

POSNER, Chief Judge.

The Indianapolis Colts and the National Football League, to which the Colts belong, brought suit for trademark infringement (15 U.S.C.A. §§ 1051 *et seq.*) against the Canadian Football League's new team in Baltimore, which wants to call itself the "Baltimore CFL Colts." (Four of the Canadian Football League's teams are American.) The plaintiffs obtained a preliminary injunction against the new team's using the name "Colts," or "Baltimore Colts," or "Baltimore CFL Colts," in connection with the playing of professional football, the broadcast of football games, or the sale of merchandise to football fans and other buyers. The ground for the injunction was that consumers of "Baltimore CFL Colts" merchandise are likely to think, mistakenly, that the new Baltimore team is an NFL team related in some fashion to the Indianapolis Colts, formerly the Baltimore Colts. From the order granting the injunction the new team and its owners appeal to us under 28 U.S.C.A. § 1292(a)(1). Since the injunction was granted, the new team has played its first two games—without a name.

A bit of history is necessary to frame the dispute. In 1952, the National Football League permitted one of its teams, the Dallas Texans, which was bankrupt, to move to Baltimore, where it was renamed the "Baltimore Colts." Under that name it became one of the most illustrious teams in the history of professional football. In 1984, the team's owner, with the permission of the NFL, moved the team to Indianapolis, and it was renamed the "Indianapolis Colts." The move, sudden and secretive, outraged the citizens of Baltimore. The city instituted litigation in a futile effort to get the team back—even tried, unsuccessfully, to get the team back by condemnation under the city's power of eminent domain—and the Colts brought a countersuit that also failed. *Indianapolis Colts v. Mayor & City Council of Baltimore*, 733 F.2d 484, 741 F.2d 954 (1984), 775 F.2d 177 (7th Cir.1985).

Nine years later, the Canadian Football League granted a franchise for a Baltimore team. Baltimoreans clamored for naming the new team the "Baltimore Colts." And so it was named—until the NFL got wind of the name and threatened legal action. The name was then changed to "Baltimore CFL Colts" and publicity launched, merchandise licensed, and other steps taken in preparation for the commencement of play this summer.

[1][2] The defendants do not argue that the balance of irreparable harm is so one-sided against them that the preliminary injunction should not have been issued even if the plaintiffs have the stronger legal position. *Curtis 1000, Inc. v. Suess*, 24 F.3d 941, 945 (7th Cir.1994). They stand foursquare on the contention that the district judge committed serious legal errors. The first they say was in holding that the Baltimore team is within the reach of Indiana's long-arm statute which is applicable to this suit by virtue of

continued

Fed.R.Civ.P. 4(k)(1)(A). The only activity of the team undertaken or planned so far in Indiana is the broadcast of its games nationwide on cable television. Since the Indiana statute reaches as far as the U.S. Constitution permits, Ind.R.Trial Pro. 4.4, we need decide only whether the due process clause of the Fourteenth Amendment forbids the degree of extraterritoriality entailed by this lawsuit. We think not, and are not even certain that the broadcasts in Indiana are critical. The Indianapolis Colts use the trademarks they seek to defend in this suit mainly in Indiana. If the trademarks are impaired, as the suit alleges, the injury will be felt mainly in Indiana. By choosing a name that might be found to be confusingly similar to that of the Indianapolis Colts, the defendants assumed the risk of injuring valuable property located in Indiana. Since there can be no tort without an injury, *Midwest Commerce Banking Co. v. Elkhart City Centre*, 4 F.3d 521, 524 (7th Cir.1993), the state in which the injury occurs is the state in which the tort occurs, and someone who commits a tort in Indiana should, one might suppose, be amenable to suit there. This conclusion is supported by the Supreme Court's decision in *Calder v. Jones*, 465 U.S. 783, 104 S.Ct. 1482, 79 L.Ed.2d 804 (1984), holding that the state in which the victim of the defendant's defamation lived had jurisdiction over the victim's defamation suit.

We need not rest on so austere a conception of the basis of personal jurisdiction. In *Calder* as in all the other cases that have come to our attention in which jurisdiction over a suit involving intellectual property (when broadly defined to include reputation, so that it includes *Calder* itself) was upheld, the defendant had done more than brought about an injury to an interest located in a particular state. The defendant had also "entered" the state in some fashion, as by the sale (in *Calder*) of the magazine containing the defamatory material. Well, we have that here too, because of the broadcasts, so we needn't decide whether the addition is indispensable. The bulk of the Indianapolis Colts' most loyal fans are, no doubt, Hoosiers, so that the largest concentration of consumers likely to be confused by broadcasts implying some affiliation between the Indianapolis Colts and the Baltimore team is in Indiana. It is true that the defendants have not yet licensed the sale of merchandise with the name "Baltimore CFL Colts" on it in Indiana, but citizens of Indiana buy merchandise in other states as well. And it

is only a matter of time before the Baltimore team will be selling its merchandise nationwide; the plaintiffs are entitled to seek injunctive relief before that happens. Certainly *the* Baltimore Colts had a national following, and we do not doubt that the resonance of the name, and not merely the clamor of the Baltimoreans, motivated the Baltimore team's choice of "Colts," out of all the appealing animals in the ark.

[3] It is as clear or clearer that venue is proper in Indiana. See 28 U.S.C.A. § 1391(b)(2); 3 J. Thomas McCarthy, *McCarthy on Trademarks and Intellectual Property* § 32.22(3)(b)(iii) (3d ed. 1994), so we can turn to the merits of the trademark dispute, cautioning the reader that the expression of views that follows is tentative, as we do not wish to prejudice the outcome of the trial on the merits.

[4] The Baltimore team wanted to call itself the "Baltimore Colts." To improve its litigating posture (we assume), it has consented to insert "CFL" between "Baltimore" and "Colts." A glance at the merchandise in the record explains why this concession to an outraged NFL has been made so readily. On several of the items "CFL" appears in small or blurred letters. And since the Canadian Football League is not well known in the United States—and "CFL" has none of the instant recognition value of "NFL"—the inclusion of the acronym in the team's name might have little impact on potential buyers even if prominently displayed. Those who know football well know that the new "Baltimore Colts" are a new CFL team wholly unrelated to the old Baltimore Colts; know also that the rules of Canadian football are different from those of American football and that teams don't move from the NFL to the CFL as they might from one conference within the NFL to the other. But those who do *not* know these things—and we shall come shortly to the question whether there are many of these football illiterates—will not be warned off by the letters "CFL." The acronym is a red herring, and the real issue is whether the new Baltimore team can appropriate the name "Baltimore Colts." The entire thrust of the defendants' argument is that it can.

[5] They make a tremendous to-do over the fact that the district judge found that the Indianapolis Colts abandoned the trademark "Baltimore Colts" when they moved to Indianapolis. Well, of course; they were no longer playing football under the name "Baltimore Colts," so could not have used the name as the team's

trademark; they could have used it on merchandise but chose not to, until 1991 (another story—and not one we need tell). When a mark is abandoned, it returns to the public domain, and is appropriable anew—in principle. In practice, because "subsequent use of [an] abandoned mark may well evoke a continuing association with the prior use, those who make subsequent use may be required to take reasonable precautions to prevent confusion." 2 McCarthy, *supra*, § 17.01[2], at p. 17–3. This precept is especially important where, as in this case, the former owner of the abandoned mark continues to market the same product or service under a similar name, though we cannot find any previous cases of this kind. No one questions the validity of "Indianapolis Colts" as the trademark of the NFL team that plays out of Indianapolis and was formerly known as the Baltimore Colts. If "Baltimore CFL Colts" is confusingly similar to "Indianapolis Colts" by virtue of the history of the Indianapolis team and the overlapping product and geographical markets served by it and by the new Baltimore team, the latter's use of the abandoned mark would infringe the Indianapolis Colts' new mark. The Colts' abandonment of a mark confusingly similar to their new mark neither broke the continuity of the team in its different locations—it was the same team, merely having a different home base and therefore a different geographical component in its name—nor entitled a third party to pick it up and use it to confuse Colts fans, and other actual or potential consumers of products and services marketed by the Colts or by other National Football League teams, with regard to the identity, sponsorship, or league affiliation of the third party, that is, the new Baltimore team. *Browning King Co. of New York, Inc. v. Browning King Co.*, 176 F.2d 105, 107 (3d Cir.1949); *Acme Valve & Fittings Co. v. Wayne*, 386 F.Supp. 1162, 1169 (S.D.Tex.1974); cf. *Nike, Inc. v. "Just Did It" Enterprises*, 6 F.3d 1225, 1228-29 (7th Cir.1993); *Boston Professional Hockey Ass'n, Inc. v. Dallas Cap & Emblem Mfg., Inc.*, 510 F.2d 1004, 1012-13 (5th Cir.1975); *National Football League Properties, Inc. v. Wichita Falls Sportswear, Inc.*, 532 F.Supp. 651 (W.D. Wash.1982); Robert C. Denicola, "Institutional Publicity Rights: An Analysis of the Merchandising of Famous Trade Symbols," 62 *N.C.L.Rev.* 603, 611-12 (1984).

Against this the defendants cite to us with great insistence *Major League Baseball Properties Inc. v. Sed Non Olet Denarius, Ltd.*, 817 F.Supp. 1103, 1128 (S.D.N.Y.1993), which, over the objection of the Los Angeles Dodgers, allowed a restaurant in Brooklyn to use the name "Brooklyn Dodger" on the ground that "the 'Brooklyn Dodgers' was a nontransportable cultural institution separate from the 'Los Angeles Dodgers.'" The defendants in our case argue that the sudden and greatly resented departure of the Baltimore Colts for Indianapolis made the name "Baltimore Colts" available to anyone who would continue the "nontransportable cultural institution" constituted by a football team located in the City of Baltimore. We think this argument very weak, and need not even try to distinguish *Sed Non Olet Denarius* since district court decisions are not authoritative in this or any court of appeals. *Colby v. J.C. Penney Co.*, 811 F.2d 1119, 1124 (7th Cir.1987). If it were a Supreme Court decision it still would not help the defendants. The "Brooklyn Dodger" was not a baseball team, and there was no risk of confusion. The case might be relevant if the Indianapolis Colts were arguing not confusion but misappropriation: that they own the goodwill associated with the name "Baltimore Colts" and the new Baltimore team is trying to take it from them. Cf. *Quaker Oats Co. v. General Mills Co.*, 134 F.2d 429, 432 (7th Cir.1943). They did make a claim of misappropriation in the district court, but that court rejected the claim and it has not been renewed on appeal. The only claim in our court is that a significant number of consumers will think the new Baltimore team the successor to, or alter ego of, or even the same team as the Baltimore Colts and therefore the Indianapolis Colts, which is the real successor. No one would think the Brooklyn Dodgers baseball team reincarnated in a restaurant.

A professional sports team is like Heraclitus's river: always changing, yet always the same. When Mr. Irsay transported his team, the Baltimore Colts, from Baltimore to Indianapolis in one night in 1984, the team remained, for a time anyway, completely intact: same players, same coaches, same front- office personnel. With the passage of time, of course, the team changed. Players retired or were traded, and were replaced. Coaches and other nonplaying personnel came and went. But as far as the record discloses there is as much institutional continuity between the Baltimore Colts of 1984 and the Indianapolis Colts of 1994 as there was between the Baltimore Colts of 1974

continued

and the Baltimore Colts of 1984. Johnny Unitas, the Baltimore Colts' most famous player, swears in his affidavit that his old team has no connection with the Indianapolis Colts, and he has even asked the Colts to expunge his name from its record books. He is angry with Irsay for moving the team. He is entitled to his anger, but it has nothing to do with this lawsuit. The Colts were Irsay's team; it was moved intact; there is no evidence it has changed more since the move than it had in the years before. There is, in contrast, no continuity, no links contractual or otherwise, nothing but a geographical site in common, between the Baltimore Colts and the Canadian Football League team that would like to use its name. Any suggestion that there is such continuity is false and potentially misleading.

Potentially; for if everyone *knows* there is no contractual or institutional continuity, no pedigree or line of descent, linking the Baltimore-Indianapolis Colts and the new CFL team that wants to call itself the "Baltimore Colts" (or, grudgingly, the "Baltimore CFL Colts"), then there is no harm, at least no harm for which the Lanham Act provides a remedy, in the new Baltimore team's appropriating the name "Baltimore Colts" to play under and sell merchandise under. If not everyone knows, there is harm. Some people who might otherwise watch the Indianapolis Colts (or some other NFL team, for remember that the NFL, representing all the teams, is a coplaintiff) on television may watch the Baltimore CFL Colts instead, thinking they are the "real" Baltimore Colts, and the NFL will lose revenue. A few (doubtless very few) people who might otherwise buy tickets to an NFL game may buy tickets to a Baltimore CFL Colts game instead. Some people who might otherwise buy merchandise stamped with the name "Indianapolis Colts" or the name of some other NFL team may buy merchandise stamped "Baltimore CFL Colts," thinking it a kin of the NFL's Baltimore Colts in the glory days of Johnny Unitas rather than a newly formed team that plays Canadian football in a Canadian football league. It would be naive to suppose that no consideration of such possibilities occurred to the owners of the new Baltimore team when they were choosing a name, though there is no evidence that it was the dominant or even a major consideration.

Confusion thus is possible, and may even have been desired; but is it likely? There is great variance in consumer competence, and it would be undesirable to impoverish the lexicon of trade names merely to protect the most gullible fringe of the consuming public. The Lanham Act does not cast the net of protection so wide. *Scandia Down Corp. v. Euroquilt, Inc.*, 772 F.2d 1423, 1428 n. 1 (7th Cir.1985); *Quaker Oats Co. v. General Mills Co., supra,* 134 F.2d at 432; 2 McCarthy, *supra,* § 23.27[4]; cf. *Gammon v. GC Services Limited Partnership,* 27 F.3d 1254 (7th Cir.1994). The legal standard under the Act has been formulated variously, but the various formulations come down to whether it is likely that the challenged mark if permitted to be used by the defendant would cause the plaintiff to lose a substantial number of consumers. Pertinent to this determination is the similarity of the marks and of the parties' products, the knowledge of the average consumer of the product, the overlap in the parties' geographical markets, and the other factors that the cases consider. The aim is to strike a balance between, on the one hand, the interest of the seller of the new product, and of the consuming public, in an arresting, attractive, and informative name that will enable the new product to compete effectively against existing ones, and, on the other hand, the interest of existing sellers, and again of the consuming public, in consumers' being able to know exactly what they are buying without having to incur substantial costs of investigation or inquiry.

To help judges strike the balance, the parties to trademark disputes frequently as here hire professionals in marketing or applied statistics to conduct surveys of consumers. 3 McCarthy, *supra,* § 32.55[2]; see also Jack P. Lipton, "Trademark Litigation: A New Look at the Use of Social Science Evidence," 29 *Ariz.L.Rev.* 639 (1987); Larry C. Jones, "Developing and Using Survey Evidence in Trademark Litigation," 19 *Memphis St.U.L.Rev.* 471 (1989). The battle of experts that ensues is frequently unedifying. Cf. *Olympia Equipment Leasing Co. v. Western Union Telegraph Co.,* 797 F.2d 370, 382 (7th Cir.1986). Many experts are willing for a generous (and sometimes for a modest) fee to bend their science in the direction from which their fee is coming. The constraints that the market in consultant services for lawyers places on this sort of behavior are weak, as shown by the fact that both experts in this case were hired and, we have no doubt, generously remunerated even though both have been criticized in previous judicial opinions. The judicial constraints on tendentious expert testimony are inherently weak because judges (and even more so juries, though that is not an issue in a trademark case) lack training or experience in the relevant fields of expert knowledge. But that is the system we have. It might be improved by asking each party's hired expert to designate a third, a neutral expert who would be appointed by the court to conduct the necessary studies. The necessary authority exists, see Fed.R.Evid. 706, but was not exercised here.

Both parties presented studies. The defendants' was prepared by Michael Rappeport and is summarized in a perfunctory affidavit by Dr. Rappeport to which the district judge gave little weight. That was a kindness. The heart of Rappeport's study was a survey that consisted of three loaded questions asked in one Baltimore mall. Rappeport has been criticized before for his methodology, *Jarret Int'l, Inc. v. Promotion in Motion, Inc.*, 826 F.Supp. 69, 73–74 (E.D.N.Y.1993), and we hope that he will take these criticisms to heart in his next courtroom appearance.

The plaintiffs' study, conducted by Jacob Jacoby, was far more substantial and the district judge found it on the whole credible. The 28-page report with its numerous appendices has all the trappings of social scientific rigor. Interviewers showed several hundred consumers in 24 malls scattered around the country, shirts and hats licensed by the defendants for sale to consumers. The shirts and hats have "Baltimore CFL Colts" stamped on them. The consumers were asked whether they were football fans, whether they watched football games on television, and whether they ever bought merchandise with a team name on it. Then they were asked, with reference to the "Baltimore CFL Colts" merchandise that they were shown, such questions as whether they knew what sport the team played, what teams it played against, what league the team was in, and whether the team or league needed someone's permission to use this name, and if so whose. If, for example, the respondent answered that the team had to get permission from the Canadian Football League, the interviewer was directed to ask the respondent whether the Canadian Football League had in turn to get permission from someone. There were other questions, none however obviously loaded, and a whole other survey, the purpose of which was to control for "noise," in which another group of mallgoers was asked the identical questions about a hypothetical team unappetizingly named the "Baltimore Horses." The idea was by comparing the answers of the two groups to see whether the source of confusion was the name "Baltimore Colts" or just the name "Baltimore," in which event the injunction would do no good since no one suggests that the new Baltimore team should be forbidden to use "Baltimore" in its name, provided the name does not also include "Colts."

Rappeport threw darts at Jacoby's study. Some landed wide. We are especially perplexed by the argument that survey research belongs to sociology rather than psychology (we leave the reader to guess the respective disciplines to which our rival experts belong); the courtroom is a peculiar site for academic turf wars. We also do not think it was improper for Jacoby to inquire about confusion between "Baltimore CFL Colts" and "Baltimore Colts," even though the Indianapolis Colts have abandoned "Baltimore Colts." If consumers believe that the new Baltimore team is the old Baltimore Colts, and the Indianapolis Colts some sort of upstart (the Johnny Unitas position), they will be less likely to buy merchandise stamped "Indianapolis Colts." But Rappeport was right to complain that the choice of "Horses" for the comparison team loaded the dice and that some of Jacoby's questions were a bit slanted. That is only to say, however, that Jacoby's survey was not perfect, and this is not news. Trials would be very short if only perfect evidence were admissible.

Jacoby's survey of consumers' reactions to the "Baltimore CFL Colts" merchandise found rather astonishing levels of confusion not plausibly attributable to the presence of the name "Baltimore" alone, since "Baltimore Horses" engendered much less. (We don't like the name "Baltimore Horses," as we have said; but we doubt that a more attractive "Baltimore" name, the "Baltimore Leopards," for example, would have generated the level of confusion that "Baltimore CFL Colts" did. *National Football League v. Wichita Falls Sportswear, Inc., supra*, 532 F.Supp. at 660.) Among self-identified football fans, 64 percent thought that the "Baltimore CFL Colts" was either the old (NFL) Baltimore Colts or the Indianapolis Colts. But perhaps this result is not so astonishing. Although most American football fans have heard of Canadian football, many probably are unfamiliar with the acronym "CFL," and as we remarked earlier it is not a very conspicuous part of the team logo stamped on the merchandise. Among fans who watch football on television, 59 percent displayed the same confusion; and

continued

even among those who watch football on cable television, which attracts a more educated audience on average and actually carries CFL games, 58 percent were confused when shown the merchandise. Among the minority not confused about who the "Baltimore CFL Colts" are, a substantial minority, ranging from 21 to 34 percent depending on the precise subsample, thought the team somehow sponsored or authorized by the Indianapolis Colts or the National Football League. It is unfortunate and perhaps a bit tricky that the subsample of consumers likely to buy merchandise with a team name on it was not limited to consumers likely to buy merchandise with a *football* team's name on it; the choice of the name "Baltimore Horses" for the comparison team was unfortunate; and no doubt there are other tricks of the survey researcher's black arts that we have missed. There is the more fundamental problem, one common to almost all consumer survey research, that people are more careful when they are laying out their money than when they are answering questions.

But with all this granted, we cannot say that the district judge committed a clear error (the standard, *Scandia Down Corp. v. Euroquilt, Inc., supra,* 772 F.2d at 1427-28) in crediting the major findings of the Jacoby study and inferring from it and the other evidence in the record that the defendants' use of the name "Baltimore CFL Colts" whether for the team or on merchandise was likely to confuse a substantial number of consumers. This means—given the defendants' failure to raise any issue concerning the respective irreparable harms from granting or denying the preliminary injunction—that

the judge's finding concerning likelihood of confusion required that the injunction issue.

The defendants argue, finally, that, even so, the injunction is overboard; it should not have forbidden them to use the word "Colts," but rather confined them to using it in conjunction with "Baltimore CFL." We are baffled by the argument. If they want to use "Colts" in conjunction with anything besides a Baltimore football team, there is nothing in this lawsuit to prevent them. The objection is precisely to their use of the word in a setting that will lead many consumers to believe it designates either the old Baltimore Colts (falsely implying that the Indianapolis Colts are not the successor to the Baltimore Colts or that the new Baltimore team is an NFL team or is approved by or affiliated with the NFL) or the Indianapolis Colts.

The defendants make some other arguments but they do not have sufficient merit to warrant discussion. The judgment of the district court granting the preliminary injunction is

AFFIRMED.

34 F.3d 410, 63 USL W 2126, 31 U.S.P.Q.2d 1811

FOOTNOTES

* The decision was released in typescript because of the desire of the new Baltimore Canadian Football League team (the appellant) to know as soon as possible what name it can play under and license merchandise under.

Reprinted with permission from West Group.

■ Ethnic Mascots

Mascots, flags, nicknames, emblems, symbols, or logos often serve as a rallying point for high school and university students and professional sports fans. However, some amateur and professional sports teams have nicknames and mascots that have become political and legal targets by individuals and organizations who allege that the **ethnic mascot** is discriminatory or offensive and should be banned or discontinued.

---

ethnic mascots   phrase used to describe athletic mascots that single out a race, gender, or culture

Professional teams such as the Atlanta Braves, Cleveland Indians, Washington Redskins, Kansas City Chiefs, and Chicago Blackhawks have been accused of being racially insensitive by continuing to use nicknames that might be condescending to the Native American culture.

Should mascots such as the Warriors, Apaches and Comanches be outlawed by the government as racially offensive or should such team nicknames be revered instead? After all, there are 11 states with Native American names and countless geographic points including lakes, rivers, and streets.[7] Should a state or local government be able to prohibit the use of ethnic team names in light of the First Amendment of the Constitution's freedom of speech protection? Recently, the State Assembly of California rejected by a vote of 35-29 a bill that would have made it the first state to prohibit government schools from naming teams after American Indian Tribes.[8]

Recent Changes Involving Mascots

While team names evoking Native American connections have a long history in American professional sports, numerous colleges around the country have reluctantly changed their names due to societal pressure and political correctness. Dartmouth College, Marquette University, Stanford University, and St. Johns University are only a few of the institutions that have abandoned an Indian mascot.[9] Heightened awareness of such issues even caused former President Bill Clinton to refuse to wear a baseball cap with the Cleveland Indians logo of Chief Wahoo on it when he threw out the first pitch of the 1994 baseball season.

The Future of Ethnic Mascots

It is uncertain whether ethnic mascots will survive legal scrutiny as being offensive. It is clear that the Civil Rights Act of 1964 prohibits discrimination on the basis of race, color, or national origin in any federally funded program.[10] Possible challenges to the use of ethnic mascots might invoke this federal statute particularly if it could be shown that the mascot created or encouraged a racially hostile environment for employees or participants. Recently, a high school in Devils Lake, North Dakota, dropped its nickname, the "Satans" after nearly 80 years of use by a 5-0 vote by the local school board.[11]

Attempts have been made to modify state laws or city ordinances to prevent the use of public stadiums by any organization that exploits any racial or ethnic group. However, it appears that societal pressure to change mascot names will supersede attempts to ask the courts for injunctions or judicial determinations to prevent such use. State governments have considered adopting legislation that outlaws such names or symbols.

■ Ambush Marketing

The term **ambush marketing** refers to activities that companies become involved in even though they are not official sponsors of such an event. For example, during Olympic years, many advertisers attempt to demonstrate to consumers that they might be official sponsors of the Olympic Games when in fact they are not. Obviously, licensing issues are important with regard to ambush marketing though this phrase is used most appropriately for an isolated athletic event rather than an ongoing sale of general merchandise.

■ The Internet and the Anticybersquatting Consumer Protection Act

The Internet has provided numerous challenges for courts with regard to protection of trademarks. Congress passed the **Anticybersquatting Consumer Protection Act (ACPA)** in 1999 to prevent an individual from registering a web domain name in order to profit from the name or mark in bad faith.[12] Numerous lawsuits have been initiated seeking a court order to prevent the use of a **domain name** without permission of the owner of the mark in an infringement action. The primary purpose of this act is again to prevent the likelihood of consumer confusion over which website is the official site. A domain name is a word followed by .com, .org, .net, .edu, .info, .biz and has been registered as part of the Internet system.[13]

Just prior to the Sydney Olympics of 2000, more than 1,800 websites were sued under the federal anticybersquatting law for using domain names that duplicate or were similar to official Olympics trademarks. The lawsuit was filed in United States District Court in Virginia on behalf of the International Olympic Committee (IOC), the United States Olympic Committee (USOC), and the Salt Lake Organizing Committee (SLOC) for the 2002 Winter Games. The word "Olympic" and its symbol of the five interlocking rings have been the subject of numerous infringement actions over the years including the use of the word in the promotion of the "Gay Olympic Games."[14]

---

ambush marketing   type of marketing in which a consumer is misled as to whether a company or sponsor is officially part of an event

Anticybersquatting Consumer Protection Act (ACPA)   1999 federal law amending the Lanham Act to create a cause of action against someone who intentionally registers an Internet domain name confusingly similar to a trademarked name

domain name   word followed by .com, .org, .net, .edu, .info, .biz, and registered as part of the Internet system

Cybersquatters

A **cybersquatter** is an individual who registers popular or trademarked names in the Internet name space with plans to either sell the names or keep them to turn a profit. The ACPA allows for substantial civil penalties against cybersquatters and enables a trademark or copyright holder to file a lawsuit to shut down a domain name in violation, even if the owner resides in a country other than the United States. Prior to the enactment of the ACPA, cybersquatters could extort companies and individuals into paying substantial sums of money in order to regain such Internet domain names.

■ Summary

Intellectual property involves protecting an owner's interest in a copyright, patent, or trademark. Federal law governs patents and trademarks and has evolved over the years, especially recently with the advent of the Internet. Intellectual property issues have become vital to the success of an organization, particularly with regard to licensing of goods that may generate profits. Team name mascots have become targets for intellectual property claims alleging disparaging emblems. Protection of domain names and other intellectual property issues on the Internet have produced the Anticybersquatting Consumer Protection Act.

■ Key Terms

ambush marketing
Anticybersquatting Consumer
    Protection Act (ACPA)
collective mark
copyright
cybersquatter
domain name
ethnic mascots
fair use

infringement
intellectual property
Lanham Act
license
patent
service mark
trademark
trade dress

cybersquatter   individual who intentionally registers an Internet domain name that is confusingly similar to a trademarked name

■ Additional Cases

A&M Records, Inc., v. Napster, Inc., 239 F.3d 1004 (9th Cir. 2001)
Abdul-Jabbar v. General Motors Corp., 85 F. 3d 407 (9th Cir. 1996)
Abercrombie & Fitch v. Hunting World, 537 F. 2d 4 (2nd Cir. 1976)
Bally Total Fitness Holding Corp. v. Faber, 29 F. Supp. 2d 1161 (C. D. Cal. 1998)
Baltimore Orioles v. Major League Baseball Players, 805 F.2d 663 (7th Cir. 1986)
Basic Books, Inc. v. Kinko's Graphics Corp., 758 F. Supp. 1522 (S.D.N.Y. 1991)
Callaway Golf Co. v. Golf Clean, Inc., 915 F. Supp. 1206 (M.D. Fla. 1995)
Dallas Cowboys Cheerleaders, Inc. v. Pussycat Cinema, Ltd., 604 F. 2d 200 (2nd Cir. 1979)
Fraser v. Major League Soccer, 97 F. Supp. 2d 130 (D.Mass. 2000)
Harjo et al. v. Pro-Football, Inc. 1999 WL 435108
Harlem Wizards v. NBA Properties, 952 F. Supp. 1084 (D.N.J. 1997)
Harley-Davidson Motor Company v. Iron Eagle of Central Florida, 973 F. Supp. 1421 (M.D. Fla. 1997)
Kellogg Co. v. Toucan Golf, Inc., 2001 U. S. Dist. LEXIS 14451 (W.D. Mich. 2001)
National Football League v. McBee & Bruno's Inc., 792 F. 2d 726 (8th Cir. 1986)
Pebble Beach Co. v. Tour 18 A. E. Ltd., 942 F. Supp. 1513 (S.D. Tex. 1996), aff'd as modified, 155 F. 3d 526 (5th Cir. 1998)
Quokka Sports, Inc. v. Cup International Ltd., 99 F. Supp. 2d 1005 (N.D. Cal. 1999)
San Francisco Arts & Athletics, Inc. v. United States Olympic Comm., 483 U. S. 522 (1987)
University of Pittsburgh v. Champion Products, Inc., 686 F. 2d 1040 (3rd Cir. 1982)
White v. Board of Regents of the University of Nebraska at Lincoln, 614 N.W.2d 330 (Neb. 2000)
World Championship Wrestling v. Titan Sports, Inc., 46 F. Supp. 2d 118 (D. Conn. 1999)

■ Review Questions

1. What is the difference between a copyright, patent, and trademark?
2. Why are sports logos so important today?
3. Are mascots that display images connected to Native Americans condescending?
4. What is *ambush marketing*?
5. Why was the Anticybersquatting Consumer Protection Act enacted?
6. Who is a cybersquatter?

■ Endnotes

1 See, e.g., The Sports Broadcasting Act, 15 U.S.C.A. § 1291.
2 In 2000, the University of Tennessee, Castles Sport/Premium Collegiate Colors, and the Collegiate Licensing Co. (CLC) launched the University of Tennessee branded paint for customers to purchase at Home Depot. It marked the first time a collegiate institution has ever licensed such a product.
3 Scott A. Bearby, *Marketing, Protection, and Enforcement of NCAA Marks*, 12 Marq. Sp. L. Rev. 543 (2002).

4 CLC is the nation's leading collegiate licensing and marketing representative. It assists collegiate licensors in protecting and controlling the use of their logos through its comprehensive trademark licensing services. The CLC Consortium consists of more than 180 individual universities, post-season bowl games, athletic conferences, the NCAA, and the Heisman Trophy.

5 See Francis X. Donnelly, *MSU Rakes in Final Four Cash*, THE DETROIT NEWS, March 28, 2000.

6 Enacted in 1946, the Lanham Act's § 2(a) bars registration of "immoral, deceptive, or scandalous matter." 15 U.S.C.A. § 1051–1127. See also, *Harjo v. Pro-Football, Inc.*, 1999 WL 435108.

7 http://www.cnn.com/2002/fyi/teachers.ednews/05/16/indian.mascots.ap/index.html

8 http://www.newsmax.com/archives/articles/2002/5/29/16/928.shtml

9 St. Johns University changed its mascot from the Redmen to the Red Storm, for example.

10 42 U.S.C.A. § 2000 (d).

11 http://fyi.cnn.com/2002/us/08/22/satans.no.more/index.html

12 A domain name is, for example, www.joanna-zeiger.com

13 Internet Corporation for Assigned Names and Numbers (ICAAN) authorities domain name registration.

14 See *International Olympic Comm. v. San Francisco Arts & Athletics, Inc.* 219 U.S.P.Q (BNA) 982, 986 (N.D. Cal. 1982), aff'd 707 F. 2d 517 (9th Cir. 1983).

CHAPTER ELEVEN

Alternative Dispute Resolution in Sports

■ Introduction

This chapter provides a fundamental understanding of the different forms of **alternative dispute resolution (ADR)** for those involved in sports law, regardless of the degree of formal legal training. Understanding how law affects the sports industry as a whole and how the legal system continues to affect daily decisions by managers, coaches, educators, administrators, athletes, and many others is obviously important. Sports managers are often concerned over liability issues when designing facilities, managing personnel, or installing exercise equipment, for example. Appreciating legal issues and the legal process is vital for the successful individual and organization at any level.

Sports law is typically studied by reading and analyzing reported cases that have been litigated in the courts. Such cases have gone to trial and have resulted in a judge's decision or jury's verdict in the public forum. ADR decisions are usually unreported, and they focus more on the parties' needs than on the legal process.

■ ADR Generally

ADR is a general term that refers to procedures for settling disputes by means other than litigation. The two basic forms of ADR are the fundamentally different concepts of arbitration and mediation. The major difference between arbitration and mediation is that in arbitration an arbitrator is a decision maker, whereas in a mediation session the mediator plays the role of settlement facilitator. Unlike ADR,

---

alternative dispute resolution (ADR)   resolving disputes via arbitration, mediation, and other alternatives to litigation

litigation is a form of dispute resolution that uses public adjudication: A judge or jury decides the result of a dispute. However, litigation is not regarded as the swiftest and most efficient method to resolve disputes, particularly if a party wishes to attempt to settle differences in a nonadversarial manner. Traditional litigation can be expensive, time consuming, and extremely frustrating for the parties. Additionally, most nonlawyers are unfamiliar with the myriad of rules related to civil procedure and evidence, and court delays and appeals can be particularly frustrating and foreign for the nonlawyer who may be used to making daily decisions in a swifter and more efficient manner. Arbitration, mediation, and other hybrid forms (such as mediation-arbitration and arbitration-mediation) may be used by unhappy parties to attempt to settle a dispute without the necessity of a trial.

ADR procedures are increasingly being used not only in sports, but also in general business disputes, marital dissolution actions, child custody debates, a wide variety of tort claims, and other disagreements that would likely otherwise involve litigation. ADR cases may involve differences over accounting methods, personnel issues, and virtually any other category that the parties agree to settle as a result of a conflict. Understanding ADR and how it differs from litigation can affect how one does business.

ADR is effective in resolving a variety of sports-related disputes. For example, ADR is often used to settle differences in interpretations or applications of CBA rules or regulations. Arbitration is common in the major sports of baseball, basketball, football, and hockey.[1] Arbitration clauses in CBAs may address individual athlete actions, medical benefits, freedoms, or salaries. Where no CBA exists, ADR may be introduced by contract and is, ultimately, a creature of contract.

Much of the reason that ADR is so effective is that the emphasis is less on lawyers and civil procedure and more on the needs of the parties themselves, particularly in mediation. Mediation does not focus on who is "right" and who is "wrong," which is a significant divergence from traditional litigation. If the attempt to resolve differences through ADR fails, one or both parties may often resort to litigation.

As courts become more crowded and access becomes more difficult, arbitration and mediation will play an even greater role in resolving disputes in the sports industry. However, litigation does play its role in our society, and litigation may be the appropriate method of dispute resolution in many cases. Such cases are usually the by-product, however, of unsuccessful settlement negotiations. An appreciation of the differences and advantages and disadvantages of litigation, arbitration, mediation, and hybrid forms of ADR is essential for those involved in sports law.

■ Federal and State Models

In the past decade much emphasis has been placed on the role of ADR, including the federal government's enactment of the Administrative Dispute Resolution Act of 1990 (ADRA), which requires all federal agencies[2] to establish policies for the use of ADR.[3] The ADRA requires federal agencies to appoint a dispute resolution specialist to

---

litigation   process of carrying on a lawsuit via the courts

consider whether, and in what circumstances, ADR procedures may benefit the general public and also help that particular administrative agency to fulfill its statutory duties more effectively. Each federal agency must develop an ADR policy following an examination of possible uses of ADR in formal and informal adjudication, rule making, enforcement actions, the issuance and revocation of licenses or permits, contract administration, litigation brought by or against the agency, and other agency actions.[4]

Prior to the ADRA, the Federal Arbitration Act[5] (FAA) and the model Uniform Arbitration Act[6] (UAA) encouraged the use of ADR to resolve disputes, and those acts remain in effect. The FAA, which was first enacted in 1925, applies to all contracts that have an arbitration clause, excluding only transportation workers.[7] The UAA has been adopted in 35 states at present since its inception in 1955.[8] The UAA creates a process whereby the existence of an agreement to arbitrate requires a court to compel arbitration on one party's motion and then requires the court to step back and take a hands-off attitude during the arbitration proceeding, reentering the dispute to confirm, modify, deny, or vacate the arbiter's award. The court does not lose its jurisdiction, but it may not interfere with the arbitration proceeding during the hands-off period.

■ Important Federal Laws

Understanding ADR requires a fundamental knowledge of Federal laws. Since, many organizations have hired an "in-house neutral" or "ombudsman" to play mediatory functions within an organization, laws such as Title VII of the Civil Rights Act of 1964,[9] the Civil Rights Act of 1991,[10] the Age Discrimination in Employment Act of 1967,[11] Section 505 of the Rehabilitation Act of 1973,[12] the Americans with Disabilities Act,[13] the Equal Pay Act,[14] and the Family and Medical Leave Act[15] are some of the major laws that serve to protect against forms of discrimination in the workplace. Managers who require employees to submit to mandatory, binding arbitration clauses in employment contracts should be aware that such forms of private justice have been upheld by the courts, and therefore human resource managers are wise to use such clauses whether in government work, private companies, and other organizations, including nonprofit groups. Since "at-will" and other nonunion employees may only seek state or federal laws for support against discrimination, harassment, and other claims, it may be wise for managers to require nonnegotiable, up-front contracts that require submission to ADR rather than litigation as it is likely more cost effective.[16]

■ Arbitration

Arbitration is the more often used form of ADR to resolve conflict in sports. **Arbitration** involves submitting of a dispute to a neutral decision maker (an arbitrator) for a final resolution of a disagreement. Arbitration is characterized as

---

arbitration   submitting a dispute to a neutral decision maker for final and binding resolution "binding" or "nonbinding" and either "mandatory" or "voluntary" depending upon the agreement between the parties. This agreement to arbitrate can be contained in a clause in an individual contract between the league and athlete as per the CBA or, for example, in an Olympic organizing committee's constitution and bylaws such as the United States Olympic Committee[17]. Arbitration may mimic a trial and is adversarial in nature, but the rules of evidence and civil procedure are relaxed and the arbitrator is in control of the process of the proceeding without judicial review. In fact, binding arbitration precludes any challenge to the decision in court, unless the arbitrator abused his or her discretion by having committed fraud or other misconduct[18]. Whether arbitration will be binding or nonbinding is determined at the outset of the arbitration process in the contractual agreement. Arbitrators' interpretations and applications of the law, then, are generally not subject to review, and their award may be made without explanation.

In 2000, the American Arbitration Association (AAA) reported, 198,491 arbitration cases were filed. This was the sixth year in a row for a record caseload.[19] Where a CBA exists, either both sides agree on one arbitrator or each side selects one arbitrator and the two arbitrators elect the third to comprise what is known as a *panel*. Arbitration hearings usually last only a few hours, and the opinions are not public record. Arbitration has long been used in labor, construction, and securities regulation and is gaining popularity in other more fundamental and general business disputes. Selection of the panel should be a joint process in which both parties have input. For example, the arbitration procedure followed by one company might provide that the employee and the company will select the arbitrator by taking turns striking names from a list obtained from a neutral administering agency (such as the AAA) until only one name remains. An arbitration policy could specify certain requirements for the arbitrator, such as minimum years of experience as an arbitrator or in the particular field or industry involved in the dispute. Having an arbitrator in whom both parties have trust might assist in bringing finality to the dispute. Another option would be to follow the panel structure often used in labor disputes under CBAs, in which each party selects a single arbitrator and the two party-selected arbitrators select a neutral chairperson.

■ The American Arbitration Association

Many athletic disputes are resolved under the auspices of the **American Arbitration Association (AAA)**. This organization is a not-for-profit educational organization dedicated to resolution of disputes of all sorts through use of arbitration, mediation, democratic elections, and other forms of ADR.

The AAA, which was formed in 1926, is headquartered in New York City but has regional offices in cities throughout the United States. More than 12,000 individuals

---

American Arbitration Association (AAA)   national organization that maintains a panel of arbitrators to hear labor and commercial disputes

are listed on the AAA's national roster of arbitrators and mediators. The arbitrators resolving amateur and professional sports disputes are former athletes, sports executives, retired judges, attorneys, agents, and more traditional labor arbitrators.

■ Mediation

Mediation is submission of a dispute to an impartial facilitator who assists the parties in negotiating a voluntary, consensual settlement of their dispute. The parties in a mediation session are virtually in complete control of the process and may walk away at any time. Mediation is about creating an environment leading to a settlement, it is ultimately about compromise and focuses substantially on the emotional needs of the parties. In order to determine the parties' needs, a mediator may have to ask, confidentially, for sensitive information about actual goals, needs, and desires of the parties.[20] A mediator can establish a base for the future relationship between the parties and can help them create a better understanding for each another. In essence, the parties decide for themselves, though they may ask the mediator for proposed solutions to the issues.

While lawyers may be present during a mediation session, the mediator plays the vital role in coordinating the process. The mediator is trained to assist and guide the parties to come to a resolution of their disputes, though there is no one "best" way to conduct a mediation session. Some mediators may refuse to allow lawyers to speak during a session. Other mediators may encourage lawyers to speak on behalf of their clients. Mediation is extremely flexible and may use "shuttle diplomacy" by employing private caucuses (i.e., meetings) in separate areas with the parties. In these private meetings, the mediator explores various options for resolving the dispute. During a caucus, each party has the chance to suggest possible solutions to the conflict, and the mediator's skills are useful in engaging with the parties to explore numerous options and suggestions for an ultimate compromise.

Some states require a mediator to be certified in order to handle a mediation session.[21] The private and confidential characteristic of mediation cannot be overemphasized by the mediator in order to encourage an open and revealing discussion leading to a possible settlement. All conversation and materials produced during a mediation session are strictly confidential, and the wise mediator has the parties sign a written statement attesting to the same. This agreement usually states that the mediator will not be called as a witness if there is subsequent litigation between the parties. The mediator also agrees not to disclose or discuss with anyone outside of the mediation session anything that occurred between the parties, while the parties agree in writing not to disclose any information regarding what happens in the mediation session without the consent of the mediator and the other party. A mediator does not have the authority to impose a solution or make a decision

---

mediation nonbinding method to resolve a dispute by involving a neutral third party who attempts to help the parties resolve their dispute

regarding the parties. Ultimately, the terms of a successful mediation will be reduced to a written contract between the parties, and any breach of that contract could then lead to litigation if either party fails to live up to its end of the bargain.

Mediation is not often used by the major professional sport leagues in the United States. CBAs focus on arbitration rather than mediation. Moving from the arbitration model to mediation would cause professional sports leagues to reexamine their relationship between players and owners and likely force these parties to agree that they are partners in a multibillion dollar industry rather than adversaries who merely participate as the result of a temporary CBA that will expire at some point in the future.

■ Med-Arb/Arb-Med and Minitrials

Mediation-arbitration, also known as **med-arb**, is a hybrid of mediation and arbitration. Med-arb is used in complex disputes that involve numerous issues.[22] The parties generally agree to resolve disputes first during a mediation phase but unresolved issues may then be presented to an arbitrator. Sometimes, the parties agree that the mediator will also serve as the arbitrator, but that is not always the case and may, in fact, be unwise. Arb-med is the reverse process of med-arb. A minitrial is a structured dispute resolution method in which senior executives or the parties involved in legal disputes meet in the presence of a neutral advisor and, after hearing presentations of the merits of each side of the dispute, attempt to formulate a voluntary settlement.[23]

■ Constitutional Concerns

While arbitration and mediation have gained great strides in the American legal system, mandatory, binding arbitration in particular has presented certain constitutional challenges for the participants, particularly in employment relationships. Congress enacted the FAA to encourage the use of arbitration in labor disputes and other contracts affecting commerce. However, the FAA has been recently characterized as a tool for employers to abuse the rights of employees by requiring up front that employees relinquish their right to pursue otherwise legitimate claims in a court of law by engaging in arbitration as their sole and exclusive remedy.[24] Mandatory, binding arbitration clauses are no longer rare provisions in employment contracts. Concerns over mandatory, binding arbitration clauses in employment agreements have created a heightened awareness that arbitration in such contracts might be grossly unfair to employees. In *Southland Corp. v. Keating*, the U.S. Supreme Court held that the FAA actually preempts state

---

med-arb hybrid form of alternative dispute resolution involving both mediation and arbitration

laws such as Wisconsin's Arbitration Act.[25] Also, in *Gilmer v. Interstate/Johnson Lane Corp.*,[26] the Supreme Court held that compulsory employment arbitration agreements can even trump the remedies available under age discrimination laws.

Arbitration also presents an interesting twist with regard to the constitutional right to a trial by jury. The **Sixth Amendment** to the Constitution provides that "in all criminal prosecutions, the accused shall enjoy the right to a speedy and public trial . . . " The **Seventh Amendment** provides that "in suits at common law, the right to a trial by jury shall be preserved." While ADR does not apply to the criminal law as a general rule, concerns over conflict between constitutional rights and waiving those rights as a condition of employment are warranted. While the Supreme Court has held that individuals may waive their constitutional rights,[27] at issue is whether an up-front contract between an employer and employee (or even a health club and a member, for example) should remain valid if the individual is essentially coerced into waiving certain rights and submitting to mandatory, binding arbitration by signing the agreement, for example. Further, while concepts such as the Fifth Amendment's due process are likely to be included in a negotiated CBA between management and labor, it is possible that due process might be waived where there is no union representation in an employment agreement, particularly where there is unequal bargaining power and the employee must accept the contract in a "take-it-or-leave it" scenario.

■ ADR in Professional Sports

In the four major professional sports, an arbitration clause is found in the respective CBAs. The arbitration clause deals with grievances and salary issues. The players are then represented by the players associations when a grievance is filed. Unlike arbitration, mediation is used rarely in team sport disputes since the collective bargaining agreement mandates arbitration as the means of settling disputes. Still, mediation might be first resort (or required) by a contractual agreement between private sponsor and a professional athlete.

In MLB, for example, arbitration is used to resolve salary disputes between owners and players. In addition to contractual grievance arbitration, the CBA between the MLBPA and the owners provides for arbitration of salary disputes. While these arbitrations are basically a form of labor arbitration in the sport context, the arbitrator is not permitted to fashion remedies or write opinions. The CBA in MLB requires "last best offer" arbitration, in which both the team and the player involved submit their last offers to an arbitrator, who must pick one of

---

Sixth Amendment "in all criminal prosecutions, the accused shall enjoy the right to a speedy and public trial"

Seventh Amendment "in suits at common law, the right to a trial by jury shall be provided"

the submitted figures. Arbitrators are limited in their ability to encourage compromise since they function as decision makers.

The CBA between the National Football League Players Association and the NFL provides for arbitration of what are again essentially labor disputes between the team and a player. The agreement between the NBA and the players association provides for arbitration of general grievances over discipline, fines, etc. In addition to the agreement between the NHL and the players association, which provides for salary arbitration, the league's bylaws call for arbitration of disputes over "equalization payments." These cases arise when one team signs another team's player as a free agent. The signing team must make an equalization payment comprising other players, future draft choices, and/or money to compensate the other team for the loss of the free agent's services. Disputes over the nature and the amount of these payments are referred to arbitration.[28]

■ ADR in Amateur Sports

National Collegiate Athletic Association

The NCAA is the premier governing body for intercollegiate athletics. Since student-athletes are not yet considered employees by United States courts and have not bargained collectively, not much attention has been given to an alternative dispute resolution process among student-athletes. However, some authors have noted that student-athletes do have a contractual relationship with the NCAA in the form of a grant-in-aid, usually called a *scholarship*. Accordingly, more than one author has suggested that ADR models might be an appropriate method to resolve disputes among student-athletes who are participants on intercollegiate athletic teams.[29]

ADR has, however, been used by the NCAA itself. In *Law v. NCAA*, the NCAA announced a $54.5 million settlement in the restricted-earnings coaches case in 1999 via mediation (see Case 12).[30] The basis of this case was that the NCAA's 1991 restricted-earnings legislation violated federal antitrust laws. Restricted-earnings coaches were limited to being compensated $12,000 during the academic year and $4,000 during the summer by member NCAA institutions as a matter of policy.[31] This policy was found to have violated federal antitrust laws. The NCAA had filed an appeal with the 10th Circuit Court of Appeals on what it argued were mistakes made by the District Court in the damages phase of the trial. The mediation services of the court became available when the petition for appeal was entered. An agreement was later reached through mediation by both parties. After almost a month-long mediation, the plaintiffs and NCAA agreed that $54.5 million in damages would be paid to plaintiffs in cash within 60 days of the date of the mediation settlement. In another famous case involving basketball coach Jerry Tarkanian and the NCAA, the case was eventually settled by mediation in April 1998, only one month after the mediation clerk for the 9th Circuit Court of Appeals contacted the parties and suggested mediation as an attempt to end the saga.[32]

The United States Olympic Committee[33]

Arbitration is the method of choice for conflict resolution in the Olympic Movement. With the enactment of the Amateur Sports Act of 1978, Congress created several organizations, including the USOC, to organize and promote the U.S. Olympic effort. The USOC has the power to appoint an amateur sports organization as the national governing body (NGB)[34] for any sport included in the Olympics or the Pan American Games. The purposes of the USOC are described in this act, which amended, renamed, and recodified the Amateur Sports Act of 1978. It is now called the Ted Stevens Olympic and Amateur Sports Act (TSOASA).[35]

The TSOASA provides that the USOC is to afford "swift resolution of conflicts and disputes involving amateur athletes, national governing bodies, and amateur sports organizations . . . "[36] Article IX of the act now requires an NGB to allow aggrieved athletes an opportunity for a hearing where they can present evidence and expect a swift and equitable resolution of their disputes. The act requires the NGB to "establish and maintain provisions in its constitution and bylaws for the swift and equitable resolution of disputes involving any of its members and relating to the opportunity of any athlete to participate in the Olympic Games."[37] This requires the NGBs to "submit to binding arbitration in any controversy involving . . . the opportunity of any amateur athlete . . . to participate in amateur athletic competition."[38] Article IX of the USOC Constitution provides that a case is actually filed against the NGB, not against another athlete, in stating that any "claim against such USOC member will be submitted to arbitration."[39]

International ADR: Court of Arbitration for Sport

In 1983, the IOC established the Court of Arbitration of Sport (CAS) to resolve issues under its jurisdiction in order to assist the process of litigation by athletes and countries for numerous disputes arising out of the Olympic Movement. The CAS was designed to be a sports-specific forum and to be the only means for Olympic athletes and the international sports federations to resolve their disputes through this final, neutral decision-making arbitration body. The International Council for Sports Arbitration (ICAS) was established to oversee the CAS to avoid perceived conflicts of interest. There are three venues to resolve disputes under the CAS: Lausanne, Sydney, and New York.[40]

CAS cases are fundamentally based upon submission to arbitration by contract. All athletes who participated in the 2000 Sydney Olympic Games were required to sign this agreement. The form contains the clause:

> I agree that any dispute in connection with the Olympic Games, not resolved after exhaustion of the legal remedies established by my NOC, the International Federation governing my sport, the Sydney Organizing Committee for the Olympic Games (SOCOG) and the IOC, shall be submitted exclusively to the Court of Arbitration for Sport (CAS) for final and binding arbitration. . . .

CAS arbitrators are bound by the procedures and rules found within its Code, which follows rules according to the Swiss Federal Code. Arbitrators must be familiar with sports law, particularly at an international level. Decisions made by arbitrators are not published but they may be if both parties agree.

Olympic ADR Cases

The AAA's history with Olympic cases goes back several years. In 1996, prior to the start of the Olympic Games in Atlanta, the AAA trained a panel of arbitrators to provide real-time dispute resolution at the Games. The arbitrators were told to be available at a moment's notice should any disputes be filed. Several cases were filed during the Games, and because of the AAA's swift response, those cases were resolved quickly. Similarly, at the request of the USOC, three arbitrators that were part of the group that was trained prior to the 1996 Games were sent to the 2000 Sydney Games to be on hand should any arbitration cases be filed. Ultimately, no cases were filed in Sydney, but the AAA's responsiveness did not go unnoticed.

Most Olympic-related cases are filed on the eve of a qualifying event or on the eve of the Olympics itself. Three days prior to the opening of the Nagano Games in 1998, an Olympic skier filed for arbitration. The AAA acted quickly and had arbitration scheduled within 24 hours. The arbitrator decided the skier was eligible for the Games. In a case that made headlines prior to the Sydney Games, wrestler Matt Lindland filed arbitration with AAA, contending that he lost the match because the other wrestler used an illegal hold. The arbitrator ordered a rematch, which the wrestler won. Ultimately, the courts decided in favor of the aggrieved arbitrator, and he won a spot at the Sydney Games.

Other high-profile cases heard by the AAA include boxing, judo, taek won do, cycling, softball, tennis, badminton, curling, speed skating, and rowing.

■ Dispute Resolution and Cyberspace

The Internet has affected the way society conducts and transacts business and has created a new marketplace of conflict. Arbitration, mediation, and their hybrid forms should be considered when dealing with disputes related to cyberspace. The Internet has created legal battles that have been litigated, such as domain name disputes, listserv debates, e-mail harassment, and fraud, slander, and libel claims. Protection of intellectual property such as copyrights and trademarks involving the Internet has essentially forced individuals and organizations to address the role that ADR might play both nationally and internationally.

With the advent of e-mail and the Internet generally, access to ADR has increased significantly as well. As a natural consequence, forms of online dispute resolution services have emerged. These "virtual" services are designed to mimic the role of human interaction to settle disputes. Theoretically, the arbitrator or mediator communicates with each side using e-mail, an online chat session, or electronic conferencing and videoconferencing when the parties have the required equipment. Some notable online ADR dispute resolution projects have included the Virtual Magistrate Project, the BBB Online Project, the Online Ombuds Office at the University of Massachusetts, and America Online's "24-hours in Cyberspace" promotion.

While such electronic forms of ADR can be successful, online ADR clearly has its advantages and disadvantages. Advantages, of course, include convenience, cost and time reductions, and reducing the likelihood of physical or verbal intimidation. Disadvantages include possible electronic security breaches, the failure to recognize the importance of face-to-face contact, lack of tone or inflection of voice and facial features, and potential misinterpretation of terms. Whether online dispute resolution in cyberspace works is still an uncertain venture, at least with the availability of technology at this point in time. Still, there is no reason why online ADR will not have its place in resolving management-player disputes in the sports arena in certain circumstances.

▪ World Intellectual Property Organization

The **World Intellectual Property Organization (WIPO)** Arbitration and Mediation Center was established in 1994 to offer arbitration and mediation services for the resolution of international commercial disputes. WIPO is headquartered in Geneva, Switzerland.[41] This center has focused on establishing a legal framework for the administration of disputes related to the Internet and electronic commerce. WIPO has arbitrated recent issues related to disputes involving sport domain names. For example, cybersquatters have often purchased domain names, usually ending with .com., .net, or .org. The cybersquatters' intent is to resell the name for a profit. Often, the cybersquatter may have violated a trademarked name or phrase of another company or organization in the process. When a dispute over a domain name arises, the WIPO is called to resolve the dispute. In one case, for example, the WIPO ordered a private company that registered the domain name "usolympicstore.com" to be surrendered to the USOC after a hearing on the matter.[42]

▪ ADR Cases

ADR has been used in many instances to resolve disputes in both amateur and professional sports. Still, as discussed earlier, legal battles in sports have had their place both nationally and internationally and have traditionally involved litigation. Figure skater Tonya Harding's case and track star Butch Reynolds' four years of litigation demonstrated the role that the courts and litigation have played in shaping the current legal landscape of sports. Litigation, however, has been costly, lengthy, and often controversial especially with regard to jurisdictional issues at the international level.

World Intellectual Property Organization (WIPO)   international organization dedicated to helping ensure that the rights of creators and owners of intellectual property are protected worldwide and that inventors and authors are recognized and rewarded for their ingenuity

■ CASE 14 *NBA Properties, Inc. v. Adirondack Software Corporation*

Administative Panel Decision
NBA Properties, Inc. v. Adirondack Software
Corporation
Case No. D2000-1211

1. THE PARTIES

The Complainant is NBA Properties, Inc., located at 645 Fifth Avenue, New York, New York 10022, U.S.A.

The Respondent is Adirondack Software Corporation, whose address is 194 Moody Avenue, Freeport, New York 11520, U.S.A.

2. THE DOMAIN NAME AND REGISTRAR

The domain name at issue is:<knicks.com>

The Registrar for the domain name is Network Solutions, Inc., of 505 Huntmar Park Drive, Herndon, Virginia 20170-5139, U.S.A.

3. PROCEDURAL HISTORY

The WIPO Arbitration and Mediation Center (the "Center") received the Complaint on September 13, 2000 by email and on September 18, 2000 in hardcopy. The Complainant paid the required fee.

On September 19, 2000, the Center sent to the Registrar a request for verification of registration data. In a response on September 24, 2000, the Registrar confirmed, *inter alia*, that it is the registrar of the domain name in dispute and that such name is registered in Respondent's name. The Registrar's response also indicated that Network Solutions' 4.0 Service Agreement was in effect.

On September 25, 2000, the Center advised the attorney for Complainant that, in view of the terms of the 4.0 Service Agreement, an amendment to the paragraph of the Complaint relating to "Mutual Jurisdiction" would be required if the case were to proceed. A copy was sent to Respondent. Complainant provided the Center with the Amendment by email on September 26, and by hard copy on September 29, 2000.

Having verified that the Complaint satisfies the formal requirements of the ICANN Uniform Domain Name Dispute Resolution Policy (the "Policy"), the Rules for Uniform Domain Name Dispute Resolution Policy (the "Rules"), and the WIPO Supplemental Rules for Uniform Domain Name Dispute Resolution Policy (the "Supplemental Rules"), the Center on September 29, 2000 sent to the Respondent, with a copy to the Complainant, a notification of the administrative proceeding. This notification was sent in accordance with Paragraph 2 of the Rules thereby discharging the Center's responsibility to employ reasonably available means calculated to achieve actual notice to Respondent. Although, the Notification sent out via courier to the Respondent at the registrant's address was returned, the Notification sent to the Technical/Zone Contact shows as delivered according to the FedEx Tracking Results on the web. Furthermore, the e-mail communications of the Notification were not returned to the Center as undeliverable.

The formal date of the commencement of this administrative proceeding is September 29, 2000.

No Response to the Complaint was received by the Center. On October 20, 2000, the Center issued a notice of Respondent's default.

The Center invited William L. Mathis to serve as a Panelist in this proceeding and he sent to the Center his Statement of Acceptance and Declaration of Impartiality and Independence. On November 13, 2000, the Center dispatched to the parties a notice of the appointment of William L. Mathis as a single member panel to decide the case.

4. FACTUAL BACKGROUND

The Complainant NBA Properties, Inc., a corporation of New York, is the exclusive licensing and merchandising agent for the National Basketball Association and its member teams, including the New York Knicks.

Copies of four federal registrations of marks are attached to the Complaint as Exhibit C. Each of them refers to at least one earlier federal registration (No. 870,255) which is said to be commonly owned but which is not mentioned in the Complaint.

All of the four attached registrations are for marks that include the word KNICKS displayed as a three dimensional arcuate body viewed from a lower level, as one might see an elevated name for an entertainment attraction or facility. Three of them depict a basketball beneath the arcuate KNICKS display, and of these, two additionally include a triangle in the background. One has the words NEW YORK immediately above KNICKS.

Three of the registrations (Nos. 1,429,344; 1,988,809; and 2,197,935) relate to the KNICKS trademarks as applied to clothing items and various kinds of bags for carrying things. The fourth (No. 1,768,640) relates to the KNICKS/basketball/triangle ensemble as a trademark applied to various goods (printed matter, clothing items, and toys and sporting goods). It also relates to the ensemble used as a service mark in connection with "entertainment services in the nature of basketball games and basketball exhibitions live in stadia and through the media of radio and television broadcasts."

The omitted registration (No. 870,255) also relates to a KNICKS mark as used in connection with "Professional Basketball Contests."

Paragraph 13 of the Complaint says that Complainant is the exclusive licensee of the federally registered trademarks, but it also represents that Madison Square Garden, L.P. is not only the owner of the trademarks but also the owner and operator of the New York Knicks basketball team. No specifics have been provided as to an agreement between Complainant and Madison Square Garden, L.P.

Paragraph 17 of the Complaint focuses on a third entity, the National Basketball Association, and its Web page at www.nba.com which provides hyperlinks to home pages of all twenty-nine NBA teams. Complainant says it "operates the home page of the New York Knicks at the URL www.nba.com/knicks."

Significantly, paragraph 17 also says that Madison Square Garden, L.P., registered the domain name "www.nyknicks.com". This domain name is said to point to the previously mentioned NBA Web site. It is not clear that the Complainant corporation is identified to Internet users who visit such sites.

With respect to the Respondent, the Complaint indicates that the disputed domain name was registered with NSI in 1995, that the Complainant's attorneys complained to NSI in 1996, and that, after attempting unsuccessfully to contact the Registrant, NSI placed the domain name in a hold status.

Complainant attempted to contact Respondent in late 1996 and early 1997. After a telephone conversation with Complainant's attorney, a representative of Respondent "executed a transfer letter, dated February 1, 1997, authorizing transfer of the knicks.com domain name from Adirondack to the NBA" (Complaint, paragraph 23).

However, the transfer letter apparently was not in the form then considered by NSI to be acceptable and it seems not to have been sent by Complainant to NSI. The record does not reflect any follow up activity over the next two years.

Complainant's attorney directed another letter to Respondent's representative in March 1999, but it was returned unclaimed. In April 1999, several telephone calls were attempted unsuccessfully.

On March 30, 2000, NSI wrote to Complainant to notify Complainant that the "hold" status of "knicks.com" would be removed unless some specified action was taken. The filing of the present Complaint was done in response to the NSI letter.

5. PARTIES' CONTENTIONS

Only the Complainant has advanced contentions.

Complainant asserts that it has rights in the trademark KNICKS, that the disputed domain name is identical to a trademark in which it has rights, that Respondent has no rights or legitimate interests in the respect of the domain name, and that the domain name was registered and is being used in bad faith.

Complainant also sets out in Paragraph 34-38 conclusory claims under Sections 43(d) and (c) of the Lanham Act. However, Paragraph 33 appears to recognize that such claims are beyond the jurisdiction of the Panel and indicates that they are offered in support of the claims actually grounded on the Policy. They have been considered in this context and there will be no further occasion to refer to them.

The relief sought by Complainant is a transfer of the disputed domain name to Complainant.

6. DISCUSSION AND FINDINGS

Complainant's Trademark Rights

The owner of the KNICKS trademarks and service marks relied upon has been shown to be Madison Square Garden, L.P., not the sole Complainant NBA Properties, Inc. Madison Square Garden, L.P., also has been identified as the owner and operator of the New York Knicks basketball team, which is source of the notoriety associated with the KNICKS marks.

The record fails to make clear what *rights in the trademark* Complainant claims to have. The rights of a licensee are contract rights with respect to, not *in*, the licensed marks. So it is also in the case of a licensing and merchandising agent.

continued

There may well be circumstances in which the contract rights possessed by an exclusive licensee vest in him substantially all the powers of an owner of the licensed property. However, such circumstances have not been shown to exist here.

The Policy is believed by the Panel to envision a transfer of a disputed domain name to a complainant/trademark owner as a route to unification of control over the uses of the domain name and the trademark. However, Complainant's request for an order transferring the disputed name to Complainant in this case would place ownership of the domain name in an entity other than the trademark owner without consent from the trademark owner.

The Panel therefore finds that the sole Complainant has not shown that it has rights in the KNICKS trademark relied upon.

Identical or Confusing Similarity

While the Complaint asserts that the disputed domain name is identical to the KNICKS trademark relied upon by Complainant, there appears to be no need to isolate "identical" from the "identical or confusingly similar" language actually used in Paragraph 4.a.(i) of the Policy.

The Panel finds that the disputed domain name knicks.com is identical or confusingly similar to the KNICKS trademark for which Complainant is a licensing and merchandising agent.

Registration and Use in Bad Faith

Paragraph 4.a.(iii) of the Policy also require that the Complainant prove that the disputed domain name "has been registered and is being used in bad faith."

Paragraph 4.b. of the Uniform Domain Name Dispute Resolution Policy under which this administrative proceeding is taking place describes some circumstances which, if found to exist, will be evidence of the registration and use of the domain name in bad faith. Four descriptions are presented in subsections (i), (ii), (iii) and (iv).

Subsection (i) describes circumstances in which a domain name was registered primarily for the purpose of selling it. Complainant does not contend that this subsection applies here. Indeed, it appears that Respondent was willing in 1997 to give the domain name to the NBA.

Subsection (ii) describes circumstances in which there is a pattern of registering domain names to prevent trademark owners from reflecting their marks in corresponding domain names. The present record does not establish the existence of such a pattern.

Subsection (iii) refers to registering a domain name to disrupt a *competitor's* business. Respondent has not been shown to be a competitor or to have a desire to disrupt the Complainant's business.

Subsection (iv) is directed to a situation in which a domain name is improperly used to attract Internet users to a web site other than the site of the owner of a similar trademark. In the present case, there is no showing that the disputed domain name has ever been used to attract Internet users to any web site.

In sum, Complainant has failed to prove that any of the circumstances described in Paragraph 4.b. of the Policy were present in this case. Nor does the Complainant provide other evidence establishing that the disputed domain name has been registered and is being used in bad faith. Accordingly, the Panel finds that Complainant has failed to prove the presence of the element referred to in Paragraph 4.a. (iii) of the Policy.

Rights and Legitimate Interests

Paragraph 4.a. of the Policy additionally requires that a complainant prove that the domain name registrant has no rights or legitimate interests in respect of the domain name.

Paragraph 32 of the Complaint addresses this issue in a conclusory way. It asserts that none of the circumstances described in Paragraph 4.c. of (i), (ii), and (iii) of the Policy existed in this case. The Panel has no basis for finding otherwise.

7. Decision

The Panel concludes (1) that Complainant has not proved that it has rights in the relied upon KNICKS trademark, and (2) that Complainant has not proved that Respondent has registered and is using the disputed domain name in bad faith.

Therefore, the Panel *denies* the requested transfer of the domain name knicks.com.

Reprinted with permission from the WIPO Arbitration and Mediation Center.

While litigation has often been the court of resort for sports disputes, the four major professional sports do have arbitration procedures in place though they prominently involve focusing on player salary disputes. In amateur sports, however, the focus of ADR appears to be rule interpretations, eligibility, and discipline disputes. Concerns for balancing athlete rights yet upholding the autonomy of an amateur sports organization's interpretations and discipline procedures were the driving forces behind the advent of the TSOASA in 1998, and the development and continuing transformation of the role of the CAS and the ICAS.

ADR has gained prominence in the most recent Olympic Games and has been effective in resolving disputes internally rather than requiring judicial review by the courts. While ADR in amateur sports continues to gain momentum, the CAS has been much more adroit at handling complaints by amateur athletes than in previous years particularly since such athletes now agree, by contract, that the CAS will be the ultimate arbiter and interpreter of international amateur rules and their enforcement at events through its Ad Hoc Division. Athletes now sign contracts in order to be eligible to participate in a sanctioned competition and the Olympic Games. A few of the more recent and significant cases are briefly summarized below.

Jessica Foschi

Swimmer Jessica Foschi tested positive in 1995 at the age of 15 for the anabolic steroid mesterolene after she placed third in the 1500-meter freestyle race at the U.S. National Swimming Championships and was required to provide a urine sample as was required for top finishers. Foschi denied she had used steroids and argued that the test results were incorrect or the sample was someone else's urine. U.S. Swimming concluded that Foschi must have been given steroids without her knowledge or was sabotaged. Foschi received two-year probation and a warning that any later positive test would result in a lifetime ban on her participation in amateur swimming. That penalty was later changed to a two-year ban. Then, U.S. Swimming reversed itself again and went back to giving her two-year probation, after FINA, the international governing body of swimming, did not suspend an Australian swimmer who tested positive for another banned substance. Foschi was allowed to participate in trials for the 1996 Atlanta Olympics, but she did not qualify for the team. Foschi then filed a demand for arbitration by the American Arbitration Association (AAA) and proceeded under the (former) Amateur Sports Act of 1978. The AAA panel decided to remove all sanctions against Foschi and concluded that U.S.S. violated fundamental fairness and were arbitrary and capricious. After lengthy legal maneuvering and appeals, in 1997, the CAS reduced her suspension to six months and ordered costs against FINA, the international governing body for swimming. Like Butch Reynolds, her case represented lack of consistency and a confusing struggle for power, jurisdiction, and rules interpretations between national and international amateur sport governing bodies and the AAA.

Ross Rebagliati

Canadian Snowboarder Ross Rebagliati competed in the sport's inaugural competition as an Olympic Sport in Nagano, Japan, in 1998. On February 8, 1998,

Rebagliati won the Gold Medal in the Men's Giant Slalom competition, but on February 11, 1998, the IOC Executive Board disqualified and took away Rebagliati's medal after he tested positive for marijuana. The Canadian Olympic Association appealed on Rebagliati's behalf. Rebagliati denied recently using the drug and proclaimed that his positive test was the result of second-hand marijuana smoke. The CAS held that under the IOC's Medical Code, the IOC had no right to disqualify Rebagliati without evidence of the required agreement between the IOC and the International Skiing Federation (ISF) to provide for marijuana testing. Under the IOC's Medical Code, a penalty could only be imposed if there was an agreement between the respective sports federation and the IOC to test for marijuana. The CAS further found that marijuana was not listed as a banned substance in the IOC's Drug Formulary Guide published for athletes participating in the Nagano games. Rebagliati had his medal restored, but the IOC Medical Commission amended the Anti-Doping Code so testing for marijuana would be conducted at the Olympic Games in the future, regardless. This case represented the technicalities associated with drug testing issues, the need to clarify ambiguous rules related to the Olympic Games, and how regulations can change as the result of ADR disputes. The case also proved how swiftly the Ad Hoc Division of the CAS could make decisions.

Matt Lindland

American amateur wrestler Keith Sieracki lost a wrestling rematch 8–0 to Matt Lindland after an arbitrator ruled that in the 2000 Greco-Roman championship match in the 167.5-pound class, Sieracki had used illegal holds by using his legs. The winner of the rematch was to represent the USA at the Sydney Olympics though Sieracki had won the original Olympic Trials match, 2–1. Lindland filed his protest over the third and final round in which Sieracki won in overtime. The Protest Committee upheld the decision, giving the victory to Sieracki. Lindland, however, appealed the Protest Committee's decision to USA Wrestling's Greco-Roman Sport Committee. Lindland's appeal was denied, but he fought further and sought arbitration. Lindland and USA Wrestling agreed to an arbitration of the dispute. Not only did Lindland win the right to a rematch due to an arbitrator's decision, but he won the rematch and later earned the silver medal in Sydney. Lindland's case represented that even with ADR there were delays in the decision-making process of rules interpretations. Additionally, it demonstrated that the use of ADR to resolve subjective, judgment calls by officials in sports might not be appropriate.

Apolo Ohno

At the 2002 Salt Lake City Olympic Games, in the final of the 2002 men's 1500-meter short-track speed skating race, a Korean skater, Kim Dong-Sung, was disqualified by the race referee for a rules violation involving blocking U.S. skater Apolo Anton Ohno. Kim crossed the finish line ahead of Ohno, but the Korean racer was immediately disqualified for the rule violation. Korean officials protested the decision of chief referee, but he declined to accept the protest. Korean officials then appealed to the CAS Ad Hoc Division insisting on a video replay analysis, but the appeal ultimately went to an arbitrator who determined that a video replay was not authorized or applicable according to the rules. While the rules of the sport involving video replay were changed later in 2002, it was established that final arbitration decisions could not be appealed or challenged further. The case again involved whether or not athletes and federations should be able to appeal the subjective, judgment calls by officials. It also demonstrated how competition rules could be modified as the direct result of legal challenges to their enforcement and interpretation.

■ Summary

Litigation is the conventional method for settling disputes. However, not all disputes require the adversarial approach to be successfully settled or to come to a resolution. Understanding the differences between arbitration, mediation, and their hybrid forms is important to students, educators, and practitioners.

In recent years, there has been an increased emphasis on using ADR to settle a variety of issues at international, federal, and state levels. While traditional litigation is often the more frequent method to resolve disputes, ADR has become a widely popular and preferred method to reach legal solutions for many involved in sports. Arbitration and mediation are usually more efficient, less costly, and more effective than litigation. Mediation is certainly more confidential. Understanding other various Federal laws is important when applying ADR.

The professional sports leagues and the Olympic Movement use ADR as a preferred method of resolving numerous contractual disputes. The advent and growth of the Internet has provided a market for the natural evolution of online ADR, though settlement negotiations that do not involve face-to-face meetings have both advantages and disadvantages for the arbitrator or mediator.

ADR is not a perfect system and presumes, especially in mediation, that both parties wish to explore a compromise. In ADR, less emphasis is placed on "win at all costs," and more emphasis is placed on problem solving and settlement. In the end, the parties often feel much more satisfied, especially if the parties are willing to compromise from the commencement of an ADR session.

■ Key Terms

Alternative Dispute
   Resolution (ADR)
American Arbitration Association (AAA)
arbitration
litigation
med-arb

mediation
Seventh Amendment
Sixth Amendment
World Intellectual Property
   Organization (WIPO)

■ Additional Cases

Circuit City Stores, Inc. v. Adams, 532 U.S. 105, 109 (2001)
Foschi v. United States Swimming, Inc. 916 F. Supp. 232 (E.D.N.Y. 1996)
Johnson v. Zerbst, 304 U.S. 458 (1938)
Law v. NCAA, 134 F.3d 1010 (10th Cir. 1998) (see Case 11)
Lindland v. United States Wrestling Ass'n, 230 F. 3d 1036, 1038 (7th Cir. 2000)
National Basketball Players Association on Behalf of Player Latrell Sprewell and Warriors Basketball Club and National Basketball Association (Freerick, Arb., March 4, 1998)
NCAA v. Tarkanian, 488 U.S. 179 (1988)
Patton v. U.S., 281 U.S. 276 (1930)
Reynolds v. Int'l Amateur Athletic Fed'n, 23 F.3d 1110 (6th Cir. 1994)
Sharpe v. National Football League Players Association, 941 F. Supp. 8 (D.D.C. 1996)
Southland Corp. v. Keating, 465 U.S. 1 (1984)
Sprewell v. Golden State Warriors, 231 F.3d 520 (9th Cir. 2000)
U.S. v. Moore, 340 U.S. 616 (1951)
WIPO *United States Olympic Committee v. MIC*, Case No. D2000–0189 (May 4, 2000)
WIPO *NCAA v. Gregory Freedman* Case No. D2000–0841 (November 10, 2000)

■ Review Questions

1. What does the phrase "alternative dispute resolution" mean?
2. Do you feel that alternative dispute resolution is effective in sport? Why or why not?
3. What are the differences between artitration and mediation?
4. Do you feel that the Court of Arbitration of Sport has been effective?
5. Why might litigation be more effective than ADR?
6. What is the American Arbitration Association?

■ Endnotes

1 *See* Gil Fried and Michael Hiller, *ADR in Youth and Intercollegiate Athletics*, 3 B.Y.U.L.Rev. 631 at 634 (1997).
2 SEC, EPA, and IRS are examples of federal administrative agencies.
3 U.S.C.A. §§571–583. The ADRA was amended in 1996. Additionally, the Alternative Dispute Resolution Act of 1998 requires all federal district courts to provide at least one form of ADR. *See* 28 U.S.C.A. §651 et seq.
4 *See also* http://www.dol.gov/asp/programs/adr/adrbrief.htm
5 9 U.S.C.A. § 1 et seq.
6 Drafted by the NCCUSL originally in 1956 and revised in 2000.

7 *Circuit City Stores, Inc. v. Adams*, 532 U.S. 105 (2001). *See also,* however, *Southland Corp. v. Keating*, 465 U.S. 1, 10 (1984).

8 For an historical review of these acts, *see* American Arbitration Association, *Past, Present and Future: Building on 70 Years of Innovation—The AAA Looks to the 21st* Century, 51 SEP Disp. Resol. J. 109 (1996).

9 42 U.S.C.A. §§ 2000e to 2000e-17.

10 2 U.S.C. A. §§ 601, 1201–1224.

11 29 U.S.C.A. §§ 621–634.

12 29 U.S.C.A. § 794 (a).

13 42 U.S.C. A. §§ 12101–12213.

14 29 U.S.C.A. §206(d).

15 29 U.S.C.A. §§ 2601–2654.

16 *See Circuit City Stores, Inc. v. Adams*, 532 U.S. 105, 109 (2001).

17 *See* USOC Constitution, art. IX, §2.

18 *See* 9 U.S.C.A. § 10 (a) for grounds to vacate arbitration awards.

19 *See* http://www.adr.org/upload/LIVESITE/About/annual_reports/annual_report_2000. pdf

20 *Id.*

21 Mediators do not have to be attorneys as a general rule but may require some form of formal training under state or federal law. However, the fact that licensed attorneys are bound by either the Model Code of Professional Responsibility or the Model Rules of Professional Conduct may create an environment even more conducive to confidential negotiations since licensed lawyers could theoretically lose their license for a violation of ethical rules. *See also,* Fiona Furlan, Edward Blumstein, David N. Hofstein, *Ethical Guidelines for Attorney-Mediators: Are Attorneys Bound by Ethical Codes for Lawyers When Acting as Mediators?*, 14 J. Am. Acad. Matrim. Law 267, 287 (1997).

22 *See,* e.g., Susan Haslip, *A Consideration of the Need for a National Dispute Resolution System for National Sport Organizations in Canada*, 11 Marq. Sports. L.Rev. 245, 270 (2001).

23 *Id* at 270.

24 Sen. Russell D. Feingold, *Mandatory Arbitration: What Process is Due?*, 39 Harv. J. on Legis. 281 (2002).

25 465 U.S. 1 (1984).

26 500 U.S. 20 (1991).

27 *See Patton v. U.S.*, 281 U.S. 276, 298 (1930); *U.S. v. Moore*, 340 U.S. 616, 621 (1951); *Johnson v. Zerbst*, 304 U.S. 458, 465 (1938) [waiving Sixth Amendment, Seventh Amendment, and assistance of counsel, respectively].

28 Thomas J. Arkell, *National Hockey League Jurisprudence: Past Present and Future*, 8 Seton Hall J. Sport L. 135, 143 (1998).

29 *See* e.g. Eric Galton, *Mediation Programs for Collegiate Sports Teams*, 53 Disp. Resol. J. 37 (1998), and http://www.rit.edu/~301www/mediation/index.html

30 *See Law v. National Collegiate Athletic Ass'n.*, 134 F. 3d 1010 (10th Cir. 1998).

31 http://www.ncaa.org/news/1999/19990315/active/3606n01.html

32 *See http://home.att.net/~rebels02/page21b_tarkncaa.html.* and *NCAA v. Tarkanian*, 488 U.S. 179 (1988).

33 USOC had previously been called the United States Olympic Association, but the name was changed in compliance with Pub. L. No. 88–407, 78 Stat. 383 (1964).

34 USA Triathlon is the NGB for the sport of triathlon in the United States, for example.

35 36 U.S.C.A. § 220506.

36 36 U.S.C.A. § 220503(8).

37 Ted Stevens Olympic and Amateur Sports Act, 36 U.S.C.A. 220501-220509, 220509. (West Supp. 2000).

38 36 U.S.C.A. § 220522(4) (B).

39 USOC Const., art IX § 2. (These are often referred to as "Article IX arbitrations").

40 Lausanne is the primary office. The New York office used to be in Denver, Colorado.

41 *See* WIPO *United States Olympic Committee v. MIC*, Case No. D2000-0189 (May 4, 2000).

42 *See* the American Arbitration Association's website for additional forms and clauses. http://www.adr.org/index2.1.jsp?JSPssid=13598&JSPsrc=upload\LIVESITE\Rules_Procedures\ADR_Guides\clausebook.html

43 George H. Friedman, *Alternative Dispute Resolution and Emerging Online Technologies: Challenges and Opportunities*, 19 Hastings Comm. & Ent. L.J. 695, 717 (1997).

CHAPTER TWELVE

Religion and Sports

▓ Introduction

The **Constitution of the United States** provides for numerous freedoms and rights. The Constitution has been amended 27 times (see Appendix B) and has provided the Supreme Court numerous opportunities to interpret its meaning.

One of the more relevant, controversial, and constitutional issues in sports is the issue and practice of religion by sports participants and fans during or around a sports contest. For example, can prayers be led prior to sports contests at private or public high schools, colleges, and universities? Do moments of silence constitute illegal prayers? The answers are not clear.

One of the basic philosophical foundations of the United States is the separation between church and state; in other words, the government may not promote, endorse, or advance a particular religion. This was an exciting and novel idea back when the United States first established itself as being free from the stronghold of England.

While the United States is amenable to the acceptance of varied religious beliefs and tenets, it is not acceptable for the state or government to impose a particular religion over another on its people. Studying religion and its impact on sports offers few certainties. This area of the law, like many areas involving sports, continues to evolve. Two clauses found in the Constitution are the focus of the subject of religion and sports: the establishment clause and the free exercise clause.

This chapter will attempt to organize the important issues involving religion, sports, and the law. Since the law in this area is ever changing and often unclear, the student should appreciate that courts have established general concepts that should be applied on a case-by-case basis.

Constitution of the United States   nation's fundamental legal document

■ First Amendment

In order to understand the basics of the freedoms afforded by our Constitution, one must start at the beginning of the Bill of Rights in the **First Amendment**. The First Amendment to the United States Constitution states:

> Congress shall make no law respecting an establishment of religion, or prohibiting the free exercise thereof; or abridging the freedom of speech, or of the press; or the right of the people peaceably to assemble, and to petition the Government for a redress of grievances.

Notice in the First Amendment the phrases "establishment of religion" and "free exercise thereof," which are referred to as the *establishment clause* and the *free exercise clause* respectively. Many refer to these two clauses as the "religion clauses" of the Constitution.

Prayers Before Sports Contests

An area of the law that continues to remain uncertain and controversial is the prayer before a sports contest. While prayers before sports contests and graduation ceremonies have been commonplace in the United States for numerous years, recent legal challenges to such organized prayers have forced the courts to address whether such prayers are constitutional. For example, do prayers prior to sports contests advance a particular religion? Do prayers advance any religion? Is there a difference between state-funded institutions and private institutions, which may in fact be traditionally religious based institutions of higher learning? Does it matter who leads the prayer? For example, is it different for students to lead a prayer as opposed to the school's administration?

Prayers at Graduation Ceremonies

It is a widely held tradition in American society that a prayer of some sort is said at high school and college graduation ceremonies. The courts appear to have dealt with school prayer more often associated with graduation ceremonies than sporting events. Still, does saying a prayer in either context advance or impose a particular religion and thereby violate the Constitution? What about a moment of silence? It appears that key to understanding the legality of prayers at graduation ceremonies is whether the prayer is voluntary or state sponsored.

First Amendment   constitutional amendment providing for freedom of the press, freedom of assembly, and freedom of religion

■ Three Tests

Courts will use several analyses to determine whether prayers in schools are valid. In sum, three tests are used:

1. **The *Lemon* test**—An action must have a secular purpose, its primary effect must neither advance nor inhibit religion, and it must not foster an excessive entanglement with religion. This has its own three-pronged test. *Lemon v. Kurtzman*, 403 U.S. 602 (1971)
2. **The Endorsement test**—The government cannot endorse, favor, promote, or prefer any religious belief or practice. *County of Allegheny v. American Civil Liberties Union*, 492 U.S. 573 (1989)
3. **The Coercion test**—The government may not coerce anyone to support or participate in religion or its exercise. *Lee v. Weisman*, 505 U.S. 577 (1992)

■ Sports-Related Cases

Chaudhuri

In *Chaudhuri v. State of Tennessee*, 130 F. 3d 232 (6th Cir. 1997), the Sixth Circuit Court of Appeals considered legal challenges to the allowance of prayers at university functions and the recitation of "The Lord's Prayer" at Tennessee State University's (TSU) graduation ceremony. A lawsuit was filed by mechanical engineering professor Dilip Chaudhuri, a Hindu. He objected to a custom of prayers being offered at graduation exercises, faculty meetings, dedication ceremonies, and guest lectures at the Nashville school.

In response, TSU officials decided that all such prayers at university events would be generic and nonsectarian. Still not satisfied, Chaudhuri then filed suit in federal district court. After he filed the lawsuit, TSU changed its policy to include a moment of silence, rather than a verbal prayer, at graduation exercises. The district court dismissed the claims. The Sixth Circuit Court of Appeals upheld and said that generic prayers have a secular purpose of dignifying or memorializing a public event, that they do not entangle church and state, and that they do not impermissibly advance or inhibit religion.

***Lemon* test**   test of constitutionality providing that an act of government must (1) be primarily secular in purpose, (2) neither advance nor inhibit religion, and (3) avoid excessive entanglement with religion

Endorsement test   legal standard in which a court considers whether the government intends to communicate, and whether an imaginary "reasonable observer" would receive, a message of "endorsement" of a particular religion and/or an act of disapproval toward any other religion

Coercion test   examination of a religious practice to determine whether pressure is applied to force or coerce individuals to participate

The Court of Appeals noted that since Mr. Chaudhuri was not required to participate in any religious exercise, his free exercise claim was without merit. The Supreme Court declined to hear the professor's challenge to "generic" prayers and moments of silence at Tennessee State University functions. Left undisturbed was a previous ruling that generic prayers and moments of silence at university events do not violate the First Amendment.

Santa Fe

Prior to 1995, a Texas student elected as Santa Fe High School's student council chaplain delivered a prayer over the public address system before each home varsity football game. Mormon and Catholic students or alumni and their mothers filed a lawsuit challenging this practice under the Establishment clause of the United States Constitution.

After the students held elections authorizing such prayers and selecting a spokesperson, the District Court entered an order modifying the policy to permit only nonsectarian, non-proselytizing prayer. In *Santa Fe Indep. Sch. Dist. v. Doe*, 530 U.S. 290 (2000) the Fifth Circuit Court of Appeals held that, even as modified by the District Court, the football prayer policy was invalid. The Supreme Court of the United States agreed and held in its 2000 decision that student-led, student-initiated prayers at public high school football games and graduation ceremonies are unconstitutional and violate the establishment clause.[1]

Adler

Adler I

Students and parents in this Florida school district challenged the school board's guidelines that allowed prayer at graduation ceremonies. The guidelines provided that graduating seniors should decide whether or not to have a brief opening or closing message at graduation ceremonies, who should give this message, and what the content of the message should be.

The stated purpose of the guidelines was to allow students alone to direct their graduation message. The words "prayer," "benediction," or "invocation" were not used in the guidelines themselves; there was no requirement in the guidelines that the message be nonsectarian. Schools delegated decision making to the students. Prayers were given at the commencement ceremonies of 10 of the 17 schools in the district.

After a lawsuit was initiated, the school district asserted that there was no violation because the school had delegated authority to the students. The defendant school board also argued that a graduation ceremony was a limited public forum, and, therefore, to not allow the students to engage in religious speech would violate the religion clauses.

The district court held that there was no violation since school officials were not involved in the decision-making process. On appeal, the 11th Circuit Court of Appeals dismissed the plaintiffs' claims for injunctive and declaratory relief because the students protesting the guidelines had graduated, rendering their claims moot.

Adler II

In May 1998, a new lawsuit (Adler II) was filed in which students with graduation dates from 1998 to 2000 were named as plaintiffs. The Florida district court again granted judgment for defendants, and the case was again appealed to the 11th Circuit. This time, the 11th Circuit reversed the district court and struck down (2–1) the Duval County school system's graduation policy. The court determined that the Duval County graduation prayer regulations were unconstitutional. The case was granted *certiorari*, and the Supreme Court vacated the judgment and remanded the case to the 11th Circuit for further consideration in light of its recent decision in *Santa Fe* which held that student-led prayers at public high school football games are unconstitutional.

The 11th Circuit reconsidered the case and reinstated its original *Adler I* decision and held that student-led prayer is acceptable in Duval County. The 11th Circuit favored the County and after reviewing the *Sante Fe* case it felt that the differences between the two cases were substantial and material. *Adler* was denied certiorari: in 2001 and therefore there is somewhat of a disparity between the cases.[2] The difference between *Adler* and *Santa Fe* is that the school policy in *Adler* allows students to speak on any topic of their choice. The message can be religious or secular. Thus, the *Adler* policy promotes student speech and is neutral and therefore constitutional. The court found that the policy was neutral toward student speech and did not inject the government into determining the content of student speech.

■ The Future of Prayer at School Events

It is still unclear whether such prayers are valid at private high schools, before college sporting events, or even at the professional level though such activities occur regularly. It is likely that private organizations that do not receive federal or state funds may say prayers of their choosing without fear of a lawsuit. However, even professional sports organizations play in publicly funded arenas which, theoretically, could be a means to establish a claim (albeit a remote one) that there has been a violation between the tradition of separation between church and state.

■ Individual Athletes and Religious Expression

What happens when individual athletes express their religious beliefs during sports contests? Does this violate the separation between church and state? When an athlete looks and points to the sky after a score, does this advance a particular religion?

---

certiorari   discretionary writ (order) issued, usually by a supreme court, telling a lower court that the case will be reviewed by the higher court

Is it legal when opposing players kneel at mid-field after a game, holding hands in prayer? Does that advance a particular religion, or is it merely a time for introspection? What about high school or college student-athletes at publicly funded institutions expressing their post-game religious prayers?

There are numerous situations that may occur around a sports context that call into question whether or not there may be a violation of the principle of separation between churds and state. Consider the following, for example:

1. A coach asks her players to join hands in prayer prior to a sports contest;
2. A school broadcasts a prayer over the stadium loudspeaker;
3. Fans in the stands pray together by bowing their heads in prayer;
4. Students at a sporting event hold their own prayer;
5. A player reads from a religious book, alone, in the team's locker room;
6. A player preaching to other members on the sidelines encouraging unity and support from a higher power.[3]

All of the above are only a few of the possible scenarios that the legal system has yet to clearly define.

No Clear-Cut Answers

Players at all levels of sports continue to express their religious beliefs and are often not penalized for doing so. For example, Sandy Koufax, a Jewish left-handed pitcher, made headlines in 1965 when he refused to pitch the first game of the World Series for the Dodgers because it fell on holiday of Yom Kippur. Along the same lines, star baseball player Shawn Green of the Los Angeles Dodgers did not participate in a game late in the season due to his recognition of Yom Kippur. Vince Lombardi, the coach of the Green Bay Packers, regularly took his team to Catholic mass every Sunday before games. Not all religious athletes, however, decide not to participate in a sports contest due to their religious affiliation or beliefs.

Still, is it right for a college coach at a publicly funded institution to require his or her athletes to attend religious services? What if a player does not wish to say a pregame prayer and is penalized for such conduct? There is no doubt that members of different religious groups "witness" their beliefs to other athletes even at public institutions. It may even be chic to associate oneself with a particular religious organization either willingly or due to pressure from one athlete to another. However, public institutions must be aware that promoting or advancing a particular religion or a religious organization, no matter how small the involvement, will likely raise eyebrows and could even be the subject matter of a passionate lawsuit.

■ Summary

One of the founding principles of American society remains the separation of church and state. Such principles can be found in the Constitution of the United States and the First Amendment, which assures the freedom of religion. While a mandatory prayer is not required before, during, or after school-sponsored graduation or most sporting events, often prayers or moments of silence are utilized as part of such events. Such prayers present extremely difficult challenges for the courts to determine whether a violation of the Constitution has occurred. It appears that there is no definitive rule in this area, but American courts employ guidelines such as the *Lemon* test, the endorsement test, and the coercion test to determine whether the state may be advancing a particular religion or religion in general and whether a public display of religion is acceptable under certain circumstances on a case-by-case basis. Still, student-led, student-initiated prayers at graduation ceremonies appear to be unconstitutional.

■ Key Terms

certiorari

Coercion test

Constitution of the United States

Endorsement test

First Amendment

Lemon test

■ Additional Cases

Adler v. Duval County Sch. Bd., 206 F.3d 1070 (11th Cir. 2000), vacated & remanded, 531 U.S. 801 (2000)

Adler v. Duval County Sch. Bd. 250 F.3d 1330 (11th Cir. 1999), cert. Denied, 122 S. Ct 664 (2001)

Brown v. Gilmore, 258 F.3d 265 (4th Cir. 2001), cert. denied, 122 S. Ct. 465 (2001)

Engel v. Vitale, 370 U.S. 421 (1962)

Jager v. Douglas County Sch. Dist., 862 F.2d 824 (11th Cir. 1989)

Jones v. Clear Creek Indep. Sch. Dist., 977 F.2d 963 (5th Cir. 1992), cert. denied, 508 U.S. 967 (1993)

Lynch v. Donnelly, 465 U.S. 668 (1984)

Wallace v. Jaffree, 472 U.S. 38 (1985)

■ Review Questions

1. Should religion be totally removed from the context of sport?
2. Do you feel that the events of September 11, 2001, have affected how American society views religion and sport?
3. What constitutional amendments are primarily at work when considering a religion and sports case?
4. What are the major "tests" that American courts have used to analyze religion and sports cases?

5. Should private schools be given different consideration for religion and sport issues than public schools? Why or why not?
6. Should teams with religious names or mascots be changed?

■ Endnotes

1 *Santa Fe Indep. Sch. Dist. v. Doe*, 530 U.S. 290 (2000).
2 *See Adler v. Dural County Sch. Bd.*, 250 F. 3d 1330 (11th Cir. 2001).
3 *See* Paul J. Batista, *Balancing the First Amendment's Establishment and Free Exercise Clauses: a Rebuttal to Alexander and Alexander*, 12 J. Legal Aspects of Sport 87 (2002).

Internet Resources

The following is a roster of resources that are applicable throughout this text.

General Law and Sports Law Research Sources

Findlaw: http://www.findlaw.com and http://news.findlaw.com/legalnews/sports/

Catalaw: http://www.catalaw.com

Westlaw: http://www.westlaw.com

Lexis: http://www.lexis.com

United States Code: http://www.law.cornell.edu/uscode/

United States Constitution: http://www.law.cornell.edu/constitution/

United States Supreme Court Cases: http://www.oyez.com/

Washburn University Law Locater: http://www.washlaw.edu/

Marquette University's Sports Links: http://www.marquette.edu/law/sports/links.html

Cornell University's Sports Links: http://www.law.cornell.edu/topics/sports.html

Sports Law Associations

ABA Forum on the Entertainment and Sports Industries:
   http://www.abanet.org/forums/entsports/home.html

American Arbitration Association: http://www.adr.org/

International Association of Sports Law: http://www.iasl.org/

The Sports Lawyers Association: http://www.sla.org

The Society for the Study of Legal Aspects of Sport and Physical Activity:
   http://www.ithaca.edu/sslaspa/links.htm

Sports Law Journals and Publications

ABA's *Entertainment and Sports Lawyer*: http://www.abanet.org/forums/entsports/e_sl.html

The Journal of the Legal Aspects of Sport: http://www.ithaca.edu/sslaspa/pubs.htm

Mark Conrad's Sports Law Newsletter: http://www.sportslawnews.com

Marquette University's Sports Law Review: http://www.mu.edu/law/sports/slj.html

Tulane University's Sports Lawyer's Journal: http://www.law.tulane.edu

Villanova University's Sports and Entertainment Law Journal:
   http://vls.law.vill.edu/students/orgs/sports/

Selected Professional Sports Organizations

ATP Tour: http://www.atptour.com/

Arena Football League: http://www.arenafootball.com/main.cfm

Major League Baseball (MLB): http://www.mlb.com/

Major League Soccer (MLS): http://www.mlsnet.com/

Minor League Baseball: http://www.minorleaguebaseball.com/

National Basketball Association (NBA): http://www.nba.com/

National Football League (NFL): http://www.nfl.com/

National Football League Player's Association (NFLPA): http://www.nflpa.org/

National Hockey League (NHL): http://www.nhl.com/

NBA Players Association: http://www.nbpa.com/

NASCAR: http://www.nascar.com/

Professional Bowlers Association (PBA): http://www.pba.org/

Professional Golfers Association (PGA): http://www.pga.org/

World Wrestling Entertainment, Inc.,: http://www.wwe.com/

Women's NBA (WNBA): http://www.wnba.com/

World Triathlon Corporation: http://www.ironmanlive.com/

Selected American Amateur Sports Organizations

National Collegiate Athletic Association (NCAA): http://www.ncaa.org

United States Olympic Committee (USOC): http://www.usoc.org

USA Anti-Doping Agency: http://www.usantidoping.org/

USA Baseball: http://www.usabaseball.com/

USA Basketball: http://www.usabasketball.com/

USA Bobsled: http://www.usabobsled.org/

USA Cycling: http://www.usacycling.org/

US Figure Skating Association: http://www.usfsa.org/

USA Gymnastics: http://www.usa-gymnastics.org/

US Rowing: http://www.usrowing.org/

US Swimming: http://www.usswim.org/

USA Track and Field: http://www.usatf.org/

USA Triathlon: http://www.usatriathlon.org/

USA Volleyball: http://www.usavolleyball.org/

USA Weightlifting: http://www.usaw.org/

USA Wrestling: http://www.usawrestling.org/

Selected International Governing Bodies

Court of Arbitration of Sport (CAS): http://www.tas-cas.org/

FIFA (Soccer): http://www.fifa.com/

FINA (Swimming) Governs swimming, diving, water polo, and synchronized swimming.: http://www.fina.org/

IAAF (Track): http://www.iaaf.org

IRB (Rugby): http://www.irb.org/

International Olympic Committee (IOC): http://www.olympic.org/

International Triathlon Union: http://www.triathlon.org/

World Anti-Doping Agency: http://www.wada-ama.org/asiakas/003/wada_english.nsf/

World Boxing Association: http://www.wbaonline.com

Selected Alternative Dispute Resolution Sites

http://www.internetneutral.com

http://www.123settle.com

http://www.eresolution.org

http://www.onlineresolution.com

http://www.webdispute.com

http://www.mediate-net.org

General Sports News

CBS Sports: http:///www.cbssportsline.com

CNN/Sports Illustrated: http://www.cnnsi.com

ESPN: http://www.espn.com

Fox Sports: http://www.foxsports.com

Sports Business Journal: http://www.sportsbusinessjournal.com/

The Sporting News: http://www.sportingnews.com/

USA Today Sports: http://www.usatoday.com/sports/sfront.htm

Amendments to the United States Constitution

The Conventions of a number of the States having, at the time of adopting the Constitution, expressed a desire, in order to prevent misconstruction or abuse of its powers, that further declaratory and restrictive clauses should be added, and as extending the ground of public confidence in the Government will best insure the beneficent ends of its institution;

Resolved, by the Senate and House of Representatives of the United States of America, in Congress assembled, two-thirds of both Houses concurring, that the following articles be proposed to the Legislatures of the several States, as amendments to the Constitution of the United States; all or any of which articles, when ratified by three-fourths of the said Legislatures, to be valid to all intents and purposes as part of the said Constitution, namely:

Amendment I

Congress shall make no law respecting an establishment of religion, or prohibiting the free exercise thereof; or abridging the freedom of speech, or of the press; or the right of the people peaceably to assemble, and to petition the government for a redress of grievances.

Amendment II

A well regulated militia, being necessary to the security of a free state, the right of the people to keep and bear arms, shall not be infringed.

Amendment III

No soldier shall, in time of peace be quartered in any house, without the consent of the owner, nor in time of war, but in a manner to be prescribed by law.

Amendment IV

The right of the people to be secure in their persons, houses, papers, and effects, against unreasonable searches and seizures, shall not be violated, and no warrants shall issue, but upon probable cause, supported by oath or affirmation, and particularly describing the place to be searched, and the persons or things to be seized.

Amendment V

No person shall be held to answer for a capital, or otherwise infamous crime, unless on a presentment or indictment of a grand jury, except in cases arising in the land or naval forces, or in the militia, when in actual service in time of war or public danger; nor shall any person be subject for the same offense to be twice put in jeopardy of life or limb; nor shall be compelled in any criminal case to be a witness against himself, nor be deprived of life, liberty, or property, without due process of law; nor shall private property be taken for public use, without just compensation.

Amendment VI

In all criminal prosecutions, the accused shall enjoy the right to a speedy and public trial, by an impartial jury of the state and district wherein the crime shall have been committed, which district shall have been previously ascertained by law, and to be informed of the nature and cause of the accusation; to be confronted with the witnesses against him; to have compulsory process for obtaining witnesses in his favor, and to have the assistance of counsel for his defense.

Amendment VII

In suits at common law, where the value in controversy shall exceed twenty dollars, the right of trial by jury shall be preserved, and no fact tried by a jury, shall be otherwise reexamined in any court of the United States, than according to the rules of the common law.

Amendment VIII

Excessive bail shall not be required, nor excessive fines imposed, nor cruel and unusual punishments inflicted.

Amendment IX

The enumeration in the Constitution, of certain rights, shall not be construed to deny or disparage others retained by the people.

Amendment X

The powers not delegated to the United States by the Constitution, nor prohibited by it to the states, are reserved to the states respectively, or to the people.

Amendment XI

(1798)

The judicial power of the United States shall not be construed to extend to any suit in law or equity, commenced or prosecuted against one of the United States by citizens of another state, or by citizens or subjects of any foreign state.

Amendment XII

(1804)

The electors shall meet in their respective states and vote by ballot for President and Vice-President, one of whom, at least, shall not be an inhabitant of the same state with themselves; they shall name in their ballots the person voted for as President, and in distinct ballots the person voted for as Vice-President, and they shall make distinct lists of all persons voted for as President, and of all persons voted for as Vice-President, and of the number of votes for each, which lists they shall sign and certify, and transmit sealed to the seat of the government of the United States, directed to the President of the Senate;—The President of the Senate shall, in the presence of the Senate and House of Representatives, open all the certificates and the votes shall then be counted;—the person having the greatest number of votes for President, shall be the President, if such number be a majority of the whole number of electors appointed; and if no person have such majority, then from the persons having the highest numbers not exceeding three on the list of those voted for as President, the House of Representatives shall choose immediately, by ballot, the President. But in choosing the President, the votes shall be taken by states, the representation from each state having one vote; a quorum for this purpose shall consist of a member or members from two-thirds of the states, and a majority of all the states shall be necessary to a choice. And if the House of Representatives shall not choose a President whenever the right of choice shall devolve upon them, before the fourth day of March next following, then the Vice-President shall act as President, as in the case of the death or other constitutional disability of the President. The person having the greatest number of votes as Vice-President, shall be the Vice-President, if such number be a majority of the whole number of electors appointed, and if no person have a majority, then from the two highest numbers on the list, the Senate shall choose the Vice-President; a quorum for the purpose shall consist of two-thirds of the whole number of Senators, and a majority of the whole number shall be necessary to a choice. But no person constitutionally ineligible to the office of President shall be eligible to that of Vice-President of the United States.

Amendment XIII

(1865)

Section 1. Neither slavery nor involuntary servitude, except as a punishment for crime whereof the party shall have been duly convicted, shall exist within the United States, or any place subject to their jurisdiction.

Section 2. Congress shall have power to enforce this article by appropriate legislation.

Amendment XIV

(1868)

Section 1. All persons born or naturalized in the United States, and subject to the jurisdiction thereof, are citizens of the United States and of the state wherein they reside. No state shall make or enforce any law which shall abridge the privileges or immunities of citizens of the United States; nor shall any state deprive any person of life, liberty, or property, without due process of law; nor deny to any person within its jurisdiction the equal protection of the laws.

Section 2. Representatives shall be apportioned among the several states according to their respective numbers, counting the whole number of persons in each state, excluding Indians not taxed. But when the right to vote at any election for the choice of electors for President and Vice President of the United States, Representatives in Congress, the executive and judicial officers of a state, or the members of the legislature thereof, is denied to any of the male inhabitants of such state, being twenty-one years of age, and citizens of the United States, or in any way abridged, except for participation in rebellion, or other crime, the basis of representation therein shall be reduced in the proportion which the number of such male citizens shall bear to the whole number of male citizens twenty-one years of age in such state.

Section 3. No person shall be a Senator or Representative in Congress, or elector of President and Vice President, or hold any office, civil or military, under the United States, or under any state, who, having previously taken an oath, as a member of Congress, or as an officer of the United States, or as a member of any state legislature, or as an executive or judicial officer of any state, to support the Constitution of the United States, shall have engaged in insurrection or rebellion against the same, or given aid or comfort to the enemies thereof. But Congress may by a vote of two-thirds of each House, remove such disability.

Section 4. The validity of the public debt of the United States, authorized by law, including debts incurred for payment of pensions and bounties for services in suppressing insurrection or rebellion, shall not be questioned. But neither the United States nor any state shall assume or pay any debt or obligation incurred in aid of insurrection or rebellion against the United States, or any claim for the loss or emancipation of any slave; but all such debts, obligations and claims shall be held illegal and void.

Section 5. The Congress shall have power to enforce, by appropriate legislation, the provisions of this article.

Amendment XV

(1870)

Section 1. The right of citizens of the United States to vote shall not be denied or abridged by the United States or by any state on account of race, color, or previous condition of servitude.

Section 2. The Congress shall have power to enforce this article by appropriate legislation.

Amendment XVI

(1913)

The Congress shall have power to lay and collect taxes on incomes, from whatever source derived, without apportionment among the several states, and without regard to any census of enumeration.

Amendment XVII

(1913)

The Senate of the United States shall be composed of two Senators from each state, elected by the people thereof, for six years; and each Senator shall have one vote. The electors in each state shall have the qualifications requisite for electors of the most numerous branch of the state legislatures.

When vacancies happen in the representation of any state in the Senate, the executive authority of such state shall issue writs of election to fill such vacancies: Provided, that the legislature of any state may empower the executive thereof to make temporary appointments until the people fill the vacancies by election as the legislature may direct.

This amendment shall not be so construed as to affect the election or term of any Senator chosen before it becomes valid as part of the Constitution.

Amendment XVIII

(1919)

Section 1. After one year from the ratification of this article the manufacture, sale, or transportation of intoxicating liquors within, the importation thereof into, or the exportation thereof from the United States and all territory subject to the jurisdiction thereof for beverage purposes is hereby prohibited.

Section 2. The Congress and the several states shall have concurrent power to enforce this article by appropriate legislation.

Section 3. This article shall be inoperative unless it shall have been ratified as an amendment to the Constitution by the legislatures of the several states, as provided in the Constitution, within seven years from the date of the submission hereof to the states by the Congress.

Amendment XIX

(1920)

The right of citizens of the United States to vote shall not be denied or abridged by the United States or by any state on account of sex.

Congress shall have power to enforce this article by appropriate legislation.

Amendment XX

(1933)

Section 1. The terms of the President and Vice President shall end at noon on the 20th day of January, and the terms of Senators and Representatives at noon on the 3rd day of January, of the years in which such terms would have ended if this article had not been ratified; and the terms of their successors shall then begin.

Section 2. The Congress shall assemble at least once in every year, and such meeting shall begin at noon on the 3rd day of January, unless they shall by law appoint a different day.

Section 3. If, at the time fixed for the beginning of the term of the President, the President elect shall have died, the Vice President elect shall become President. If a President shall not have been chosen before the time fixed for the beginning of his term, or if the President elect shall have failed to qualify, then the Vice President elect shall act as President until a President shall have qualified; and the Congress may by law provide for the case wherein neither a President elect nor a Vice President elect shall have qualified, declaring who shall then act as President, or the manner in which one who is to act shall be selected, and such person shall act accordingly until a President or Vice President shall have qualified.

Section 4. The Congress may by law provide for the case of the death of any of the persons from whom the House of Representatives may choose a President whenever the right of choice shall have devolved upon them, and for the case of the death of any of the persons from whom the Senate may choose a Vice President whenever the right of choice shall have devolved upon them.

Section 5. Sections 1 and 2 shall take effect on the 15th day of October following the ratification of this article.

Section 6. This article shall be inoperative unless it shall have been ratified as an amendment to the Constitution by the legislatures of three-fourths of the several states within seven years from the date of its submission.

Amendment XXI

(1933)

Section 1. The eighteenth article of amendment to the Constitution of the United States is hereby repealed.

Section 2. The transportation or importation into any state, territory, or possession of the United States for delivery or use therein of intoxicating liquors, in violation of the laws thereof, is hereby prohibited.

Section 3. This article shall be inoperative unless it shall have been ratified as an amendment to the Constitution by conventions in the several states, as provided in the Constitution, within seven years from the date of the submission hereof to the states by the Congress.

Amendment XXII

(1951)

Section 1. No person shall be elected to the office of the President more than twice, and no person who has held the office of President, or acted as President, for more than two years of a term to which some other person was elected President shall be elected to the office of the President more than once. But this article shall not apply to any person holding the office of President when this article was proposed by the Congress, and shall not prevent any person who may be holding the office of President, or acting as President, during the term within which this article becomes operative from holding the office of President or acting as President during the remainder of such term.

Section 2. This article shall be inoperative unless it shall have been ratified as an amendment to the Constitution by the legislatures of three-fourths of the several states within seven years from the date of its submission to the states by the Congress.

Amendment XXIII

(1961)

Section 1. The District constituting the seat of government of the United States shall appoint in such manner as the Congress may direct:

A number of electors of President and Vice President equal to the whole number of Senators and Representatives in Congress to which the District would be entitled if it were a state, but in no event more than the least populous state; they shall be in addition to those appointed by the states, but they shall be considered, for the purposes of the election of President and Vice President, to be electors appointed by a state; and they shall meet in the District and perform such duties as provided by the twelfth article of amendment.

Section 2. The Congress shall have power to enforce this article by appropriate legislation.

Amendment XXIV

(1964)

Section 1. The right of citizens of the United States to vote in any primary or other election for President or Vice President, for electors for President or Vice President, or for Senator or Representative in Congress, shall not be denied or abridged by the United States or any state by reason of failure to pay any poll tax or other tax.

Section 2. The Congress shall have power to enforce this article by appropriate legislation.

Amendment XXV

(1967)

Section 1. In case of the removal of the President from office or of his death or resignation, the Vice President shall become President.

Section 2. Whenever there is a vacancy in the office of the Vice President, the President shall nominate a Vice President who shall take office upon confirmation by a majority vote of both Houses of Congress.

Section 3. Whenever the President transmits to the President pro tempore of the Senate and the Speaker of the House of Representatives his written declaration that he is unable to discharge the powers and duties of his office, and until he transmits to them a written declaration to the contrary, such powers and duties shall be discharged by the Vice President as Acting President.

Section 4. Whenever the Vice President and a majority of either the principal officers of the executive departments or of such other body as Congress may by law provide, transmit to the President pro tempore of the Senate and the Speaker of the House of Representatives their written declaration that the President is unable to discharge the powers and duties of his office, the Vice President shall immediately assume the powers and duties of the office as Acting President.

Thereafter, when the President transmits to the President pro tempore of the Senate and the Speaker of the House of Representatives his written declaration that no inability exists, he shall resume the powers and duties of his office unless the Vice President and a majority of either the principal officers of the executive department or of such other body as Congress may by law provide, transmit within four days to the President pro tempore of the Senate and the Speaker of the House of Representatives their written declaration that the President is unable to discharge the powers and duties of his office. Thereupon Congress shall decide the issue, assembling within forty-eight hours for that purpose if not in session. If the Congress, within twenty-one days after receipt of the latter written declaration, or, if Congress is not in session, within twenty-one days after Congress is required to assemble, determines by two-thirds vote of both Houses that the President is unable to discharge the powers and duties of his office, the Vice President shall continue to discharge the same as Acting President; otherwise, the President shall resume the powers and duties of his office.

Amendment XXVI

(1971)

Section 1. The right of citizens of the United States, who are 18 years of age or older, to vote, shall not be denied or abridged by the United States or any state on account of age.

Section 2. The Congress shall have the power to enforce this article by appropriate legislation.

Amendment XXVII

(1992)

No law, varying the compensation for the services of the Senators and Representatives, shall take effect until an election of Representatives shall have intervened.

Glossary

Fourteenth Amendment   prohibition against states abridging the rights guaranteed under the United States Constitution

1980 Olympic Boycott   President Jimmy Carter's refusal to send a United States team to the Summer Olympic Games in Moscow

acceptance   agreement to the terms of an offer that creates a legally binding agreement

actus reus   criminal act; one of two elements of every crime (see *mens rea*); literally, the "act thing"

Age Discrimination in Employment Act (ADEA)   1967 law that prohibits job discrimination based on age against people age 40 and older

agent   individual authorized to act on behalf of a principal

aggravated crime   crime involving use of a weapon and/or causing serious bodily injury to another

alternative dispute resolution (ADR)   resolving disputes via arbitration, mediation, and other alternatives to litigation

Amateur Sports Act of 1978   American amateur sports act that established guidelines for athletes and the United States Olympic Committee

ambush marketing   type of marketing in which a consumer is misled as to whether a company or sponsor is officially part of an event

American Arbitration Association (AAA)   national organization that maintains a panel of arbitrators to hear labor and commercial disputes

Americans with Disabilities Act (ADA) of 1990   federal law imposing obligations on employers and other providers of public transport, telecommunications, and public accommodations to accommodate persons with disabilities; 42 U.S.C.A. § 12101 et seq.

Anticybersquatting Consumer Protection Act (ACPA)   1999 federal law amending the Lanham Act to create a cause of action against someone who intentionally registers an Internet domain name confusingly similar to a trademarked name

antitrust   term used to describe any contract, combination, or conspiracy that illegally restrains trade and/or promotes anticompetitive behavior

appearance contract   agreement that the athlete will appear in person on behalf of a sponsor's promotion

arbitration   submitting a dispute to a neutral decision maker for final and binding resolution

assault   willful attempt or threat to inflict injury; usually associated with battery; both a crime and a tort

Basic Agreement   term often used to describe the CBA between Major League Baseball players and owners

battery   crime involving unlawful physical contact with another person; both a crime and a tort

beyond a reasonable doubt   the test the government (state) must prove in a criminal case

boilerplate   fixed or standard contract terms that generally are not negotiable

breach of the implied warranty of fitness for a particular purpose   implied warranty that arises when a seller of goods knows the particular purpose for which the purchaser needs the goods

breach of warranty of merchantability   implied promise that a product will be merchantable and fit for its ordinary use

certiorari   discretionary writ (order) issued usually by a supreme court telling a lower court that the case will be reviewed by the higher court

Clayton Act   1914 federal law that allows the government or a private plaintiff to obtain an injunction against anticompetitive behavior

coercion test   examination of a religious practice to determine whether pressure is applied to force or coerce individuals to participate; unconstitutional coercion occurs when (1) the government directs (2) a formal religious exercise (3) in such a way as to oblige the participation of objectors; based on *Lee v. Weisman*, 505 U.S. 577 (1992)

collective bargaining agreement (CBA)   contract between a league and players association; more generally, a contract between management and labor in a union context

collective bargaining   process of negotiating a contract between management and labor in the union context

collective mark   trademark of an association, union, or other group

commercial misappropriation   tort of intentionally using a person's name, image, or likeness, without permission, for personal gain and profit

comparative negligence (fault)   standard in which damages are awarded based on the degree of fault among plaintiff and defendant; typically, plaintiff's degree of fault must be 49 percent or less than the defendant to recover damages

compensatory damages   remedy to compensate a plaintiff for actual out-of-pocket loss or expense due to negligence or breach of contract

consequential damages   damages for an injury arising from special circumstances that were not ordinarily foreseeable but result from the consequences of an act by a defendant

consideration   the price, usually in monetary terms, of a promise

Constitution of the United States   America's fundamental legal document

contact sports   sports such as football, wrestling, and lacrosse that inherently involve hostile, even violent physical struggles as part of the game's rules

contract   legally binding agreement

contributory negligence   failure of plaintiffs to take reasonable precautions for their own safety; has been replaced in many jurisdictions by comparative negligence

copyright   property right in an original work of authorship such as literary, musical, artistic, or photographic work

Court of Arbitration of Sport (CAS)   body that addresses complaints of athletes, coaches, and federations under the jurisdiction of the Olympics

crimes affecting the public health and welfare   including blackmail, illegal gambling, and prostitution

crimes against property   including arson, trespass, vandalism, and theft

crimes against the government   including tax evasion, treason, RICO violations, and terrorism

crimes against the person   including assault, battery, robbery, murder, rape, and kidnapping

Curt Flood Act of 1998   federal law that revokes part of a 1922 United States Supreme Court decision exempting baseball owners from antitrust laws; the original exemption, based on the idea that baseball was not a business, prevented players from suing owners over anticompetitive practices; allows players to sue owners, but only over contract negotiations and only if the players union first disbands

cybersquatter   individual who intentionally registers an Internet domain name that is confusingly similar to a trademarked name

damages   generally, amount of money recoverable by a person for a loss or injury, usually due to negligence or a breach of contract

defamation of character   intentional tort whereby a false statement is published (libel) or spoken (slander) about the plaintiff

defenses to crimes   category in which the criminal defendant alleges lack of intent to commit a crime, self-defense, or another reason to plead not guilty to a criminal charge

Department of Health, Education and Welfare (HEW)   former federal agency originally charged with enforcing Title IX provisions

domain name   word followd by .com, .org, .net, .edu, .info, .biz, and registered as part of the Internet system

due process   Fifth Amendment right to a hearing before a person's life, liberty, or property is taken away by the government or other entity, if a contract entitles them to due process

effective accommodation   third-prong test under Title IX that determines whether the interests and abilities of the underrepresented gender have been fully and effectively accommodated by the present state of the athletic program

endorsement contract   contract in which a sponsor agrees to pay a fee or provide product to an athlete in exchange for using the athlete's name or image in its promotions

endorsement test   legal standard in which a court considers whether the government intends to communicate, and whether an imaginary "reasonable observer" would receive, a message of "endorsement" of a particular religion and/or an act of disapproval toward any other religion

Equal Employment Opportunity Commission (EEOC)   federal agency responsible for enforcing federal antidiscrimination laws

Equal Pay Act of 1963   federal law mandating, with some exceptions, that all who perform substantially the same work must be paid equally; 29 U.S.C.A. § 206

equal protection   clause in the 14th Amendment that states that the government must treat a person or class of persons the same in similar circumstances

Equity in Athletics Disclosure Act (EADA)   federal law requiring public disclosure of financial records of college and university records related to athletic expenditures

erythropoietin (EPO)   performance-enhancing hormone affecting red blood cells

ethnic mascots   phrase used to describe athletic mascots that single out a race, gender, or culture

exclusive contract   agreement for sole rights to sponsor, promote, and advertise between an agent and athlete

fair use   term used in the copyright context that allows reasonable yet limited use of a work without the author's prior permission

Family and Medical Leave Act (FMLA)   1993 federal law that guarantees employees unpaid time off from work for childbirth, adoption, and medically related emergencies

fan   person passionate about a favorite player, team, or league; short for "fanatic"

Federal Trade Commission (FTC)   federal agency that enforces laws against false, deceptive, and other unfair advertising and trade practices

felony   crime punishable by more than one year in prison

fiduciary   one who owes another a higher duty of good faith and care

Fifth Amendment   the requirement for a "due process" hearing before a person's life, liberty, or property is taken away; this amendment to the United States Constitution also provides the right against self-incrimination

First Amendment   constitutional amendment providing for freedom of the press, freedom of assembly, and freedom of religion

Fourth Amendment   United States Constitutional amendment prohibiting the government from conducting a search of a person's body or home without the individual's consent, a warrant, or a contract; referred to as the "search and seizure" amendment

gender equity   concept associated with Title IX, evaluating whether equal opportunities to participate in intercollegiate athletics are available to both men and women

gross negligence   failure to use a small amount of care to avoid harm to a plaintiff

health club contract   agreement typically regulated by state consumer protection acts to protect health club members from potential abuses

history of expansion   second-prong test under Title IX on whether a collegiate institution can show a history of continuing practice of program expansion for the underrepresented gender

human growth hormone (HGH)   hormone that affects all body systems and plays a major role in muscle growth and development

impairment   diminishment of physical or mental capabilities

implied contract   contract created by the courts as an obligation in the absence of an agreement to prevent unjust enrichment by one of the parties; sometimes called a *quasi* contract

Individuals with Disabilities Education Act (IDEA)   federal law, amended in 1997, mandating that all children with disabilities have available to them a free, appropriate public education that emphasizes special education and related services designed to meet their unique needs and prepare them for employment and independent living

infringement act that interferes with one of the exclusive rights of a patent, copyright, or trademark owner

insurance contract in which a company agrees to compensate the insured for loss due to perils or other liability

intellectual property category of law pertaining to trademark, copyright, and patent rights

intent desire to bring about a particular result

intentional infliction of emotional distress intentional tort in which the defendant causes emotional distress by extreme or outrageous conduct

intentional interference with contractual relations intentional tort of interfering with a known contractual relationship with the intent to induce one of the parties to breach

intentional tort tort closely associated with crimes in which the tortfeasor intended to commit an injury to another

International Federation (IF) sport-specific regulatory body that sets international rules under the jurisdiction of the IOC

International Olympic Committee (IOC) organization responsible for managing the Olympic Movement; based in Lausanne, Switzerland

Lanham Act 1946 federal act that provides for a national system of registration of trademarks

Lemon test test of constitutionality providing that an act of government must (1) be primarily secular in purpose, (2) neither advance nor inhibit religion, and (3) avoid excessive entanglement with religion; see *Lemon v. Kurtzman*, 403 U.S. 602 (1971)

letter of intent form prospective student athletes sign committing to attend a college or university

license revocable permission to commit an act such as copying a trademark

liquidated damages agreed-upon remedy in a contract in the event of a breach

litigation process of carrying on a lawsuit via the courts

Lloyd Bloom sports agent accused of racketeering, conspiracy, and fraud in recruiting student athletes

lockout temporary withholding of work by the employer to resolve a labor dispute

malpractice negligence by a professional person, such as a lawyer or physician

med-arb hybrid form of alternative dispute resolution involving mediation and arbitration

mediation nonbinding method to resolve a dispute by involving a neutral third party who attempts to help the parties resolve their dispute without litigation

meeting of the minds phrase used to describe agreement between offeror and offeree

mens rea criminal intent to commit a crime; one of two elements of every crime (see *actus reus*); literally, the "mind thing"

misdemeanor crime punishable by up to one year in county jail

mitigation of damages reducing or keeping one's damages to a minimum

MLB Major League Baseball

MLBPA Major League Baseball Players Association

Model Code of Professional Responsibility model act for ethical conduct by attorneys adopted by the American Bar Association in 1969

Model Rules of Professional Conduct approved by the American Bar Association in 1983, these rules have been adopted by many states to replace the Model Code

National Governing Body (NGB) sport-specific regulatory body for a particular country, such as United States Swimming

National Labor Relations Act (NLRA) federal act regulating relations between employers and employees; 29 U.S.C.A. § 151 et seq.

National Labor Relations Board (NLRB) federal agency created by the NLRA to regulate employer and employee relations, particularly in the union context

National Olympic Committee (NOC) designated national organization responsible for managing the affairs of a particular country's Olympic teams

NBA National Basketball Association

NBPA National Basketball Players Association

NCAA National Collegiate Athletic Association, based in Indianapolis, Indiana

NCCUSL National Conference of Commissioners on Uniform State Laws

negligence failure to act as an ordinary, reasonably prudent person would

NFL National Football League

NFLPA National Football League Players Association

NHL National Hockey League

NHLPA National Hockey League Players Association

no fly zone areas established by the Federal Aviation Administration in which airplanes and helicopters may not travel without prior consent

nonexclusive contract agreement allowing either party to pursue other similar contractual relationships

nonstatutory labor exception general term describing any union-management agreement that was a product of good faith negotiation and will therefore receive protection from federal antitrust laws

Norby Walters sports agent accused of racketeering, conspiracy, and fraud for recruiting student athletes

Norris-LaGuardia Act 1932 federal law that forbids federal courts from abusing the injunctive process and to prevent employers from abusing the courts to obtain injunctions on union activities

offer element of contract that creates the power of acceptance in the offeree

offeree one who receives an offer and has the power to accept

offeror one who makes an offer

Office of Civil Rights (OCR) federal agency that enforces Title IX provisions

Olympic Movement term used to describe the underlying goals and themes of the Olympic Games and the International Olympic Committee

patent federal government's grant for the exclusive right to use, make, or sell an invention if the device is novel, useful, and nonobvious; 35 U.S.C.A. § 101 et seq.

per se rule analysis rule that holds that certain types of trade agreements or arrangements are inherently anticompetitive and therefore illegal

performance-enhancing drug drug or substance ingested, injected, or inhaled by an athlete to increase muscle growth, repair, or development or any substance used to decrease the effects of fatigue

personal services contract special nonassignable contract providing unique talents, abilities, and skills

preponderance of the evidence test in a civil case that plaintiff must prove the defendant is "more likely than not" responsible for the injuries sustained

principal one who grants another, an agent, the right to act on his or her behalf

products liability tort law focusing on a defect in design, manufacture, or warning

professional sports counseling panels groups formed by colleges and universities to advise student athletes on potential careers in professional sports

punitive damages damages designed to punish the misconduct of a civil defendant; not available for breach of contract; sometimes referred to as *exemplary damages*

quantum meruit term used to describe amount of compensation that must be paid under an implied contract to prevent unjust enrichment; literally means "as much as he or she deserved"

quota mandated proportional share often associated with Title IX analysis

reasonable accommodation adaptations or adjustments employers must make to comply with the ADA to accommodate the interests of a person with disabilities without undue hardship

reasonable person standard test used to determine whether, in hindsight, a person acted reasonably

recklessness such a high degree of carelessness that most courts view the harm to the plaintiff as intentional, making punitive damage awards likely

Rehabilitation Act of 1973 precursor to the American Disabilities Act stating that "no otherwise qualified handicapped individual in the United

States . . . shall, solely by reason of . . . handicap, be excluded from participation in, be denied the benefits of, or be subjected to discrimination under any program or activity receiving federal financial assistance"

remedies one of various methods to enforce a contract if a breach or default occurs

rescind to cancel or nullify a contract due to another's breach

RICO Racketeer Influenced and Corrupt Organizations Act, which spells out laws against organized crime

rule of reason rule that holds that only unreasonable restraints of trade violate Section 1 of the Sherman Antitrust Act

scope of employment responsibilities or activities an employee carries out on behalf of an employer

service mark trademark of a services provider

Sixth Amendment "in all criminal prosecutions, the accused shall enjoy the right to a speedy and public trial"

Seventh Amendment "in suits at common law, the right to a trial by jury shall be provided"

sexual harassment form of employment discrimination that consists of images or verbal or physical abuse sexual in nature and unwelcome

Sherman Antitrust Act 1890 federal anti-monopoly law that prohibits interference with interstate production and distribution of goods; 15 U.S.C.A. § 1 et seq.

specific performance remedy as ordered by a court to enforce a contract in its exact form where money damages would be an inadequate form of compensation for a breach

sports agent individual who represents the interests of a professional athlete

sports bribery illegal influence over an athlete, coach, referee, or other participant to affect the outcome of a sports event

sports gambling (gaming) illegal in most states and of particular interest to professional and amateur sports leagues

sports official individual who referees a professional or amateur sports contest; sports officials are usually compensated for their services

standard player contract (SPK) boilerplate contract between a league and a professional athlete

statute of limitation amount of time a plaintiff has to file a lawsuit

strict (absolute) liability liability for an activity that involves an ultra-hazardous activity

strike cessation of work by union members to obtain benefits or prevent abuses in the workplace

student-athlete student who participates as an individual or member of a college or university team; student athletes must comply with NCAA or other eligibility rules

substantial proportionality first-prong test under Title IX that reviews whether intercollegiate level participation for male and female students is provided in numbers substantially proportionate to respective enrollments

Ted Stevens Olympic and Amateur Sports Act (TSOASA) of 1998 amendments to the Amateur Sports Act of 1978 giving amateur athletes more specific competition rights and recognizing the role and needs of athletes with disabilities

ticket scalping buying tickets to sports events and then reselling them for a profit, usually well in excess of face value

Title IX of the Education Amendments of 1972 federal law prohibiting gender discrimination in athletic programs at institutions that receive federal funds; 20 U.S.C.A. § 16819 (a)

Title VII of the Civil Rights Act of 1964 provides that discrimination is illegal based upon race, color, religion, sex, or national origin

tort civil (noncriminal) injury or wrong that violates a legal duty owed to another

trademark word, phrase, logo, or symbol used to distinguish a product from others

trade dress the total image and appearance of a product or service

undue hardship analysis under ADA that would provide a defense for an employer that must pay excessive costs to accommodate a person's disability

Uniform Athlete Agents Act (UAAA) model state law governing sports agents authored by the National Conference of Commissioners on Uniform State Laws

Uniform Commercial Code (UCC) model act drafted to provide certainty in governing the sale of goods, commercial paper, secured transactions, etc.; adopted by all states in whole or in part

universal rule concept whereby courts expect that all spectators who watch baseball or softball games have a reasonable expectation that foul balls are part of the risk of watching a game

USOC United States Olympic Committee

valid term used to describe a legally binding contract

void contract that is not enforceable

voidable contract that may be voided by one of the parties

waiver the voluntary relinquishment of some legal rights; also called *disclaimer, release,* or *exculpatory clause*

WNBA Women's National Basketball Association

workers compensation system designed to compensate employees injured on the job in the course of their employment

World Intellectual Property Organization (WIPO) international organization dedicated to helping ensure that the rights of creators and owners of intellectual property are protected worldwide and that inventors and authors are recognized and rewarded for their ingenuity

wrongful death death caused by a tort

Index